MW01596831

Maynard S. Bird

✦

The Saga of a Maine Son

Rose Bird Waterman

iUniverse, Inc.

New York Lincoln Shanghai

Maynard S. Bird
The Saga of a Maine Son

iUniverse books may be ordered through booksellers or by contacting:

iUniverse
2021 Pine Lake Road, Suite 100
Lincoln, NE 68512
www.iuniverse.com
1-800-Authors (1-800-288-4677)

ISBN: 0-595-34572-7

Printed in the United States of America

*"As life is action and passion,
it is required of a man that he should share
the passion and action of his time
at the peril of being judged not to have lived."*

Oliver Wendell Holmes

For my daughters, Elizabeth, Clarissa and Teresa, whose interest in family history inspired this work.

Contents

FOREWORD. xi

CHAPTER 1 3

CHAPTER 2 14

CHAPTER 3 21

CHAPTER 4 30

CHAPTER 5 38

CHAPTER 6 48

CHAPTER 7 58

CHAPTER 8 67

CHAPTER 9 78

CHAPTER 10 86

CHAPTER 11. 97

CHAPTER 12 107

CHAPTER 13 114

CHAPTER 14 122

CHAPTER 15 130

CHAPTER 16 141

CHAPTER 17 156

CHAPTER 18 163

CHAPTER 19 174

CHAPTER 20 190

CHAPTER 21 195

CHAPTER 22 203

CHAPTER 23 212

CHAPTER 24 219

CHAPTER 25 228

CHAPTER 26 237

CHAPTER 27 244

CHAPTER 28 253

CHAPTER 29 265

CHAPTER 30 275

CHAPTER 31 283

CHAPTER 32 291

CHAPTER 33 300

EPILOGUE 311

Endnotes 313

FOREWORD

The origin of this story stemmed from my desire to leave my children (and grandchildren) a record of their heritage. They had never known their paternal grandfather or grandmother, so if they were ever going to have any knowledge of their roots in the Bird family, it was up to me to provide it. In writing of my father's life, I found an opportunity to best portray the qualities of independence and willingness to accept and respond to challenges that so often characterize the Maine native.

As I delved into the history of my father, Maynard Sumner Bird, it became evident that even my knowledge of his early life, (he was fifty-two when I was born), was woefully lacking. I knew that he had progressed from a small town Maine boy, to a man of wealth and some importance in American financial markets. Also, I discovered that his unique personality and business acumen set him apart from others in his family; it, therefore, made him the most suitable person through whom to interpret the internal relationships among the Birds. In my search for details of his life, I found that local historians had forgotten the significant role he had played in the late nineteenth and early twentieth centuries in the Rockland (Maine) community. This discovery provided the impetus to write a fuller account of his life than I had earlier anticipated.

In trying to reconstruct my father's life, I have been hampered by a lack of original documents. Maynard was not a diarist, but he did keep precise records, (or I assume he did), of his business dealings. Unfortunately, at a low point in his life, when he was in his eighties, he, inexplicably, had all records and personal papers destroyed. Thus, I have had to rely on newspaper articles, advertisements and oral accounts passed down from relatives and friends over the course of time. Twice, I was able to acquire first hand material: the first time was the discovery of my father's "Adventures" that he wrote at the behest of a nephew; and the other time was the acquisition of a collection of postcards and a letter written by my mother. I am sure that had I had the time, opportunity and energy, I could find many more accounts of his activities in the Maine newspapers, State records, and possibly personal documents.

As it turned out, I was able to write a cohesive story that, while frequently not supported by records, was based on knowledge of actual events in my father's life.

Some incidents were created to fit likely situations or those that had to exist. Others, such as his courtship of my mother, sprang from my, (not so fertile), imagination. Her death presented a problem because it was so painful that my father never spoke about it; and my grandmother only told me the barest details. Rather than fictionalize the event, I have inserted my own interpretation, gleaned from the meager records available.

Characters have been invented where the need is obvious and essential to the story. Fictitious names have been given to persons who existed, but whose real names have been lost or forgotten. In the case of Walter Hammons, all indications are that he was in some way connected with the Maynard S. Bird Company and its brokerage office at 120 Exchange Street in Portland; I have, therefore, taken the liberty of identifying him as one of my father's 'boys'.

Footnotes have been included where appropriate; and, in order to clarify complex family relationships, genealogical charts have been added to show those individuals (both Birds and Tylers) mentioned in the text.

I am indebted to many relatives—some I did not even know I had and others with whom I had lost touch. To Larry Bird—no, not the basketball player but the son of my first cousin Theodore (Ted) Bird—I owe immeasurable thanks for hours spent in the Rockland Public Library photocopying old news articles and advertisements. Thanks are also due to Carolyn Bird Murray, the daughter of my cousin Fred Bird, for discovering, and passing on, Maynard's account of his "Adventures". Evelyn Cobb MacDougall sent me my mother's letter and the post cards of their wedding trip to the Orient. Marjorie Bird Richardson, another Bird descendant, provided pictures and information on the family; and Jane Bird Stearns, daughter of William Case Bird, filled me in on my father's influence on her father's life. Although he may have forgotten the correspondence by this time, Richard (Rick) Bird, a great-grandson of my father's brother, Elmer, provided me with some details of The John Bird Company. Thanks, too, to the present John Bird, his wife, Mary Alice, and cousin, Sidney Richardson. They all contributed in one way or another. My thanks to our daughters, Elizabeth Kally and Clarissa Henderson who have both been supportive of the undertaking.

I am indebted to George Martin, author of *The Damrosch Dynasty* and authority on opera, for information on the Institute of Musical Art in New York City, the forerunner of the present day Juilliard School, where my mother studied. He also contributed information on schedules and performances of the Metropolitan Opera Company.

I owe a debt of gratitude to Sharon Walklett, a dear friend and computer wizard, for her help in putting this book together so that it could be transmitted online.

If I have omitted anybody to whom thanks are due, I excuse myself on the grounds of advancing age. (What better excuse is there?)

And finally, I could not have produced this work without the support and encouragement of my dear, dear husband, Ed Waterman. Without his contributions of editing and, in some cases, writing, there would have been no book.

Rose Bird Waterman
Kennett Square, PA
January 2005

The Bird Family Tree

All-in-One Tree of Maynard Sumner Bird

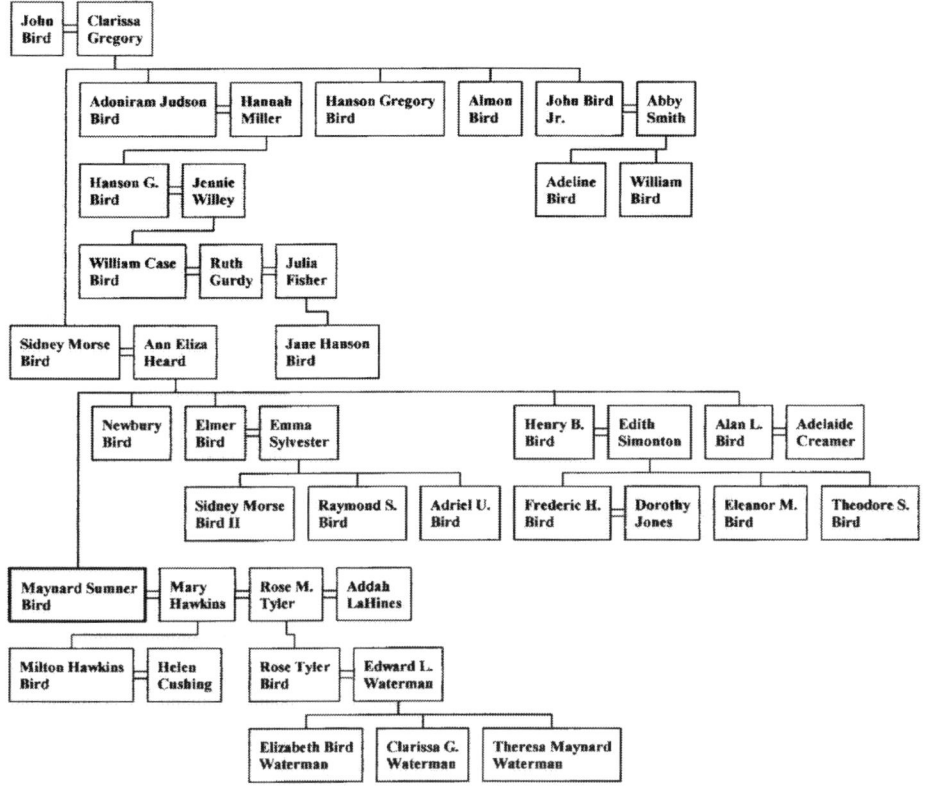

1

The Rockland Gazette, July 17, 1869
Born to Mr. and Mrs. Sidney M. Bird of Camden Road, The Highlands, a son, Maynard Sumner. Little Maynard joins his two older brothers, Newbury and Elmer.
Mr. Bird is a partner with his brother, John Bird Jr., in the John Bird Company founded by their father. Mr. Bird is also President of the North National Bank. Mrs. Bird is the former Ann Eliza Heard of Ash Point and Blackington's Corner. Both Mr. and Mrs. Bird are active members of the First Baptist Church of Rockland.

◆　　　◆　　　◆

Thus, inauspiciously, did Maynard Bird enter the life of Rockland, an equally inauspicious small city on the rugged Maine coast. Rockland, situated at the mouth of the Penobscot River, had originally been part of Thomaston known as Shore Village. In 1848 it adopted the name of East Thomaston in order to distinguish itself from the rest of Thomaston. The new town included the commercial area around the waterfront of a deepwater harbor, as well as an inland area known as "the Highlands". Like a child determined to assert its independence, it rechristened itself The Town of Rockland in 1850. The new decade marked the beginning of an era of great business growth and prosperity. The traditional industries of shipbuilding and fishing became subordinate to the ever-increasing importance of the lime industry: the quarrying of limestone and its conversion into lime. Lime was shipped from Rockland's magnificent harbor, which was rivaled only by Portland's as the most important seaport on the Atlantic coast east of Boston. In addition to the smaller ships called "limeburners", the harbor was filled with ships of all sizes; captained by experienced men; ready to transport goods of Maine and the Nation to all parts of the world. Somehow, the title of 'town' didn't reflect the status that its residents felt it deserved; so in 1854 Rockland incorporated itself into The City of Rockland, and everybody was satisfied.

The Bird family, into which Maynard was born, had established roots in Rockland by marrying into a family of earlier settlers—the Gregorys. Although

3

farmers, hunters, trappers and fishermen had harvested the bounty of the land and the sea for more than a hundred years, not until 1769 did the first permanent settler, Isaiah Tolman, arrive with his numerous offspring. The Tolmans made their home on 500 acres at the foot of Dodge's Mountain (originally Mt. Madambettox), on the shores of Chickawauka (Madambettox) Pond. Then, in 1770, William Gregory moved his family from Fort St. George to 400 acres adjacent to the Tolmans in an area of Camden that later became Rockport. The Gregory land lay immediately behind Clam Cove (now called Glen Cove) and extended westward close to the boundary of Rockland. Thus the Gregorys had as their nearest neighbor Isaiah Tolman's family.

William Gregory had eight children. The fifth child, a son, was named after his father. This William was born in Walpole, Massachusetts in 1761 before his father's emigration to the Maine area. (Maine was part of Massachusetts until 1821 when it became a state as part of the Missouri Compromise.) As an adult the second William became a sea captain, and in due course commanded a number of vessels built at Shore Village, that he probably used as his home port since it was closer to his home in Clam Cove than the harbor in Camden. The ships he sailed freighted cargo down the Maine coast to Boston and beyond, although it is doubtful that they sailed to distant foreign ports. In Boston, where stays to off-load and take on cargo would have been the longest and most frequent, he made friends through business dealings; and renewed acquaintances with the Gregory family in his Walpole birthplace.

◆   ◆   ◆

John Bird, who would become the patriarch of the Bird family, was born somewhere near Framingham, Massachusetts. As an infant, he was surreptitiously left on the doorstep of a home in that town operated by a woman known to take in orphans and illegitimate children, who were called foundlings. The baby's only identification was a note that read: "His name is John Bird". In 1805 young John Bird, barely eight years old, had lived in this foster home since birth. There were now a number of reasons for him to leave. He had become too big and active to stay in a home that cared only for younger children; and since he had started school and made friends with other boys, parents and teachers were beginning to be curious about his origins. His mother, who had previously paid for his keep, may have concluded that if John lived elsewhere there was less likelihood of embarrassment for her in Framingham or the vicinity.

Whatever the reason, inquiries were made among friends and others in maritime trade that led ultimately to Captain Gregory. Capt. William's down-east character and rectitude as well as his Walpole connections assured those interested that the boy would suffer no harm at his hands. The Captain, impressed with the boy's intelligence and good behavior, and probably for a reasonable fee, agreed to take him to Maine. He felt certain that one of his numerous brothers or sisters could easily make room for another sturdy, healthy boy willing to work for his keep. William had only one child, but his brother John, who was also known as Captain—a title earned as a result of service during the Revolution—had fathered nine children. The fourth, a girl, was named Clarissa. The Gregory homes were close together and John Bird may have lived at both William's and Capt. John's at one time or another. In any event, he certainly knew Clarissa from an early age.

The arrival of the young orphan, as the Gregorys preferred to call him, at Clam Cove in 1805 marks the beginning of the Bird name in the area. John claimed to have been born on December 25, 1797, but that may reflect the decision of an orphan to pick a suitable date for a birthday not knowing with certainty the actual date. Settled with the Gregorys, John Bird found this new foster family much more to his liking than the one in Framingham. For the first time in his short life he lived in a stable family environment; one that furnished him not only with room and board, but saw to his education, and taught him a trade.

In those days, children attended district one-room schools where they were taught the 3 R's. John went to school with assorted Gregory children, including Clarissa who was only a few months younger than he was. The boy proved to be industrious, energetic, learned quickly and gave every evidence of a superior intellect. He may also have had the ready wit and appealing personality that was passed on to many of his descendants. The earliest pictorial record is a tintype of him in his middle years. It shows a handsome man with dark hair, intelligent brown eyes and a ruddy, clean-shaven complexion. Of moderate height with a thin wiry frame, he no doubt carried himself with an air of dignity and independence. A man who could walk three miles to his store and back every day and work his farm, as John did in the 1820's before he moved to Rockland, is not going to carry any excess weight.

When John arrived in Clam Cove, he found himself part of a family which already numbered eight children. The two oldest Gregory children, Mary, 13 and Frances 11 were in charge of the house, since their mother, Elizabeth's time was taken up with caring for the younger children: Celinda, 4, the toddler, Hanson, and infant Hiram. Within another year the ninth, (and blessedly the last) child,

Isaac, would be born. That left William, nine going on ten, John Jr. just six, and finally Clarissa, at seven the one closest in age to the new arrival. John Bird felt right at home with these children, although he also felt somewhat superior to the younger ones, having already been exposed to the big city of Boston and having traveled all the way to this distant part of Massachusetts. In any event, he found himself quickly absorbed into the ebb and flow of life on a country farm. It fell to Clarissa as the closest in age to John Bird, who was now called John B. to distinguish him from John Gregory or John G., to break in the new boy.

A farm such as the Gregory's was nearly self-sufficient. Much of the land had already been cleared in order to grow staple crops of oats and corn. Live stock included plow horses or a yoke of oxen, at least one riding horse, one or two milk cows, pigs, chickens and possibly some sheep. The proximity of salt water meant a variety of fish available for the much-needed protein in the family diet. Haddock and cod could be dried, smoked or salted and stored for winter use. Game included an abundance of deer and moose and even the occasional bear which could be killed with the muzzle loading guns of the day. Pheasants, ducks and geese were trapped, and small game, such as rabbits, was plentiful. Every home, even those in Shore Village, had a kitchen garden, that produced beans, peas, squash, potatoes and other root vegetables. These were kept in cold cellars during the winter or preserved in jars for winter consumption; butter and cheese were also stored. Fields not in cultivation produced two crops of hay in most years; the excess, after feeding the live stock, could be sold to town dwellers unable to provide for it themselves. In the summertime there were blueberries, wild raspberries and lovely, sweet, little wild strawberries in the fields and rocky outcroppings of the land. Apple trees and an occasional pear tree provided additional fruit, all of which could be preserved for winter's need. But nature's bounty required husbanding, a chore which fell to the children in large families. With Clarissa's guidance, John Bird soon became adept at the routine chores of farm life. It was the beginning of their lifelong association—as children, as sweethearts, as husband and wife and parents.

After the age of 12 or 13 boys were needed to operate the farms or they went to sea as their fathers had done, but in many instances they were apprenticed to learn a trade. (Girls may have stayed in school longer, but if they were needed at home, as both Clarissa's older sisters were, their formal schooling was also over by age thirteen.) It was John's lot to learn a trade. The flourishing industry of quarrying and burning limestone to produce lime used in construction in the booming cities to the south required wooden barrels, called casks, for shipping containers. The perceptive Gregorys apprenticed John to a cooper. When John was 15 or16 he had a trade much in demand in the surrounding area. With steady work for good wages he not only achieved his independence, but also compensated the Gregorys for his care.

With the enterprise and acumen that characterized his adult career, young John was not long satisfied to work for mere wages, even those of a skilled journeyman cooper. A deal with one of the owners of the abundant forest land gave him a source of wood that he cut himself for staves and heads for his own barrel shop. Whatever wood was not usable for barrels could be sold to sawmills or for fuel for the hungry lime kilns. The extra profits from cutting his own wood helped to hasten the day when he could buy the cleared land from which he had profited. Within a few years, John was farming his own tract in the vicinity of Clam Clove and the Camden Road. Here he likely raised crops that were the least labor intensive, leaving him time for his cooper's shop and for his next venture. Hay and fodder-corn were required for the hundreds of draft horses used in the lime industry, and hay from Maine was shipped in great quantities to Boston and New York. Straw was required for insulation in ice houses at nearby ponds and in the ships that carried ice to the big cities. Potatoes and other root vegetables found a ready market feeding workers in quarries and lime kilns and provisioning the many ships that carried the lime southward. John also earned a little money acting as tax collector in the Clam Cove area of Camden.

By the time he reached the age of 24 in 1821, through hard work and an ability to take advantage of opportunity, John Bird had assured himself of a steady income and a modest amount of capital. He had his own home now in Clam Cove—a place where he could bring a wife. There was never any question in John's mind as to who his wife would be—it had always been Clarissa. Ever since they were children, there had been a bond between them, which as they grew older, became unbreakable. John relied on Clarissa for advice and support, while Clarissa admired John's independence, intelligence and the determination he had shown in overcoming the handicap of being an orphan.

Of all John Gregory's children, Clarissa was the least likely to conform to a submissive pattern of female behavior. Somewhat of a tomboy as a child, she had grown into a strong minded, motivated adult. To judge from the same tintype that showed John in middle age, Clarissa was not a beautiful woman, but one whose face reflected intelligence and character. Pictures cannot describe what a person looks like when they speak or smile; at such a time her face may have become very animated and attractive. If she inherited the Gregory geniality, she undoubtedly had wit and humor. Her features were sharp and her eyes, her most prominent feature, were heavy lidded, a characteristic, that she handed down to sons and grandsons. She may also have bequeathed a prominent "Roman nose" which appeared in many of her offspring in successive generations. Whatever her appearance, she was, as one writer put it "a woman of remarkable force of character, to whose assistance much of Mr. Bird's future success was due."[1]

In 1821 Mary and Frances Gregory were already married: Frances to Jeremiah Berry of Rockland, and Mary to Ebenezer Cleaveland from Camden. Clarissa's older brother, William, was also married and now lived in Camden. That left Clarissa at age 23 the oldest child still living at home. Had she and John not already been planning to marry, she would surely have been considered an old maid. But marry him she did in the spring of 1821 in a Baptist ceremony, at the new, interdenominational Meeting House, (also called the Brick Church), on Limerock Street near what was then the Camden Road (now Old County Road). All the Gregorys, even old William then nearly 90 attended their wedding. Mary and Frances and their husbands were there and so were Frances' three children: the youngest, William, still an infant. Some of the Tolmans, attended as well as members of the Keene family who were neighbors of the Gregorys.

Once married and settled in their home at Clam Cove, Clarissa and John started planning for their future. They discussed business matters and they continued to do so throughout the rest of their married life. At this time, John was taking most of his casks down to the lime kilns at Shore Village. With new kilns being built all the time, the couple realized that it was possible to accept shares of a future, or already producing, lime kiln in payment for the casks John made. This proved to be a timely idea. It was not long before John became a partner in, and later owner of, a number of kilns. By 1825, in addition to manufacturing lime, he also opened a small store, which catered to the teamsters who hauled the lime and the workers who processed it.

Blackington's Corner, situated at the intersection of the Camden road and the inland road to Hope and Warren, lay about two miles from John's home. On his way to the kilns at Shore Village, the Corner presented other advantages to the budding Bird businessman. It was an area of considerable traffic for it was the most direct route to either Camden or Thomaston from Shore Village and inland points. The Corner was also on the direct mail route between Portland and Bangor. (Although Shore Village was developing into the main commercial and shipping center for the area, there was as yet no direct road along the shore to either town.) Many lime-burning kilns were situated along the shore of the harbor, but there were also a number around Blackington's Corner. Considering the traffic going past the Corner, John Bird could see the opportunity it offered for some sort of a general store that would supply the needs of the growing local population as well as travelers and quarry workmen. Probably as early as 1825 [2] he made arrangements to open his store. The site he chose was on the southwest corner of the intersection. (Currently the intersection of Maverick St. and Lakeview Drive.) At first, the store stocked basic food items imported from elsewhere, such as molasses, sugar, spices and tobacco, all in bulk. Hardware, pots and pans, yard goods and other domestic items progressively expanded the store's inventory. Over the years the store grew, and as it grew its business changed from strictly retail to predominately wholesale. In 1855 it took the name of The John Bird Company. By the time John Bird died the company he had founded was one of the region's most successful, and would carry his name for more than a hundred years.

Even before his marriage, John had invested small sums in syndicated shipbuilding ventures—the earliest in 1819 was a small ketch or sloop called *The Fly*. Additionally, there were a number of other small boats in which he had shares. In 1827, with his friends Tolman, Keene, and Thorndike, he became a part owner of the 108-ton schooner, *Peggy Thomas*. At first most of these ships were used to carry lime, but with the success of the grocery business, larger ships were used for the transportation of the John Bird Company products. John would continue to invest in shipping and lime until the end of his life. Both ventures contributed generously to his eventual wealth. In 1854, as one of Rockland's principal businessmen, he led in the organization of the North Bank and served as its president until his death.

The marriage of John and Clarissa fulfilled their deepest desires. Within a year their first child, a boy, was born. They named him Adoniram Judson after the famous Baptist missionary. This child would always be called A.J., since Adoniram seemed too much of a mouthful for such a small child. Another boy, named Hanson after Clarissa's brother, Hanson P. Gregory,[3] was born in 1823. Then came Almon in 1825, followed by John Jr. in 1827. In the next twelve years, five daughters were born to John and Clarissa, four of whom survived to adulthood, while only the fifth died in infancy. Considering the frequency of infant mortality at that time, it is remarkable that so many of the Bird children not only survived but also became strong healthy individuals living in some cases to very old ages.

The final addition to their family was another boy who was named Sidney, and who would be the father of Maynard. Of the five boys, only John, Jr. and Sidney followed in their father's footsteps by becoming partners in the John Bird Company and carrying on the other business ventures that John Bird had started.

By the time of Sidney's birth in 1840 all his brothers were pretty well grown up, with the exception of John Jr. who was 13. Adoniram was already active in the lime business and would shortly open his own store at the north end of Shore Village. Hanson, a year younger than Adoniram, made the sea his career following in the footsteps of his notable uncle and namesake. Records show Hanson as a part owner and sometimes captain of many of the Maine built ships in the Bird family fleet: a fleet that was expanding along with the other Bird enterprises. Almon Bird, the third son, was content to follow in his father's footsteps in the role of shopkeeper. Whether his goals were more limited than those of his brothers or whether he was differently motivated, he seems never to have sought anything beyond managing the original Bird store at Blackington's Corner. In later years Almon's son Ulysses would join his father at the store, eventually becoming an owner. Almon's marriage to Sarah Keene produced one other son, Leslie, whose offspring were far more numerous than those of the rest of that Bird generation, but in the 20th Century they seemed to have migrated to different parts of Maine and the country in general.

Despite the age difference between the brothers, Sidney was closest to John Jr. It was hard not to like John. He was gregarious, witty and a born salesman, able to hold his audience spellbound with Downeast yarns and tall tales. Also, he seems to have inherited the Bird intelligence and a willingness to work hard. These characteristics were sufficient to earn him a partnership in The John Bird Company at the age of 28 in 1855. For 37 years, John Jr. continued to play a significant role in the continued expansion and success of the family company. If his business life was successful, his private life had elements of tragedy. Married to Abby Smith of Worcester, Massachusetts when he was nearly 30, the couple produced two children within three years—Adeline and William. After that, there was a succession of still births and infant deaths, until their last child, Sumner, was born in 1874. Abby died in 1878 whether from consumption, the scourge of many Maine communities, or from constant childbearing. She was followed less than ten years later by Sumner, probably another consumption victim. A stone that reads "No Sects in Heaven" marks Abby's grave. We are left to wonder what form of prejudice she endured and whether death may not have been a welcome release from the trials of her life. John married a second time but fathered no more children.

Sidney's birth barely a year after the death of an infant daughter made him particularly precious to Clarissa. As an infant and toddler he was tended by older sisters and treated as a special child by the girls. If he avoided being spoiled it was because the family in general were far too busy with the normal chores and business activities to waste time on him. The size of the family gave a sense of security to all the children and the growing importance of the Bird ventures in the town impressed each member with a sense of pride in their place in the community. The influence in Sidney's life of his sisters was replaced by that of his father and brothers by the time he was a teenager. The boy was showing the same characteristics of enterprise and energy that marked his father's life. These qualities were combined with those of his mother of decisiveness, self-discipline and authority. If there was a touch of arrogance in Sidney's personality, future events conspired to remove it.

Sidney's education was that of any other boy his age. From the age of four or five he attended schools in the neighborhood including the nearby Highland School located almost directly across the Thomaston-Camden road from the Bird store. No high school or academy as yet existed in the area; the closest one was an academy in Thomaston that provided some form of advanced education. In any event, Sidney's formal education ended when he was 18. Between the years at the Highland School, working at the family store after school hours, and learning about finance through his father's interest in the North Bank, as well as experience in the other Bird enterprises, the boy had a far more complete education than most of his contemporaries. Whether his father recognized the boy's ability and was consciously grooming him as his successor, there is no doubt that he accorded Sidney far greater participation at an earlier age in the family businesses than his others sons. John Jr. had not become a partner in the John Bird Company until he was 28, but Sidney achieved that distinction when he was 22 in 1862.

◆   ◆   ◆

By that time (1862) Sidney was already married and a father of two children. Little is known about his courtship of Ann Eliza Heard—generally called Annie—except the facts of their marriage and their subsequent life. The Heard family came from original settlers at Ash Point, a community of seafarers and fishermen about 10 miles from Shore Village. It was Annie's misfortune that her father, Alvan Heard, died in 1846 when she was only four years old. Her mother, the former Eliza Hall, subsequently remarried a widower, Captain David Haskell II, of South Thomaston. As a small child, Annie went to live in a family where she had no standing except as the child of a second wife. Captain Haskell died in 1854 and Annie's mother followed two years later leaving her 15-year-old daughter an orphan, dependent on the support and benevolence of relatives. The Heard family offered no sanctuary, but fortunately, her mother's sister, Nancy Hall Brown, who lived at Blackington's Corner, took in the orphan girl.[4] Annie probably completed her education at the Highland School. She could have met Sidney either at school or perhaps in the Bird store where Sidney worked.

After a childhood and youth of being dependent on others for her livelihood, Annie yearned for the stability of a family like the Bird's. A picture of Annie, taken in the 1860's shows a woman with a not unpleasing, but serious face. She stands behind a Victorian style sofa, with her hand on the wood carved frame in her plaid taffeta crinoline skirt and dark balloon sleeved shirt waist; the white edge of the blouse at the neck is highlighted by a cameo. Her dark hair, in the style of the period, is parted in the middle and draped over her ears framing and enhancing the oval of her face. Deep set eyes, a straight regular nose and a firm mouth produce a solemn appearance in one so young.

Sidney at 19 was the handsome scion of a prominent local family. A picture taken at the same time as Annie's shows a serious appearing young man with a high forehead, thick black hair and full beard. Brown eyes under slightly hooded lids seem to conceal emotions while still evidencing intelligence and dignity. He had a straight, high-bridged nose curving slightly over a sensuous mouth that in later years was masked by a mustache His nose, inherited from Clarissa, he passed on to his son, Maynard. Sidney, like his parents and brothers was of medium height. The picture shows him rather formally dressed in the manner of the Victorian mid-century male, and if one is to compare it with a picture taken in his later years, he seems to have been a stylish and meticulous dresser.

Sidney Morse Bird married Ann Eliza Heard on September 25, 1859 in a Baptist ceremony performed by The Rev. Joseph Kalloch. The ceremony was performed at the home of the bride's aunt, Mrs. Brown. Whether this was a joyous occasion or one brought on by necessity, the fact was that the bride was nearly five months pregnant. In order to give a semblance of respectability to the occasion, the parents of the groom were present, as were one or more of the groom's brothers. Considering the social mores of the day, it is doubtful that many outsiders were invited. However, the union turned out to be a happy one. Annie found the love, security and family stability she had yearned for, while Sidney, despite the need for such a marriage, was a fond husband and loving father. They settled in a small house near the corner of Cedar Street and the Camden Road. Here their first child, Newbury Alvan was born in January 1860. A second son, Elmer followed in May of 1861.

◆   ◆   ◆

John Bird died on September 15, 1868 after a long illness. His obituary best sums up the significance of his life: "Mr Bird has for several years been one of the most prominent business men of our city, and from nothing, [he] gained from his own industry a large property. He was a man of great diligence, good judgement and unblemished moral character, a constant attendant upon the services of the church [Baptist] of which he was a member, and a kind father and husband."[5]

Maynard, the third son of Sidney and Annie, was born 10-months after John Bird's death. Of all John's descendents, he would exhibit most vividly his grandfather's traits of "diligence, good judgement and unblemished moral character."

2

Rockland Gazette: August 17, 1875
Born to Mr. and Mrs. Sidney Bird of Old County Road, The Highlands, this city, a son named Henry Borstel. Henry will join his three older brothers, Newbury, Elmer and Maynard in this branch of the Bird family.

Mr. Bird is a partner in the John M. Bird Company, and President of the North Bank where he succeeded his father who founded the bank. Mr. Bird is also active in Republican politics.

Rockland Gazette: August 27, 1875
Died in this city, Newbury Alvin Bird age 15 years, 8 months and 4 days, eldest son of Mr. and Mrs. Sidney Bird of Old County Road, The Highlands, after a long, wasting illness. Services will be private at the Bird homestead.

◆　　◆　　◆

Maynard Bird was barely six when these events occurred. Up to this time he had led what could be considered a normal life for a boy living in the small Maine city. In the years since the death of his grandfather, the first John Bird, ten months before Maynard's birth, the Bird's had become increasingly prosperous and recognized figures in the Rockland community. His father, Sidney, and the rest of the numerous Bird clan were demonstrating that the road to fame and wealth was through owning one's own business; promoting new products and services spreading throughout the country; and, most particularly, building affiliations with other able venturers.

Sidney Bird and his older brothers, John and Adoniram, (A.J.), were the principal partners in the family company, founded by their father and now flourishing far beyond the expectations of its founder. From a small neighborhood store, it was developing into a large, regional retailer and wholesaler of foodstuffs, dry goods and general merchandise. Except for areas immediately around Rockland, product distribution was made by ship—either bought or built—to towns up and down the Maine coast. The Bird family continued their interest in ships and shipbuilding, and now owned a considerable fleet of ships[6] that were used to carry an increasing variety of other cargoes.

Family members were also heavily involved in the lime business, the backbone of the regional economy. Lime burning provided abundant employment at good wages; a profit flow that enriched leading families, and a liberal coating of black ash and white lime dust. (If there was a connection between the lime business, air pollution and the incidence of lung inflammation, no one seemed to notice.) Some of the Bird ships were used for lime shipment, although the same ship could not be used for both the carrying of lime and company merchandise. Although the Civil War blockade had cut the production of lime by half, business had rapidly recovered in the years immediately following the war. In 1868 Rockland's lime production had passed the million-cask mark for the year. In 1871, the Bird's joined with other principal lime producers, including Francis Cobb and William A. Farnsworth, to form the Cobb Lime Company. This company became the leading manufacturer of lime in the state. Despite the Panic of 1873, which hit the lime business hard, the Bird's other businesses prospered.

As the family fortunes flourished, Sidney felt they needed to build a home that would adequately accomodatehis growing family, and, also, reflected his importance in the community. The site chosen for the "The Homestead" and later known as "The Bird House" was a nine-acre lot next to the Achorn Cemetery on the Thomaston-Camden road no more than 500 yards from Blackington's Corner. Construction started in 1868, although it had not been finished at the time Maynard was born. Well set back from the road, it was reached by a drive lined on both sides with a row of trees. "Heavy timbers went into the frame which was set on hand fitted granite blocks whose seams were filled with melted lead."[7] The front door was set back behind a porch. Windows on either side and on the second floor gave a balanced appearance to the façade. Chimneys on either end of a hipped-roof, which was, in turn, crowned with the railing of a 'widow's walk', completed an imposing appearance. At the end of the driveway, but somewhat to the rear of the house, was a barn and carriage house.

The interior was as spacious as the exterior was imposing. Four bedrooms were thought to be sufficient for the growing family. Downstairs there were two adjoining parlors separated by sliding doors. Additionally, a music room for Annie; a dining room, two kitchens and a washroom comprised the rest of the living space. Great care was given to the interior with wood paneling in the front hall; a finely carved stair railing; and in the parlors, elaborate mantel carvings done by local craftsmen as was the stucco work in several rooms.

For Sidney, as it would be for his son, Maynard, in later years, a house was a symbol of stability, strength and importance. Sidney succeeded in building one that dwarfed all others in the area. What he could not have foreseen in 1868 was that the center of residential Rockland would move closer to the business section of town. By the time of his death in 1907, his beautiful home was already part of a neighborhood which was declining—one made up of small Cape Cod houses, ramshackle two story farm houses, and commercial properties. Ultimately, in the 1970's the "Bird House" would be demolished and an uninspired 2-story colonial built in its place. But that was far in the future and for Maynard and his brothers who lived in this grand home in 1875, the present, as exemplified by their father's success, could not fail to exemplify for the boys the importance of their father's position in the community.

Maynard was barely a year old when the family moved into The Homestead; so, as far as he was concerned, he never knew another house. His earliest memories were of the area surrounding the house. In the big barn cows, horses and carriages filled the ground space, while above in the loft there was hay just meant for boys to tumble in. The Bird store up the road a piece where his mother, Annie, frequently took him, was one of his favorite spots. He loved the smell of the store: an amalgam of scents that emanated from the spices, picked up a touch of tobacco, sweetened with the smell of molasses, and coated overall with a musky store-like aroma of bare worn wooden floors. His mother or one of his uncles would sit him on a high stool amid the barrels of crackers, flour, tobacco and beans. There were hogsheads of molasses, bags of white sugar brought in by ship from far away islands, and every once in a while, when a ship came in from Florida or another tropical place, oranges, lemons and limes. Shelves full of curious pieces of hardware were on one side and on the other there were bolts of fabrics and ribbons and all sorts of sewing things that attracted his mother. There were pots and pans hanging from hooks on the wall, and a variety of household necessities without which no Maine housewife could possibly keep house.

In the store, Maynard could watch and listen to the coterie of old men, for whom the store was a second home, as they told endless yarns that he was still too young to understand. He may have known intuitively that, whether true or not, these stories formed the pattern and core of the world he lived in. Occasionally, one of the men would get up to cut himself another piece of chewing tobacco from a twist hanging from the counter. At such times the little boy might be handed a stick of black licorice or a piece of horehound candy from a glass jar strategically located on the counter next to the tobacco, with the admonition, "Here's summat for you Sonny, don't eat it all t'once." One thing that aroused the child's interest in particular was the ability of these store sitters to hit the spittoon located ten feet or more from their circle of chairs. A good spitter could aim a stream of tobacco juice into the dead center of the spittoon. What was even more remarkable was the gong sound made when the expectoration, slightly off target, hit the lip of the spittoon before falling into the bowl. Some of these ancients were more proficient at this than others and were recognized for their skill by the Downeast congratulation, "That were a good un, Jawn!"

Whether Maynard realized that this was his family's store or not was immaterial. It was a wonderful place for a small boy to go. But one thing Maynard did know was that not having any brothers or sisters near his own age was an advantage because his mother would usually take him with her to do her errands, or even to visit with neighbors. On any of these trips he was always the center of attention. A small slight child with dark brown eyes under heavy lids, he looked in this respect like his grandmother, Clarissa. He had a straight, determined mouth under a nose, prominent even at such a young age, a well-shaped jaw and straight, almost black hair above a broad forehead. His serious appearance belied the fact that he was actually a very happy child—one who always appealed to others and would always continue to do so.

By the summer of 1875 things had begun to change. Maynard probably noticed earlier that his brother Newbury took up more and more of his mother's time. Newbury seemed to stay in bed a lot, and Maynard would often hear him coughing both during the night and day. Annie spent more and more time with Newbury, and after a night when the coughing was particularly bad, the morning would see the hired girl, arms full of bloody sheets, hustling to the washroom to start another days washing. Often, Annie, herself, would take to her bed after such a night leaving Maynard in the care of his brother Elmer. More to Maynard's liking was when he was taken to his Uncle John's house across the street. Here he could play with baby Sumner and be cared for by his cousin Addie (Adeline), who at 11 was a fully capable 'little mother'.

The year had been hard on Annie Bird—one that she would never forget. Before Christmas Annie knew that she was once again pregnant. This should have been seen as a joyous event since it was more than five years since Maynard had been born. Unfortunately, however, the good news was offset by the failing condition of her oldest child. It had been obvious to Annie and Sidney for sometime that Newbury was suffering from tuberculosis, (then called consumption), which during the 19th century was particularly prevalent in the Maine seacoast communities. Annie was not aware of the seriousness of her son's condition when she became pregnant. No matter what remedies they applied, the feverish eyes, flushed face, uncontrolled coughing, combined with a constant low-grade temperature persisted. The doctors recommended lots of fresh air and sunshine, but a Maine winter is not conducive to these elements. By the time better, warmer weather arrived in late May and June, the disease was already too far advanced for that treatment to be effective.

Any concern Maynard might have had was forgotten when he learned that he was to have a new sister or brother. His father told him that this was a 'blessed event' and it would be an occasion for family rejoicing. Maynard was excited by the thought that he would now have a brother or sister to play with. Elmer, who was already 14, when not in school, could be found working at the Store. Despite all the nearby aunts, uncles and cousins, there was no one in his own family just Maynard's age. Shortly after his sixth birthday, the baby arrived, but when he was allowed into his mother's room, he quickly realized that it would be a long time before the squirming bundle of red flesh by her side turned into someone he could play with. "What's its name?" asked Maynard.

"IT is a boy," answered his mother. "Heaven has blessed us with a fine boy and we're going to call him Henry Borstel."

"When will he be big enough to come out and play?" was the next question although Maynard already knew the answer.

His mother just smiled and said, "You wait, Maynard, he'll be big enough before you know it. Now you go out and tell your friends about your new baby brother."

◆   ◆   ◆

A little more than a week later, Maynard's father took him to Newbury's room to say goodbye. "Where's he going?" Maynard asked.

"God is going to take him to heaven," Sidney replied.

When Maynard went into Newbury's room, he found his brother in bed, so pale and thin. "Are you really going to heaven, Newbury?" Maynard asked.

Sidney tried to hush Maynard up, but Newbury just nodded his head. Then he seemed to rouse himself and spoke gently but in a faint voice to his brother. "You be a good boy, Maynard. You can have my jackknife if you want, I won't be needing it." Then he started to cough again and Maynard was taken out of the room.

All of this was confusing to the six-year old boy. He wondered if God had given them the new baby because God wanted Newbury to come live with Him in heaven. It didn't seem like a fair exchange—a little bitty baby for Newbury who was all grown up.

The next day there was a big box on sawhorses in one of the parlors and Newbury's body had been put in it. Maynard's father and mother sat in the other parlor—his mother holding Henry, looking tired and sad. There was a big black wreath on the front door and lots of flowers that people who came and spoke to his father and mother had brought. They also brought lots of food so that no one had to cook. Many of the people who came cried. Elmer stayed near his father, but Maynard, who didn't like to have his head patted by the men visitors or be kissed by the ladies, retreated to the kitchen where his cousin, Addie, found him.

The two children wandered out to the barn where they discussed the situation. Addie, who felt qualified to speak authoritatively on the matter of death because her mother had endured a number of infant deaths, took it upon herself to enlighten Maynard on the subject.

"You know, Maynie," she said, "don't feel badly about Newbury's death. Mama says children die because God doesn't want them to be sick so he takes them to Heaven where they can get well."

"Well, did God make Newbury sick so he could take him to Heaven? And why did He wait so long?" Maynard sounded far from convinced. "The children your Mama lost were all babies. Newbury was fifteen years old!"

"Well, don't you see," Addie said a little impatiently, "our babies weren't well to start out with, and God thought it was better to take them right away so they wouldn't have to suffer." As an afterthought, she added triumphantly, "Your Mama got your new brother, Henry in exchange, didn't she!"

"What did your Mama get in exchange?" Maynard was not to be deterred in his line of reasoning. "God didn't take you or William in exchange did He!"

"Course not!" Addie had it all worked out. "Father told Mama he'd give her more babies to take the place of the little ones who died. And he did. Only some of them didn't last. Now we've got Sumner and he's lasting. He's going on two now, so there!"

Maynard was not up to disputing his cousin. All in all, he decided, maybe it was just as well not to get sick. Later, it occurred to him to wonder how Addie knew that her father gave her mother babies. His mother had said that Heaven—that must mean God—had blessed them by sending Henry. If that was the case, what did his father have to do with getting babies for his mother? Maynard's six-year old brain was not yet ready to solve this puzzle.

"C'mon Addie," he said tiring of all this talk about God, babies and death, "Let's go see if the apples on that 'ol' apple tree behind the barn are ripe yet!"

◆   ◆   ◆

A day later the minister from the church came and said some prayers. Then a lid was put on the box with Newbury in it, and taken to the cemetery next door. There the box was put in a hole dug in the ground and covered with dirt.

As Maynard stood next to his mother, holding her hand, he wondered how Newbury was ever going to get to Heaven packed up in that box, but his brother Elmer told him that Newbury was already in Heaven; that it was his spirit that went not his body. This puzzled Maynard even more because no one had ever told him that Newbury had a spirit. Perhaps that was why Newbury had given him the jackknife. Evidently spirits didn't use knives in heaven.

Finally he put these thoughts out of his mind. There were other things to think about, especially going back to school in a few days. He knew he would find some new boys to play with there.

3

Henry's birth had a profound and longer lasting effect on Maynard than Newbury's death. He was no longer the baby of the family, but was relegated to the position of Elmer's younger brother. Eight years Maynard's senior, Elmer was already working occasionally in the 'Store' and would, in a few years, make The John Bird Company his career. Maynard automatically assumed the role of big brother, first to Henry and three years later to Alan. But perhaps because of the circumstances of Henry's birth, Maynard was, throughout his life, closer to Henry than to Alan

Annie Bird, still mourning the tragic loss of her eldest child, was preoccupied with infant, Henry, leaving less time and attention for Maynard. He seems to have understood intuitively that Henry meant more to his mother than just another baby. In a story entitled "Baby Beauty Contest" written for Henry on his 80th birthday in 1955, Maynard expresses this understanding: *"Henry was born at a time that meant a great deal to Mother. He was the wonder baby—light hair, sort of blue eyes and a fair complexion—into a family of dark-haired and dark-eyed brothers. ' "Heaven Born Child"' was the way he was spoken of."*

The years following Henry's birth in 1875 were years of increasing affluence and importance for the Bird family in the commercial, political and social life of Rockland, Maine. Sidney, with his brothers John, and Adoniram, was expanding the scope of The John Bird Company by concentrating exclusively on wholesale operations. With the fleet of ships, owned wholly or in part by the Bird family and managed to a large extent by brother Hanson, the company was shipping goods up and down the Maine coast to small communities not reachable by rail or road. More and more, John was traveling to buy merchandise for the Bird enterprises, leaving Sidney in charge of day to day operations. Adoniram controlled the family's lime business, while Almon worked in and later managed the Highlands store when the company moved its headquarters into Rockland proper in 1883.

Sidney was more farsighted than his brothers; he was one of the few local businessmen who saw "a prosperous venture in the establishment of an electric street [trolley] railroad. Other men, shrewd and conservative, were much less sanguine of its success".[8] During his lifetime, Sidney promoted or helped form the Rock-

21

land, Thomaston and Camden Street Railway as well as the Camden and Rockland Water Company serving as president of the latter. He was also active in local Republican politics and served two terms on the Rockland City Council. Later, he served three terms in the Maine State Legislature and on the Maine Governor's Council.

Family life was built around Sidney's schedule. He was usually preoccupied with various business matters, and local politics; state politics meant that he spent less and less time at home. When at home, it was not unusual for him to leave home early on a weekday morning driving a horse and buggy, first to attend to matters at the Highland store. Then he would continue down Maverick Street to the North Bank located, as its name implied, at the north end of town. He might stop at the docks to consult on shipments of goods for the Company—either incoming or outbound. When he arrived home in time for supper—usually served at about 5:30 or 6:00PM—the evening would be spent, as with most families, in reading, possibly card games or cribbage, and even music if anyone was so inclined. (The Bird family never inclined to any real musical ability.) Infants and little children under a certain age were expected to be in bed sometime soon after the rest of the family had eaten. Children Maynard's age and older were allowed to stay up later—or at least until evening prayers had been said.

Prayer was an integral part of New England family life and there is no reason to think the Birds differed in this respect. The day was started with prayers, and prayers were said before each meal. Most families adhered to one or another of the Protestant denominations with Congregationalists predominating, Baptists the second most numerous and Methodists a distant third. The Bird family was distinctive in one respect—they were what would be known today as a 'mixed marriage'. Annie was a staunch Baptist, while Sidney, although of Baptist roots, was now leaning toward Congregationalism. This caused some low-key conflict between the husband and wife as when Annie objected to Sidney's playing cards on Sunday. Sidney's response was, "The Bible says 'God made Sunday a day of rest' and I guess He's not going to object too much if I find playing cards a restful activity." Nevertheless, the family always attended the Baptist church en masse each Sunday morning. Living a considerable distance from either the Congregational or Baptist churches, that were situated across from each other on opposite corners of Summer and Main Streets, it was inconvenient to attend Sunday evening prayer meetings—this to the unqualified relief of Maynard's father.

Sunday activities really started on Saturday with the Saturday night bath; so that by early evening the children, at least, had been scrubbed and polished to a fare-thee-well. Until such a time as running water and indoor plumbing was installed in the Bird homestead, baths were usually taken in a big tub set up in the kitchen and filled with hot water from buckets heated on the stove. In some large families, the children would have to reuse the bath water after a younger—or older—sibling had had first crack. The Birds, however, considering their status in Rockland society, eschewed this practice, and anyway, their family wasn't large enough to require such restriction. By the 1890s if not before, Maynard's home boasted of modern plumbing, doing away with kitchen bathing and the outhouse as well. Saturday night supper was always baked beans cooked all day in an earthenware pot, with a generous supply of salt pork and covered with molasses mixed with brown sugar. Creamed salt finnan haddie (salted haddock) was also a staple of Saturday night supper. Thus, well fed and well scrubbed, the family members were deemed morally and corporately prepared for the Sabbath.

With a new baby and a husband immersed in business activities, Annie Bird was expected to take care of the home, the children and provide a restful retreat for her busy spouse. Since their house was the largest and most imposing structure in the neighborhood, there was obviously more work involved in taking care of it plus the barn with its livestock, and the vegetable garden—still a required feature of every good New England home. This was more than one person could handle, so Maynard's mother undoubtedly had help both in the house and outside starting with the children who were assigned chores. While Elmer still had some responsibilities, Maynard at six was old enough to take on some easier chores like feeding the chickens and collecting their eggs. As he grew older he graduated to milking the cow, feeding the horses and occasionally cleaning out their stalls. He didn't like the latter and complained constantly that it left him and his clothes smelling like a barn. (The fastidiousness he later displayed in his dress and appearance had its roots, no doubt, in his efforts to erase the barn smell from his person.) Occasionally the boys might be called on to pick some peas or beans for dinner—that is if they could be found at the time they were needed. Little boys have a knack of not being in evidence when called on to do something they don't want to do. The Bird family had the resources, and used them, to hire outside help to assist in running such a large house and grounds. In small New England communities it was customary to hire a local person to assist around the house. This 'person' might be a young daughter of one of the families nearby, or perhaps an older woman who, for whatever reason, was willing to do day work for a local family. Such help was not considered a servant but more like a family friend who was simply helping out. This practice of hiring local help continued well into the 20th Century, even though at the end of the 19th Century foreign immigration, especially Finnish immigration, provided a new source of labor to replace neighborhood friends. Nevertheless, there continued to be a more familiar relationship between employer and employee than could be seen in urban areas along the East Coast. In later life, Maynard had the knack of joking with household help while still maintaining a certain amount of reserve as befitted the head of the household. Children brought up in families where this relationship existed looked on a long-time cook or housekeeper as part of the family. In his later years, Henry and his wife, Edith, had Ida who literally ran the house for them. She was beloved by Henry's children as well as by all the others who knew her. Alan and his wife, Adelaide, had a wonderful cook named Pauline—a pastry chef par excellence. Birthday cakes were works of art, and fat, jolly Pauline with her sparkling blue eyes was often called on to play Santa Claus to children in the neighborhood.

Annie Bird surely had help for cooking, laundry and housekeeping. For the outdoors there was a hired man to take care of the kitchen garden, the barn and livestock—at least those duties that were not the responsibility of Elmer and Maynard, and later Henry and Alan. When the house was built wood-burning fireplaces heated it, and Franklin stoves placed in rooms without fireplaces. Cooking was done on cast iron stoves fueled with wood, and it would be the task of the children to keep the wood box filled with newly chopped wood. However, the Bird house converted to coal when that commodity became available sometime later in 19th Century.

Whether heated by wood or coal, every Maine house required a vigorous 'spring cleaning' to rid itself of the winter's accumulation of dirt or, in the case of coal heat, coal dust. Annie hired the same team of women every year—one or two, but occasionally three—whose pride in their "Spring Cleaning" profession was evident in the authority with which they attacked their objective and organized their assault. Like all true professionals, family and cleaners alike addressed each other as "Mrs." or "Miss". They, would arrive on the appointed day, usually Monday, armed with an assortment of brooms, mops, buckets, rags and carpet beaters. For the rest of the week the house would be in turmoil. The women, their heads covered with cotton scarves, rolled up carpets and rugs; took them outdoors, where they were hung over clotheslines. There, with the women exhorting them to hit "hahdah", younger boys beat the rugs until both carpets and boys disappeared in a cloud of dust. The older boys, veterans of earlier 'spring cleaning' campaigns, had suddenly recalled important business elsewhere. Although vacuum cleaners had been invented, it was the opinion of the "pros" that all they did was turn the dust over. Especially since the dirt that had found a comfortable home in a braided or hooked rug could be dislodged only by scrubbing in hot water and air drying in sun and breeze. Furniture was covered with sheets and moved to the center of each room in order to allow the lady cleaners to wash the walls and ceilings. The ample feminine buttocks of the Windows Squad projected over windowsills until every windowpane glittered like a diamond. Curtains were removed and if they were washable they went to the wash bucket. Otherwise they were sent to the clotheslines for the same, but more delicate, treatment than the carpets. Beds were stripped and mattresses and pillows treated to shaking and beating—outdoors if possible. Every nook and cranny was subjected to the application of soap, hot water, brooms and mops. Paneled doors, mantelpieces, and other natural woodwork were polished to a high gloss with a mixture of lemon juice and linseed oil. Glass globes and lamp chimneys and shades were subject to careful washing and polishing by the more experienced technicians. ("Lizzie, you leave them lamp shades alone now. Mrs. Bird don't want no one touching 'em but me.") Each day, promptly at noon, the entire team and those of the family who had not escaped earlier, gathered at the big kitchen table for a dinner that would have sated a crew of quarry hands.

By the end of the week, with everyone exhausted, father and children were allowed to resume their usual routines in the usual places. But with a parting exhortation from the Force Commander that everything was now clean and had better be kept that way if they knew what was good for them. Maynard would remember 'spring cleaning' for the rest of his life despite the fact that the practice in its most violent form had been abandoned in the urban environments in which he later lived.

◆   ◆   ◆

Another event that made a big difference in Maynard's life while he was still at the knee pants age was the birth of his brother Alan in March of 1878, almost three years after Henry's arrival. Maynard had become more independent when Henry was born but there was still that closeness to his mother that neither of his younger brothers could claim. After all, HE and Elmer were the ones who remembered Newbury, and his brother's death may have made a more vivid impression on Maynard than on Elmer. Neither Henry nor Alan could claim this memory. To them, Newbury would always be someone who had been part of the family, but with whom they had no connection.

While Alan's birth loosened the bonds Maynard had with his mother still further, it had the effect of strengthening those with his father. Sidney probably remembered his own childhood: the youngest of nine children with all his brothers grown or nearly so, and realized that had he not been taken under the wing of his brother John, his life might have been quite different. When Alan arrived to complete the family, Sidney made it his business to show his middle son special attention. He would take Maynard with him to the bank, where given a piece of paper, a pencil and a seat on a teller's stool, the little boy would amuse himself for hours. At the same time, the child learned from the teller or other employees, how interest worked, and how by charging more interest on loans than it paid to depositors, the bank earned a profit. He learned how deposits were made and how money was withdrawn; and he watched the bookkeepers with their fine script, enter transactions in great big ledgers.

When his father went to the docks to supervise loading or unloading, Maynard begged to help the men who carried bales of tobacco or bags of flour on and off the ships. Sidney told him it was all right as long as he didn't get in the way. So the little boy would tug on the shirt of a big, burly, bearded man and plead, "Let me help, let me help!" And often he would be given some small bundle to take aboard. As he grew older, Maynard's help was enlisted to check bills of lading or invoices for goods sent to the company. Like most boys living in a sea side environment, he could easily identify ships by their rigging or shape. More often than not, he would see one or more ships belonging to a member of his family. Of course the one that gave him the greatest thrill was the S.M. Bird, named after his father. Perhaps one day he would have a ship named after him.

Sea Street, the location of many of the wharves, offered other learning opportunities that may not have set well with Maynard's mother. Sidney warned his son that some of the language picked up from the dock handlers was not to be repeated at home; he explained to his son that this kind of language was unfit for the ears of the gentler sex under any circumstance. The teamsters who drove the quarry wagons, past the Bird homestead and down to the shore could swear a blue streak and the presence of small boys was no inhibitor. Sea Street had been the principal 'red light' district in Rockland from the earliest times so that boys learned, early or late, the trade carried on by some of its residents. Although Maine became 'dry' long before Prohibition, in Maynard's youth there were still plenty of taverns in town whose trade, in addition to food and (questionable) lodging, provided some form of liquid refreshment to slake a seafarer's thirst.

Thus, Maynard's education continued to expand.

◆　　　◆　　　◆

In those days, even though there were no kindergartens, children were sent to the village school as early as four. No restrictions were placed on age, and a child was ready for school when his parents said he was ready. When he was four Maynard was sent to the Highland School—the same school attended by his father, his uncles and his brothers. Since the school was no more than 500 yards down the road, the Bird children had no need of transportation. They could walk picking up other children on the way—all arriving more or less in time to get to their seats when the teacher, standing at the threshold of the school door, rang the bell signaling the beginning of the class day.

Highland School, although considered a one-room school, may actually have had two large classrooms—one on the ground floor called the lower school for the younger children, and another upstairs called the grammar school for children aged ten to thirteen or fourteen. Although a grade system had been instituted in most of the Rockland schools by 1865, the Highland school continued to separate children into a primary division on the ground floor and an intermediate division on the second floor. At the time Maynard attended the Highland School, it was unique in one respect: it was the only one room school left in town. "Each room was taught by a harassed and over-worked woman, who with upwards of twenty recitations a day in essentials, had no time to attend to the frills and extras even although she had known anything about them or discerned any value therein."[9] Until 1873 when the city school committee started requiring all teachers to have attended normal school, most Rockland teachers qualified by graduating from high school—preferably Rockland High School. If they had proved successful in their pedagogy and still able to withstand the stress of each day's teaching they had tenure for as long as they wished.

Maynard was a good student and early demonstrated a quickness of mind unusual in a child his age. By the time he was seven or eight he had learned to write a cursive script which would later become handsomely distinctive, if somewhat illegible to others. Much learning was taught by rote with the literal repetition of lines and paragraphs. The McGuffy Reader was still in use, with a liberal sprinkling of more noted authors and works for the children to memorize. The Bible was used to some extent, but secular writings such as *Washington's Inaugural Address,* Lincoln's *Gettysburg Address,* and even selections from Shakespeare were foisted on children as young as eight years old. The selections may have been far beyond the comprehension of the young readers, but they were prescribed reading. The memorization of the prose and verse left an indelible mark on many young minds. Witness Maynard's acquisition of the complete works of Shakespeare copyrighted in 1880, when, as a young, upwardly mobile, business man, he sought to establish a home library.

In arithmetic, after having mastered the basics of addition and subtraction, the student concentrated on the multiplication tables—also known as 'the times tables'. For the older students fractions and the decimal system followed. Early on Maynard understood relationships between numbers; how to calculate in fractions and percentages; and as later became evident, how to use mathematics to assess value in business matters. Whether this talent was enriched by his experience in the Store as he watched an uncle add up the amounts purchased, or from his father's banking career, he quickly mastered the basics of arithmetic and was frequently called upon by a harassed teacher to help younger students.

One area of a child's education in Maine that was given great emphasis was geography. This is understandable when one realizes how much of the general commerce of the Maine Coast was focused on transportation by water to distant parts of the world. The days of the Clipper Ships, many built in Maine ports, were followed by the 'Down-Easters' of Maynard's youth and young manhood. No child in Rockland could be unaware of all the kinds of ships from the small ketch to the majestic Down Easters when one glimpse of Rockland's harbor would present a panorama of all kinds of sail. It would be a dull boy over five who could not identify each ship in the harbor by its rigging whether a barqentine, brig, schooner, (often pronounced "skunner" in Maine jargon), or a full rigged 'Down Easter'. Geography, therefore, presented few problems to Rockland children. Identifying places such as Honolulu, Hong Kong and even Calcutta on the rather tattered map that was the staple of every classroom was literally child's play. They knew these places because they knew sailors, captains and mates who had been to them and brought home stories to tell about them. Maynard knew that his Uncle Hanson had been all over the world as a sea captain, and that he had a cousin, Clara Borstel, who had been born aboard a ship at sea off the coast of India in 1867.

History to a child going to school only twenty years after the Civil War was a subject alive and thriving. Who could forget the tales told by war veterans, who like many veterans of other wars, were eager to recount their feats of bravery and courage, or to bewail the scourges of disease and death to which they had been exposed. Then there were always parades at Memorial Day and Fourth of July in which the veterans proudly donned their uniforms to march down Main Street. Bands played, flags waved, and little boys ran after the men trying to imitate their marching gait and their salutes. Rockland and nearby Rockport boasted of at least seven veterans of the 20th Maine including a cousin, Samuel H. Gregory, a nephew of Maynard's grandmother, Clarissa. Furthermore, Rockland had its own HERO in the person of Major General Hiram G. Berry who was killed at Chancellorsville in the spring of 1863. To this day his life-sized statue stands guard in Achorn Cemetery over many lesser souls.

Rockland, as befitted the third largest city outside of Portland and Bangor, led the way in education by building a public High School in 1868.[10] Up to that time, children of high school age attended special classes taught by male teachers. During the Civil War women took their place at nearly all levels, but with the return of veterans, the gender distribution changed somewhat. For although most primary teachers were still women, men began to regain their former standing especially in the higher grades where their ability to maintain discipline was thought (not necessarily correctly) to be superior to the 'gentler sex'. Maynard, therefore, continued his education at the Rockland High School, located then, as it was for many years into the 20th Century, on Lincoln Street between Summer Street and Beech Street.[11] A child entering the Rockland school system, as Maynard did, around the age of four, could, with steady progress, graduate from high school by the age of seventeen.

Although college was not yet an option in the Bird family, Sidney was beginning to realize from his experience in the state legislature, that some sort of advanced schooling would give his son the social polish and business connections that might be needed in later life. William Bird, John Jr.'s son, had been sent away to Phillips Exeter Academy in New Hampshire. Not to be outdone, Sidney decreed a year at the same school for Maynard. As the future would show, it was money well spent. [12]

Thus, by 1887 Maynard Bird came back to go to work, as foreordained, at The John Bird Company.

4

Maynard gave little if any thought to college after his year at Exeter. Neither his father nor his older brother, Elmer, had gone to college, which at that time attracted only those who aspired to be lawyers, doctors or teachers. It was a foregone conclusion that Maynard would go into business. Where to start was all that needed to be resolved. He had already had experience at the North Bank where his father was president, and where he had impressed others with his quickness of mind and his mathematical aptitude. Furthermore, during his school years he had taken advantage of every opportunity to hang around The John Bird Company operations. First at the store at Blackington's Corner, then at the company's new location in what had become 'downtown' Rockland. This move, in 1883, marked a major change in the way the company did business. "At this time they discontinued retailing and nearly everybody marveled at the boldness of the firm in entirely shutting off the retail trade for that of a 'jobbing' or strictly wholesale business."[13]

Also, there were times while still in school during his summer holidays that he sailed on one or another of the Bird coastal ships delivering goods to the islands and other out-of-the-way places along the coast. These small towns and villages relied on the provisions brought by ship to stock their stores. With his gregarious personality, ready wit and warm smile, Maynard had no difficulty in making friends at many a stop on the meandering voyages of his family's ships. Whether he realized it or not, these traits of salesmanship, and the contacts he made would later lead to quite a different kind of career.

The choice to start in banking or the wholesale grocery business presented no problem. Despite the prophets around town The John Bird Company was expanding by leaps and bounds and financial control was sorely needed. Maynard started as an assistant bookkeeper under Ernest Stubbs, then the head bookkeeper, later the company's treasurer. Maynard's first assignment was to handle Accounts Receivable and Payable, eventually expanding to Purchasing and Inventory control. As time went on, his knowledge of all parts of the business expanded to cover everything the company did, one might say, from the bottom deck up. For the next five or six years, Maynard's business life revolved around the Company and its activities.

These were also years of expansion in all areas of commerce and manufacturing. The lime quarries were making fortunes for many people including some in the Bird family. In 1888, after years of discussion, construction was started on a railroad to transport the quarried lime rock down to the shore kilns for burning. When it was finished in 1893 it replaced the 140 teams of horses and wagons that hauled rock from the quarries, making as many as four trips a day.[14] Kilns were being modified to burn coal and later oil thereby becoming more efficient. Ships were still used as for lime transportation to the markets where their cargo was used in the building construction industry. Some lime shippers thought that barging lime to market might prove safer and avoid the hazard of fire that plagued the ships. This idea went nowhere since many of the major shippers, the Birds included, also owned lime ships and were loath to abandon them.

Working at the Bird Co. office in the center of Rockland, Maynard saw evidences of commercial vitality all around him. From his office window he could see, in addition to the smoking lime kilns that lined the shore, the wharves where dozens of ships were taking on casks of lime, lumber and goods for delivery along the coast—many were Bird company vessels. Other ships might be off-loading merchandise from Boston and other cities along the eastern seaboard. Big new passenger vessels were landing or boarding passengers from Bangor, Boston and New York. Looking inland, Maynard watched shoppers bustling in and out of the new stores that lined a half-mile of Main Street whose pavement of granite blocks made its all-weather surface the equal of any Main Street in Maine.

Streetcars ran down the center of Main Street, and brought shoppers and workers from as far as Thomaston, Warren and Camden; for Rockland had become the major commercial center between Bath and Bangor. Trolley cars were still horse-drawn in the 1880's, but during the 90's would be electrified by the construction of a generating plant to provide power. It had been one of Sidney's pet projects to see the trolleys that served the Thomaston-Camden Road, now called Old County Road, connected by a spur line down Maverick Street to join the Main Street line.

Although shipbuilding reached its peak in the 1850's and 60's, this industry was booming in Rockland in the 1880's and 90's along with everything else. The age of the clipper ship that had produced Rockland's most famous ship, *The Red Jacket*[15] had given way to the 'Down Easters'. Ranging from 1500 to 2000 tons, they were full-rigged ships with anywhere from four to six masts, wide of beam and economical to operate. They were best used for carrying grain down the East Coast and around the Horn to the West Coast. In their early years they could be seen in ports as far distant as Hong Kong and Calcutta.

From the 1880's until World War I, Rockland boasted at least five shipyards. There was the Cobb-Butler shipyard that launched a number of four and six masters in the early 1900's. The launching of one of these large ships was occasion for celebration. Engraved invitations were sent out and "as many as 200 invited guests [who] boarded the ship to ride down the ways, and a banquet usually followed the festivities, often at the popular Crescent Beach Inn."[16] Other yards, however, made a good living out of building smaller craft—barkentines, brigs and schooners that were the bread and butter ships for local labor. The best known shipyard was Snow's which specialized in smaller schooners like the 110 ton *Catawamteak,* named for the Indian word "Great Landing Place" as Lermond's Cove had originally been called. Ships like this carried molasses, sugar and stone in the West Indies trade in addition to trade goods.

Maynard now found himself involved with numerous members of the family. There was Uncle Adoniram, the oldest and the titular head of the family, whose major interest was the lime business. Then came Uncle John who was president of the company and chief buyer. Father Sidney headed operations, and Cousin William, Uncle John's son, became a partner in the firm in 1886. In 1890, Maynard's brother, Elmer, also became a partner. Up to the time the company moved downtown (1883) Elmer had worked at the Blackington's Corner store, which Uncle Almon managed. This store was subsequently sold to Almon's son, Ulysses. The downtown facility was expanded in 1890 to include a spice mill, with Elmer in charge. It was established "in order [for customers] to be assured that its spice products and extracts were absolutely pure and produced under personal supervision of the firm…"[17]. This operation also included the roasting and grinding of coffee. The spice mill later became a division of the company and carried the trademark *Three Crow Brand,* illustrated by three crows perched on a rail fence.

In 1891 the Bird Company incorporated. By agreement among the former partners, William and Elmer each received 10% of the stock, and Maynard and Ernest Stubbs, long-time head bookkeeper, got 5 shares apiece.[18] Uncle, John became president, with Maynard's father, Sidney, as vice-president and Ernest Stubbs as Treasurer. Elmer and Cousin William were both directors with specific assignments; Maynard was also a director.

As for the rest of the immediate family, Maynard's younger brother, Henry, though still in school, would join the company within a few years. Alan, the youngest of the Bird brothers, was still too young to be considered in the company hierarchy; there was talk of sending him to college when he graduated from high school. (Alan later became a lawyer, and, for many years handled the John

Bird Company's legal work.) Also, Elmer, who had married Emma Sylvester in 1882, now had two young sons for whom places in the company might have to be found. Taking all this into account, Maynard could see that, although there might eventually be a place for him in the company that could provide a good living, it would be a long, slow climb to the leadership to which he aspired.

However, in 1891, he had other things on his mind. Although he had devoted himself assiduously to learning the Bird Company business since leaving school, he had not neglected other aspects of his life. Besides his voyages on the coastal ships, he had traveled to Portland with his father several times when Sidney had gone there on banking business. In consequence of his experience in the state legislature, Sidney had many friends in state government; trips to Augusta gave Maynard opportunities to meet some them. With his genial personality, intelligence and cordiality, Maynard made friends wherever he went. Elmer was still the older and better known of Sidney's sons, but Maynard was beginning to be noticed as 'a comer'.

Neither did Maynard neglect his social contacts. Always popular with his contemporaries, he now commenced to take part in the family's activity in the Rockland social scene. The Sidney Bird family had always been involved in Rockland's social life which included lectures, theater productions and concerts that made up Rockland's winter social season. The Farwell Opera house held as many as 1200 people and was one of the sites for these events. Other programs took place in the Masonic Hall and the Odd Fellows Hall on Spring Street. Churches, too, made their facilities available for community affairs—most notably the Universalist Church on Union Street. Rockland had its own city band organized in 1875, The Rockland Military Band and the Farnum's Boys Band followed a year or so later. Hardly an occasion went by without one or another of these bands being called on to provide music.

In 1889 a group of citizens founded the Shakespeare Society of Rockland for the purpose of studying and performing at least two of Shakespeare's plays during the year. When their schedule was changed to offer a modern play instead of all Shakespeare, it was because either they or their audience had had their fill of the "Shakespeare only" schedule. Other clubs included the Rubenstein Music Club formed in 1892 and named for the Russian composer Anton Rubenstein. Maynard had no musical talent to speak of, but he loved plays and music. Although his taste ran to the popular forms of both, he supported the more 'high-brow' offerings when he thought they were beneficial to his social or business position.

The Bird family never missed the annual Rockland Fireman's Ball held every fall and preceded by a fireman's parade. Most families allowed their small children to attend the parade—an exciting affair for little boys in particular. The Dirigo and Defiance Companies brought out their equipment of horse-drawn hose and ladders flanked by the firemen themselves in their shining helmets. The fire horses, which had been curried to a fare-thee-well and decked out in harnesses in which every piece of brass sparkled, seemed to catch the spirit of the occasion, tossing their heads from side to side as they pranced down Main Street. Small boys always excited by anything to do with a parade took up their positions along side the marching fireman. Many an envious glance was cast at those few boys who had the good fortune, whether through family connections or other influences, to ride besides one of the drivers of the fire wagons.

Attendance at the ball was of course limited to adults. Although no one in Rockland would have been pretentious enough to call it a 'coming out party', for many a young girl this was the first occasion she had to appear as a mature young lady. For young men, and Maynard was surely one of them, now dressed in more formal attire, the ball offered the opportunity to meet with girls, albeit under the watchful eyes of mothers and grandmothers, in an atmosphere of closeness and communication not previously allowed.

In the summertime, social life revolved to a much greater extent around the outdoors. After the long, cold winter and an endless, muddy spring, people of all ages took advantage of opportunities to be outdoors. Picnics and rides to shore areas were particularly popular. If a family had a horse and carriage, as the Birds did, a leisurely drive to Crescent Beach and lunch at the Inn would consume a summer Sunday. Swimming was often included in an outing that went to Chickawauka Pond or one of the shore resorts. Some steamship lines ran day excursions to islands in Penobscot Bay. This appealed to groups of young people since it did away with the formality of a chaperone. Many a couple, if they had had the foresight to pack a lunch, would separate themselves from the group and take a leisurely walk into the woods where they could picnic under a tree or in some secluded glade. Thus: many a youthful romance bloomed and was sometimes consummated.

Summer was also the tourist season—especially the months of July and August, (as they still are today), when visitors from Boston, New York and Philadelphia came by train to shore points in New Hampshire and Maine. The railroad had already been extended to Rockland from Bath, and trains equipped with several 'sleepah' cars called 'Pullmans' after their originator, disgorged passengers ready to spend a month or more in the healthful seaside atmosphere of the Maine coast. "An important moment in Rockland's social history occurred with the grand opening of the Bay Point Hotel in 1889."[19] The hotel, developed on land at Jameson's Point on the north side of Rockland harbor, would be the showplace of the area. Not only did it enhance the tourist trade, it became a source of employment for many local people. Maynard, already fully occupied in business at the time it was built, was invited to the grand opening as were other members of Rockland's elite. The Bay Point immediately became a place where one could escort a young lady to one of the *Thè Dansant*s, as the tea dance was the called. Evening dances and galas offered other opportunities to young, socially acceptable, Rockland bachelors. To their eyes, the attractive young girls who came there with their parents were more glamorous and sophisticated than their local counterparts.

Maynard had no trouble attracting girls whether of the local or out-of-town variety. He was not an outstandingly handsome boy, somewhat short of stature, but well built, and all his life women found him interesting, whether for his charm and humor, or perhaps because he flattered them and made them feel important. In fact, by the time he was twenty-one, he was probably one of the most eligible bachelors in the Rockland area. Some of his boyhood friends were, by that time, married and had settled down to raise families. His brother, Elmer had married at twenty-one and so had several other of his male relatives. There is no indication that there was any pressure on Maynard to marry, but he might have begun to feel that it was time to 'take the leap'. So it was that sometime, perhaps in his twenty-first year or earlier, Maynard met and fell in love with one of the visiting young woman—Mary Elizabeth Hawkins.

The Hawkins family came to Maine each summer from Vineland, New Jersey, and had taken a cottage at Ingraham's Hill for many years. Mary's mother, Ella Hawkins, had Maine connections dating back to the 18th century which accounted for their Maine vacation. Mrs. Hawkins was also a member of the Prince family—one of the most important and affluent families in Vineland. To add to her sense of importance, she was related through the marriage of her brother to the Surgeon General of the Confederate Army—to whom history awards no honor.

Mary's father, Thomas Hawkins, had a more plebeian pedigree than his wife: he was born in Boonton Falls, New Jersey and was a veteran of the Civil War on the Union side having served as a private in 4th Massachusetts Regiment. However, he died in 1890, so the widow and her daughter stayed at the Bay View Hotel the summer of 1891.

Mary was close to Maynard's age. A fairly short girl of medium build, she was very pretty with dark hair and sparkling brown eyes; her vivacious manner masked a rather shallow intellect, but what twenty-one year old man bothers about a girl's mind? She had style and was good company; and Maynard found her very appealing and far more sophisticated than the girls he knew around Rockland. The proximity of Vineland to two of the country's largest cities, New York and Philadelphia, gave her an air of worldliness, which impressed him. He always appreciated these qualities and perhaps he had dreams, even then, of branching out of Rockland and Maine. He concluded that Mary, with her more polished manners, would make a superior companion in achieving that end.

Mary, on the other hand, could not have failed to be attracted to a young man who was as charming and as eligible as Maynard. In her eyes, even if he came from a small provincial city, he had developed social graces that would in no way embarrass her with her friends in New Jersey. Besides, he had pledged his love to her in a manner that no girl of her generation could deny.

Ella Hawkins might have made a different choice for a son-in-law, but she was well impressed by the Bird family's position in the Rockland social scene as well as their obvious affluence. Annie and Sidney had no objection to the marriage. In fact, they were relieved, feeling that their son had already had plenty of time to sow his wild oats. Memories of their own marriage may have haunted them, and they didn't want Maynard to repeat their mistake by making a marriage of necessity. If either family had any misgivings about how Mary would fit into Rockland life, it was not voiced at that time.

The marriage took place in the Vineland Baptist church on September 9, 1891. Maynard's best man was George Crockett with whom he had grown up. Eugene Kimball, also a longtime friend, served as an usher. The rest of the wedding party, (4 bridesmaids, 3 ushers, and a maid-of-honor), were either friends or relatives of Mary's. Maynard's parents, his brothers, Henry and Alan, and Sidney's niece, Lola Messer made up the Rockland contingent. Elmer stayed in Rockland since travel with a wife and three small children was not a thing to be undertaken unless the stay at the destination was of some length. Determined not to be outdone by her in-laws-to-be, Annie had a new dress made in the latest fashion especially for the event. Mrs. Hawkins, for her part, arranged for a special railroad car to meet them in Philadelphia, bring them to Vineland, and again take them back the day after the wedding. The trip from Rockland was arduous enough so the use of a private railroad car was a luxury that was greatly appreciated. This was the first introduction to New York City and Philadelphia for many in the Rockland wedding party.

The wedding was an elaborate affair, as was the reception at the Hawkins home after the ceremony.[20] The newlyweds left Vineland by train for Philadelphia and then extended their trip to the Catskills. Returning to Rockland, they took up residence at 43 Rankin Street, where they were at home on October 7, 14 and 21, "and will be welcomed here by a legion of friends who hold bride and groom in the highest esteem, and who are eager to offer their sincerest congratulations".[21]

Maynard, as a married man, now began to consider his future. The seeds of change were starting to germinate; during the next year the seeds would sprout. Two years after his marriage, Maynard would no longer be an assistant bookkeeper for The John Bird Company.

5

The years of 1892 to 1893 were ones of many changes in the lives of the Bird family of Rockland, Maine.

The first event was the death on January 21st at the age of 72 of Adoniram, eldest son of the first John Bird. His health had been failing for several years. On his death his son Adoniram, Jr., or A.J., to distinguish him from his father carried on the lime business. Although Adoniram had been head of The John Bird Company after his father's death, John Bird, Jr. had been running the company and was made president when the business incorporated at the beginning of the decade.

Adoniram's death was the final blow for Clarissa, who, at 92 had survived the deaths of both Hanson and Laura in the '80s. Her death followed her oldest son's by less than a month. Her funeral was attended by all the Bird clan living in the area; for the passing of the matriarch marked the last tie to the first John and the founding of his line.

After the interment in the family plot, the family moved from the gravesite to the Sidney Bird home—the closest and largest place available to accommodate them all. For Maynard it was a reminder of Newbury's funeral especially when he encountered Addy Bird, his childhood companion. Addy was by this time married to Clarence McIntire and lived in Rockport.

"You remember me, Addie?" Maynard said.

"'Course I do, Maynie," was the response.

"I was just thinking of you, Addie," Maynard said as he fondly grasped her arm and steered her into a corner away from the other relatives.

"I hope you were thinking nice thoughts, Maynie," she responded with a smile. "I'll bet they were of Newbury's funeral. By this time, you should know where babies come from."

Maynard chuckled. "I'm not so sure you knew where they came from then either. I'll bet you just made a lot of that stuff up."

"Addy smiled and changed the subject. "It's sort of sad, Clarissa passing,"

"I guess so, but she was pretty old." Maynard responded unemotionally. He seldom thought of his grandmother and then only as a rather distant figure; "She

38

wasn't much of a grandmother to us boys. Maybe Father saw her, but I don't ever remember her coming to our house."

Addy was puzzled by the discrepancy between her memories and Maynard's. "That's funny, Father saw a lot of her and so did Mother before she died. William and I loved listening to her stories about the Revolution; how her father fought in something up around Castine; and then the sort of tavern he ran for a while afterwards. Father always said that she exaggerated, but whether true or not, she was a great story-teller, and people say my father takes after her."

It seemed to Maynard that Addie always left him with some puzzle to resolve. Here it was again: why did his grandmother pay attention to Uncle John's family and not to his? It was a question that was not answered to his satisfaction at that time.

At this point, Mary found them and was introduced to Addie and the conversation continued on other subjects.

When they parted, Maynard put his arm around Addie. "It's good to see you again, Addie. We don't see enough of you now that you live in Rockport." As an afterthought he added, "But, I have one favor to ask of you. Now that we're both grown up, don't you think it's time you called me Maynard.? Maynie was for when we were kids."

Adeline grinned at him and winked at Mary. "Shuah, Maynie, er, Maynard," she teased him. "You're too important now for such a nickname

She turned to Mary who was frowning as if his relative had insulted her husband. "Don't pay any attention to us, Mary. We go back a long way, and Maynard knows there's more between us than just a nickname."

On their way home, Mary asked, "Did anyone else ever call you Maynie, dear?"

"No, and I hope no one ever does. I hate nicknames, but I can forgive Addie almost anything." Then he added rather wistfully, "She was my friend when I was little and especially after Newbury died when I needed someone to talk to."

◆ ◆ ◆

A month after Clarissa's death, another of her sons, John Bird Jr., died in New Orleans while on a buying trip for raw materials for the spice business. This was a blow to Sidney personally, for John Jr. had been a driving force in the company after their father's death in 1868. John and Sidney had worked well together in the successful development of the company. While his brother was alive, Sidney had been free to involve himself in state politics in addition to serving as president of the North Bank. Now Sidney, as the senior member of the family, would become president, responsible for the entire operation of The John Bird Company. William, John's son, and Elmer were next in line for promotion. Which one of the two would become vice-president? Eventually it was Elmer who, though younger than his cousin, got the job. This decision was to have far reaching consequences for the ultimate future of the business, but at the time, perhaps Maynard was the only one who gave any thought to the company and his future in it.

By fall of 1892, when Maynard learned that he would be a father in June, he began to consider that if he were to advance in business as he hoped to, he would have to find a more promising avenue of opportunity than the family business. The Company was too small a stage for his ambition—a stage where his brothers, cousins and probably nephews, would soon be vying for dominance. He wanted to compete, but not at the expense of family. He had his own family to support and was determined to provide Mary with all the comforts—even extravagances—which he knew she had had in Vineland but missed in Rockland. Therefore, the sooner he made the change the better.

By this time, he had learned the importance of finance, credit and insurance in the operation of businesses. He understood how growth and profitability were accelerated by the judicious use of the company's cash reserves and bank credit to attract credit-worthy customers and command the respect of the best suppliers. His responsibility for management of insurance coverage for ships, cargoes, real estate and lime burning investments had taught him a great deal. As he looked around Rockland, he noted that the insurance brokers there tended to be passive representatives of insurance companies in distant cities, who merely issued coverage ordered through their agencies and rarely, if ever, visited outlying towns. Most agencies were adjuncts of other business such as real estate, steamship agencies and the like. He found that he knew more than the brokers with whom he dealt on Bird Co. business; he knew that many properties and businesses were uninsured or under insured. New types of ventures required new types of protection, and coverage was not being sold aggressively. There was a need in town for a new, dynamic insurance business. And Maynard didn't see why he shouldn't take advantage of it.

He had been talking to friends and business acquaintances in order to gauge their interest in a possible new insurance venture. One of these was George Barney who already had some experience in insurance and was responsive to Maynard's enthusiasm and persuasiveness. Barney was older than Maynard and his age, plus his previous business experience, would give the new venture stability in the eyes of potential customers. Maynard had his eye on the small insurance agency of L.G. Moffitt. He felt that Barney would be able to set up an office, solicit clients and negotiate new agency contracts with insurance companies. Maynard's contribution would be his (by now) extensive array of business contacts cultivated in the last five years through the Bird company affairs; and he also hoped to bring with him all The John Bird Company's substantial insurance business. There was still the need for capital to buy Moffitt out. Neither Maynard nor Barney had sufficient funds for this purpose. In addition, there was rent to be paid, and funds to cover the expenses of operation for at least a year and needed new equipment.

Maynard realized that there was nothing else for it but to talk to his father who was the unarguably the best source of financing for a new venture. Whether Sidney would help by cosigning a note for a loan from the North Bank or perhaps lend them money directly, either way, Maynard felt his father was the key to finding start-up funds. It was undoubtedly difficult for this 24-year old to be dealing on such a critical matter with an older seasoned businessman, even if that man was his father. He had always stood a little in awe of him, despite the fact that he admired him and respected his intelligence and ability. The question in Maynard's mind was whether in this instance his youth would work to his advantage, especially when combined with his intense determination to succeed.

The conversation took place in the president's office at the Bird Company's headquarters. Maynard found his father seated behind an oak desk, on one side of which papers of all sorts were kept in an orderly pile by the weight of a scrimshawed whale's tooth. A single personal touch was a picture of Annie Bird taken shortly after their marriage. Additional papers lay in front of Sidney ready for signing. A pen with a nib lay at the foot of an ink well stand in the center. Maynard made a mental note to get his father one of those new-fangled Waterman fountain pens like the ones he'd seen in Portland. Behind the desk was a picture of the first John Bird and beside it a framed statement, entitled "How to be Rich".

Maynard remembered this statement from when it hung in the old Blackington's Corner store—a gift from one of his grandfather's friends. (It had followed the company to the downtown location, and served as good-luck charm for the prosperity of the company.) As he looked at this reminder of his grandfather, he was struck for the first time by some of the concepts that mirrored his own thoughts. Especially, the admonishment, "Never misrepresent for those whom you deceive will not return." And again, "Deal uprightly with all men to gain their confidence."[22] This, then, was the way to establish a reputation for honesty and integrity. He wished he'd known his grandfather; he must have been a man of great character and determination to achieve so much. If these ideas had made the first Bird rich, maybe it could do the same for one of his grandsons.

Maynard tried to start the conversation off casually by suggesting that the company should have a telephone in the president's office.

"No", Sidney said, "even though I have a telephone at home I don't want to be bothered at work with that thing ringing in my ear all the time. It's that young Belle Cullen's[23] job to do the answering. Keep her busy, I should think."

Maynard made another mental note that his new venture would have more than one telephone with the first one on his own desk. He knew that the use of the telephone was becoming more and more popular, and it was only a matter of time before every office would have multiple instruments.

Enough of avoiding the subject of his visit. Trying to appear casual, Maynard remarked, "Father, I have a proposition I'd like you to consider".

Sidney, of course, had already heard about his son's ideas for an insurance business, but he felt it better to pretend ignorance and let him explain the plan in his own words. (Rockland was, after all, a small place and news got around quickly.) He was certainly aware of Maynard's talents and ambitions, and wanted to encourage him. Of all his boys, Sidney felt that this one would be the one to go furthest. Elmer was competent, a good manager and a worthy successor to head the company when the time came. But Elmer showed none of the drive and understanding of complex situations that were part of Maynard's character. Elmer had married a Rockland girl and was not about to leave for greener pastures. On the other hand, Maynard had married an out-of-state girl who would have no objection if, as Sidney now reflected, Maynard might eventually find Rockland too small a place to exercise his talents. Sidney had also noticed that this son resembled his late brother, John, in many ways. He had John's wit and talent for telling a 'downeast' yarn, but unlike John, he frequently used this gift to achieve a predetermined result. Like John, Maynard had the born salesman's ability to convince a prospect of the desirability of his product. In addition, he was a good organizer, and had already developed what Sidney believed were Bird characteristics: honesty and integrity. If he was stubborn—well, stubbornness seemed to be a common trait in the Bird family, but one which shouldn't necessarily be a handicap. There were times, Sidney thought, when stubbornness could be used to good advantage.

Altogether, the father was proud of this son and was ready to offer his support, he was also curious to see what kind of a proposal Maynard would come up with.

So, lighting another of his innumerable cigars he said, between puffs, "What's on your mind, my boy?"

As he listened to Maynard outline the steps he and George Barney planned to take to get a new business started, his son's ideas were not only appealing, but well thought out. Reacting to his father's obvious approval, Maynard decided to ask directly for the money and just assume that there would be no impediment to getting the insurance business.

Sidney had expected that Maynard would want the company's insurance for the new agency, but he wasn't enthusiastic about personally lending him money. For a variety of reasons he felt that either lending the money or underwriting a loan was not a good way to start an independent career. He pointed out that the Bird Company had not fully recovered from John's death. He may even have called Maynard's attention to the framed "How to Get Rich" advice hanging behind his desk as it related to credit.

"Maynard, if I sign a note for you, it will make me, in effect, a partner in your company. Is that what you want? I sort of thought you wanted to get out from under the family yoke."

"No, Father, that is not what I want", Maynard replied sharply as he realized the implications of unwanted family involvement. "It may be alright for the John Bird Company to keep taking in family members, but I'm not interested in competing with my brothers and their children—or even you, Father—because that's what it's going to come to eventually as I'm sure you realize."

Sidney nodded. He was well aware that Elmer and his family would take precedence over Maynard whose family was still, literally, in the formative stage. And he doubted that if Maynard stayed in the company, he and Elmer could work well together.

Accepting his father's acknowledgement of a defacto situation, he continued earnestly, "I want to do something that will succeed through my own efforts".

Sidney smiled. He was secretly pleased that his son was ambitious and motivated enough to strike out on his own. After further discussion, and at Sidney's suggestion, it was agreed that a third partner, whose role would be to provide the needed funds, might be the best solution.[24] Sidney also agreed to send the new company a large part, although not all, of the John Bird Company's insurance business.

"You know, Maynard, I can't just pull all of the insurance out of other companies," Sidney said. "But you'll get your fair share, and if you handle things right, you'll get more."

Seeing a look of disappointment on his son's face, Sidney added, "I'll also do what I can to steer business your way."

This in itself was more than enough to make Maynard feel that he had succeeded in his negotiations with his father. Sidney's implied backing and his willingness to send him business was just as valuable as all the Bird Company's insurance.

Maynard had earlier made the acquaintance of a man named Rice who had connection with the Moffit Agency. With the concurrence of George Barney, Rice was approached and agreed to provide the capital funding needed, and also to use his influence in obtaining the Moffit firm at a reasonable price. In recognition of the part he would play, the new firm was named Rice, Bird & Barney.[25]

◆   ◆   ◆

Maynard and Mary had taken up residence, after their marriage, in the house on Rankin Street which, although adequate, was old and not located in the best part of town. As Mary discovered in her first winter in Rockland, the house tended to be drafty and cold during the months of snow and ice. She complained constantly of the smell of fish from the wharves, the rattle and clanking of the wagons going by the house; and worst of all, the pollution in the air caused by burning lime. Maynard was sympathetic to her complaints if a little surprised. He probably hadn't given much thought to how the workings of the lime industry might affect someone who had never encountered it before. Lime, it's quarrying, transportation, burning and shipping were part and parcel of his life. The Bird fortune was, after all, partly built on the lime industry, and that industry had made Rockland "The Lime Capitol of the United States"—if not the world.

Mary was desperately lonely; she was finding that living in Rockland was a lot different than staying at the Bay View or in a rented cottage for the summer. There was not the congeniality that she had assumed would be forthcoming when she married into one of the town's most prominent families. Maine people have often been accused of 'stand-offishness' and there is certain validity in this accusation. This may be due to the fact that Maine in its early days was geographically isolated from the rest of the country. It had a frontier character and its people a frontier mentality, it is a fact that the Maine native "will reserve any judgement until newcomers are, as he puts it, "summered and wintered".[26] Mary's ties were primarily with her in-laws and the Baptist Church. Here in Rockland, she lacked the companionship and with it the self-confidence she had known in Vineland. Her later behavior may have stemmed, in part, from these circumstances. When she became pregnant in the fall of 1892, the drawbacks of the Rankin Street house and her sense of social isolation were magnified. She felt herself imprisoned in a place where she had no friends, and could not get out. Furthermore, until the time of her marriage, she had never been parted from her mother whose influence had been paramount in her life. Even without the pregnancy, she would have had a hard time adjusting to life in a small Maine town.

Her first shock may have been the Maine winter—long and cold, so much colder than Vineland. Snow drifts deep around the doors and windows, ice on every puddle and pond, and everlasting cold in a poorly heated house; so that Mary spent her days bundled in blankets as close to the fireplace or stove as she could get. When in despair she had decided that winter would never end, spring arrived or tried to. Then Mary became acquainted with Maine's fifth season: the Mud Season. Now she could go outdoors, but only where duck-board walks made it possible not to sink ankle deep in mud.

No first pregnancy is ever easy, and in the late Victorian era Mary would have found the changes accompanying pregnancy particularly disturbing. Young women her age seldom knew much about their bodies and how they functioned. Thus the morning sickness, the swelling breasts and the distention of her abdomen after the fourth month, while perfectly normal, were a source of dismay, ignorant as she was of nature's methods of reproduction. She was no doubt counting on her mother to be with her at the time of the birth, and she knew she could count on Annie Bird for help. However, Rockland had, as yet, no general hospital, although there were several private hospitals and maternity homes. Many babies were born at home; the mother attended by either a doctor or midwife. Whether Mary planned to have her baby at home or in a maternity home, she would still be among strangers, in a town that did not have the modern facilities she had known in Vineland, where, if the need had arisen, she could go to Philadelphia for her lying-in. Living in what she still considered an alien world only aggravated her anxiety.

If Maynard remembered his mother's pregnancies with Henry and Alan, it could only have been a vague memory; but it seemed to him that his mother had made the 'blessed event' one to look forward to. Like most new fathers-to-be, he felt some degree of apprehension as Mary's physical and emotional balances began to change. He often came home after a day's work to find her, still in her negligee, hair uncombed, beds unmade and no supper in evidence. These signs of personal and household neglect disturbed his fastidious nature. He sincerely wanted to be a good husband and father, but was oblivious to some of his wife's problems, absorbed as he was in his work, the prospect of a new venture, and his already established ties in the area. Rockland was his birthplace and had always been his home; his roots were Maine roots. Along with his native independence and self-confidence, he had the additional feeling of belonging that often characterizes the Maine native. He may not have realized that pregnancy and her perceived failure to be accepted in the town's social life all combined to make Mary lonely and unhappy. He did his best to take her to the plays, musicals and social events of the winter season, but often she would feel ill, or imagined herself too large and her clothes too ill fitting to be seen in public.

On June 14, 1893, Maynard and Mary became parents of a baby boy who was named Milton. It was a name new to the Bird family. It didn't sound like a Maine name, saturated as the area was with biblical nomenclature and Anglo-Saxon derivatives. In later life, Maynard was known to express regret that he had not given the child his own name; but he had acquiesced in Mary's choice in the excitement of becoming a father. (As it turned out, he had no further opportunity to name a child, for this would be their only child and his only son.)

Mary's mother, Ella Hawkins, who Maynard referred to as "Mother Hawkins" as was then the custom, arrived shortly before the birth. The new mother had considerable assistance—perhaps more than she needed—from the new grandmother in taking care of the infant. Maynard had not had many opportunities to judge his mother-in-law before the marriage. Now he found her forcefulness verged on the autocratic. In a few days she had completely reorganized their small home; given directions to the girl Mary had hired; and taken over much of the care of the baby. Even Annie Bird found that her good offices were not needed, and Maynard was relegated to the position of bystander. It was not until Ella Hawkins left at the end of the summer that Maynard began to feel that he could be of some use and to enjoy the novel idea of parenthood.

Although the baby was healthy, he did his share of crying. Mary fussed over him constantly—not unusual for a new mother with her first child. There was no source of guidance for her after her mother left. She was reduced to following the advice of older women who subscribed to family nostrums, which, whether good or bad, had been used for generations. Babies, she was told, always had colic and they cried. Why should little Milton be different? "Don't worry, the baby will stop crying after three or four months, they always do," said her neighbor, Mrs. Perry. It was then that she finally sought the advice and help of her mother-in-law, who not surprisingly had been made to feel unneeded when she had originally tried to help. Annie Bird was not one to turn away from her son's wife, but their relationship never became a warm one.

During that winter, (1893–94), Maynard tried to spend more time with Mary and the baby, even though he sensed that Mary had her own ideas of child care and didn't want his help. Whenever, in an effort to be helpful, he tried to care for Milton, his efforts seemed unappreciated. Nevertheless, he adored the child, especially in the first few years. Milton was a good-looking baby with dark hair and dark eyes like the Birds, but the shape of his face and head seemed to resemble the Hawkins side of the family. Both parents delighted in showing the child to family and friends, and Mary especially, reveled in the compliments meant for the baby, but in her eyes surely a confirmation of her proficiency as a mother.

By the end of 1893, Maynard had assumed two new careers—first becoming a father and then an independent businessman. For the first two years he devoted only part of his time to the insurance business, relying still on his salary from The John Bird Company. But it was not long before he gave up that job and devoted his whole effort to the increasing business of Rice, Bird & Barney.

6

With the June 1893 opening of the Rice, Bird & Barney agency, Maynard began what he would later call his *Adventures*. An interesting insight into his personality is his definition of each achievement of a new personal goal as an "adventure". Obviously the challenge and its achievement were more important to him than the wealth it brought.

George Barney had already been busy at the Moffitt Agency office in the Syndicate Block[27] on Main Street. Much needed to be done, including changing the sign to reflect the new agents and owners. In September, Maynard reduced his time at the Bird Company in order to spend a part of it at the agency. In the process, he transferred some of the promised Bird Company insurance business as well as his father's and uncles' personal insurance. In addition to working part time at the Bird Company, he held onto the company stock and remained a member of the Board of Directors for many years.

Despite the 'Panic' of 1893, Rockland prospered, perhaps not as vigorously as previously, but still enough so that Rice, Bird & Barney grew. At the end of their second year, Maynard and his partners could look forward to a rosy future with few or no clouds on the horizon. After three years Maynard and George Barney had sufficient capital to buy out Rice, and change the name of the agency to Bird & Barney.

The agency was a success from the beginning so that when in 1896 Rice left, Maynard could turn over whatever work he still had with the Bird Company to a new associate and, with Barney, devote all his efforts to the insurance business. In a community, where adequate insurance coverage was more the exception than the rule, the partners did not lack for promising prospects. They signed up all their ready contacts, and solicited real estate owners, lime companies, ship owners and various commercial businesses, working the Bird name and its association to the utmost. The new department stores became clients and Maynard went after the public transportation and utility companies that were emerging and expanding in Rockland, the surrounding towns and nearby islands. The first and, possibly the most important utility to give them business, was the Camden & Rockland Water Company, of which Sideny was a director.

Now familiar with fire and casualty coverage, Maynard could accurately appraise a prospect's needs, and thereby present a convincing proposal, backed up by persuasive explanation and his appealing personality. He was also willing to take the time and make the effort to understand what he was selling so that he soon established a reputation for knowing what he was talking about. In addition, liability insurance was a new product and an extremely profitable one. He was later to tell his nephew, Frederic Bird, "We were successful in obtaining the agency of Travelers Life and Accident for Maine [and] by our success with them, we were appointed generals [general agents] for Maine, excepting Cumberland Co. which was under Barney's charge…Barney was given the state agency and I took over the Rockland agency."[28] Probably it was at this time (1897) that George Barney moved to Portland where he was still in the insurance business as late as 1920.

Barney's departure left Maynard as the sole owner of a full service agency and he promptly changed the name to Maynard S. Bird & Company. Under the new name the firm continued to prosper and readily obtained contracts with insurance companies, such as Aetna located in Hartford, Connecticut. Aetna already held Bird business but Maynard was not averse to inferring that the business could go elsewhere if he were not their agent. Other companies also welcomed the new agency when they were shown its business growth. Well-known companies were located no nearer than Portland and most as far as Boston, Hartford, and even New York. Signing them up, and solidifying his own personal relationships with them required visits to home offices. In the course of such visits, Maynard initiated valuable friendships, learned new aspects of insurance, and probably enjoyed his earliest exciting views of the great cities that would become magnets for his ambition. Older and mature executives were impressed with the personable and energetic young man from Downeast, and his new agency; in consequence, they looked with favor on his agency and referred new prospects in the Rockland area to him. By February 1904, a notice in the Courier Gazette announced that the agency represented nineteen fire insurance companies "which are among the oldest and strongest doing business in the United States".[29]

With the departure of George Barney, Maynard found a replacement in H. Nelson McDougall, a Scotsman who had emigrated from Prince Edward Island. This was a fortuitous decision on Maynard's part, for McDougall had been working up to that time in a grocery store; he turned out to be a loyal and extremely capable employee and later a partner. Subsequently, Maynard felt confident enough of his future to leave the offices of the Syndicate Building and take the ground floor space at a new building at 14 School Street. This "was considered by the townspeople as a bold move".[30] It was hardly as bold a move as what Maynard later called his "Second Adventure"

◆   ◆   ◆

The last decade of the 19th Century and the first of the 20th were periods of great expansion in commerce and industry. New companies, fueled by an explosion in technology, sprang up almost over night. Telephone companies, in particular were sprouting like mushrooms throughout all regions of New England. In the Rockland area, and beyond, every one of them was a potential insurance customer as Maynard was soon to realize.

In the 1890's Vinalhaven, one of the islands at the mouth of the Penobscot River, was a new, prosperous community, due in large part to the granite and fishing industries. Maynard found it a very fertile field for insurance and made frequent trips there, spending one or two days each time. Neither Vinalhaven nor its sister island, North Haven, had any connection to the mainland except one round trip daily by a slow steamer; so he usually stayed with friends whom he had known from earlier Bird Company business visits.

Maynard had the ability to make friends easily with his insurance customers, and also enjoyed spending time with the islanders. There was a casual, down-to-earth air about them that reminded him of earlier days at the Blackington's Corner store. One customer—and friend—was a man named Fred Walls, whose lean and angular frame and weather-lined face bespoke the granite quarries that were his life's blood. Fred had done well with granite, and by local standards, was well off. During the course of a conversation on one of Maynard's visits to the island, Fred brought up the subject of communication.

"You know, Maynard, staying in touch with the mainland is getting more important every day. Not just to those of us who quarry, but people out here in general. We're feeling sort of short-changed. Here we are supplying first quality granite to much of New England, and not getting much in return."

With a smile and a chuckle Maynard replied, "You must be making some money on that granite aren't you, Fred, or are you just talking poor?"

"Not at all, Maynard," Fred sounded hurt. "You know me better than that. I was thinking on how we might go 'bout getting some telephone service out heah. Seems to me that if a telephone cable was laid between us and Rockland everyone would benefit, including you."

Never one to turn away from an opportunity, Maynard said, "That's interesting, Fred. I see your point; let me give it some thought. Maybe I can talk to someone when I get back to the mainland."

On the boat returning to Rockland the next day, Maynard pondered Fred's suggestion about telephone service to the islands. Try as he might he could see no downside to the idea. If a transatlantic cable could be laid, surely it wouldn't be much of a job to lay one to Vinalhaven. As always, once he had made up his mind on action, he embraced the undertaking enthusiastically. He knew little about how it would be done and what it would cost, but assumed that the New England Telephone & Telegraph (N.E.T.& T.), which served Rockland, would welcome the opportunity to expand their customer base. His first move was to get in touch with the district manager. Much to his surprise, he got a very cool reception: N.E.T.& T. was not interested in serving the islands; the number of subscribers there were not sufficient to warrant spending the money to lay a cable.

To tell Maynard that a thing couldn't be done was like waving a red flag at a bull—it only made him more determined to push the idea. His next effort was to tackle the N.E.T.&T. at a higher rung of the executive ladder. Through a friend who, coincidentally, was the company's local attorney, he was once again turned down. According to his friend, the executive contacted said the cable would not work and that the company would have nothing to do with it.

Still not discouraged, Maynard found he was running out of options. As a last resort, he contacted another friend in N.E.T.& T, a man who was also an engineer, but who had an interest in a private telephone company in New Hampshire. He agreed to approach the Washburn Wire Company, manufacturers of wire and cable as to the feasibility of laying the cable. Finally after a considerable wait, the answer came back: Yes, laying a cable between Rockland and Vinalhaven, (and perhaps—other islands at the same time), was possible.

Now, it was a question of raising money to do the job. Fred Walls was as good as his word and got subscriptions from the islanders. In Rockland, Maynard enlisted the support of his father and his father's associates—especially those who had supported Sidney in the street railway venture and those on the board of the Water Company. Both efforts were successful, and the result was that the cable was laid. Customers were easily obtained putting to rest N.E.T.& T.'s argument that there would be too few to make service economical. The new company did have to offer rates that undercut those of N.E.T.& T. to attract customers, but Maynard figured their overhead would be lower than the larger company's which would make up the difference. Of course, laying the cable was only the beginning. Exchanges had to be established at either end; lines had to be strung to bring service to customers; permits from the town governments had to be obtained; personnel had to be hired; and many other problems had to be resolved before actual operation could begin.

According to Maynard, "It was root hog or die!" He worked hard and a study showed that if service were provided to surrounding towns, it would be a talking point to Rockland merchants. Exchanges were established in Thomaston and Waldoboro that had never had them before, connecting them with the surrounding rural territory.[31]

But the fledgling telephone company—temporarily named the Eastern Telephone Company—was not out of the woods yet, and neither was Maynard. There was still work to be done. When service was expanded outside of Rockland city limits to Thomaston and Waldoboro, Maynard found that they had run a foul of a law that required any public service company wishing to cover the state, or any part of it, to obtain the right of eminent domain through an act of the Maine Legislature. Once again, he consulted his father, as the best source of advice, on how to go about getting such an act through the Legislature.

As an old hand in state politics, Sidney started out by saying, "The first thing you have to do Maynard, is to get someone in each house to sponsor the legislation; then the proposed legislation goes to the appropriate committee for consideration.

Maynard stroked his chin and nodded. This is what he had expected. "But how does it get passed?" he asked his father. "Doesn't it have to have sponsors in both houses to push it?"

"You bet it does," Sidney smiled as he fiddled with the pen on his desk. "That's the hard part. I can give you some names, but you, Maynard, need to do this yourself." He paused, then, with a twinkle in his eye, he continued. "What I'm telling you is that you should run for the legislature; this is your baby. You won't have any trouble getting elected; I can see to that. Then you can do your own steering."

So Maynard's two-year stint (1899–1901) in the Maine Legislature as one of two representatives from Rockland, resulted in the passage of an act that gave authorization of eminent domain to the Eastern Telephone Company. It wasn't easy! Up against the political clout and money of the Bell System of which N.E.T.& T. was a part, Maynard's group twisted political arms and called in every political I.O.U. in their possession. Sidney Bird's political connections were utilized to their fullest and other deals were made on a 'quid pro quo' basis.

According to Maynard it was "some fight." In describing it to Fred Bird some years later, he said, "We licked them in the house 95 to 92 and in the Senate 14 to 8. This was against the biggest lobby ever known in the capital."

With the authorization now to expand throughout the state, Eastern bought out an independent company in Farmington, applied for rights in Lewiston and Auburn and other cities that were not friendly to the Bell System. As a result of its efforts to monopolize the State's telephone system Bell had suffered. This was particularly true of their failure to serve the rural sections that had provided the push for Maynard's group. Ultimately, a new president in the Bell System realized that it would be better to join groups like Maynard's rather than to continue the fight. To this end, Bell approached Eastern for an interchange contract, which resulted in setting up a new company known as Knox Telephone & Telegraph. George Sherwin, President of N.E.T.& T. became president of the new company holding 51% interest for the Bell System, while Maynard became General Manager with a 49% interest.

By 1904, Maynard found that the telephone business was taking up too much of his time. He had other ideas for a new undertaking—one that would prove as profitable, if not more so, than either the telephone or the insurance business. Eventually, the Knox company became part of the Bell System in 1914—the same system that had formerly been its adversary. Maynard, thereby, became a large stockholder in the Bell system.

◆   ◆   ◆

What Maynard had in mind when he withdrew from the telephone company he called his "Third Adventure".

In both his insurance business and his involvement in the telephone industry, Maynard became aware of the need for capital. When he had raised money for the telephone cable, he found that his father and others had excess cash that they were willing to invest in a venture that would earn them more than keeping it in a bank account. Many of the rapidly expanding commercial and manufacturing ventures either had ready cash to invest or were short of capital and needed money for expansion. Insurance companies needed to keep their rapidly growing reserves profitably invested, and were heavy buyers in the bond market. Many were earning more on their investments than on insurance premiums. In the larger cities, even Portland, stock brokers traded securities—both stocks and bonds—to investors among the general public through their own offices and branches. Many customers were the same people to whom the agencies sold insurance. Insurance companies particularly favored railroad bonds for their high yields and relative security. Railroads were expanding dynamically, carrying ever-increasing amounts of freight and numbers of passengers; they enjoyed enormous political influence; and their rates were relatively free of regulation. The big companies were absorbing, by acquisition and coercion, smaller independent feeders and connecting roads. Additionally, street railways as a means of local and inter-city transportation were booming. Their needs in financing were the same as the regular railroads only to a lesser extent. Water companies and municipalities were also expanding and in need of financing. This was the beginning of the 'electric age' when cities and even towns and villages were looking forward to an electric light on every street corner and every home illuminated.

For all this, capital was needed beyond the ability and willingness of banks to provide. Bonds were the way to go! Not only did they absorb money from insurance company reserves, but also from the savings and nest eggs of the general public. An ever-increasing number of middle class working people and small businessmen owned a few bonds, happy with the returns, which were so much greater than savings bank interest.

It did not take Maynard long to realize that the securities market had great potential as a source of income. After his experience with raising money for the Telephone Company, he had a better idea of the need for capital. He was quick to learn that insurance companies were eager for investment opportunities to invest their large reserves. Not only were his insurance clients potential securities customers, but there was money to be made by initiating and underwriting new bond issues to be sold to banks as well as to individual investors. Initially, the sale of bonds was a sideline to insurance sales of the Maynard S. Bird Company; subsequently, as the securities business grew, it became evident that investments were destined to become a major part of the company's business, rather than merely a profitable sideline.

Between 1901 and 1907, the Maynard S. Bird Company advertised its bond offerings regularly in the Courier-Gazette. Early on Maynard realized the value of advertisements, and those placed in both local and other more distant newspapers were large and attention getting. Offerings included bonds for Rockland, Thomaston and Camden Street Railway; City of Pittsfield, Mass. Sewer Bonds; City of Boston bonds; Augusta Water Co. bonds; Camden & Rockland Water Company bonds, and many others. Although the majority of the bonds were of Maine companies, both municipal and utility, an October 1904 listing offers City of New York and City of Boston bonds, and even "Underground Electric Railways

Company of London, (otherwise known as "The Tube"), 5 per cent. Profit Sharing Secured, Coupon Gold Notes due 1908"

As the agency grew to include the brokerage of securities, it would need another major executive. "W. C. Ladd was added to the firm in 1909." Up to that time, Walter Ladd had worked at the Rockland Hardware Co. According to his son, E. Clifford Ladd, Maynard walked into the hardware store one day and, out of a clear blue sky, offered his father a job in the insurance business. Maynard must have seen qualities in the young man that would make a good insurance salesman, for Walter Ladd stayed with the company for 42 years until his death in 1956. By that time through mergers, acquisitions and changes, the firm was known as W. C. Ladd & Sons.[32] It is interesting to note that both McDougall and Ladd, who were to become partners and owners of the insurance company fifteen years later were hired by Maynard from relatively ordinary jobs. Both met or exceeded all of Maynard's expectations in their later careers in business. In later years, Maynard never ceased to dwell proudly on the success of men he had hired and who had gone on to greater business achievements.

With reliance on telephone and telegraph for speedy communication, bonds and stocks could be traded from Rockland readily on the New York and Boston exchanges. Maynard needed an outside brokerage firm to facilitate this kind of trading. Enter the firm of Bond & Goodwin, securities dealers with headquarters in Boston, but with offices in New York and a seat on the New York Stock Exchange. It was arranged for them to maintain a desk in Maynard's office. A young man named Hellier, who appeared to have the sales skills and energy that Maynard sought, was hired to staff this desk. Hellier went on the payroll of Bond & Goodwin and worked as their representative at the Bird office. Maynard probably realized at that point that he was moving toward becoming a stockbroker and investment banker—a move that would change the rest of his life.

In fact there seemed to be no limit to the securities available and what could be offered. Whether the sole underwriter of an issue, as was probably the case in some of the Maine securities, or as a participant in larger offerings, Maynard had found a source of increasing income and wealth as an investment banker.

"The Fourth Adventure": Around 1903 another business opportunity presented itself, one that Maynard was quick to take advantage of. While in the State Legislature, his contacts had included the state treasurer and members of legislative finance committees. If he could establish or control a full service bank, his contacts were willing to use it as a depository for State funds. State funds required no payment of interest, but, on the other hand, could be loaned to provide bank income. There is no question that the bank was Maynard's idea. He had noted in his efforts to raise money for the telephone company, as well as in his securities sales, that local banks were handicapped by limited resources both in borrowing and lending. As he had done eleven years before in starting an insurance agency, he took care to find supporters for the undertaking. Organized in 1903, *The Security Trust Company* with Maynard S. Bird, President, and Jarvis Perry, Treasurer, the bank could claim deposits of $113,477.00 by September 1st of its initial year. The bank's Board of Directors included Maynard's father, Sidney, as well as William T. Cobb, later to become governor of Maine, and many other prominent Rockland businessmen. The bank paid "3 ½% compound interest on time deposits" and advertised itself as "…well equipped, progressive yet conservative,…[pre]pared to transact all branches of domestic banking."[33] By 1909, after only six years of operation, The Security Trust Company could boast of assets of $895,052.99. Initially located at the corner of Limerock and Main streets, it eventually, in 1912, had its own building at the corner of what is now Museum Street and Main Street. It is an imposing building in classic Roman style, which, if one looked carefully, closely resembled the Aetna building shown on the Maynard S. Bird & Company letterhead.[34] A double-faced Telechron clock anchored to the northeast front corner of the building proclaimed the name—Security Trust Company—in bold letters below the clock face.[35]

During these early years, Maynard reached out locally and statewide to expand his business contacts. He became a Mason, joining the Aurora Lodge, Rockland's oldest and most prestigious Masonic group. His political activity included the chairmanship of the Rockland Republican Caucus in 1900. This was the election year in which William Jennings Bryan ran against William McKinley for president, and the year in which Bryan made his famous 'Cross of Gold' speech. Considering the number of 'Gold Bonds' the Maynard S. Bird Company would later offer for sale, it is not hard to understand why the Democrat's silver platform was anathema to Maynard. He remained a staunch supporter of the Grand Old Party until the day he died. Rockland was then, and has been ever since, a stronghold of Republican sentiment.

Maynard's agency was only seven years old, and he himself only thirty-one, but his influence in the insurance business was apparent when in 1900 he organized The 1st Annual Convention of Maine State Association of Local Fire Insurance Agents held in Rockland at the Thorndike Hotel. Maynard, who had been influential in organizing the association, was elected its president at the convention. More than 60 people attended the event, an impressive number for a city as small as Rockland. According to the Rockland Courier-Gazette, the Thorndike Hotel strained its resources to their limits to make the event an historic one. The menu included oysters, salmon, lobster salad, filet of beef, squab, as well as an assortment of vegetables, condiments and desserts. The wonder is that any delegate survived the meal to live another day, much less attend the next year's convention in Lewiston. The Entertainment Committee carried out its part of the evening by printing the menus and the program in the form of a fire insurance policy. Speeches were made, cigars were smoked, and toasts, possibly of a spirituous nature, were drunk until around midnight when the affair was adjourned with a call for "three rousing cheers for the new officers, which were heartily given".[36]

On February 1, 1906 the Maynard S. Bird & Co. opened for business at their new location at 14 School Street in the new Thorndike & Hix Building. The previous October a newspaper article describing the new building and its tenants said that occupancy was expected by December 1, 1905. The delay in re-locating Maynard's firm may have been due to time needed for "the fine set of offices [to be] finished for his brokerage and insurance business".[37] This, then, was to be the home of Maynard S. Bird & Co. and its successor companies until the year 2003. The builder provided a vault "equipped with steel safety deposit boxes large enough to contain a complete set of books...". [38] It is possible that Maynard may have suggested the idea of a vault, since policies and bonds associated with his business necessitated fireproof storage. In addition to being a symbol of security and prestige in this small town, the value of the vault proved its usefulness when a fire on February 22, 1915 destroyed the building leaving only its vault unscathed.

Now, after sixteen years, Maynard's flourishing insurance and brokerage businesses had fulfilled his objective of establishing an independent presence in Rockland. He had built a reputation for integrity, honesty, and reliability that did justice to the precepts which had guided The John Bird Company to success. In an advertisement designed to allay investment fears as a result of the Stock Market Panic of 1907 and to promote the sale of Belfast Water Company bonds, the following surely reflected Maynard's personal view of the future. "...bear in mind that the United States has tremendous resources unequalled by any nation in the world. We are simply on the threshold of our opportunities..."[39] The door was open, and Maynard intended to cross the threshold and follow the path to future success.

7

The last decades of the 19th Century were the 'Gilded Age'. Great fortunes were made by the Rockefellers in oil, J. Pierpont Morgan in banking and railroads, Cornelius Vanderbilt, also in railroads, and Andrew Carnegie and Elbert H. Gary in steel. Their tactics earned them the epithetical titles of 'Robber Barons'. They formed monopolistic corporations through which they controlled the major industries of the United States.; their fortunes were derived from the oppression of labor for the benefit of a few.

It was also a time when an incredible number of new inventions and products flooded the markets, making life more comfortable for those with the means to obtain them. Telephones and telegraphs; electricity for street lighting and home illumination; and indoor plumbing and public water systems to name a few. Houses were being built or modernized to include running water in bathrooms and kitchens. Rail transportation meant quicker and easier communication and access between major cities. Railroads also meant a flood of products from all parts of the country and from abroad as well. When the Grand Trunk Railroad was finished in the late 90's, connecting Montreal in Canada to Portland, Maine, it meant that Canadian products could easily be sent to the United States and transshipped abroad. The reverse was also applied to goods coming into the docks of Portland that could be shipped throughout Canada and other cities in the United States. Smaller cities and towns were linked by electric railways (trolleys) of which Maynard's father was a great proponent.

Automobiles put in an appearance—first in Germany when Daimler built both the Daimler and the Benz. Later in the U. S. came the Oldsmobile, built by a man named Olds, and then the Packard also named after its builder. By 1898 there were fifty car manufacturers; by 1908 there were 241.

These first cars and others like them were owned and driven mainly by the well to do. Roads were still dirt tracks and impassable for cars under adverse conditions. Breakdowns and frequent flat tires had to be repaired on the spot often to the accompanying derisive shouts of "Git a hoss" from an audience of small boys. In Rockland, Dr. Charles Britto, who lived on Chestnut Street, became the first purchaser of not one, but two automobiles in 1900.[40] We do not know when Maynard acquired his first car, but knowing Maynard, it was probably shortly

58

after Dr. Britto and undoubtedly was one of the more stylish cars. Still the temptation to be one of the early operators of a motor car certainly fits in with Maynard's image as an up-and-coming young man.

The age of the airplane could be envisioned when the Wright brothers made their first flight at Kitty Hawk in December, 1903. Later, the next year they took their plane on a series of celebratory hops around Ohio. Even at the St. Louis World's Fair the same year, a prize was offered for Aeronautic Achievement—a prize which, unfortunately, nobody won. But it was a start![41]

The population of the United States was also growing. In the two decades between 1890 and 1910, the census counted almost 30 million new residents in the 45 states. Many were immigrants from Europe to the East Coast, and to a lesser extent to the West Coast from Japan and China. They were welcomed at first to supply the labor demanded by growth of industry and development. By 1910 discrimination against these new arrivals from the Orient in the form of quotas and other exclusionary means had reached a peak. Their immigration created a political problem, which seemed to concern few except politicians from California, who tried in every way possible to stop the "yellow tide". Nevertheless, immigrants were fanning out all over the country and along the eastern seaboard where the numbers were greatest, they came mainly from Europe

The State of Maine was growing too, but the state was still sparsely settled with only about 24.8 persons per square mile in 1910. Rockland grew apace with population peaking at about 12,000 in the second decade of the new century. Although there were some Polish and Italian newcomers in the Rockland area, it was the Finns, who, starting shortly after the Civil War, were the largest immigrant group. They came to the region because of the granite quarries in the area of Long Cove on the road to Port Clyde, and on the islands of Vinalhaven and Hurricane. Both Finnish men and women worked hard—the men in the quarries and the women as household help. As they accumulated money they bought land and settle along the River Road. Today the names of Harjula, Honokonen and Hahl still appear on barns and mail boxes along that road. In 1895 there was a large increase in Finnish immigration to the region. These Finns were predominantly farmers and had money to buy land; after clearing the land of lumber, that they sold to the lime kilns, they turned to blueberry farming.[42]

The lime business was booming, and would continue to do so, even though in 1903 cement became a more popular use for lime rock. Still with the completion of the Limerock Railroad in 1890, lime in some form or other would still constitute the principal industry in Rockland until more modern building materials such as 'dry wall' eliminated the business as a major source of income and employment. But in Maynard's youth there was no disputing that Rockland was "The Lime Capital of the United States".

Maynard also observed that shipping and shipbuilding were changing. No longer could the Bird family count on a fleet of ships to carry lime to distant cities. These older craft were being replaced with lime barges towed to market by tugs. However, small coasters were still a popular means of transportation for Bird Company products to reach communities where there were no decent roads or where transportation by water was still shorter, cheaper and quicker than hauling by cart or wagon. Fishing in wooden boats or sail powered ships was still a major industry as it always had been and would continue to be for many years to come.

Other sources of income included two crops of hay that Maine's fields could produce and shipment of ice by water to major cities along the coast. Hay, a staple of horses' diets, was also used for numerous forms of insulation. Ice from Chickawaukee Pond was cut in late winter and stored in an icehouse at the west end of the pond. Later it would be packed in a covering of hay or straw and loaded onto 'coasters' for delivery as far down the coast as Boston. The ubiquitous icebox was still found in most homes, and the biweekly (sometimes more often in the summertime) ice delivery by the iceman with his horse and cart was as commonplace as the daily delivery of a newspaper is today. The electric icebox had not yet been invented, nor had anyone given much thought to the automobile displacing the horse as a common means of transport. The production of both hay and ice, although not as significant as lime and fishing, formed an important part of the economic life of Maine

◆   ◆   ◆

The Bird family was growing along with everything else. Maynard's brother, Elmer, now had four children. The oldest was named after his grandfather, becoming the second Sidney Morse Bird. Raymond was Elmer's second child and a little girl named Gertrude followed Raymond. Gerttrude was "a blue baby" and died from a congenital heart defect when she was fourteen. The youngest, another boy named Adriel, arrived in 1893—a little more than a month after Milton put in his appearance. However, the fact that Elmer had produced three sons reinforced Maynard's conviction that the family company would not have room for all the relatives available. Later, when Adriel showed the initiative and drive that had been a hallmark of Bird success, Maynard was one of the first to offer his support. If Maynard had any reservations about Elmer in later years, it was the persistent rumor that there was more than a business relationship between him and his secretary, Clara Foskitt.

In fact, Elmer continued to work diligently at the John Bird Company that was expanding and doing well. Partly this was due to the flourishing spice business that was placed wholly under Elmer's supervision. The company ground its own spices in a mill located behind the Farwell Opera House, and later roasted and ground its own coffee. Ultimately, the spice and extract business—registered under its trademark "Three Crow Brand"—would become the leading money-maker for the Bird Company. However, Maynard did not begrudge Elmer his family or his success. If the company prospered so did Maynard's business, and as a director he was undoubtedly keen on the new decision by the company to erect its own building. The Bird Block, located on Sea Street,[43] opened its doors for business with a grand reception on January 10th, 1899 to which all the most important figures in Rockland's business community were invited. Maynard, as a stockholder and director, attended along with other members of the family.

Maynard's brother, Henry, (the Heaven Born Child), after graduating from Peekskill Military Academy, went to work in the family company in 1895; one more Bird to feed at the trough. But Maynard did not see in Henry the challenge or the same dynamism that was later evident in Adriel. Of his three brothers, Henry was probably Maynard's favorite. Henry was made of softer stuff than the other Bird brothers: he made friends easily and was well known and liked around Rockland; he had the Bird charm without the sharp edges that appeared in the others. Intelligent and hard working once he settled down, his ambition never overrode his concern for his family. His marriage in 1899 to Edith Simonton proved to be the most loving and enduring union of any in the family. They had four children—two boys and two girls. Henry's second child was a girl—one of the few in a family of boys—who they named Eleanor; but the second daughter, Grace Adelaide, died in infancy. Again, the preponderance of male offspring boded ill for the Bird Company's future. Not all could be supported by the wholesale grocery business.

Alan, Maynard's youngest brother and the last of Sidney and Annie's children, may have felt that, in this family of brothers widely separated in age, he had been an afterthought. As a child he tagged along with his brother, Henry, until Henry went away to school. Then, on his own and without the guidance of older siblings, Alan became more obstreperous and soon made a name for himself—with others—as a practical joker and occasionally unruly. As if in an effort to make up for their lack of attentiveness, Alan was sent to college (University of Maine, class of 1900) the only one of Sidney's boys to get a higher education. A year or so later, Alan followed up his bachelor's degree by studying law in the law office of former Governor F. A. Powers in Houlton, the principal city of Aroostook County. A personal letter from Sidney to Powers makes it clear that there was a close association between the two men, and that Sidney was soliciting Powers' support for Alan to help him through his bar exams. Evidently the John Bird Company was full up with Birds by the time Alan became a lawyer, and started his practice by handling legal affairs for the family company for a number of years. For a while after he got his law degree, he developed the reputation as a playboy. At this time (1899 and on) he became friendly with Glen Lawrence and Blanche Smith (known as B.B.). The triumvirate delighted in hunting and fishing parties away from the restrictions of family and society.

Despite the fact that Maine had adopted laws prohibiting the public sale and consumption of liquor well before the Federal law came into existence, liquor was available to those who wanted it. An area that raises as big an apple crop as Maine does could hardly avoid applejack as one of the many uses of that abundant fruit. Certainly other liquor was available including rum from the West Indies smuggled into Maine ports. If some of the Bird men drank too much, it was considered a mark of youth. Most people took the "boys will be boys" attitude, that is until the drinking got out of hand, which unfortunately it did with some young men including a number in the Bird family. If Alan was one of them, it was a habit he discarded in later life becoming a complete teetotaler after the age of forty. In any event, Alan's doings were of little concern to Maynard except as they reflected on the Bird reputation in the community.

On the whole, Maynard made a point of remaining on good terms with all the Bird family. If there were rumors of a misdoing by one or another of his brothers, he tried to remain neutral and steer away from confrontational situations. He was still young and had not as yet completely established his business. In the '90s older men with whom he had to deal, frequently saw him as "Sidney's boy", and if not patronizing, treated him as not quite seasoned. That is not to say that he condoned illicit or immoral behavior; he may have turned a blind eye to the misdeeds of some of his younger relatives as long as they did not become too blatant.

◆   ◆   ◆

By 1894 Maynard had moved his family to 23 Maple Street where they occupied a half of a two-family house. This represented the fulfillment of Maynard's promise to Mary that, after the miserable winters in Rockland before Milton was born, they would move to a more suitable home.

Despite the move, Maynard's home life still presented problems. One of them was his mother-in-law. Ella Hawkins had a domineering personality. She had taken to visiting them every summer and had decided it was more convenient to stay with her daughter in the larger accommodations on Maple Street than at the Bay Point Hotel. (Anyway, why should she spend so much money when her daughter had a perfectly good guestroom?) With her arrival, Mary reverted to the role of obedient child, following her mother's dictates from raising Milton to managing her husband. Maynard found that he was no longer the head of his household; nothing he did seemed to suit his mother-in-law; and his wife's compliance with her mother's instructions left him with no choice but to either accept her role or ask her to leave.

Maynard's resentment of Ella Hawkins' interference in their domestic affairs was only part of the problem. He found her social arrogance intolerable. She never missed an occasion to boast of her family connections to notables in both the Revolution and the Civil War. That many connections to the latter war were Confederate certainly did not endear her to Maine's staunchly Union sympathies. She left no doubt in people's minds that she considered the Prince family, from which she descended, far superior to any family in Rockland, especially the Birds. For Maynard, who was proud of his family and their achievements in only two generations, Ella's condescension only fueled the fire of his dislike. He knew that his mother and father were too tactful to be critical, but he was aware by their manner that they held Ella in as much contempt as he did.

After a particularly unpleasant evening when Annie and Sidney had joined them for supper, and Ella had made some particularly disparaging remarks about Rockland and its residents in general, Maynard decided the time had come to take action. After his parents' left—probably earlier than they had planned—Maynard drew Ella aside while Mary was putting Milton to bed.

He was very angry but made a great effort not to show it. "Mother Hawkins," he said, "it seems that you don't like Rockland; you don't like my parents, and from the way you talk, I suspect that you don't like me. You are making our home—Mary's and mine—very unpleasant, so I think we would all be happier if you moved to the Bay Point for the rest of your stay."

"Do you mean to tell me that you're asking me to leave?" she said, glaring at him and drawing herself up to her full five foot three inches, which was still more than two inches shorter than Maynard.

Maynard was not one to be intimidated. "We think that will be better for everyone." He felt he had his temper under control now and spoke very calmly. "I have noticed that Mary gets upset when you're here, since you don't seem to approve of the way she handles Milton, and you obviously don't think enough of my family to treat them with the most basic courtesy, the sooner you go, the better." Maynard had made his point, but he wondered what Mary would say. It didn't matter what she thought, he was just fed up with Ella Hawkins and wanted her gone.

"I've never been so insulted in my life." Ella was now the one who was offended and feeling sorry for herself. You can't make me leave. I'll tell Mary how you've treated me. She won't stand for this."

Maynard decided that he'd better end the conversation before Mary returned from putting Milton to bed. "Around this house, what I say goes. I can assure you, Mary will do as I tell her, and I insist that you leave by tomorrow morning. I'm sure the Bay Point will have a room for you until you're ready to go back to Vineland." He turned on his heel and went upstairs.

Mary reacted with shock as Maynard had expected. At first all she could say was, "Oh, oh! But she's my mother, Maynard, how could you do such a thing."

Trying to suppress his still simmering anger, he put his arm around her and said in as gentle a voice as possible, "Mary, dear, you know your mother aggravates you. I can tell that when she's here and I come home that she's gotten you all upset."

"I know, Maynard, but that doesn't mean I don't love her. She's my mother!" Tears were beginning to fill her large, soft, brown eyes.

"It's done, Mary. We'll talk more about it after she's left. This is our home and I want it to be a happy one for both of us. Right now I am not happy and when she's here I don't think you are."

Maynard started to turn away, but Mary caught his arm. "If you love me, Maynard, please don't do this."

But it was too late. He had made up his mind and there was no changing it. They were to discuss it many times after that, but Maynard stuck to his guns and Ella Hawkins never entered their home again. She continued to come to Rockland in the summer for a few more years, but Mary would see her only at the Bay Point, where she held court with a number of old friends from earlier days. Mary no doubt resented Maynard's actions even though she, too, felt that her mother was overbearing. After a few years, Ella stopped coming to Rockland, and if Mary missed her, no one else did.

◆　　◆　　◆

Almost since the inception of Rice, Bird & Barney, Maynard traveled a great deal. For a while he could make day trips to surrounding communities in search of new business, but his trips to the islands, as has already been noted, involved at least an overnight stay and sometimes longer. Once Maynard became involved in developing Eastern Telephone and then as a representative to the State Legislature, he was often away from Rockland from Monday to Friday. Since the break over Ella Hawkins, relations between Maynard and Mary had never been the same, although to the casual observer they were still a very devoted couple. Maynard knew that Mary resented his action, but, with his strong sense of self-justification, he convinced himself that it had been for the best.

The combination of his travel and the rejection of his mother-in-law caused a rift between Mary and Maynard that never healed. There was no longer any intimacy between them, she was colder toward him than formerly, and he realized after a number of rebuffs that she had no desire for any more children. He may have found companionship elsewhere; if so he was very discreet for there was never any gossip in Rockland.

By 1899 when Milton started school Mary had been accepted and had adjusted to her role in Rockland as Maynard's wife. That her husband was doing so well and was becoming a person of note in town did much to ease her unhappiness. Little by little, with the help of her mother-in-law, Annie, she had become part of the community. She followed Annie's example and joined the Baptist Church, was active in their Dorcas Club, and made serious efforts to make friends with some of the leading women of the town. Now that she had more space to entertain, she delighted in giving little tea parties to some of the women whom she felt were important in Rockland society. Ida Crie, whose husband, R. Anson, was in the family hardware business, was one whose taste in home décor—heavily draped windows, overstuffed furniture and rooms cluttered with bric-a-brac—Mary tried to emulate. There was also Lucy Cobb, whose husband, William, later was elected governor

With Maynard so often out of town Mary was free to devote all her love, care and attention on Milton. She dressed him in the most outlandish outfits: little sailor suits with a matching berét. Short pants when other children were wearing knickers. If he came home crying with his knees scraped and his pants torn or dirtied, she was there to take him in her arms and comfort him. It was always the fault of "those big bad boys who picked on her little darling." She complained to

Maynard as if she expected him to find the miscreants and punish them for her son.

"Mary, no wonder he gets in trouble", Maynard said when she appealed to him for help. "Look at the way you dress him. No other boy goes to school dressed in a silly outfit like that. Milton goes to school just asking for trouble, and he gets it. He needs to be taught to fight back or he'll wind up a sissy."

"Well, if you'd stay around a little more and pay some attention to him—and to me", she added hotly, (Mary could have a temper when she felt unjustly aggrieved), "he might wind up like some of your nephews, rough, and tough with dirty fingernails and banged up knees. I guess that's what you want."

"Better that than to have him wind up a 'Mama's boy'. You know what I mean, Mary. I want our son to be a real boy. So what will a few scrapes and bruises do to hurt him? He's got to learn to fight back and you've got to learn not to send him out looking like a girl."

Maynard could think of nothing more to say, and Mary let the matter drop. But it bothered both of them for a long while. Whatever the reason, Milton never made many friends in Rockland, and those friendships were mostly women. Many years later another member of the Bird family who had known Milton would refer to him as "a queer duck".

◆   ◆   ◆

And so the 19th century came to a close. Except for the sinking of the battleship Maine at the entrance of Havana harbor, the Spanish-American War had had little effect on the people of Rockland or on Maine in general. McKinley, a dyed in the wool Republican, was elected to the White House. Gold as a rock solid support of the dollar, made the currency safe from the depredation of the 'silver men' led by William Jennings Bryan. In Rockland, the Maynard Bird family prospered, as did most of the other members of the family. Nothing could now stop their continued success. The future looked as bright as a new silver dollar.

8

The 20th Century swept in and over Maynard like a tidal wave of wealth and opportunity. In eight short years he had established a flourishing insurance business. He concentrated increasingly on the production and marketing of bonds, mainly for new and growing businesses. He had enlarged the scope of his activities and his clientele through his activity in the telephone companies and now, was General Manager (with a 49% stake) of The Knox County Telephone Company, a subsidiary of the Bell network. Already, (1903), he was president of the newest commercial bank in Rockland. Thanks to his brief stint in the State Legislature, his influence in business circles throughout the state, but especially in Portland, had increased. Later, he retired on very favorable financial terms from the day to day management of the Telephone Company to devote more time to the insurance and securities operations that were becoming the mainstays of his growing wealth. The high volume of deposits and demands for credit that the bank attracted, due in part to Maynard's growing business importance, also ensured growth of a profitable loan portfolio. As already noted, the bank qualified as a state depository providing capital at little or no cost. Finally, it also provided a 'tie-in' with Maynard's other undertakings, enhancing profitability for all three.

Another factor that played a part in Maynard's rising success was the expanding Maine summer population. Ever since the late 1870s, Bar Harbor, and the Maine coast and islands in general, had become popular as summer retreats for the wealthy and famous of the big eastern seaboard cities. Summer homes were sprouting up in Camden, Rockport and on the islands of North Haven, Vinalhaven and Isleboro. In 1902 The Bay Point Hotel was sold to the Ricker family owners of the famous Poland Springs House and Mansion House. The hotel was greatly expanded to 200 rooms and renamed the Samoset and, as expected, provided for an expansion in the summer trade. It boasted a 310-seat dining room famous for its cuisine, and a manager direct from New York's Waldorf Astoria. At this time a golf course and a salt-water swimming pool were also added. The completion of the mile-long Rockland breakwater in 1895 gave hotel visitors an opportunity to stroll out to the lighthouse as an afternoon's diversion. Visitors during the months of July and August—"the Social Season"—were known to reserve their rooms a year in advance for stays of no less than a month.[44] As might be expected, the summer season provided Rockland residents with employment opportunities and local businessmen with a new source of trade. Maynard was not slow to take advantage of this situation. The summer homes—often called "cottages" despite their size—needed insurance; their owners needed a local bank in which to deposit funds; and, most important, all summer residents, whether owners or visitors at the hotel, were potential buyers of securities. With his growing stature in the business community, his fashionable appearance, poise and ingratiating charm, Maynard involved himself with many summer visitors of social and business prominence.

In the early days of the new century, he was increasingly aware of the changes in Rockland's growth patterns. During the past twenty years, more and more businesses were building along Main Street as Rockland developed as a commercial center and the traffic between Thomaston and the Rockland waterfront sought a shorter, faster and more direct route. Thus an alternate road came into use bypassing Old County Road and leading directly to Rockland's Main Street via Park Street. These two factors combined to promote a shift in the population from the area of the Bird Homestead on Old County Road (and Blackington's Corner) to new streets within walking distance of the business section. Unfortunately, clairvoyance was not a Bird characteristic. If it had been, Maynard or one of his brothers might have realized that, in the long run, the once grand dame of Rockland's homes—the elegant and imposing Bird family homestead—would be increasingly surrounded by smaller houses, workshops and dilapidated farms of lesser value. It was left as a beautiful ship among a fleet of fishing boats.[45]

The first area to reflect expansion was the North End where lots along the streets intersecting on North Main were quickly built up—some with large houses of the porch and tower variety. Unfortunately, the pollution emitted by the lime kilns, and the odor of fish from the nearby wharves soon reduced the desirability of the North End as a site for more impressive homes. Since the road from Thomaston became Park Street when it entered Rockland, a new street named Broadway branched off Park Street several blocks before the latter intersected Main. Broadway skirted the downtown area completely. It was in this area to the north and west of the business district that most of the new homes were being built in the late 1890's.

As if to emulate their father, all of Sidney's sons built homes of increasing distinction. Elmer already occupied a fine house at the corner of Broadway, and Masonic Streets; it would not be long before Henry and Alan would build imposing homes further along Broadway. By 1901 with the growth of his income, Maynard felt that his social and political stature warranted a better home. Throughout his life he sensed that a house, properly designed, would be the means of reflecting his status in the community. He may not have consciously articulated this idea, but as the years passed and he built or owned several homes, each one conveyed the same message "This is who I am". He was not trying to upstage any of his relatives or friends in town—he was too shrewd for that—but his pride of family and position dictated to some extent the kind of house he felt would be appropriate.

Mary was delighted with the idea of a new home. While the house on Maple Street was comfortable enough, it was still a twin house, of which she and Maynard occupied half—a half they didn't even own. To Mary, the prospect of a larger home all her own made up somewhat for her husband's frequent absences. Maynard abetted Mary's enthusiasm with the promise that she could take charge of the furnishings, even going to Portland to a <u>decorator</u> if she wanted to. In addition, she would be able to entertain at larger and more elaborate parties; and, of course, they would need more help to maintain a larger place. He may have thought that it would also give Mary some other outlet for her energy than the smothering attention she lavished on Milton.

Maynard had his eye on an existing house on a large double lot at 19 Beech Street. This street ran from Broadway to Union Street and was still sparsely settled. Despite the fact that the well-known Maine architect, John Calvin Stevens, had built a home in 1897 for Maynard's cousin, William, and followed that with the Bird Block in 1898, Maynard was too preoccupied with business matters to think of starting from scratch. The purchase was made in Mary's name in January, 1902.

The house was late Victorian 'Queen Anne' style, built in 1896. There was a number of this type in Rockland: three story, cross-gabled with a tower nestled in the L of the gable, brown scalloped shingle siding, and a wide front porch. The interior was spacious enough on the first floor to satisfy husband and wife's predilection for entertaining. The second floor had four bedrooms, two bathrooms and a fireplace in the master bedroom. On the third floor two servants' rooms took care of the possibility of full time, live-in help. The very consideration of such an arrangement was a far cry from the time when Annie Bird would make do with the assistance of a neighborhood woman and a yardman to take care of livestock and gardens. Maynard undoubtedly made changes to suit his own taste. The kitchen contained all the latest equipment, including a coal burning stove, an ice-box and a large sink with both hot and cold running water. Heating was by a coal-burning furnace in the cellar that supplied hot water to radiators throughout the house. (Maynard made sure that Mary would never again have to live in a cold, drafty house.) There were <u>two</u> telephones—one upstairs and one down—electric lights throughout and every available new appliance or design feature.

John Bird 1797(8)-1868   Clarissa Gregory Bird 1798-1892

John Bird's Store at Blackington's Corner 1832

Sidney Morse Bird (1840-1907)

Annie Eliza Bird (1841-1922)

Highland Homestead

Maynard S. Bird,
Age 8 (Approximately)

Maynard S. Bird, Company (left) School Street, Rockland, Maine (1906)

Bird Block, Tillson Avenue (Formely Sea Street)
Rockland, Maine (1898)

19 Beech Street, Rockland, Maine

Milton Hawkins Bird
From 1912 Exeter Year Book

Sidney Morse Bird & Sons
From Left: Elmer, Henry, Alan, Maynard, Sidney

Mary chose to decorate the interior in a manner that mimicked that of her friend Ida Crie. The doors, moldings and wood trim were oak stained a golden brown, since this was fashionable at the time. Floors were wood stained a darker color than the woodwork. Fortunately, the era of dark overdraped windows and overstuffed furnishings was becoming passè, so the furnishings and drapes were lighter and the furniture to some extent more comfortable than the 90's style. Settees and armchairs still called for an erect position for anyone choosing to sit in them. Upstairs, Maynard and Mary's room had a large heavy double bed and other pieces to match. Milton had his own room and a playroom as well. Only Ella Hawkins was excluded from the use of the guestroom.

A stable for Mary's horse and carriage that she still favored as a means of transportation was located at the western end of the property. There was also a stall for Milton's pony, and, of course, space for Maynard's automobile. Between the barn and the house there was a combination vegetable/flower garden. Rockland was not as yet so citified that people had given up the kitchen garden and the fruits and vegetables it produced. Canning and preserving still provided a source of winter food and no good housewife could do without a cellar for cold storage of off-season foods.

To Maynard the effect of the new house on Mary was cause for satisfaction and pleasure. He felt that he had finally lived up to her expectations, or perhaps it was the fulfillment of a dream she had been nurturing unbeknownst to him. He noticed that she seemed to have regained the sparkle and effervescence that had attracted him in the first place. The trips to Portland to consult with the decorator were occasions greatly looked forward to, and after a while, Mary began to shop for clothes there as well. Maynard even suggested that she open a charge account at Porteous, Mitchell and Braun where she would get special attention as a result of his connections with the store's owners. He began to urge her to join him on trips to Portland and Augusta where he would see to it that people he knew from state government dealings would entertain them. Mary agreed to the Portland trips for she saw Portland as the center of the state society. Not quite like Philadelphia, but the best she could expect for Maine. Augusta was another matter. She had never been attracted to politics nor did she understand Maynard's interest in them. Her tastes ran more, she felt, to the artistic in life. She enjoyed plays, concerts and book reviews. In her mind political circles, whether local or state wide, seemed populated with men (and their wives) of much lower social order than the intellectual and artistic circles she aspired to. Of course, the Cobb family of Rockland was different. Everyone who knew them respected them. Mary and her friends considered Lucy Cobb, the wife of William T. Cobb, to be the leader of Rockland society. When Cobb ran for governor in 1904[46] (and was elected) the Bird's new home provided a setting in which Mary, displaying all her social skills, could entertain on their behalf. She could show off some of her lovely linens, china and crystal, wedding presents that had been hidden or packed away until an appropriate occasion deserved their use.

The fact was that Mary had finally settled into the 'downeast' environment. This transformation was due, in no small part, to Maynard's rise in business and political circles. But Mary herself had changed. She no longer felt her identity depended on her mother and her mother's pretensions. (Although it is questionable whether she ever forgave Maynard for banishing her mother from their home.) For better or worse, Mary had put down roots in Maine, and was finding that life wasn't so bad after all. She had put aside her air of superiority because she was smart enough to realize that it only left her with few friends and isolated her from the people she needed to make her life endurable. She was at heart a friendly, generous person and responded enthusiastically to these qualities in others. In addition to her church, she had branched out into various organized charities. In later years she devoted much time to the local "Home for Friendless Boys"[47] and eventually was elected to its board of directors. It is probably fair to say that by 1906 she was a well-established, well-regarded matron in Rockland. Combined with Maynard's gregariousness and charm, they made a popular couple to both year round residents and summer visitors, many of whom became Maynard's clients and friends.

If Maynard's marriage was less than fully gratifying, he never let it be seen. When he realized that he and Mary would have no more children, he lavished on Milton every material benefit a boy could want. He knew that Milton was developing much more under his mother's influence than did most boys, but he satisfied himself that Milton would have more opportunity than Elmer's children—especially Adriel, who was the same age as Milton and much more prone to boyish fun and high spirited mischief.

For boys growing up in those days, life was spent mainly outdoors. There was sledding and skating in winter. Spring meant testing the ice (and often falling in) to see if it would still hold you. Summer was the time to be pulling lobsters from under Owl's Head rocks; swimming in Chikawauka Pond or in the ocean in water so cold that naked boyish skins turned blue, and for climbing trees, fishing and games of Cowboys and Indians. When a boy was serving his inescapable school sentence, there were spitballs to be aimed at classmates, girl's pigtails to be tied together, or better yet, to dip surreptitiously in inkwells. Outdoors at recess there were the usual games of tag and hide and seek. There were fights after which a boy would have to explain to his mother how he ripped the knee of his pants or got a black eye, earlier flourished before his friends as a badge of honor. Milton never became part of the boys' crowd; he tried to avoid the fights but there were still times when he came home crying and complaining that the gang had called him 'a sissy' or worse yet 'a mama's boy'.

If Mary complained to her husband on behalf of her son, Maynard was likely to retort, "I warned you that this would happen, Mary. You've only yourself to blame!"

But these instances were becoming less frequent. The fact that Milton was a good student, generally near the top of his class at the McLain School made up somewhat for his failure to mix with other boys his age. He liked school and liked learning. In this he took after Mary who found pleasure in reading, albeit mostly novels. Milton had his pony, and rode often with some of the boys and girls who were his friends. But, as Maynard watched his son grow up, he believed, from his experience at Exeter, that Milton would do better if he were sent away to school for his high school years. He had not broached the subject to Mary because he feared her opposition to her son's leaving home. However, the time would come sooner than Maynard expected, and helped by support from an unexpected source, when the decision had to be made.

◆   ◆   ◆

Sometime around 1903 or 1904 Sidney gathered his sons together for a group studio portrait. When it was completed, each son was given a large, framed print that Sidney hoped they would hand down to their descendants. They are posed around a marble-topped drum table with books open and scattered on it. Sidney is seated on the right opposite Elmer. Henry is seated next to Elmer, while Alan and Maynard stand. They are all well-dressed—three of them including Maynard, have watch chains anchored in waistcoat buttonholes, with the watch presumably hidden in a vest or trouser pocket. However, Maynard is the best dressed of them all. He wears a new-fangled wing collar with a well-tied bow tie. (Bow ties were to be his trademark throughout his life.) By comparison, Elmer wears a similar collar that appears a little large and a tie not quite as stylish or as well tied. Maynard's clothes are more fashionable and better fitting than his brothers and he seems more at ease in them. Always identifiable by his head cocked to the right, his hair has a neater cut and his mustache more carefully trimmed. The fastidiousness that he showed as a boy rebelling against doing barn chores now becomes apparent in his appearance. He already reflects the polish and influence of a more cosmopolitan environment. One might say that he had 'arrived'.

9

The Rockland Courier-Gazette—September 24, 1907
The death of HON. SIDNEY M. BIRD removes one long prominent in business circles of our city, the desire has been expressed
on many sides that the business houses unite in some testimonial of regard and sorrow.

In furtherance of this suggestion, and that the action may be concerted, I have been desired to suggest that so far as possible, business be suspended throughout the city from 2 to 4 o'clock Tuesday, Sept. 24, the afternoon of the funeral.
H. JONES, Mayor

Hon, Sidney M. Bird died Saturday evening at his home at the Highlands, age 67 years. Funeral services will be held from the late residence Tuesday afternoon at 3 o'clock. Rev. W. C. Barrows of Biddeford, a former pastor of the First Baptist church will officiate. In compliance with the mayor's proclamation, above printed, it is expected that there will be a general closing of stores and offices that the business men may pay their last tributes to a distinguished fellow citizen.

◆　　◆　　◆

Sidney's death did not come as a surprise to Maynard. For sometime now, his father had suffered increasingly from a malignancy of the throat and Maynard, thinking of the innumerable cigars his father had smoked, suspected they might have been a contributing cause of the disease. In 1902 Sidney had been operated on to remove the growth. At first it appeared that the surgery was successful—he and Annie had made a trip abroad taking Alan with them. But the illness came back despite the efforts of doctors as far away as Boston. He and Annie had even gone to Florida one winter in the hope that warmer weather might help. All four brothers stood by helplessly as their father became weaker and weaker. A trained nurse had been hired so that Annie could get some relief from the constant strain of caring for her husband. Finally death came somewhat unexpectedly after an outing on a glorious fall day. The crisp fresh air and the autumn colors announced that if life must end, it should do so with as much natural beauty as possible. Maynard wondered if his father was grateful for this small favor.

Maynard sat in somber stillness as the Reverend Barrows eulogized his father. He could not help thinking about the influence Sidney had played in his life. More than just a father, Maynard knew he had lost a friend and a wise mentor. Sidney had known Maynard perhaps better than Maynard knew himself. It seemed to Maynard that, although his father made every effort to treat his sons equitably, there was always a special bond between them that his brothers did not share. It started when Henry was born and Annie was preoccupied with a new baby, and at the same time grieving over the loss of her first-born, Newbury. Then it was Sidney who had taken Maynard with him to the store or to the bank to relieve his wife's stress. Even at such a young age, Maynard had found the bank much more interesting than the store. Was it then, he wondered, that he had first appreciated the power that money conferred on someone who knew how to use it and make it work for him?

Had Sidney appreciated Maynard's aspirations beyond those of his brothers? Was that why Sidney had been willing to open doors for Maynard that might otherwise have stayed shut? Maynard thought so. He recalled Sidney's encouragement when he was approached about the insurance business. Maynard had not forgotten, either, his father's backing for the funding of the Vinalhaven telephone cable. Without Sidney's help and that of his father's friends could he—Maynard—ever have raised the money by himself? And what about the fight in the State Legislature—the one to acquire the right of eminent domain for the fledgling telephone company? Maynard remembered how hard he and others had worked to line up votes, but maybe, as he now thought about it, it was his father's state-wide political reputation that tipped the scales in their favor

As Maynard listened, all the most important people in the state eulogized his father. Governor Cobb, Congressman Littlefield, father of Maynard's contemporary, Charlie Littlefield, and the Hon. J.E. Moore all spoke glowingly of Sidney. What Maynard appreciated most were the words spoken by Billy White. Here was a friend and contemporary of his speaking of his father in terms of admiration and respect, and they rang truer to Maynard than those delivered by older speakers. The words—<u>loyalty</u> and <u>integrity</u>—so frequently used—became transformed and stamped indelibly on Maynard's mind. He knew that he had been blessed to have such a father—a man whose life had been one of courage, determination and honesty. To be the heir to such a reputation was an ideal worth living up to and Maynard quietly vowed to achieve it.

Finally, the mourners moved on to Achorn Cemetery and the space reserved in the Bird Family plot for Sidney's casket. As Maynard stood beside his mother her hand in his, he knew that her thoughts merged with his in the faith that her husband's sons would carry the Bird name on to greater distinction. His thoughts also dwelt on Newbury. He felt he knew what went through his mother's mind as she saw her husband laid beside her oldest son. With a feeling of profound love, Maynard squeezed his mother's hand hoping she would understand that he shared her feelings. His father was truly gone now. Once again, Maynard realized that he had been left a legacy, a standard, to live up to for the rest of his life.

◆   ◆   ◆

Several days after the funeral, a lawyer, other than Alan, read Sidney's will since Alan was one of the beneficiaries. The will was perfectly straight forward reflecting the logic of Sidney's mind and the equity of his disposition. Maynard's mother, Annie, would get the Homestead and a generous amount of money—to be held in trust—for her to live on. Additionally there would be money to keep up the house and grounds as long as she lived there. After a number of individual bequests the remainder of the estate, which included Sidney's holdings in the John Bird Company and other local operations, was to be distributed equally among the four sons. Maynard and his brother Elmer were named co-executors and co-trustees for the Annie E. Bird trust. Smaller bequests were made to a number of local charities, to long-time employees, and to friends or retainers.[48] Two of Sidney's grandsons received bequests. To his namesake, Sidney M. Bird II, Elmer's oldest son, he gave $1000. To Maynard's son, Milton, he left $1050 specifying that it be used for the boy's education.

This bequest for Milton's education both surprised and pleased Maynard. It was as if his father was making amends to Maynard for not providing him with a better education. Maynard wondered if his father had recognized that Milton's personality and character were different from those of his male cousins, and that his interests tended more toward intellectual pursuits than did theirs. The bequest brought up the question of sending Milton away to school; a subject Maynard could no longer avoid discussing with Mary. Maynard figured that Mary would be pleased that Sidney had thought well enough of Milton to include him in the will. She would also be quick to notice that neither Raymond nor Adriel, Elmer's other sons, had been included. Mary's relations with her brother-in-law's family were, for various reasons, always a little tense, and as a result, she grasped every opportunity to assert the superiority of her family to that of Elmer and Emma's. As it turned out, Maynard's expectation of Mary's reaction proved correct and without any serious objection on Mary's part, Milton was duly enrolled in Maynard's alma mater, Phillips Exeter Academy, for the 1908 fall term.

The fall and winter of 1907 were busy times for Maynard absorbed as he was in various business undertakings, and, at the same time, working with Elmer as co-executor of Sidney's will. As he and his brother examined their father's assets, Maynard realized that Sidney had left a sizeable estate.[49] On November 19th the brothers posted a $150,000 bond as principals and trustees for Annie E. Bird, Henry B. Bird and Alan L. Bird. There were ample resources to fulfill the terms of the trust for Maynard's mother and all the other smaller bequests before considering how to handle the balance of Sidney's estate. At the time they filed their accounting in March, 1908, they asked the probate court to exempt them from filing a complete inventory of the estate, thereby protecting from public view the value of The John Bird Company. (The Company had undoubtedly increased considerably in value in the 17 years between the deaths of John, Jr. and Sidney.) Maynard remembered all too well the occasion when his father had been quite annoyed with his mother because she had hoarded her dividend checks, refusing to cash them for fear people in town would know how much money she had. He and Elmer felt the same way about publishing an inventory of the estate. In the Rockland community it was just as well to keep a close-mouthed approach to letting others know how much you were worth. Also, because the time consumed in settling Sidney's estate was diverting his energies from the expansion of his own businesses, Maynard was anxious to finalize the accounting and get on to other things. In this Elmer concurred, since he was involved in the reorganization of The John Bird Company of which he was now president.

◆   ◆   ◆

As a man of considerable energy, well organized and intellectually very acute, Maynard had become accustomed to involvement in several simultaneous undertakings. After all, the insurance business had opened the door to the telephone companies, and the two-year stint in the State Legislature enlarged his political horizons. Raising capital to finance the telephone cable to Vinalhaven made him aware of the general need for increased capitalization of utilities as well as other businesses. This had gotten him into the issuance of new securities and brokerage of those in the secondary market. Founding the Security Trust Company only increased his standing in the business community as a fully diversified financier.

Initially Rockland and the surrounding towns and villages had provided a sufficient source for new bond issues, and the local population a plentiful market for their purchase. But Maynard realized that, sooner or later, he would have to find other and larger markets if he expected the investment banking business to grow. He was already developing new dealings in Portland and its surroundings, and was sometimes spending several days a week in Portland and Boston to do so. He had established contact with the Boston investment-banking firm of Bond & Goodwin. Young Hellier,[50] who Maynard thought of as another of his 'discoveries', now manned a Bond & Goodwin desk in the School Street office. Tom Baxter and Ed Fenno both partners in Bond & Goodwin,[51] encouraged Maynard, to come to Portland and open an office there promising him leads and backing if he did so.

Since Maynard could no longer discuss his plans with his father as he had so often done in the past, he thought it might be well to talk to his mother about his future. Mary was only interested in his business activities as the source of income and social contacts. But Annie, more perceptive, had always understood her son's needs and motivations. One day in early May, when the buds on the trees and bushes were just beginning to green-up and there was a softness in the air that presaged spring, Maynard took an afternoon drive out to the Homestead to see his mother. He found her outdoors near the kitchen garden, obviously planning her spring planting.

"Maynard, what a surprise! What brings you out here on a work day?" she exclaimed when she saw him get out of the car—he was then driving an Oldsmobile

Maynard smiled at her reaction. "I didn't realize that you kept track of my comings and goings, Mother. Just thought you might like to take a spin in the car."

Annie frowned and replied somewhat testily, "You know I don't like those darned autos. They make too much noise and they smell something awful. I don't think you came all the way out here just to take me for a ride. What's on your mind?"

"Let's go sit on the back porch. I see you've got a couple kitchen chairs out there." Maynard noted that the chairs had obviously seen better days. "Don't you want to buy some new furniture for the kitchen instead of using this old, beaten up stuff? You sit in that chair many more times and you'll find yourself sitting on the floor when it gives way." He knew his mother would follow her own choices no matter what he said.

As he expected, his mother ignored the question and settled herself in a chair whose caned seat was sagging and otherwise showing considerable wear. She waited patiently while her son brushed off the other chair, which was only slightly less worn and disreputable. She had noted that his clothes were, as always, stylish and well cut, and that in every respect he was carefully groomed.

After a little more small talk, Maynard got to the subject of his visit. "Mother, now that Father is gone, I've come to you for advice." He paused and tugged at his chin, a habit he'd developed when he was pondering how to get started.

"I know Father talked to you about his affairs, and I'd like to feel that I could do the same" he said rather diffidently. It was true, Maynard realized, even as the words came out of his mouth. Sidney had always confided in his wife and had great respect for her advice and opinion. He wished he could have the same relationship with Mary, but even if she sat and listened to him, she wouldn't understand what he was talking about.

As they sat there in the warm afternoon sun, Maynard explained to his mother how his business was growing and that he felt that he must expand even if it meant leaving the Rockland area.

"I'm getting into the securities business in a major way, Mother, which means I need to locate in an area where there are more opportunities. I'm thinking about moving my office to Portland where I'll be closer to larger banks and to the Boston financial scene."

Annie nodded her head. "I'm not quite sure how you handle so many things, Maynard. You seem to have your fingers in an awful lot of pies. Are you sure you're not spreading yourself too thin?"

"Possibly! I've given up the telephone manager position. It was taking up too much time and besides, I already have a good appreciation in the stock so I'll just hang on to that. The company got someone else to run it."

Annie didn't say anything so Maynard went on trying to explain what he wanted to do. "Jarvis Perry or someone else can take over the presidency of the bank although I'll stay on the board. That leaves the insurance business here and I think Nelson can handle that."

Annie still didn't comment and Maynard wondered whether she was even interested. "Do you want to hear more, Mother?"

"Of course. I'm just digesting what you've been saying."

"If I go to Portland, there will be more opportunity to underwrite larger offerings. Most of what I get around here are small potatoes and the big banks don't want to take them. The larger the issue, the more money everyone makes. I've even got the opportunity to underwrite a large bond issue for the the Bath Ironworks."

"You don't need to go to Portland for that if you've already got the Ironworks business, do you?" It was more of a statement than a question.

Maynard scratched his head as he pondered what next to say. "You know I've been dealing with a firm named Bond & Goodwin who have offices in Boston. They want me to be closer to the Boston area and have offered me a partnership. I don't think I'll take it, but I need their influence and connections to get ahead."

When Maynard finished, Annie cleared her throat, paused as she looked out over the fields and let her eyes take in the view of Dodge's Mountain. Finally, after what seemed to her son an interminable pause, she said, "I've found it's never good to give advice unless you're asked for it. So, what is it you want me to say Maynard? You seem to have pretty well made up your mind."

Maynard sighed. "I guess I just wanted to talk this over with you and get your approval, or at least get your opinion."

Annie thought for a moment and then spoke rather deliberately. "Your father and I always knew that you would reach out for greener fields. You married Mary rather than a local girl who might have tied you down here. You could have had your choice of any one of many of the girls from around here, which would have made it harder to move on. Ever since you started in business you've been 'expanding' as you put it. I'm not being critical, that's just the way you are. Always looking for the next opportunity—the next adventure." She smiled as she said this, knowing she had touched a familiar cord in her son's nature. "But one thing I hope you will never forget—you come from Maine, and Rockland is where your roots are. If I had a crystal ball I would tell you that you would travel far and have many adventures. But I would also tell you not to forget that this is your home."

Maynard pondered his mother's words and knew she was right. He could never completely sever his ties to his hometown, and have someone say he had grown too big for his britches. "I guess I could keep the Rockland office open and just open a branch in Portland" he suggested. "I could spend part of my time there—maybe the winter months—and then be here in the warm weather when the summer people come."

Annie smiled to herself as she watched her son's mind work out a new approach to his problem. "How do you think Mary will feel about this," she asked?

"Oh, I think Mary will go along if I explain that we will be spending only the busiest social months there. She likes Portland and is beginning to make friends there. Also, it will be closer to Exeter where Milton will go this fall. She can go visit him much easier than if she were here," Maynard answered.

Their conversation continued for a while longer with Maynard talking about family matters and his mother listening.

When finally he got up to go, Annie stopped him with another question, "By the way, Maynard, you've talked a lot about these 'Bond & Goodwin' people. I wonder if, with a name like that, they are really a reliable company for you to be dealing with? Perhaps "Bond", "Good" and "win" are just catchwords to shine 'em up with a look of big city reliability. Remember that the Birds have always staked their reputations on their own names. I hope that you continue to do the same."

Although Maynard laughed at his mother's humorous critique, he recognized the underlying message there. It was just like her to use the play on words to remind him of basic moral values. He took her words seriously, nevertheless.

He had the last word, just the same. "Do as I told you Mother, get some new kitchen chairs before you fall off the porch and break your neck."

As he drove away, he knew she would ignore his advice and decided to talk to Mary about picking out a new set. The old ones could go to the old Tolman place now being used as a Poor Farm and they'd be glad of the gift. Some one there could fix them up, put in new caning and make them usable.

On the other hand, he would follow her advice and continue to use his name—The Maynard S. Bird Company—when he opened the Portland office.

10

On a cold, gray, late April morning in 1911, Maynard stood at the rail of the promenade deck of *S.S. Mauretania* as she plowed through the equally gray seas of the North Atlantic two days out of Southampton headed for New York. Although the ship was not setting any record on this crossing, she was still doing better than 25 knots as duly noted in the ship's morning bulletin. A pretty good clip, Maynard thought for such a large ship.[52] The seven foot swells and the occasional white cap were enough to discourage many other passengers from joining him as he kept his morning vigil. He was still a 'morning' person—a habit retained from life in Rockland. In business, he found he could organize and prioritize his thoughts better if he had some uninterrupted time to himself, either at the office or at home before other activities made demands on him. It gave him a step up on his competitors, and whether on land or sea—a matter of the early BIRD getting the worm. Maynard smiled as he turned over in his mind this play on words.

This morning he had left Mary in bed in the stateroom, feeling a bit queasy. This might have been due as much to eating too well as a guest at the Captain's table the preceding evening as to the rough sea. The honor of the invitation was due in part to a recommendation from a titled business associate in England, but more probably to their status as occupants of a choice first class stateroom. The generous tips Maynard had seen fit to distribute to the Dining Room Maitre d' had also been effective. For Mary, to sit at the Captain's Table, if only for one night, represented social acceptance and was, perhaps, the climax of her trip. She had dressed herself up in her fanciest gown; had her hair arranged by the ship's coiffeur, (Maynard wondered why they couldn't call the rather effeminate man who did Mary's hair, a hairdresser just like they did in Portland). She had taken her best jewelry—the lovely garnet necklace and earrings Maynard had given her—out of the ship's safe deposit box to wear for the occasion. If the stays of her corset were a little too tight, (Mary had been gaining weight lately), they didn't seem to inhibit her appetite to any degree. He had to admit, though, that the occasion had brought out the best of Mary's sociability. At dinner she had made friends with a number of the women, while Maynard involved himself in business conversation with some of the male guests at the table. By the time they left

86

the dining room and joined other acquaintances in the ballroom for dancing, they both felt assured that the evening had been a social triumph.

The trip had been a success, no doubt about it. He had, through letters of introduction, been able to meet a number of prominent businessmen in London, and had managed to make arrangements for private placement of several large blocks of U.S securities as well as acquiring some British offerings which would do well at home. He remembered with satisfaction how he had sold gold notes with a 5% coupon for the London Underground Electric Railway back in 1904. They had sold easily, of course with an interest rate 2 points above the going rate. Since then he had handled other foreign offerings. The British securities were always sound and he was sure that the crop he had garnered in London would be successful.

Aside from business, both he and Mary had enjoyed England. Like all first time tourists they visited the Tower; St. Paul's, Westminster Abbey; and Maynard had been invited to The House of Commons where he sat as a guest in the visitor's gallery. In his business dealings, the dignity and civility of his British contacts had impressed him. So he had been somewhat surprised and not a little amused to find the conduct of the English lawmakers in the House of Commons both rowdy and crude. The back-benchers had no compunction about yelling epithets at an opposing speaker; interruptions in the form of boos were frequent as the members lounged with cigars in mouths and feet propped up on the rail in front of their seats. By comparison, the Maine legislature was as dignified as a Baptist church service.

Another highlight of their trip had been when they were invited <u>down</u> to one of the country houses for a weekend house party. It didn't seem to matter that the country home they visited was in the Cotswolds north of London. It appeared that any place outside of London was 'down'. Maynard accepted this geographical peculiarity in the same manner as he accepted the fact that the natives of his home state always identified Maine as 'downeast'. They had both been impressed with the English style of living   the spacious houses staffed with servants whose job it seemed was to anticipate your needs even before you could think of them yourself.

Mary had seemed a little uneasy at first with the opulence. "What would they think of a butler in Rockland?" she asked and then giggled as she said, "Can't you just see Clara's husband, Mr. Harjula,[53] dolled up in a boiled shirt, white gloves and tails trying to serve dinner?"

Maynard laughed with her, but just the same, he thought, *I am going to have enough money some day soon so that I can afford a house as grand as this one, and a butler and other servants to go with it if I want them. Maybe not in Rockland—no certainly not in Rockland—but Portland would be another matter'.* Portland society was much more sophisticated than Rockland, and he knew that if his business continued to grow as it had in the last two years, there was no limit to where he could go or, for that matter, what he could afford.

While in London, Maynard had ordered suits from one of the fashionable custom English tailors on London's exclusive Saville Row. Somewhat of a dandy, he enjoyed superior, well fitting clothes made from finely textured fabrics. He had admired the meticulous tailoring seen on British bankers, and was pleased to find that this firm came to the United States at least twice a year to serve its patrons, so he could have the final fitting done in Boston later in the summer. In addition he ordered a half dozen monogrammed shirts and a number of silk foulard ties. Although he still clung to his preference for bow ties, he would not be found wanting on the occasion something dressier was called for.

Now, with the Old World receding behind him at each surge of the ship's bow, his thoughts reverted to home—to past successes, to plans for a future in which opportunities seemed, at this point, unlimited.

◆   ◆   ◆

In 1909 Maynard had begun the process of moving the securities business to Portland. By 1911 an office of the Maynard S. Bird Company was operating at 82 Exchange Street in the heart of Portland's business district. Portland, at this time, was probably about seven or eight times the size of Rockland. Nelson McDougall his early and valued partner in Rockland, also spent time in Portland office. McDougall still remained responsible for the Rockland operation, since it was felt that Ladd had not been with the company long enough to assume full charge. It was Maynard's intention that in Portland he would deal primarily with securities leaving the Rockland office to handle the bulk of the insurance business. It turned out that rather than diminishing either operation, both were enhanced by the division. His company was becoming the largest insurance broker in Rockland. Investment banking was the principal business of the Portland office. (By 1914 the branch needed larger quarters and moved to 120 Exchange Street, where they occupied the ground floor office #101. Here the brokerage would stay for years even when carried on by Maynard's successors.)[54]

As his reputation as an investment banker specializing in utility and public service issues grew, Maynard attracted an increasing number of underwriting opportunities many of them through Bond & Goodwin; some were in such large amounts that he would take only a portion of the issue. If he took the whole issue, he had no trouble placing it with a large bank in Boston. Independently, he still had the 'bread and butter' business of the smaller companies on which his reputation had been founded. However, the steadily increasing requirements of small utilities seeking expansion capital in amounts as little as $10,000 and a few as big as $50,000 presented a problem. The Maine bankers who knew Maynard best were squeezed between legal restraints and corporate regulations limiting total loans from one class of borrower. Bankers in large Boston banks, where his contacts were newer, were not interested in small issues that required too much paper work for the return they brought.

What to do about these small issues? Maynard had been mulling over the problem for quite sometime—even during the trip to England and after his return. One day at a point of deep frustration, the solution popped into his mind as if an otherwise hidden switch had been activated. He immediately contacted Charlie Higgins, a loan officer at the American Trust Company in Boston, with whom he had dealt on some previous underwriting business.

"Charlie," Maynard said abruptly, not bothering with any small talk about the market or other business. "I need to talk to a vice president in your bank—someone who can make decisions. I have a proposal for him that I know will be of interest."

"Hold on, Maynard," Charlie responded. "What's the big rush? Didn't you just get back from England? Have they turned sterling into gold over there? You sound all excited."

"Maynard took a deep breath and decided to soft pedal the conversation. "Well, I've been doing business with your bank for a while now and I like the way you operate. But if it's going to be too much trouble for you, I'm sure I can take the deal someplace else."

"Alright, Maynard—I get the message. Let me see if I can get hold of Mr. Boone. He's the principal VP in charge of loans. Guess that's who you want? Do you want to fill me in on the proposal so I can tell him why you want to see him?"

"Just set up a meeting with Boone and I'll tell you about it before we see him," Maynard replied. He thought it best to play his cards fairly close to his vest on this one.

As good as his word, Charlie made the appointment for the following week. When Maynard met him at the bank, the young loan officer was itching to find out what was going on.

"How would you like to bring the bank $3,000,000 in new 6% loan business?" Maynard paused, "And what would they think of you if you did?"

Charlie's eyes almost popped out of his head! He knew that on previous occasions his bosses had been impressed with Maynard's financial creativity—so often lacking in the stodgy banking environment.

"Wow!" was all Charlie could say. "We'd better go see Boone right away." And the two men proceeded to the office of Vice President John A Boone in charge of utility loans.

Boone was a big, gruff, rather paunchy man whose most memorable feature was an enormous walrus mustache. He recalled that Maynard had impressed him well at an earlier meeting. Now, his interest was quickly aroused by Maynard's scheme to package small loans to AAA quality utilities of which there were dozens throughout the northeastern states of Maine, New Hampshire and Vermont.

"You're probably getting $3\frac{3}{4}\%$ to $4\frac{1}{4}\%$ on the utility loans you make," Maynard said. "But I can do a lot better for you."

Boone scowled and his moustache scowled with him. "Sounds just like another scheme to give us loans we don't want anyway."

"Not at all," Maynard asserted. "You'll have just one large loan and probably never even meet the individual borrowers. And my company, MSB Financial Services (born only at that moment) will consolidate payments and bring you one semi-annual check. Furthermore, I will guarantee payment."

"And what about the rate? I can't take this unproven scheme at 4%." Boone was not about to give in too easily, although he was already intrigued by idea.

"That's the best part," Maynard's eyes sparkled. "Those utilities are so hungry for money that they're already paying 7% to local banks—that is when they can find banks that will take their paper. I can charge them $6\frac{1}{4}\%$—the $\frac{1}{4}\%$ a servicing fee—while American Trust gets the loan at 6%. So you see there'll be very little for the bank to do."

The Vice-president was silent for a few minutes; then a half smile flickered behind the moustache—for a Boston banker an extreme display of excitement. "Of course, I still have a lot of questions and will need more information. You know the bank has to approve this, but Charlie and I will take it to the next loan committee meeting."

After a bit more discussion about the plan, Boone said, "Charlie, will you excuse us, please."

When Charlie left the VP smiled broadly—or as broadly as the moustache would allow. "Great presentation, Maynard! I wish some of my business school wizards here had that kind of initiative.

Maynard had one more suggestion. "You may be right, Boone, about the need for creativity in banking, but Charlie has been very helpful to me in the past, so I hope he will get some credit for this project."

"Don't worry Maynard, Charlie is going to do well with this bank." With that, the two shook hands and Maynard made his way back to Charlie's office.

He found Charlie waiting for him in a state of contained excitement. He grabbed Maynard's arm and said, "I've never seen old 'Stone Face' so cordial. Why he even smiled! It usually takes three months to get something before the Loan Committee, and here he's promising you he'll take it to the <u>next</u> meeting! It's as good as approved, Maynard."

Maynard, too, was elated with his success. "Charlie, I can see us being exclusive for all utility bonds sold in the market, and at that rate, the bank can get a premium—maybe as much as 5%. Now, I've got to go back to Portland and organize the MSB Financial Services Company." He winked at Charlie who looked a little confused.

"You mean…" Charlie's voice trailed off.

"Just thought it up today." Maynard burst into laughter. "Pretty good idea, if I do say so myself!"

Maynard always thought of this venture into creative financing as a 'New Adventure' to be added it to the others that were the foundations of his success. With the packaging of small utility loans he was on track to achieve true wealth.

◆　　　◆　　　◆

In the four years since Sidney's death, the fortunes of the Bird family generally had grown steadily. Elmer as head of The John Bird Company had picked up where his father had left off. Elmer's oldest son, Sidney (II) had joined the business, and no doubt, the second son, Raymond, would soon be involved. If Maynard had any concerns about Elmer and his management of the Company, it was that Elmer was not expanding the company as fast as Maynard thought possible. But, on the whole the company seemed to be doing well and despite being a major stockholder, Maynard, preferred not to get involved in company affairs; it was better to let Elmer run things as he wished.

Henry, by this time, had already advanced in influence in the company, and had been given responsibility for the relatively new and productive canning operation. After more than nine years of marriage, Henry and Edith produced their first child in 1908, a son named Frederic after Edith's father. Then, having at last found the key to procreation, they continued with a daughter, Eleanor, in 1909 and a second son, Theodore, in 1910.

Alan's law practice, founded on his relations with The John Bird Company and energized through his father's position with the Rockland Water Company, was thriving. Alan, now well past thirty (1910) had enjoyed a bachelor's life a bit too long, the family thought. There had been rumors of a lot of drinking with his buddies, BB Smith and Glen Lawrence. So far there had been no serious consequences, but most agreed that it was just a matter of time. If everyone felt that it was time for Alan to settle down, it still came as quite a shock when, on April 20, 1910, Alan married Adelaide Craemer of Thomaston. As if to underline the family's displeasure, brother Henry was the sole Bird family member at the wedding.[55] Why this seeming act of disapproval? The Craemers were decent, hard working people. If they had not achieved the "refinement" and social status the Birds ascribed to themselves, they lived an honest, if somewhat ordinary—some would say hand to mouth—existence farming a small acreage in the country in back of Thomaston. Before the marriage, Adelaide, in a departure from the accepted norm of her new female in-laws, had worked as a bookkeeper for a Rockland business.

If, the Birds—and in particular—Elmer's family looked down on Alan's bride, had they forgotten their own roots in the first John Bird's illegitimacy barely two generations ago? Then there was the situation of Sidney's marriage to Annie when she was already five months pregnant; by now, it had become a poorly kept secret, if a secret at all. In the fifty years since John Bird had died, family bonds had weakened. Sidney's sons had combined to form themselves into self-anointed heads over the remaining family. This trait of dynastic arrogance was to color familial relationships for a number of generations to come.

Maynard had been in Portland at the time of the marriage, and so could be excused for not attending. He was familiar, however, with the way small town gossip could disparage the marriage as one of necessity. Since this did not seem to be the case, Maynard could see no fundamental objection. But he was concerned that members of his family had seen fit to show their displeasure by not attending the wedding. This he felt would ultimately cause unwanted family alienation. As he got to know his new sister-in-law, he recognized a bright, alert mind, and a disposition well suited to reigning in her new husband's excesses. Throughout his life, Maynard appreciated intelligence and ability without regard to gender. These were characteristics of which Adelaide could always boast. As time went on and Maynard's respect and trust of Adelaide grew, he would put in her care one of his most treasured possessions.

Like most of his contemporaries, Maynard hewed to the white, Anglo-Saxon, Protestant ethic. He was prejudiced against Catholics, Jews and of course, the colored, but so was everyone else he knew. Maine was still, to some extent, isolated from other eastern seaboard states. By the beginning of the 20th century, most towns had Catholics, and the larger towns and cities small Jewish communities. Immigrants to the state came from some of the Baltic countries including Finland and Poland, but they were white. The Finns in Maine tended to stick together and were Protestant, while the Poles were absorbed into the growing Catholic population, fueled to a greater degree by the steady influx of French Canadians. Few if any colored, as the former black southern slave population were then called, had migrated to Maine. There had been some migration of colored from the Caribbean islands mostly to Portland by ship, but they were few in number.

Aside from these institutional prejudices, however, Maynard tended to judge people by their abilities—and this was especially true of women. At a time when they were thought of more as homemakers, subordinate to men in the world of affairs, Maynard recognized that there were women who, in some instances, had qualities that exceeded those of men. In this he differed from others in his family.

◆   ◆   ◆

During these years of business expansion, Maynard and Mary occupied a suite of rooms in Portland, during the winter months, at the Lafayette Hotel on Congress Street. They still maintained the house in Rockland for the summer months—Maynard's friends among the wealthy summer visitors always played a part in his ideas for business expansion. Mary's mother's summer visits had long since ceased. (Had her son-in-law's success diminished her own importance in her daughter's eyes?) In Portland, they had become part of the social elite and were seen at many of the winter performances of opera, plays and concerts. They were also frequent guests at the elegant homes on the Western Promenade, and reciprocated the Lafayette. Mary found herself thriving in an environment where she didn't feel the strictures of in-law oversight. Her husband was popular—perhaps even a little too popular Mary thought—with some of the ladies. If this was jealousy, there was never an instance that she could find to complain about him. If she was extravagant, Maynard was more often than not indulgent of her excesses. In so many ways these years were probably the happiest of Mary's life.

Milton entered Phillips Exeter Academy in the fall of 1908 as planned where, after a rather rocky start the first marking period, he began to excel in most of his subjects.[56] Languages, literature and history seemed to be his forte; he was weaker in mathematics and science. Milton's extra-curricular activities were limited to a few sports and occasional class offices. The one activity that may have surprised his family was his membership in the Academy Banjo Club. Any musical aptitude must have been inherited from Mary, since Maynard could never boast of any talent even though he enjoyed dancing and the popular music of the day. Just the same, Maynard was pleased with his son's apparent scholastic ability, and hoped that time would convert him into the businessman he so ardently desired. By the time he left Exeter in 1912, Milton had become the epitome of the polished, upper class, private school graduate in dress, appearance and behavior. His graduation picture shows a handsome young man resembling his father around the eyes, but with a more sensuous mouth perhaps inherited from his mother. In Rockland his contemporary cousins, may have found this transformation too effete for their taste thus bringing back the old taunting that had earlier been Milton's lot. [57]

Despite his good grades at Exeter, getting into college was another matter. For some reason after leaving Exeter, Milton did not go immediately to college. He did not go to Bowdoin where so many of the Bird family had thrived, but selected Harvard instead; this can be ascribed to a certain snobbishness on the part of both father and son. At any rate he needed the tutoring of one W. W. Nolen of Cambridge in order to be accepted at Harvard in June of 1913.[58] Although never a distinguished student, Milton maintained a B average while majoring in philosophy. He received a B. S. degree from Harvard at the 1917 Commencement.[59] During these years, he lived with Maynard and Mary at the Lafayette when home on winter vacations. However, Boston became a second home for him when not with his parents. Maynard did his best during these years to make a salesman out of his son, even listing him as employed by The Maynard S. Bird Company at 120 Exchange Street.[60] Unfortunately, it became more and more apparent that Milton, knowing he was not cut out for his father's business, resisted any effort to make him a part of it.

◆   ◆   ◆

When war broke out in Europe in August 1914, Maynard's investment banking business was thriving. Even though most of his business acquaintances in Maine, Boston and New York felt it would be a short war, the need for capital to prosecute it was not lost on any of them. As the war continued into fall 1914, then the winter and into spring of 1915, it became apparent that the United

States must become a major supplier to the combatants. Most people along the Eastern Seaboard were wholeheartedly in support of the Allies, while large German immigrant populations in major cities in the center of the country naturally hewed to the side of the Central Powers. The Wilson administration was firmly in favor of keeping the United States out of war. The President saw himself and the United States as the means to lead the European nations to a "peace without victory". All that went by the boards with the sinking on May 17, 1915 of the *Luisitania* by a German submarine in the North Atlantic[61]. Ties with Germany were severely strained, and only the fact that the United States was in no way prepared for war, and the German government, realizing its mistake, immediately ceased attacks on ships in neutral waters, averted conflict.

As a life long Republican, Maynard was fundamentally opposed to any Democratic administration and Wilson specifically, who he regarded as an ivory tower intellectual. But he and others of the same political bent quickly saw the advantages of staying out of the European conflict while profiting from it at the same time. Maynard was already a principal underwriter for many large capital offerings. Starting with his utility packaging, and continuing with other capital offerings such as The Bath Ironworks, he was well known in financial circles in New England. With a war in Europe there was no dearth of opportunity in financing other ventures. He had set up his MSB Financial Services a division of The Maynard S. Bird Company and had increased the office staff with the addition of a talented young man named Walter Hammons. Nelson McDougall was encouraged to spend more time in Portland leaving the Rockland office to Walter Ladd's supervision. Maynard's income was increasing at a rate that even surprised him—he was becoming a very wealthy man.

September 9, 1916 marked the 25th or silver anniversary of Maynard and Mary's marriage. Maynard figured if it was called a SILVER anniversary then SILVER it would be in every way. He ordered a complete sterling silver service from Boston that was replete with every article available that would fit on a tray so large that only a butler could carry it. Maybe that was when Maynard seriously considered having a butler—an English one, of course, not Mr. Harjula as Mary had once drolly suggested. All of this silver was heavily embossed and monogrammed with Mary's initials (*MBH*) in classic script. Other gifts of silver from relatives, business associates and employees poured in many of them in the same pattern as the silver service.

By this time, Maynard and Mary had spent more than six years as Portland residents in the Lafayette Hotel suite. Although the hotel was a perfectly acceptable address in Portland, it could not compete with ownership of property, whether a mansion on the Western Promenade or land in the fast growing suburb of Falmouth Foreside. At the Lafayette, although the service was good, the beds were unusually hard, or so Maynard would tell his friends in later years. Neither he nor Mary ever expected that the hotel would become a permanent home. Mary still considered Rockland her home, having acquired, by dint of perseverance, the status she sought in that community. Maynard on the other hand had come to the conclusion that a Portland residence or one nearby would enhance his business connections as well as his social standing. After some investigation, he found property on Cumberland Foreside: fourteen acres stretching from Foreside Road to Casco Bay. On the estate, located near the road but with a magnificent view of the Bay, was a large imposing brick mansion. (Maynard always thought the land lay in Falmouth, which according to his lights was slightly more exclusive than Cumberland.). By the time that he and Mary celebrated their 25th wedding anniversary he had purchased the estate and was preparing to renovate the house.

But then the unexpected happened, as it so often does, and changed all their future plans. Mary became ill—seriously ill. It probably started as a pain in her lower abdomen; years of wearing corsets with boned stays had contributed to the occasional 'tummy ache'. Mary was also at the menopause age, and had passed the pain off as a common female complaint. But the pain persisted, even though she tried to hide it. By the time she sought medical advice it was too late. She was diagnosed with incurable cancer.[62]

11

The Rockland Courier-Gazette—April 13, 1917

MRS MAYNARD S. BIRD
Mary Elizabeth (Hawkins), wife of Maynard S. Bird, died in Portland Tuesday afternoon after a long illness. Mrs. Bird was the daughter of Thomas and Ella (Prince) Hawkins, formerly of Vineland, N. J.

She was of a temperament warm-hearted and generous, constantly bestowing kindness in many deserved directions and taking special interest in organized charities.

The funeral services were held at the family home on Beech street Thursday afternoon, Rev. Charles A. Moore, D.D. of Bangor, formerly pastor of the Congregational church here and a close and long-time personal friend of the family, officiating. Interment was in the family lot in Achorn cemetery. Besides her husband, Mrs. Bird is survived by a son, Milton H. Bird.

◆   ◆   ◆

It was with a sense of relief mixed with feelings of guilt that Maynard stood by Mary's grave at Achorn Cemetery while Dr. Moore intoned the final words over Mary's coffin. Relief—because Mary's suffering was at last over. Guilt—because he wondered if he had done all he could have through the years of their marriage to make Mary happy. He suspected that maybe he hadn't, but of course, now he would never know.

Although Maynard was not usually introspective, Mary's death made him ask himself questions about their relationship that he had previously avoided. It wasn't so much whether he had done enough for her—he felt that in a material sense he had done more than enough. In another sense, though, there had always been a disconnect between them. Mary's interests were not his, and despite sincere efforts on his part, Maynard could find little of interest in the trivia (as he saw it) that occupied Mary's mind and daily attention. Yes, they had enjoyed many of the same social contacts, although at times Mary showed a marked dislike for his political connections. She would entertain, at Maynard's request, some of his contacts she considered "common"; she preferred to include, if possible, people like the Cobbs who were obviously a cut above the run-of-the-mill politicos. However, she was completely uninterested in her husband's business affairs. Maynard had tried to explain to her the business of laying a cable to Vinalhaven and how he had been able to raise money for the project—what it would mean in terms of establishing a telephone company. As he talked, about this and other matters, Mary would interrupt with an excuse that she had to speak to the cook or finish some minor detail of the arrangements for their Saturday night entertainment. Milton was really their only topic of mutual interest and that more often than not elicited disagreement. Rather than argue about their son's upbringing Maynard preferred to give in to Mary's point of view. If by doing so, he relinquished control over the boy, well, at least he kept peace at home. Now that was all past, and not being one to dwell on past events, Maynard's thoughts turned to more immediate past and problems posed by Mary's death.

◆   ◆   ◆

It had been a long, sad, stressful winter for everyone as Mary slowly wasted away. It was not until early November after he had bought the Cumberland Foreside property[63] that he became aware that Mary was really sick. She never talked to him about her ailments because she considered them 'female problems' unsuitable for discussion with men—even with her husband. Maynard supposed that most women, if they were ladies, kept these matters to themselves and took it as a matter of course that Mary followed this pattern. Now, he realized that Mary's distaste for physical intimacy was a reflection of her prudishness about her body and her health. After Milton was born and their marriage became totally devoid of intimacy, Mary led him to believe that she could have no more children. Maynard accepted this as best he could; he devoted his energies instead to building up his business and with it his fortune.

It came as a shock, therefore, when one day he received a call at his office from their family doctor asking him to come in for a talk. Mary had finally, albeit it reluctantly, sought medical help. According to the doctor all signs pointed to cancer in some part of her reproductive system. He suggested that she have an operation as soon as possible. Hoping against hope, Maynard had taken her to specialists in Boston with the same result. An operation did take place, but only revealed a massive growth already spread to the point that it was inoperable.

Maynard wondered, if Mary had really felt well at their 25th Anniversary party. For the evening, they had rented the Masonic Hall in Rockland; an orchestra had been hired and the hall decorated with a profusion of flowers. Dressed in her finest ball gown with all her jewelry displayed, Mary stood next to Maynard in the receiving line welcoming their friends and guests from all over the state. After an hour of this, she asked for a chair and continued to greet people sitting down. When the orchestra started to play a fox trot, Mary, who loved to dance, smiled up at her husband and with a coquettish air reminiscent of her youthful days said, "Aren't you going to ask this old lady to dance, Maynard?"

And dance they did until both became breathless and glowing with pleasure. At that point, as he looked at her, all Maynard could see was the vivacious, bewitching girl he had married so many years ago—the girl with the sparkling eyes and alluring smile. Forgotten were the arguments and disagreements that had soured their marriage. Forgotten was the alienation from the Rockland community that Mary had endured in the early years. Forgotten, too, was the estrangement from her mother whose criticism of Rockland in general, and of Maynard in particular, had finally made her persona non grata in their home.

At Christmas time when they returned to Rockland, as they always did, Mary's pain had increased to the point where she spent a great deal of time in bed curled up with an ice pack wrapped in towels on her stomach. When the medication she took eased the pain sufficiently, she would dress and make an appearance for lunch or dinner trying to appear as normal as usual. For this Christmas, if it was to be Mary's last, Maynard was determined to have the house on Beech Street decorated the way Mary had always done it before. Garlands of pine bows hung above each doorway and across each mantelpiece; a huge spruce tree in the living room bow window was trimmed with strings of cranberries and popped corn, while mostly hand-made ornaments, collected over the preceding twenty-five years, filled every branch and twig of the tree. As an insurance man, and very alert to fire hazards of all kinds, Maynard vetoed the placing of candles on the tree, but candles decorated the dining room table for the Christmas banquet and, where possible, were placed in windows looking out on the street.

Milton came home for Christmas somewhat reluctantly. The holiday season in Boston meant many dances, receptions and other social events that he was loathe to miss. He had made a number of contacts in Boston—some among the upper crust of Boston society; but his father's insistence that he return to Rockland gave him no chance to refuse. Maynard had not told Milton of the seriousness of his mother's condition for he felt that an explanation would be easier for him to make on the spot. Once at home, he took his son aside and without mincing words told him of his mother's condition. He made clear that this was probably Mary's last Christmas and that they all must make it the best ever for her sake. Milton was shocked by the decline in his mother's health, although as yet she didn't seem to show any signs of failing. His first question, one that Maynard was prepared for, came out rather bluntly. "Father, how long has Mother been this way?"

Quietly, Maynard answered him. "I've only known about it since November, but I think it had been going on for some time before that."

"She didn't seem to be sick last September at the party. Was she then? You brought her to Boston in November, but you never told me then that it was for anything more than a check-up." Milton was angry—angrier than his father had ever seen him.

"Your mother didn't want me to tell you then. She was afraid it would interrupt your studies," Maynard said somewhat defensively. "What would you have done if I had told you? I suspected she was sick at the party," he continued, "but she hadn't told me or anyone else. Your mother loved parties, and nothing was going to spoil it for her. She enjoyed the party and she wanted everyone else to have a good time. I didn't even know she was sick until after I bought the Cumberland Foreside property."

"Would you have bought it if you'd known she was sick?"

This was a question Maynard had been asking himself without finding an acceptable answer. He was only fooling himself by pretending that it was for Mary. It was as much for him as for her. It was what he wanted—the fulfillment of a dream. "I don't know", he said, "Maybe I'll keep it so that the renovations that have to be done will keep her occupied. I can always sell it if I don't live in it.

It was time to change the subject to one Milton would find more pertinent. "What do your friends at Harvard think of the situation in Europe?" he asked. "Do they think we're going to get into the war?"

"There's a lot of interest in it and most of the fellows think we will have to get in on the side of the Allies. It's only a matter of time before those Huns do something stupid like sinking one of our ships with a torpedo from their damn submarines. If it happens while I'm still in college, I'll sign up immediately. Navy probably. We should have gotten in when they sank *The Luisitania*, but that mealy-mouthed president of ours backed off." Milton sounded quite war like in his comments.

Maynard didn't dispute his son's remarks, because he realized that it would not sit well with him had he known how much his father had benefited from the influx of investments as a result of the war. Maynard had long ago abandoned any hope that Milton would follow in his business footsteps. Also, there was a considerable amount of truth in what Milton had said. He knew that the British were extended financially to the breaking point and that their orders for war materiel were being filled by American firms solely on the basis of past goodwill and the hope that the United States would enter the war on their side.

Back in Portland after Christmas, as Mary's condition deteriorated during the winter months, Maynard spent many hours with her, either by her bed or sitting next to her in a chair. He would tell her about the people he had seen, especially those who had asked for her. When the weather was good, he took her out for rides—sometimes as far as Cumberland Foreside where he would show her the house and the beautiful stretch of land they now owned. They would talk about the house, the changes they would make and the parties they would have there with the butler and all the servants in attendance. He tried everything to distract her, but too often the pain was overwhelming. At those times the nurse would give Mary an injection of morphine for relief. Little by little she became bedridden.

◆　　　◆　　　◆

Milton's words would prove prophetic in ways not even Maynard could have imagined. The Germans did do something stupid and it appeared as headlines in the morning papers on Thursday, March 1. The [New York] *Times* proclaimed:

GERMANY SEEKS ALLIANCE AGAINST U.S.
ASKS JAPAN AND MEXICO TO JOIN HER.[64]

The country was in an uproar, and as Milton had predicted, the Germans had finally done something so stupid that even the German press in cities like Milwaukee and Kansas City denounced the action "as a direct threat against the body of America." As the Omaha *World Herald* stated, "The issue shifts from Germany against Great Britain to Germany against the United States".[65] When the United States ship *Algonquin* was torpedoed and sunk in the North Atlantic on March 12th by a German U-boat, and later two others were sunk in the same manner, the declaration of war awaited only the reconvening of Congress which was scheduled for April 2nd.

In the meantime, Milton was as good as his word. Whether he went home due to his mother's terminal condition or because of the imminent outbreak of war, he wasted no time in enlisting as a seaman first class in the U. S. Naval Reserve on

March 29 in Portland. Subsequently, Harvard granted Milton and other seniors like him, their degrees and they became members of the Class of 1917. On April 6, the United States declared war against Germany and its allies. Fortunately for Milton, being called to active duty meant that he was assigned to a patrol boat in Casco Bay. This way he could go home to the Lafayette Hotel when off duty and was frequently given leave to return home to be with his dying mother.

That Mary hung on as long as she did may have been due to the need to have her son nearby. In her waking moments when not heavily sedated, she would call for him and hold his hand as he sat beside her. Her wasted body and drawn gray face showed little of her former vibrancy. Only her eyes would light up when Milton came near. For Maynard to have his son nearby was a great relief. He had carried the burden of his wife's illness almost alone for many months now. The weeks before her death were weeks of great strain but at least he could share them with his son. In retrospect, father and son had never been closer.

Mary died on Tuesday afternoon, April 10th. On Wednesday, there was a brief prayer meeting in the Lafayette parlors so that her Portland friends could pay their last respects. The Portland papers said: "Mr and Mrs. Bird came to Portland from Rockland about seven years ago and since that time and until the illness of Mrs. Bird, [they] have been prominent in the social life of the city…"[66] Afterwards, Maynard and Milton accompanied the casket to Rockland there the final services were held.

◆　　　◆　　　◆

When the funeral was finally over, the family returned to the Beech Street house. Not since Sidney's death had there been so many of the Bird family together at one time, nor would it ever happen again. Adriel, Elmer's youngest son served as an usher, as did William Case Bird, the son of Maynard's first cousin, Hanson Gregory Bird II. Maynard thought well of both young men, but especially William whom he had assisted financially through a year at Exeter in 1907 and the four years at Boston Tech[67] until his graduation in 1912. William had then accepted a civil engineering job in Oklahoma. However, when he contracted malaria there, he gave up the job and returned to Rockland just before war broke out. Maynard was to keep track of William for many years assisting him wherever possible through business contacts.[68] Maynard also thought well of Adriel who had only recently graduated from Bowdoin but would soon join the army. Maynard saw in him many of the salesmanship characteristics inherited from his grandfather and uncles, and was sure that Elmer had noticed the same thing. Sooner or later, Adriel would be absorbed into the John Bird Company where he would do well. Sidney and Raymond were already there, the former being groomed to head the operation when Elmer retired. Maynard wondered how much longer the company could sustain the constant addition of the younger generation of Birds.

The talk among the Bird men after the funeral was all about the war and what it would mean to their businesses. Maynard knew that he would have to go back to Portland as soon as possible. He realized that this would mean making Portland his home base because there the security and investment banking business was thriving. He also wanted to be closer to Boston and to the Bond & Goodwin headquarters where there would be more action in a war economy. During the following two years, Maynard made frequent trips to Rockland to keep tabs on the insurance business. Walter Ladd had turned into a first rate insurance man and was making a name for himself and the firm throughout Maine.

. Maynard had pretty much decided that he would now move into the Foreside house even while renovations were taking place. For the time being he would keep the house on Beech Street but look for a buyer. He and Mary had lived at the Lafayette for seven years because Mary didn't want to give up their connection with Rockland where she felt secure in her place in the community. In Rockland, she was recognized as a senior member of the town's society, and she had made it clear to Maynard that she was unwilling to start over again in Portland.

It wasn't until the summer of 1918 that a buyer for the Beech Street house in the person of Nelson McDougall, appeared. Nothing could have suited Maynard better. Nelson had been his strong right arm for many years even though, as Maynard later wrote to Walter Ladd, he had "hired McDougall off of some farmer's grocery wagon, and believe me he was green".[69] Once the sale was concluded and the furnishings either shipped to Portland, or left for the new owner, Maynard found himself relieved of much of the responsibility for operation of the insurance agency. He still had business interests in the Security Trust Company and the John Bird Company; he an Elmer were also trustees of the Annie Bird Trust—all of this involved frequent trips to Rockland.

Despite Mary's death and his new status as a single man, he had committed himself to living at Cumberland Foreside, which he persisted in misidentifying as Falmouth Foreside . The property had been acquired from the estate of Abba Burnham,[70] one of many Burnhams descended from the original settlers of the area. The house had been designed and built around 1890 by another member of the Burnham clan, young George Burnham, who in subsequent years would design many notable buildings both in Portland and its suburbs.[71]

It may seem odd for a man recently widowed to live alone in a mansion—for that is what it was. Maynard was spending an increasing amount of time in Boston and was considering an apartment there. He had never consciously thought about remarrying, although he realized that at 48 he could be considered a real 'catch' by the single women in his social circle. In the years after Mary's death he was frequently invited to dinner parties where his hostess would seat him next to a newly minted divorcée or widow, or, rather unsubtly, a single lady of indeterminate age. At the time he was too preoccupied with his business affairs and the renovations of the house to pay much attention to any overtures—if that's what they were.

Although Maynard had admired the English Country houses he had seen in England, he was satisfied with his new home's design that fell into the French Eclectic style—popular in the first decade of the 20th Century. Set back some 200 yards from the street, there was a hedge that protected it from the casual sightseer. A long semi-circular drive stopped at the front door, then continued on past an east service wing to a garage and stables. Built of brick, the house had "a massive hipped roof…with the ridge paralleling the front of the house dominating the symmetrical façade with [a] centered entryway."[72] Three chimneys rose at the ends of the main building—two on the north and one (in the living room) on the south. The main floor was designed for entertaining with windows on the east that afforded a spectacular view of Casco Bay. On entry, a coatroom and lavatory were hidden behind a three-landing staircase. Maynard's study was behind the coat room. To the right of an entry hall that ran the width of the house, there was a living room; and on the left a formal dining room A butler's pantry, kitchen and a servant's hall completed the main floor. Upstairs there were four bedrooms including the master suite, and three bathrooms. Three servants' rooms were reached by a backstairway A third floor had as yet no designated use.

Despite the fact that he gave Cumberland as his residence while renovations were in progress, Maynard leased part of a twin house at 72 Bowdoin Street, just off the Western Promenade, for a winter residence. The Western Promenade was at that time the most fashionable address in Portland. It also had the advantage that it was close to a number of Maynard's friends living on the Promenade . Although he still continued to list Milton as part of the family, Milton, by the fall of 1917 had completed his officer's training at Annapolis and had been commissioned an Ensign in the U. S. Navy. By May of 1918, he had been promoted to Lt.j.g. (junior grade) and transferred from the battleship *New Jersey* to the destroyer *Whipple* for patrol duty in the European theater. Although Maynard worried about his son's safety, he felt some reassurance that at least Milton wasn't serving in the trenches, which, from all Maynard could find out, were far more dangerous.

During this time, Maynard listed himself as an investment banker, at which he was doing very well. While weekdays were taken up with business appointments and trips to Boston and other cities, his leisure hours too often left him alone and lonely. He joined the Portland Country Club, not far from the Cumberland property, whose main building was designed by the same architect, George Burnham, who had designed Maynard's new home. He attended various concerts and recitals in the city, and tried to carry on the social life that he and Mary had so successfully established. However, this was interrupted by an event that no one could have foreseen, least of all Maynard Bird.

The year 1918 saw a plague of influenza sweep over the whole world. Although there had been an outbreak of 'the flu' during the spring months it was mainly a three-day affair of aches, pains and fever. Having started in Spain, it seemed to affect troops fighting in Europe as well as the American soldiers on their way to the war. After the middle of June it seemed to disappear and no one gave it much more thought. But in Boston in August it reappeared with frightening and lethal results. Highly contagious, it spread with uncontrolled rapidity to all parts of the country—with special emphasis on Army camps and cities where large groups congregated. "Within a month after the flu arrived in Philadelphia nearly 11,000 people died from the disease."[73] It seemed to attack people in certain age groups—the young (under 5) and the elderly (70–74)—but the odd thing, only to be discovered later, was that those people in the 20 to 40 age bracket—ones in good health—seemed to be much more susceptible to the disease. In the United States alone more than half a million people died of the 'flu', while worldwide at least 20 million perished.[74]

Maynard was living at the Foreside during the summer months, and reduced his visits to Boston to a minimum to avoid the heat. So he did not recognize the disaster in the making until he read about the deaths from the disease in Boston, and its spread to Fort Devens, 30 miles northwest of the city. Once the country became aware of the deadliness of the influenza epidemic, all public events were cancelled in the major cities and gatherings of any sort were banned. Portland probably followed these same procedures, urging businessmen, including Maynard, to curtail their contacts to only those most vitally needed. Needless to say, Maynard did no travelling to Boston during the rest of the year. His age protected him to a certain extent and restrictions whether self-imposed or by public imposition saw him through the worst of the plague.

It is ironic that the Influenza Plague should have killed more American soldiers than were killed in battle. By November, the worst of the plague was over, and so was the war. On November 11, 1918 at 11AM an armistice was signed in a railroad car near the battlefield of Compeigne, France, and the "War to End All Wars" was over. The irony, of course, was that no one could foresee that the same railroad car would play a similar role with the antagonists reversed 25 years later in another war

No more guns were fired and the scythe of death from warfare and plague that had decimated the populations of the world was laid aside. The United States of America, with barely 100,000 in losses from battle could count four times that number from Influenza. The country had become a world power, but whether Maynard and his colleagues in the business world recognized the country's new international status is problematic. The year 1919 would bring changes for him that of course he could not foresee, but always the optimist he hoped for the best and, with his ingrained self-assurance, felt that he would be deservedly rewarded. And so it turned out.

12

1919—The clouds of war and pestilence, (those two Horsemen of the Apocalypse), had dissipated. Guns were silent; influenza was retreating in most parts of the world; and with a vast sigh of relief, soldiers left the quagmire of trenches to return home to their families. In America, if at first they had trouble finding work, the economy soon revived sufficiently to offer opportunities to the veterans. Peace was the watchword of the day when on January 18 the Paris Peace Conference got underway. Great Britain sent Prime Minister David Lloyd-George and the United States, President Wilson; Vittorio Orlando of Italy and Georges Clemenceau of France made up 'The Big Four' who would, in five months time, create a League of Nations and a Peace Treaty for Germany to sign. The German military and civilian representatives—the authoritarian Kaiser had long since abdicated—signed this treaty, although with bitter resentment, on the 28th of June in the magnificent Hall of Mirrors at the Palace of Versailles outside of Paris, an ironic reminder of France's own history of royal dictatorship.

The United States, flush with capital as the bankers of the war, turned its energies into the expansion of industry both new and old. The war had proven the value and use of motor vehicles, not only for troop and supply transportation (when they didn't get swallowed up by the mud), but now for peacetime use. This meant mass producing more cars and building more roads. And then there was the airplane! If there was any form of combat that rose above the calamity of trench warfare by adding a touch of glamour to the conflict, it was the aerial dogfights between opposing pilot aces on both sides. It didn't take long for resourceful minds to promote the commercial use of air transportation. On February 9th the first round trip passenger flight between Paris and London took place, and in July the British dirigible R-34 made a round trip crossing of the Atlantic. The United States would not be far behind. In a few years mail would be carried by air from coast to coast and passenger service would soon follow.

After a brief downturn, the economy started to boom. Consumer goods, in short supply during the war, once again crammed store shelves ready to be snapped up by eager buyers. Older companies that had deferred needed expansion and renovation until after the war were now competing with new ones; both old and new crowded markets with new products and services; all were seeking

107

investment capital. While most of these opportunities were legitimate, there would always be the unscrupulous individual ready to take advantage of an American public flush with money accumulated during wartime shortages. Eager to reap the benefits of an expanding economy, people were willing to put money into even the most risky undertakings to the regret of many investors. Charles (Carlos) Ponzi was one of the most artful of these con men with his pyramid scheme. But greed was becoming rampant and the national government itself would be tarred with the brush of corruption in the "Teapot Dome" scandal.

There were some labor problems epitomized by the strike of Boston police in the summer of 1919, but organized labor had not yet found a strong voice in American affairs. If there was any cloud on the horizon, it was a by-product of the Russian Revolution to which Americans had paid little attention in 1917, except to note that it had taken Russia out of the war. However, by 1919 anarchy, which the public associated with the violence of the Russian upheaval, became a burning topic in every day discourse. Immigrants from European countries, who might have been tainted with socialist or anarchist ideas, were looked upon with suspicion. Another two years would see the trial of Sacco and Vanzetti consume the attention of the entire nation.

The Maynard S. Bird Company was not slow to take advantage of the need for investment capital to fuel commercial and industrial expansion. Electric, gas, and oil companies needed investment to expand; telephone companies needed more money to service the increase in subscribers; railroads needed more rolling stock; and water companies needed to build more mains. Considering that twenty years before Maynard had gotten his start in the investment business by raising money for a telephone company, utility underwriting had been and still was his core business. He found that the Maynard S. Bird Company was being deluged with utility and other security offerings and it was only a matter of selecting the best ones to offer to his already select clientele. Large issues were often placed with Boston banks. Maynard's earlier association with American Trust had already paid off handsomely and would continue to do so. His company was now well enough established in Portland so that he was also getting other underwriting opportunities for industrial expansion. The company continued to have close ties with Bond & Goodwin, and although Maynard had been asked to join the partnership, he had declined, recalling his mother's advice about keeping the Bird name.

Early in February of 1919, Milton resigned his commission in the U.S. Navy having served honorably in the United States and overseas for nearly two years. Obviously not interested in returning to his father's business in Portland, as had been first suggested, he was induced, instead, to take a position with Bond & Goodwin in their Boston office. He reasoned that if he had to go into the securities business at all, Boston offered a more inviting work environment. There, at least, he had friends from his years at Harvard who would make life a lot more enjoyable. Although he probably hated to admit it, Maynard must have known by this time that his son was not cut out to be a securities salesman. As it turned out, Milton's stay at Bond & Goodwin did not last long. In November he married into the prestigious and wealthy Cushing family.[75] After that, he didn't need his father's support and never would again.

In July 1919, Maynard celebrated his 50th birthday in Rockland with his mother and brothers. He didn't feel his age. His energy and drive were those of a man twenty years younger. Rockland no longer offered the opportunities that it had twenty years ago when he had used those opportunities to his advantage. Now he had moved on while his brothers had anchored themselves in the familiar waters of their hometown. Alan and Henry had built houses side by side on Broadway. Both had employed the services of John Calvin Stevens, who was becoming known as Maine's premier architect. (Many thought that George Burnham, the architect who had created Maynard's house on the Foresdie, was equal to or better than Stevens, but since Burnham committed suicide at an early age, the relative merits of the two became moot.)

Henry and Edith's three children were old enough now to call Maynard 'uncle'; Elmer's three sons were already grown men. Surprisingly, Alan and Adelaide had produced no children in the nine years of their marriage even though Alan loved children and they him. Looking back on the furor their marriage had caused, Maynard wondered what it had all been about. Adelaide continued to impress him with her sound judgement and common sense. From Maynard's point of view, she had been a fine influence on Alan.

There were also family affairs to attend to in Rockland. Maynard's mother, Annie, had decided to give up The Homestead in the Highlands. She finally had to admit that it was foolish for an old lady nearly eighty years old to be "rattling around by herself in that great big house". Her sons found an apartment for her in a building at 27 School Street that she felt would be suitable. Now she would be close to the Post Office and only a few doors away from Maynard's company's office at 14 School Street.

"But Mother", Maynard pointed out, "I don't live in Rockland anymore, and when I am here I can always stay at the Thorndike or the Samoset. In between times, all you need to do is pick up the phone and call me in Portland."

"That's all right", Annie replied, "but at least those people in that office know where you can be reached. I like the idea of being near your office, it's like being near you."

Annie probably realized that when she left the Homestead, Maynard was symbolically leaving it with her; not only that, but he was leaving Rockland as well. She could no longer remind him that Rockland was his home as she had done a decade before. He had been away too long. The house was his last concrete tie to his birthplace.

With the move there was also the matter of selling the property, but that was solved when Clint Gifford came along and thought it would be great for his growing family.[76] Although the place didn't sell for what he and Elmer had hoped it would, Maynard realized, as perhaps Elmer didn't, that the property could easily become a real estate white elephant and they had better take what they could get. These transactions had necessitated another accounting by the brothers as executors of their father's estate and of the trust they had set up for their mother. In this instance, only small cash distributions were made, for the bulk of the trust obtained income from the John Bird Company and other investments.

Other Rockland business included attending a board meeting of The John Bird Company of which he was still a director. By this time, all Elmer's sons were company employees while Alan was still the company attorney, and owned his share of stock received from his father's estate. Henry, on the other hand, had left the Bird Company in 1917 to set up the Medomak Canning Company in nearby Waldoboro. Maynard, Alan and Nelson McDougall were among the stockholders. Henry gave, as his reason for leaving the family company that he wanted to build a business that he could leave to his children. Henry remained a stockholder in the Bird Company for many years. He remained on good terms with Elmer, who was now a majority stockholder, and who was obviously grooming his son Sidney for the presidency when he, Elmer, retired in the near future.

The John Bird Company was not the only source of the Sidney Bird's family's assets. They had a large stake in the Water Company and controlled the North Bank that the original John Bird had founded. Although he still held his share of Bird Company stock, Maynard's interests in Rockland were primarily concentrated in the insurance/brokerage business and the Security Trust Company, both of which were flourishing. In divesting himself of telephone stock a few years back he had reaped a lush harvest from the initial planting. Other members of the diverse family had kept their stake in the lime business, and some of Almon's and A.J. Bird's descendants ran local grocery stores; another was a mail carrier whose wife clerked in the post office. Obviously, not all the later generations had inherited the entrepreneurial abilities of their forebears.

◆   ◆   ◆

When Maynard returned to Portland from Rockland, it was with a sigh of relief. Perhaps he had been away too long, but Rockland seemed so provincial, (which of course it was), compared to Portland and Boston. He cared about his family—at least the immediate ones—and especially his mother. He realized that as new generations were born and became part of the growing family tree, there already were some he barely knew. He also had the feeling that there was no longer the community of shared interests between him and his brothers that they had enjoyed as younger men. He guessed this was natural because, since Mary's death, Portland was more his home than Rockland. Only when he saw his nephews and niece, Eleanor, enjoying the friends and activities that their hometown town had to offer, did he wish that his own son could have formed similar roots. But it was too late for Milton. He had provided him with the education and associations far from Rockland and in doing so had unwittingly contributed to the separation.

All in all, even though it was occasionally lonely, Maynard enjoyed his life in Portland. When the renovations were complete and the house completely furnished, he was looking forward to being able to invite his friends to see the finished product. He had already hired part of a staff that included a chauffeur, Mike Hanratty, because he thought it was simpler to have a car and driver available for transportation into and around town. His cook was a local woman, Ruth Brewster, from the Freeport area; he had no intention of giving up the 'downeast' cooking he was so fond of. In Boston he had contacted an employment agency to provide him with a butler and maid. Although he seldom thought a great deal about Mary after two years as a widower, he smiled now as he thought how she would have loved the idea of a real English butler and maid.

They came as a couple with names to suit their positions—Whiteway and Nancy. The surprising thing was that they seemed to get along with Ruth Brewster, a dyed-in-the-wool Yankee. Whiteway called Ruth "Cook" as he would have done in an English house, but she failed to reciprocate by calling him "Mr. Whiteway" as he had expected. Nancy, on the other hand, accepted the informality of an American household and called Ruth by her given name. It was a slightly different matter between the two English servants and the Irish chauffeur. Mike's Irish background was sufficient to foster a distinct coolness between the two historical enemies. Ruth acted as go-between and was often the bearer of instructions such as "Whiteway, wants you to bring in more wood for the living room fireplace." When she found that Mike didn't take orders from the butler readily, she tactfully switched the wording to "The living room fireplace needs more wood, Mike. Think you can find time to get some?" The answer as usual was "Yes".

◆   ◆   ◆

Now that the influenza epidemic was at last snuffed out, public gatherings were once again permitted. In the fall of 1919, Maynard could look forward to parties, concerts, and plays that made up Portland's social and artistic season. Mary had usually dragged him to some of these affairs insisting that they would enhance his appreciation of the finer aspects of life. Churches, once closed until the ban on meetings was lifted, resumed their regular schedule of Sunday services and other appropriate activities. Maynard had never been a religious man, although he and all his family had been brought up Baptists. Religion was just something you did—everyone did! You were brought up with it and took it for granted. Of course there were the Catholics whose faith seemed to ooze out of their pores on Sundays, while at other times was the least of their concerns. Annie Bird still attended the First Baptist Church in Rockland, as did a few other Bird descendants. More and more, though, Maynard and his brothers were choosing Congregational churches, often patronized by friends and members of their social circle. In Portland, Maynard found that many of his friends and business acquaintances were members of the State Street Congregational Church.[77] He may have been interested in the minister's sermons if they reinforced his preconceptions of God's message to Maynard Bird.

Certainly he was not expecting anything out of the ordinary when he settled himself in a pew midway down the center aisle one crisp fall morning in early October 1919. During the service he listened half-heartedly to the minister's sermon, that had been less than inspiring. It was hard to pay attention when the subject matter seemed to be a repetition of the Epistle selection, which, if you understood it the first time didn't need to be repeated. The sermon must have concluded while his mind drifted off on other matters, for suddenly he heard the most beautiful soprano voice coming from the choir stalls in the Chancel. The singer was a tall, beautiful young woman with dark eyes, dark hair, and creamy complexion unmarred by any artificiality. Her voice seemed to speak only to Maynard and held him entranced until the final note. He must find out who she was, and could hardly wait to ask her name when he was greeted by the Rev. Dr. Leavitt at the door.

"Why that's Rose Tyler," Dr. Leavitt, responded to Maynard's question. "She was formerly our resident soprano, but has been singing at a Congregational churches in New London, Connecticut and Boston the last few years. Whenever she's in Portland, she always favors us with her voice for at least one Sunday. Why here she is now," he continued, as Maynard turned to see the lovely Miss Tyler approaching them.

In that moment Maynard knew, instinctively, that somehow he and Rose Tyler were destined for each other.

13

"Miss Tyler, may I introduce Mr. Maynard Bird", Dr. Leavitt said as Rose approached from the choir room where she had changed from her robe to her street apparel. "Mr. Bird has been telling me how much he enjoyed your singing at this morning's service."

Rose was really in a hurry to leave; she was due for Sunday dinner with her parents at their home on Longfellow Street by one o'clock. The service had been a little longer than usual and now if she stopped very long to talk she would miss the trolley that left Congress Square at 12:40PM. Nevertheless, she could not ignore Dr. Leavitt's summons even though he sometimes talked longer than she cared to listen. So she smiled pleasantly at the stranger with the hope that she could slip away soon without offending anyone.

As Mr. Bird enthusiastically shook her gloved hand, she found she was looking at a man somewhat older than most of the men who had hitherto sought her attentions. He was well dressed in a smart well-cut suit of fine light wool gabardine. (Rose was particular about her own clothes, buying or having made only those that were in the latest style. Her mother called her a 'clothes horse' and maybe she was, but her own sense style made her conscious of the appearance and style of others.) Mr. Bird was slightly shorter than she was. She thought his face handsome with a high forehead, and slightly graying hair, (but then so was hers as a result of that typhoid she'd had fifteen years ago). His neatly clipped mustache failed to hide a pleasant smile on a generous mouth. A high-bridged nose accounted for his strong, independent appearance. But her attention was especially drawn to his eyes that were wonderfully expressive—the best feature of his face, she thought. Deep set, they spoke of humor, intelligence and understanding.

After a few pleasantries, Dr. Leavitt was lured away by other parishioners, and Rose was left to talk to Mr. Bird. Glancing at a watch pinned to the lapel of her smart looking brown suit, she realized that she must leave. "Please excuse me, Mr. Bird, but I have a dinner engagement with my family and must leave now or I'll be late."

"Perhaps I can offer you a ride, Miss Tyler. I have my car here and would be happy to be of service", Maynard replied.

Rose was a little taken back. She hadn't meant to sound as if she was begging transportation. She really didn't know this man well enough to accept a ride alone with him, but, she told herself that, after all, they had been properly introduced by a minister, so where was the harm? "How kind of you, Mr. Bird, but I'm sure it will be out of your way.

"Not at all, Miss Tyler, and it's not out of my way. Please let me have this pleasure in addition to that your singing has already given me. By the way", he said laughingly, "where <u>do</u> your parents live?"

"My parents live off of Brighton Avenue past 'The Oaks', but truly, I don't want to bother you," Rose tried to sound emphatic to put an end to the conversation.

But Maynard wasn't about to take "No" for an answer. "Nonsense," he said, "that isn't far and I can save you a lot of time."

Since she couldn't think of anymore excuses, Rose graciously yielded and accepted his arm as he escorted her from the church. His car turned out to be an Oldsmobile touring car, in beautiful condition with a chauffeur standing beside it. Rose was quite surprised. None of her friends, unless it was Mabel Foster who lived on Danforth Street off the Western Promenade, had chauffeurs. Some, but not many, drove their own cars, but hardly anyone had a chauffeur!

Once they had seated themselves in the rear of the car. Rose opened the conversation. "Where do <u>you</u> live, Mr. Bird?" she asked

Maynard told her about the house he had built on the Foreside road in Cumberland. His obvious enthusiasm delighted Rose.

Trying to be tactful and at the same time obtain a little more information about this interesting man, she asked, "Have you and your wife lived there long?"

"My wife is dead", Maynard answered soberly, "and I live there alone, although my mother comes to visit from Rockland occasionally. During the winter, I rent a house on Bowdoin Street." He paused, hoping to elicit further information, as she seemed rather reserved. "Do you live with your parents, Miss Tyler?"

"Yes, at present I do, although I have been working in both Boston and New London, Connecticut where I stay with my sister." Rose was now embarrassed feeling that she had been too forward in asking such a personal question and had gotten it right back in exchange. His wife had probably died of the flu from which there had been so many deaths. She was not surprised to hear of one more.

The conversation turned to her singing and to her career in general. Rose didn't feel it necessary, however, to tell this man that she was at a point in her career where she had to make some decisions. The best singing parts were in opera and New York was the place to find them. But despite having a manager for the last three years, she had gotten only a few concert engagements for private groups in New York. She had had several concert engagements in Boston in addition to her position at the Central Congregational Church there. Also there were the usual concerts available in New London. But the flu last year had created an upheaval in the concert and opera world everywhere.

Rose knew that she could go back to Boston and New London, but she also knew that if she wanted to sing in opera she had to go to New York where, if she was lucky, she might land a job singing at the Metropolitan in the chorus. All the divas the Met wanted were foreign-born singers, like Nellie Melba, although Geraldine Farrar was English-speaking. Of course, the great Caruso was in a class by himself. How she would love to sing with him. She knew she could learn the Italian operas; already her repertoire included arias from Verdi, Rossini and Puccini. Nobody, but nobody, sang Wagner anymore; the war had created deep antagonism toward the Germans and anything German that had not waned even a year later. Besides, Rose knew that her voice was not robust enough to sing Wagner, even if she had wanted to. But going to New York would mean more study and a place to live, both of which cost money—money which she didn't have a lot of right now.

Before she realized it they had arrived at her parents home. As the car drew up at the front door, Maynard took Rose's hand in a gesture of farewell. "I hope you will allow me to see you again, Miss Tyler", he said. "You might like to go for a drive and perhaps stop for tea some place."

"I would like that very much", she said almost automatically as if it was the most natural thing in the world to have met a man a half hour ago and agree to go out with him again. But why not! She hadn't met any one quite as engaging for a long while. He seemed genuinely interested in her, and, thank heaven, he wasn't involved in music. She was getting a little tired of listening to the music aficionados with their constant critiques of this tenor or that contralto. She supposed they talked about her the same way when she was not around.

With that, the chauffeur opened the door and handed her down. She turned and gave Maynard one more of her dazzling smiles and thanked him once again for the ride then hurried up the steps and into the house.

What an enchanting smile, Maynard thought. As he drove off, he realized that he had failed to ask her if she had a telephone and how he could get in touch with her. Never mind, he'd find her and she would come with him for a drive and to tea. Rose Tyler was all he could think of and in so doing the world was suddenly much brighter.

◆　　　◆　　　◆

On arrival home, Rose let herself into the house and removed her hat in the vestibule before starting for the kitchen to help her mother. Glancing into the parlor, she saw her father sitting in his easy chair reading the Sunday paper. "Hello Pa," she said as she went down the hallway that connected the front entrance with the kitchen. There she found Jennie Tyler in the last stages of preparing Sunday dinner.

Rose's father had been standing at a window in the parlor when Rose arrived in Maynard's car. Before she came by he had resumed his seat in the easy chair rather than let her think he had been spying on her. At 74 Joe Tyler was still an imposing figure. He carried himself in the erect manner of his youth when he had measured just under six feet; of course he had shrunk some since then—but not so badly as some of his friends. Although now bald, he had once had a full head of black hair like Rose's; but he still had the same deep black eyes as his daughter. His fingers were becoming arthritic, which impaired his ability to play the cello—one of his favorite pastimes. Altogether though, he thought, he wasn't in such bad shape for an old man

He put down his paper when Rose spoke to him. He had never gotten over the wonder that this lovely young woman was part of him. Nor had he ever expected to be blessed with a child as talented, even though he knew himself to have some talent—not just as a cellist. He could play a number of other instruments as well. After all, he had been General Chamberlain's bugler throughout the war. He and the General had been through a lot together—from Antietam, Gettysburg to the surrender at Appomattox. He still had the little cross he had whittled there with the date and his name on it.[78] When it came time for the remnants of Lee's army to surrender their weapons, General Grant had given General Chamberlain's brigade the honor of accepting the surrender. Chamberlain had ordered him, Joe Tyler, to sound the bugle call from 'order arms' to the marching salute of 'carry arms' in honor of a valiant foe. As long as he lived he would never forget the Johnnie Rebs, ragged, and worn, many without shoes, laying down their arms at the feet of the Union soldiers.[79]

But that was nearly 55 years ago. A lot had happened since then. Even though he and Jennie had married late when he was forty, it was certainly a much more satisfying marriage than his first one. He had been too young then, just back from the war and still a little wet behind the ears as far as women were concerned. Anyway, she had died and their daughter had taken off for Philadelphia[80]. He didn't care—he and Jennie had three fine children. Ann, the oldest, so much like her mother, was married now with a child of her own. The boy, Carroll, the youngest, had acquitted himself well in this last war—a war so different from the one he remembered. And then there was Rose. He didn't like to play favorites, but certainly she was the most interesting and talented of the three.

Even as a little child she had loved to climb up on the piano stool and play with the keys. It wasn't long before he had taught her to play simple little tunes, and then she started to sing them as she played. Jennie had objected to spending the money on music lessons for Rose. After all, she said, Joe had taught himself, and certainly he could teach Rose. But Joe knew that Rose would surpass him in the musical world, and he was determined that she have the best instruction Portland had to offer—especially when her voice started to develop.

Joe's musings were interrupted by Rose's voice from the kitchen, "Come to dinnah, Pa!" He could smell the roast pork and hoped the meal would also include sauerkraut, but he doubted it. Jennie didn't like to cook kraut because as she said "It smells up the house" and right now Joe couldn't smell it.

Once they were seated at the dining room table—a table Joe had made himself out of white oak to match the sideboard[81]—and 'Grace' had been said, Joe remarked, "You came home in a pretty fancy car—chauffeur and all that. You got a new admirer from the looks of it, Miss Rose?"

"What were you doing, Pa, peeking out the window?" She didn't like to be spied on even though she knew her father meant no harm. "His name is Maynard Bird, Pa, and Dr. Leavitt introduced us at church", Rose explained. "He's very nice and I may go out for a drive with him again—at least he invited me to."

"He'll have to make it soon. You said you were going back to Ann's on Friday?" Jennie said.

"I suppose so. At least they're expecting me", Rose remarked. For the present she decided to put off any discussion about her future. She loved being with her sister and especially with Ann's darling little daughter, Evelyn, now five years old. In the meantime she would have a chance to see her friends and perhaps go for a ride with that nice Mr. Bird.

"Well tell us about him", Joe said. "You must have learned something about him while you rode around in that fancy car."

"I know that he's a widower and that his wife died, but he didn't say when", Rose answered. "I suppose it may have been the flu. He has a house out on the Foreside that he's very enthusiastic about. I gathered that you could see the Bay from the back yard so it must be near the water. He's also a banker and has an office at 120 Exchange Street. Dr. Leavitt seemed to think very highly of him, although I don't ever remember seeing him in church before. I think he comes from Rockland because he said his mother comes from there to visit him here."

"How old is he and does he have any children?" asked Jennie, ever the practical one.

"Really, Ma, how much did you expect me to find out in a fifteen minute ride, and anyway, it would have been rude to ask", Rose answered rather sharply. "It's not as if I was going to marry the man—we've only just met and I'm sure he has lots of other things on his mind besides me."

But in that she was quite wrong.

◆   ◆   ◆

After leaving Rose at her family's home, Maynard proceeded to the Lafayette Hotel where he was in the habit of having his Sunday dinner, all the while puzzling over how he could find out more about Rose Tyler. It occurred to him that Helen Whitney, the wife of one of his clients, might be a member of something called "The Rossini Club" to which Rose had mentioned she belonged. Although Maynard was not sure, he vaguely remembered hearing that Rossini was a composer of opera music.[82] Helen Whitney was fond of music and supported many charitable musical events. She was also a member of the State Street Church and therefore must know something about Rose. After dinner, Maynard decided to pay a call on the Whitneys who lived near the Western Promenade.

Maynard had picked the ideal person to inform him about Rose. Helen was a member of the Rossini Club, and Rose was its youngest member. Helen was also quite intrigued that this eligible bachelor had found a young woman who interested him and as a result she happily told him all she knew about Rose.

"Rose is the second child of Joseph and Jennie Tyler," Helen began. "I don't know much about her mother, except that she comes originally from Calais and was a Hastings before she married. Jennie Tyler is Joe's second wife, by the way, and I don't know anything about the first one. Joe made his living as a skilled cabinet and furniture maker. I'm not sure who he worked for or whether if he worked independently, but his hobby, if you can call it that, is music. He is a fine musician—plays the cello now and then in local orchestras. I did hear that when he was in the 20th Maine during the Civil War, he was General Chamberlain's bugler. Rose must have inherited his talent. She went to Deering High School, but contracted typhoid when she was about sixteen. I think she lost a year of school then. She had already been taking singing lessons from local teachers.

Again, I'm not sure who they all were, but Harriet Foster Chadwick comes to mind.

Maynard was puzzled. From what he had seen and heard of Rose, he had judged her to be a well-trained professional with all the polish and sophistication of a lady. "But she couldn't have gotten all her training right here in Portland," he said.

"Oh my no", Helen responded. "She's had training at the Damrosch School[83] in New York. She left high school in the middle of her last year after Walter Damrosch heard her sing in an amateur school production. It was a great opportunity for her—she does have a beautiful voice and she's such a nice person. Do you know, she came back from New York just to sing at her high school class graduation exercises even though she wasn't graduating. They were thrilled to have her. It's a shame the school didn't give her a diploma anyway. But then, I guess she got one from the Damrosch School. Rose was, and perhaps still is, a pupil of William L. Whitney in Boston."[84]

"How long was she at the school in New York?" Maynard asked.

"Oh, I guess a year or perhaps a year and a half. I do know that the State Street Church hired her as soprano soloist in 1909", Helen went on. "She is very popular in Portland and has sung in opera and given many concerts. You did know, didn't you, that she has been singing in Boston and also New London, Connecticut, at churches in both places?" Helen paused for a moment waiting for a remark from Maynard. When none was forthcoming, she continued.

"All of us in the Rossini Club were very sorry to lose her. At her last concert here before leaving Portland, we gave her a pin of sapphires and pearls which she still wears. The Portland Choral Society also gave her a gift. I think it was a gold piece." (This was said in a manner that made plain that Helen thought the gift of The Rossini Club far outshone that of the Choral Society.)

"Do you know whether she plans to go back to Boston or New London?" Maynard asked. "She was a little vague about it, and I didn't want to question her too much. After all we had just met."

"I'm not sure what she plans to do, but maybe I'll find out this week. Inez Turner[85] is giving a Bridge Party for her on Thursday, so if she's going back to New London, she surely won't go before then. Rose loves to play bridge. In fact she's pretty good at most card games," Helen concluded.

Maynard decided not to push the questioning any further so the rest of the afternoon was spent quite pleasantly discussing other matters with both husband and wife. As he was leaving, Helen walked with him to the front door. "Maynard", she said, "why don't I arrange a little dinner party and invite Rose. That way, you can have another opportunity to get to know her better."

"Helen, that would be wonderful and very thoughtful of you. How did you guess that I was anxious to become better acquainted with her?"

"Oh, Maynard, you are obvious some times." Helen laughed. "I know you came here this afternoon just to quiz me about Rose. You can't pull the wool over my eyes!"

"Why Helen," he responded with a chuckle, "you know I enjoy your company under any circumstance, and before you take it back, I'm accepting your invitation right now. What better way to get acquainted with someone than in your charming home."

As he rode home, his mind was full of plans for future meetings with Rose Tyler

14

Had Maynard been more introspective, he might have pondered over the coincidence that led him to The State Street Church that morning of all mornings in October. It had been a spur of the moment decision to abandon an hour or two in his garden at the Foreside for the spiritual uplift of the church. His reaction to hearing Rose sing and their subsequent meeting had convinced him that she was to be in his future. Since Mary's death he had been lonely for he enjoyed women and liked the part they played in his life. He had become used to Mary even though she had not furnished the affection he yearned for in a mate. But she had provided a measure of companionship that he missed. In Rose's beauty and talent combined with her apparent intelligence and poise, Maynard saw the kind of mate he had always desired.

Once his mind was made up, he was not one to let grass grow under his feet. On arriving at his office Monday morning, he immediately had a secretary check to see whether the Tyler's had a telephone. Finding that they did he waited until mid-morning to call and reconfirm their engagement for the next afternoon. Mulling over a suitable place to take Rose to tea, he called the Black Point Inn at Prout's Neck where he made arrangements for an early tea. Now, with everything in readiness for their next meeting, Maynard could only pray for good weather, good roads and a drive without a flat or breakdown. God would have to take care of the first two requirements, although He had some doubts about God's influence on road conditions. Any automobile malfunctions he left up to Mike Hanratty whose rather remarkable mechanical talents had seen them through a number of motorcar predicaments.

Maynard took great care in preparing for his outing with Rose. He realized, perhaps for the first time, that there was a considerable difference in their ages. It would have been indelicate to ask Helen Whitney of Rose's age, so he had to guess that she was probably close to thirty[86] given the time she had been singing both in Portland and New London. In order to look as youthful as possible, Maynard selected a tweed tattersall jacket with a black pattern on a light gray background to go with a pair of darker gray flannel trousers. With his self-collared shirt he wore his customary gingham bow tie. As he looked at himself in the full-

122

length mirror in his dressing room he was satisfied that his appearance was conservative but youthful enough to impress a younger woman.

Promptly at 1:30pm the Oldsmobile touring car with the top partially retracted arrived at 169 Longfellow Street. Mike was sent to escort Rose to the car where she joined Maynard in the back seat. Rose had decided that warmth took the place of style on this outing, and had worn and a warm calf length knitted blue wool sports coat. She had also worn a practical pull-on style hat with a narrow brim and deep crown and was hoping that it would stay put and not blow away in the wind.

Concerned for her comfort, Maynard asked, "Will you be warm enough, Miss Tyler? I brought along a couple of lap robes just in case it gets colder."

"Mr. Bird, I'll be just fine," she responded. "You picked a wonderful day to go for a drive. Where are we going, or are you going to keep it a secret?"

"I think I'll let you guess," Maynard said teasingly. In truth it was a beautiful clear, warm day for mid-October. The maple leaves in their crimson glory, contrasting with the dark evergreens, lent a feeling of excitement to their excursion. Maynard thought the autumnal beauty was a good omen for what he hoped would be their mutual friendship—and possibly something more.

At first their conversation was restrained by their lack of familiarity with each other. After a few comments about the weather, the car and their destination, Maynard looked at Rose and said earnestly, "Miss Tyler, may I call you 'Rose?" Rose laughed, a lovely bell-like laugh, and said "Only if I may call you Maynard. Or do you have a nickname you would rather I use?"

"Of course, just call me Maynard. I've never had a nickname, or at least one that I liked", he said, remembering his childhood when Addie called him Maynie, and his schoolmates had called him 'Maybird'. "Does anyone call you Rosie?"

"Oh heavens no!" Rose replied. "My father would be furious if he heard anyone call me that. He says Rosie sounds like an Irish immigrant name." Rose stopped and covered her mouth as she looked at the chauffeur whose red hair and freckled, pug nose left no doubt of his Irish heritage.

It was Maynard's turn to laugh, even though he appreciated and understood her embarrassment. "Don't worry, Mike probably didn't hear you at the speed we're going and the wind in his face. Even if he did, he would think you meant it as a compliment. He's very proud of being Irish."

With the conversational ice broken, the rest of the trip to Prout's Neck passed quickly for both of them. They told each other something about their families and their interests. Rose found out that, unlike her previous impression, Maynard's wife had died more than two years before and not of the flu as she had assumed. She learned that he had a son who had served in the navy during the war. This led her to mention her brother, Carroll, who had also served overseas but in the army.

Maynard, on the other hand, was eager to learn of her life in New London and Boston. Without seeming too curious, (which of course he was), he said, "You must enjoy New London more than Portland to have stayed there as long as you have. I always thought Portland, next to Boston or New York, offered more in the way of musical opportunities than any other New England city."

"That's true," Rose responded with a smile that seem to say, 'I know what you're getting at and maybe I'll just tease you a little with a little exaggeration of the goings on there'. "I really spend more time in Boston than New London, but because my sister and her husband live in New London, and have ever since their marriage, I consider it my second home. My sister Ann's husband, Skip—that's his nickname; his real name is Ernest—is an automobile representative for the Studebaker Company. They have a darling daughter, Evelyn, who is my god-child. I've enjoyed New London, and, surprisingly, there's a lot going on there, or there was before the war.

"Ann and Skip have many friends", Rose continued, "and they've seen to it that I've been introduced to a number of them. Of course I meet people at church and at concerts too. There was a whole artist's group there for a number of summers. You may have heard of James O'Neill, the famous actor.[87] The O'Neill's have a summer place in New London, and I knew their son, Eugene. Ann didn't like him because he drank too much, but I thought he was interest-ing. When he was reasonably sober he wrote plays—some of them pretty good. He may yet turn out to be well known as a playwright. The last I heard of him, he was in New York where a group of his friends were producing some of his plays."

Rose decided not to mention that there had been a number of O'Neill's friends in New London who had taken her out and with whom she was quite friendly. So she steered the conversation away from New London. "I am also in Boston frequently. That's where my voice teacher lives. I sing at the Central Con-gregational Church and have had a number of other engagements there. At least I did before the flu epidemic."

"Do you plan to return to either place soon?" Maynard asked. Thinking ahead, he wanted to know how he could see more of her.

"Really, Maynard, I don't know." Rose was distracted by his question. She had been procrastinating making any decision on her future. "I have to return to straighten out some business with the church where I sang. Whether I will continue to sing in either Boston or New London is another question."

Maynard felt it was not appropriate to push the issue any further. Anyway, Mike had brought them safely to The Black Point Inn at Prout's Neck, so Maynard said, jokingly, "You forgot to guess where we were going, Rose."

"No I didn't," Rose said indignantly. "I knew from the moment we crossed the river into South Portland that we were going somewhere along the shore. I just couldn't decide whether it would be Cape Elizabeth or Prout's Neck." Then she continued a little sheepishly, "Actually, I didn't think the Black Point Inn would still be open, so I didn't say anything in order not to embarrass you when you found it was closed."

With this Maynard roared with laughter. "You didn't really think I'd bring you all the way down here without calling ahead to see that the place was open. We may have the place all to ourselves, but that's alright, they're expecting us."

A table had been set for them in the lounge where they could enjoy the warmth of the fireplace and the beauty of the sea. As it was late in the season; Maynard was right that they had the place almost to themselves.

Now, it was Rose's turn to listen while Maynard recounted anecdotes dealing with his business ventures. Many of his stories were embellished with bits of 'downeast' humor—humor that only someone from Maine, who had lived elsewhere in more sophisticated surroundings, could appreciate. Rose liked the balance that he showed between the folksy wit of his native environment and that of the more polished circles in which he obviously now moved. She was finding her escort more interesting than she had expected, although she couldn't quite put her finger on why this was so.

The afternoon passed quickly for both of them. Before they knew it the time had come to leave the Inn and start their journey back to Portland. Mike had taken the opportunity of pulling the top shut because with the sun lowering in the sky there was more of a chill in the air. Now the lap robes came in handy. On arrival at the Tyler home, Maynard asked, "Will I have another opportunity to see you before you return to New London? Perhaps you would like to go out to dinner."

"I've really enjoyed this afternoon immensely," Rose responded, "but in answer to your question, I haven't made up my mind yet about returning to New London. I think they expect me on Saturday this week" Then with a wistful smile, Rose turned and said, "Why don't you call me on Thursday. I should have made some definite plans by that time."

This time Maynard himself got out of the car to escort Rose to the door. He was elated that she herself had offered him a chance to see her again.

◆   ◆   ◆

Rose had been quite sincere when she told Maynard that she'd enjoyed the afternoon with him. It had been a long while since she found such pleasure in a man's company. She had memories, of course, of other men who had shown an interest in her. Long ago, when she was just beginning her career, Frank Jackson had wanted to marry her. The trouble with Frank was that he wanted her to give up her career before it had hardly started. Frank was a singer too, with a fine tenor voice, but singing would never be his profession. He had married Jeanette Emerson and gone into his father's hardware business. So much for his vows of undying devotion when she turned him down! Then there was Ed Keefe, one of Gene O'Neill's friends. But Ann's dislike of anyone connected with the O'Neill's made any relationship with Ed difficult. Just the same she had kept his picture in her little gold locket; she would always remember him as special. What with losses from the war and the flu epidemic, Rose had pretty much decided that it was either build on her career or resign herself to church singing with the occasional concert. There was not enough money in the latter and she couldn't go on being a burden to either her parents or her sister. She intended when she returned to New London to visit New York and see if there was any possibility of getting work there. Boston was another option that should be explored. She had contacts there through her voice teacher, William Whitney. Perhaps he could help her find something or someone in Boston that would revitalize her career.

Her mind drifted from the disturbing thoughts of her future to the afternoon spent with Maynard and how truly enjoyable it had been. He was easy to talk to and easy to listen to, and not critical of her ideas as were so many men when her opinions differed from theirs; above all she liked Maynard's sense of humor. She had laughed at some of his stories more than she had in a long time. She had just about decided that if he called on Thursday she would postpone going to New London and accept his invitation to dinner.

◆   ◆   ◆

When Rose arrived at Inez Turner's bridge party on Thursday morning, the first person she ran into was Helen Whitney who cornered her before she could even take off her coat.

Helen's eyes were sparkling and a big smile lit up her face. "Rose, you certainly have an admirer in Maynard Bird. He paid us a visit Sunday afternoon and wanted to know all about you."

. "You mean he came to *your* house on Sunday?" Rose was almost speechless with surprise. "Dr. Leavitt only introduced us after Sunday morning's service. He gave me a ride home."

"He was really taken with you. He wanted to know all about you. You don't mind if I told him a little about your background, do you? I hope you found him pleasant enough because I promised him I would have you over for dinner." Helen paused, wondering perhaps whether Rose had found Maynard as attractive as he had her.

"Yes, I liked him; he was charming and interesting, but I never dreamed you knew him," Rose stammered.

"Then you will come to dinner—how about this Saturday evening? Oh, I forgot, you're not going back to New London right away are you?" Helen was now the one who seemed confused.

"Oh no, Saturday will be alright. In fact I had decided to stay over the weekend anyway. I may even sing at the eleven o'clock service again." Rose saw no reason to tell Helen that she had only this minute decided to stay longer in Portland. Partly it was because of Maynard's and now Helen's invitation. Nor did she want to tell Helen that she had spent Tuesday afternoon with him as well. Let Helen continue to think she was a matchmaker.

Inez calling them to the bridge table interrupted their conversation. "I'd rather you didn't say anything about this to the girls, Helen," Rose said.

"It will be our secret for the time being," Helen replied.

◆   ◆   ◆

Maynard was delighted to find that Helen had been as good as her word. When he arrived at the Tyler home Saturday evening, he decided to go to the door himself rather than to rely on Mike. The door was opened by a tall, impressive man in his seventies whose resemblance to his daughter, Rose, was apparent. "You must be Maynard Bird," he said, "I'm Joe Tyler. Won't you come in and sit down, Rose will be ready in a minute. Just like a woman, always a little late."

Maynard was ushered into a sitting room furnished with comfortable easy chairs, an upright piano, and a long divan opposite the piano. In one corner to the left of the piano, a cello rested against a straight-backed chair as if the musician had been interrupted in the midst of a performance. If Maynard had not already known, he could not fail to recognize the symbols of a musical family.

Before he could do more than acknowledge Joe Tyler's greeting, Rose appeared in the doorway. She had taken pains with her outfit that evening; her dress was made of lavender georgette with sheer net sleeves banded in a darker-hued lavender satin. The hemline fell about three inches above her ankles and the waistline, belted with a matching satin belt, gave her a willowy appearance. The neckline was cut square and fashionably low accenting her graceful neck and shoulders. Around her neck she wore a string of amethyst beads and in her ears small amethyst earrings. The heels of her black pumps made her at least two inches taller than Maynard, but that did not seem to bother either one of them. In fact, the expression of pleasure on Maynard's face when he saw her, was reward enough for the time and effort she had spent dressing.

Helen's dinner party was a great success. Rose, to whom some of the guests, although friends of Maynard's were strangers to her, felt completely at ease with all of them. As a climax to the evening, and as a thank you to Helen for arranging the party, Rose graciously agreed to entertain them with a few songs after dessert and coffee. She had thought to sing only one or two but found that she could not refuse a third and even a fourth.

On the way home, Rose felt she must tell Maynard of her decision—made that afternoon in response to a wire from her sister Ann—to return to New London. "Maynard," she said, "I've decided to go back to New London on the morning train Monday." She paused, feeling that she had been too abrupt. "I have to settle with the church in Boston where I sing, and then from New London, I can more easily get to New York. I can't tell you how much I've enjoyed this past week and our acquaintance." This was said very earnestly as if to make up for her past bluntness.

Maynard reached over and took Rose's hand as it lay in her lap. "This week has meant a lot to me, too, Rose. I want us to continue our friendship, even if it means seeing you, perhaps in Boston or New London. I go to Boston frequently on business, and there are many concerts, plays and other things there that we could do together." For once Maynard felt he had not expressed himself as well as he could, but he was determined not to let this lovely woman drift away.

Rose was a little surprised at the emotion in his voice and her own reaction to what he had said. She found she wanted to see more of this man without any expectation of where it might lead. Just being with him felt right. "I am in Boston for voice lessons and hopefully for other engagements. Perhaps we could see each other there," she replied, not too sure of her own voice.

"I hope you will let me write to you, then," he said.

"Of course, nothing would make me happier. Oh, Maynard, what a wonderful week it's been!" was Rose's reply. "By the way, I think I'll be singing in church tomorrow: will you be there?"

"Of course," was his answer, as if she hardly needed to have asked the question.

With that they parted. For Maynard, the trip back to the big house on Cumberland Foreside was a journey of dreams. Now with so much to look forward to he prayed that nothing would be allowed to interfere.

15

The Cobb family greeted Rose's return to New London with much enthusiasm. Little Evelyn[88] who at four and a half was already devoted to her Aunt Rose, clung to her Auntie's skirts, plaintively asking, "Did you bring me a present?"

"Of course sweetheart, but let Auntie catch her breath and you'll see what a wonderful surprise I have for you," The surprise turned out to be a Raggedy Andy doll to go with the Raggedy Ann doll that the little girl already had. The new doll hardly left its new owner's arms for the next several days.

Rose was glad to be back in her sister's home with time in the next few days to recount her latest news. Some of it was not encouraging, for she had not been able to tie down a position at any of the Portland churches where a professional singer might have been hired. "Most of the church people I talked to had really not recovered from the upheaval that the flu and the war created," she told Ann. " I did sing a couple of times at the State Street Church, but even there they are considering converting to an all volunteer choir with the organist as director. Perhaps, I'll have better luck here."

But Ann shook her head. "I think it's the same here—at least with the Congregational churches, but there's no harm in contacting them. Maybe something will turn up."

Rose mentioned her intention to visit New York and see if she could resurrect some of her contacts there. Then she said as casually as possible, "I met an interesting man last week in Portland." And with that she told Ann all about her meetings with Maynard.

Ann listened intently, and finally said, "Rose, you sound as if you really have a crush on him. Didn't you say he's much older than you are and also that he's pretty rich. Are you sure you're not being carried away by all that glamour?"

Rose ran her hand through her hair—a habit she had lately developed when not sure of her response. "You know me better than that Ann. When have I ever been taken in by money? Besides, he comes from a very conventional family in Rockland. The money must be fairly recently come by and I guess he just enjoys spending it."

Ann shook her head. "I believe you, but don't let yourself get carried away, Rose."

130

"I must say, I was a little overwhelmed when he took me home from church that first day in a chauffeur driven car. But he has nice friends" Then pausing momentarily, she continued, "Oh, by the way, did I tell you that Helen Whitney gave a small dinner party for me and invited Maynard?" She paused and smiled as she corrected herself. "Or maybe it was the other way around: the party was for Maynard and she invited me!"

Ann laughed "Did you consider it was for both of you?" She dropped the subject, but she couldn't wait to tell Skip about the budding romance. In this she was more farseeing than her sister.

Their conversation continued about other matters for a while longer until Ann excused herself to make dinner. But the talk had left a kernel of doubt in Rose's mind. Yes, she liked Maynard, and yes, she hoped she'd see more of him. But she didn't want people to think she was chasing after him for his money. At this point she didn't even consider what kind of role Maynard might play in her life. Up to now, she had always been able to support herself with her singing, but it was getting harder and harder to find engagements. At 31 she should be at the height of her career—or—she would be seen as over-the-hill. She was hoping that New York or Boston would offer better chances than Portland and New London, otherwise, she would have to rely on her parents for help. This was something she didn't want to do for it would be admitting defeat. She decided that first she would do whatever needed to be done to enhance her career; and, as a last resort, she could always give voice lessons in Portland.

In the coming weeks, Rose found that there was still no openings at any of the churches in New London. Nor did there seem to be any musical presentations scheduled around town. She made a trip to New York where she paid a call on Robert Johnston, her agent. He was not encouraging. The season had already started, he said, and he knew of nothing in particular that would be suitable for Rose. She was irritated at this response since Johnston had done precious little for her so far, and he should have been seeking opportunities for her earlier in the summer or fall when musical schedules were being made up. Of course it didn't cost anything to keep him as her 'agent', but she realized that she shouldn't expect much help from him.

She also called on a contact at The Institute of Musical Art—otherwise known as The Damrosch School. Nothing was available there either. At that time Mr. (Frank) Damrosch was in the process of preparing for the November concert of The Musical Art Society, a choral group that sang à capella works of the 16th and 17th centuries.[89] Rose knew her voice was not suited to à capella singing—it was too strong and didn't blend in well with a choral group—so she had never participated in the Society's concerts. She was beginning to realize that she had misjudged how much the war and the influenza epidemic had disrupted the music world. If she needed any further proof, she certainly got it when she visited the Met. Their schedule had already been made up and there were no openings in chorus parts. She left her name anyway in the hope (which proved vain) that someone might get sick and drop out and thereby leave an opening for her.

So it was a dispirited soprano with an empty basket of hopes that returned to New London. There, however, she found a letter from Maynard, asking if she would consider meeting him in Boston the following week. He mentioned a popular play that had opened prior to it's run in New York, and went further to suggest that he could find accommodations for her at the Parker House. Although she couldn't accept his offer of accommodations, Rose immediately responded that she would be delighted to see him again, as she had planned to go to Boston anyway. There she told him she would stay with her voice teacher and his wife, William and Mary Whitney.

◆   ◆   ◆

In the weeks since Rose left Portland, Maynard's company had been swamped with business. The Portland branch was thriving with opportunities for underwriting new bond issues and sales of securities. Maynard's adventure in packaging small issues of utility stocks had paid off handsomely, and he was now able to place these consolidated offerings with a number of large banks in both Portland and Boston. He still had close ties to Bond & Goodwin, and could always count on selling some of the securities for which they were participating underwriters. Nelson McDougall now spent much of his time in the Portland office, leaving the operation in Rockland in the capable hands of Walter Ladd. Also, young Walter Hammons was becoming a real asset to the Portland office. And why shouldn't he be? He came from a good Maine family with connections all through the state. Maynard felt himself lucky to have the 'boy'.[90] The office bustled with several clerks and telephones rang constantly. Although the firm did relatively little business in stocks, (that would change later), a ticker tape machine occupied a place of prominence for the convenience of investors who wished to keep up with the stock markets in both Boston and New York.

Maynard alternated with McDougall in visiting the Rockland office. It gave him a chance to see his mother who had adjusted to living in the apartment on School Street. There she was near enough to everyone and everything in town and could keep up with all the goings-on, gossip and news that contributed to the vitality of small town life. For Maynard now saw Rockland as a 'small-town'. He was still on the board of the John Bird Company and attended the board meetings whenever possible. The company seemed to be going along well enough with young Sidney about to take over the president's reins from his father. Although he said nothing at board meetings, Maynard felt that the company needed new blood, new energy and new drive, which he feared would not be forthcoming from this Sidney.

As Maynard looked around the only family members he thought showed enough ability to eventually run the company were Elmer's youngest son, Adriel, and perhaps his cousin, Hanson's boy, William. Adriel was bright enough, but freshly back from military service he had yet to settle down, marry and establish himself in the town.[91] On the other hand William with his engineering degree from MIT had shown ability in other areas, and seemed smart enough to learn the grocery business quickly. Maynard knew, however, that it was unlikely William would find a place in the company since Elmer now had a controlling interest and would favor his own sons before anyone else. As far as Maynard was concerned, as long as the company could support his mother's needs—and there seemed no doubt that it could—he would stay well enough out of the family affairs. Henry seemed to be prospering in the canning business, while Alan, through his family and political connections, was now known as one of the smartest lawyers in Knox County.

Maynard never stayed long in Rockland anymore. (Actually he found it somewhat boring and ingrown.) His family connections still meant a lot to him, especially his mother; his business had been founded in Rockland and he thought of it as his home base. More and more, however, he felt himself destined for a larger stage. His affairs took him ever more frequently to Boston for several days at a time. Even New York was not out of the question although with his newly minted interest in Rose, he put that idea on hold.

When he realized that Milton's wedding to Helen Cushing was set for November 29th—the Saturday after Thanksgiving, it occurred to him that the days preceding the holiday might be his best opportunity to see Rose. Just the excuse he had been looking for to invite her to meet him in Boston. Her acceptance of his invitation delighted him. While they had been separated, he had given some thought to his relationship with Rose. He had, through rather devious means, discovered her age. In one respect the gap of nineteen years was discouraging. What could she ever see in him—a man old enough to be her father. On the other hand, Rose had never married, and maybe, just maybe, this was the point in her life when marriage would appeal to her. In any event, Rose had already indicated that she enjoyed his company, and Maynard had enough self-confidence to believe that Rose would find him attractive

Their meeting in Boston was a great success. They seemed to pick up where they had left off in Portland. It gave Rose a chance to seek out job opportunities during the day, while Maynard tied up some loose ends of his own. Besides the play that he had mentioned, they went to a vaudeville show and a movie; Rose had never been to either one and laughed enthusiastically at the vaudeville skits. Full-length movies (mostly of a romantic kind) were already popular, especially with stars like Mary Pickford and Douglas Fairbanks. (Rudolph Valentino had yet to initiate the swooning woman syndrome.) Maynard and Rose found this new media exciting and enjoyable. They dined at some of Boston's best restaurants, and went to a 'thé dansant' at the elegant Copley Plaza. Maynard loved to dance and found in Rose an enthusiastic partner. They found a lot to talk about: Rose introduced Maynard to William Whitney, and Maynard introduced Rose to his son, Milton and his fiancèe, Helen. If Rose noted an air of snobbery about Helen whose family prided themselves on their social position as part of Boston's upper crust, she gave no sign of disapproval.

Although Rose enjoyed the time spent with Maynard, the trip to Boston had not produced anything noteworthy in the way of concert engagements. She had visited several churches to see if they had any openings for sopranos, but found nothing encouraging. One Congregational church thought they might have an opening in the spring, and she should keep in touch. So it was with a heavy heart that she returned to New London. She could not continue to live at Ann's without paying for her upkeep. The result was that she decided to return to Portland for the Christmas holidays and maybe stay there because she had more contacts in the musical world there. In her thank-you note to Maynard, she told him that she had decided to return to Portland and hoped that she would see him there at Christmas time.

◆   ◆   ◆

Nothing could have suited Maynard better. Rose had hardly arrived back in Portland before she heard from him. From then on, whenever he was in town, he would call and suggest dinner, a film, a concert or some sort of entertainment. During the winter he was living in the rented house on Bowdoin Street, and although he had talked a lot about the Foreside place, he had not taken Rose to see it. This was due in part, aside from the weather, to the house being only partially furnished. Much of the furniture had come from Rockland and had been kept in storage until the renovations were finished. When the furniture was taken out of storage, it was arranged helter-skelter in the various rooms. Maynard didn't like the way it looked, and was considering a trip to Boston after the Christmas holidays where he planned to hire an interior decorator and purchase additional furnishings. He didn't want Rose to see the house in its present state, but only when he could be sure that she would marry him. He hadn't asked her yet and was still worried that she might turn him down. There might be someone else—someone who had been away or worse yet—unable to marry her. Maybe she would get a wonderful offer to sing in New York or Boston and her career would take off again. All of these thoughts went through his mind, and for the first time in his life he felt unsure of himself.

His spirits rose, however, when Rose invited him to have Christmas dinner with her family, an invitation that he accepted eagerly. On Christmas Eve, she was to sing a solo at the State Street Church and of course Maynard planned to be there too. Her solo was *O Holy Night* sung at the midnight service. It was the first service of its kind since the war when the threat of the flu had cancelled all services at Christmas time 1918. As her clear, exquisite voice sang the words, "O holy night, O Night Divine", it was enough to make Maynard, sitting in a front pew, thrill with delight. He had never realized that music could affect him that way. After the service, on their way home, bundled up with lap robes in the car, he tried to explain to Rose how her singing affected him, and found himself tongue-tied. After several attempts, he gave up and put his arm around her, kissing her gently on the cheek, and managed to say, "Thank you for your beautiful singing."

Rose had invited Maynard to Christmas dinner as an opportunity to introduce him to her parents in an informal setting that would make them all feel more at ease. He had already met her father, although rather briefly and she wanted both her parents to get to know him. She may not have realized that to her parents this signified her seriousness about her relationship with Maynard. She knew that she was thinking of him more and more and with considerable fondness. She couldn't help but question whether this was because she truly cared about him, or because she was at a stage in her life when her faltering career was less important than the need for the love and companionship of a mate. As she drifted off to sleep on Christmas Eve, she reflected on the kiss that Maynard had given her on the way home. Should she, perhaps, have kissed him back or in some way shown her acceptance of his gesture? She probably had but she was not sure.

On Christmas day, Maynard arrived at the Tyler house loaded down with gifts, the largest of which he had entrusted to Mike's capable hands. This big box contained a portable victrola[92], which he thought would be appropriate for the whole family. Knowing that Caruso was Rose's favorite tenor (as he was everyone's), he had decided to make her a special gift of five of Caruso's most famous recordings. The presents were duly deposited in front of the tree in the parlor, and Rose introduced Maynard to her mother, Jennie, and her brother Carroll, who had yet to meet his sister's new beau. Maynard urged Jennie to open the big box, and when she saw its contents, let out a delighted cry of "Oh, how wonderful! Thank you, Maynard."

Maynard smiled at Jennie's reaction. "I thought the whole family might enjoy it, but you need some records to play. Rose, why don't you open the other package that just might fill the bill."

As Rose carefully unwound the wrappings, she gasped when she saw the records and realized what they were. She looked at Maynard who was sitting beside her and with her sparkling smile said, "That's the most wonderful present you could have given me," With that, she leaned over and kissed him on the cheek.

Carroll, who was taken by surprise by this show of affection, let out a whistle. "Wow, you don't even need mistletoe, do you Sis?"

Everyone laughed at this remark and the ice—if there had been any except for that outdoors—was broken.

It was a happy gathering as the five of them sat down to a bountiful meal. Although no spirits were served for Joe was a teetotaler, the day's importance was celebrated with toasts in sparkling cider. Jennie noted the happiness on her daughter's face and realized that Rose had finally found a man she could love. Indeed, happiness filled their home and it was a Christmas they would all remember.

Christmas night Rose lay awake a long while pondering the events of the day. She thought about the gifts of the victrola and the cherished Caruso records. How thoughtful of Maynard to pick something that meant a lot to her. This was a man who seemed to read her thoughts and tried to fulfill her wishes. As she tossed restlessly in her bed, turning over in her mind her feelings for him, her career didn't seem as important as it once did. She felt like the doll in the ballet *Coppelia* that had a key in her back. Maynard would wind her up and she would come alive. When he was gone, she felt lifeless, waiting for him to come back to wind her up again. She had never felt like this about any other man. All of a sudden she sat bolt upright in bed—of course, she must be in love with him! And he must love her too, from all the signs and signals he had given. If he wanted to marry her, then why hadn't he asked? And Rose realized she wanted to be asked more than anything else.

On New Year's Eve, Maynard and Rose were invited to the home of the Browns's on the Western Promenade for dancing and a late supper to celebrate the coming year. Rose dressed carefully in a new dress she had bought with her Christmas money. The bodice, with its low square-cut neckline and wide band shoulder straps of black crepe de chine, displayed her graceful neck and arms to advantage. The crepe de chine skirt fell to about four inches above her ankles and was covered with an overskirt of black net. A large black net bow in the back was held in place vertically by a wide belt around her waist of gold silk embroidered with a floral design in greens and purples. She knew the black pumps with the two-inch heels she was wearing would make her taller than Maynard, but she had no other shoes to go with the dress. He didn't seem to mind the difference in their heights so why should she? As she was dressing, her mother came in to help her with her hair.

As Jennie combed and arranged Rose's thick, lustrous, black hair with it's faint streaks of gray around the temples, she looked at the reflection of her daughter in the dressing table mirror. "You look particularly lovely tonight, Rose. A penny for your thought's."

"I think they're worth much more that a penny, Ma. I was thinking about Maynard. Do you suppose he might want to marry me?" was Rose's response.

"I know you've been thinking about him a lot, dear," her mother replied. "Have you decided to give up a career for marriage, then?"

"Perhaps. All of a sudden Maynard seems more important than continuing with a career. Not that I'm going to stop singing. Singing is my life. It's almost a necessity—a spiritual necessity. I could never give it up completely. I would still like to do some concerts and church singing occasionally. But a career is just not that important anymore. And you know, Ma, I don't think Maynard would mind if I accepted a few engagements. He's genuinely interested and encouraging about my singing. Of course it wouldn't be for the money. I could do some programs for charity. If there is one thing that bothers me it is that people might think I married him for his money; he's awfully rich!"

Jennie nodded her head in a gesture of understanding. "I don't think anyone will accuse you of being a gold-digger, but don't you think you had better wait until he's asked your father for your hand?"

"Oh, Ma, that's so old-fashioned. No one does that anymore."

"Just the same, I think Maynard is sort of old-fashioned, and I'll wager he goes to your father before he speaks to you," Jennie answered.

They made a handsome couple when they arrived at the Brown's. Maynard was dressed in the new style of less formal dinner jacket worn with a black bow tie, a wing collar and starched shirtfront. Rose, with a corsage of white roses Maynard had given her, caused every head to turn when she entered the ballroom. It was not just her beauty and grace, nor the elegance of her outfit, nor even her training as a performer, although that certainly helped, but a certain indefinable presence that commanded everyone's attention. Another woman might have elicited a certain amount of envy or jealousy from others of her sex, but Rose's charm and friendliness was enough to dispel any such emotions. Maynard seemed to enjoy the notice Rose evoked as they greeted their host and hostess and then mingled with the other guests until the dancing began.

At the stroke of twelve, the lights went out and each couple wished each other a Happy New Year in whatever form suited them. Maynard having foreseen the occasion had maneuvered Rose into a private corner of the room. When the lights went out he put his arms around her and kissed her passionately, and Rose returned his kiss with the same passion. As he looked into her eyes still holding her close, he said, "Rose, I love you."

"And I love you too, Maynard," was Rose's reply.

◆   ◆   ◆

After the New Year, Maynard's business took him on an extended trip to a number of cities where he—or Bond and Goodwin—had business. While he was gone, he made a point of writing to Rose several times a week. She had responded with notes and cards to him whenever he stopped long enough in one place to receive mail. On his return to Portland in the early part of February, it was to find that Rose had gone to New London to visit her sister. Although anxious to see her again, he took advantage of her absence to visit the Tylers with the idea of having a talk with Joe.

The Tyler family, once they realized that Maynard was serious about Rose, and that Rose reciprocated the feeling, had opened up their home to him. They liked him and enjoyed his company, and they frequently asked him to Sunday dinner after church. (This ended the Lafayette Hotel Sunday meals that were becoming less and less appealing to him.) After dinner at the Tyler's, he and Joe would sit in the parlor while Rose, if she was there, and her mother washed up the dishes and straightened up the dining room. Maynard found that he enjoyed listening to the old man's stories of the Civil War, especially his recounting of the fight at Little Round Top on the second day at Gettysburg. The story became more and more gory each time it was told. Maynard assumed that Joe was exaggerating the way most of the veterans did, but that in no way lessened his interest in the story.[93]

But on this particular Sunday afternoon in February with Rose away, Maynard had other things he wanted to talk about so he commenced the conversation as soon as they left the table. "Joe, Rose tells me that you are quite a bit older than Jennie."

"Ayah, that's so. First wife died," was the laconic answer. "Met Jennie after that. She's a bit younger."

"I don't mean to pry," Maynard said, "but how <u>much</u> difference is there in your ages?"

"Well, let's see. I was born in '45, and I think Jennie came in about '63 or thereabouts. Never seems to have made any difference though. Did you know, she's a <u>real daughter</u> of the War of 1812?"

Maynard wasn't about to let himself get hooked into more war talk from the old soldier. There was nothing for it but to come right out and tell Joe what was on his mind. "Joe," he said, "you've probably guessed that I'm pretty fond of Rose, and would like to marry her."

"I kind of 'spected as much," was the reply. "Why don't you go ahead and ask her?"

"I thought maybe you could give me some advice," Maynard responded. "There's nineteen years difference in our ages, and I'm worried that that might make a difference—that I'm too old for her."

"Don't see why it should. Didn't make no difference with Jennie and me. We've gotten along just fine, and I think she'd tell you the same." Joe seemed to think this settled everything as far as he was concerned. Maynard decided that was all the answer he was going to get—and on thinking about it, it was enough.

When, a little later, Jennie joined them, Joe put aside his Sunday paper and said to his wife, "Jen, this here young man wants to marry our Rose. What do you think o'that?"

"I think it's just fine," was the response. Turning to Maynard, "I was wondering when you'd get around to it!" She said this with a smile on her face and a twinkle in her eye.

Maynard broke into laughter. "If I didn't know better, I'd think you two had known all along that I wanted to marry Rose."

"Of course we did," they said almost in unison. Then Jennie continued, "I wonder Rose waited for you so long to pop the question. She loves you Maynard, I'm sure of that; so you'd better not waste anymore time in asking her."

Maynard needed no further encouragement. No sooner had Rose returned from New London than he invited her to have dinner with him at a small, elegant restaurant in the West End (now long gone). He had dispensed with Mike's services for the evening so that he was driving himself when he picked her up. We can only imagine what transpired on this evening. Perhaps it was dinner at a small candle-lit table for two with soft romantic music in the background. Although the details were never divulged, when they returned somewhat later that evening, Rose went straight to her parents' room without bothering to find out if they were awake. (Fortunately, they were.) There, still glowing from the excitement of the evening and it's romantic outcome, she stood in the doorway wreathed in smiles, and announced in a manner that left no doubt of her joy, "Maynard has asked me to marry him and I have accepted!" And with that, she left the room, humming the famous aria from Rigoletto, *Caro nome.*

16

Rockland. March 22nd, 1920
My dear Miss Tyler:

It is with great satisfaction that I learned when I was in Portland, that you and Maynard desided (sic) to try the matrimonial life together, and I wish you both much happiness. I shall be very pleased to have another daughter and I think he will be a happier man. I think he is very lonely as he is, and what I learned of you—think you will be a very companionable wife.

I trust you and I will be the best of friends and enjoy each other's company.

With much love to you
Sincerely yours,
Annie E. Bird

Rose and Maynard decided to wait to announce their engagement. Rose was committed to concert dates in New London and had agreed to sing there at St. James Episcopal Church during the month of March. Maynard, too, had business obligations that necessitated a considerable amount of travel to both Boston and New York. They agreed that Maynard would visit in New London to meet the Cobb family before a general announcement was made. In the meantime, Maynard had told his mother of his anticipated marriage making her the first relative in Rockland to hear the news.

One matter, however, needed to be cleared up, before Rose left for New London and that was the date of the wedding. She and Maynard had discussed a possible date in June, but for the other details of place and time the Tyler family needed to be consulted. Maynard was becoming a frequent guest at 169 Longfellow Street for Sunday dinners; so in late February after one of Jennie's bounteous Sunday dinners, the family gathered in the living room to discuss wedding plans.

Rose initiated the conversation by saying to her parents, "You know that Maynard and I have been considering a June wedding, but we wanted your opinion on what kind of a wedding we should have."

Joe fiddled with his newspaper obviously leaving the question up to Jennie, who said rather diffidently, "Well, it's your wedding, Rose—that is it's yours and Maynard's—so what were you thinking of?"

Maynard could see that neither Joe nor Jennie wanted to offer any initial proposals. He guessed they might be embarrassed to suggest any limitation on the amount they could spend for the affair, but at the same time probably wanted something nice for Rose. Tactfully, he entered the conversation.

"I think, since this is my second marriage, even though I know it will be the first one for Rose, that I would feel more comfortable with a small family type wedding, rather than a more elaborate one." He stopped, waiting to see what kind of reaction he got from the Tylers.

Trying to encourage her parents' comments on the subject, Rose quickly seconded Maynard's statement. "I don't want a big wedding, Ma. After all, it isn't as if I was just twenty and getting married to a childhood sweetheart. I'm thirty-one and too old for that kind of ceremony. Besides, if we did have a big wedding, Maynard and I know so many people between us that we'd have to hire the Pythian Hall to take care of them all."

Joe looked up from his paper, cleared his throat and said, "Rose, dear, we want only the best for you and if <u>you</u> want a small wedding, I'm all for it. We gave Ann and Skip a nice wedding and we want to do the same for you."

Rose, touched by the loving tone of her father's voice as well as by his words, got up from her chair, and going over to her father's seat, gave him a kiss on the cheek. "I know you do, Pa, and I'm really grateful you care so much." She didn't go back to her own seat beside Maynard, but settled down on the floor by Joe's feet with her hand laid gracefully on his knee.

"We could have a small wedding here," volunteered Jennie. She was already calculating how she could get all the people in from both families who might be invited. "How many people are you two planning to invite, Rose?"

"Well, Ann and Skip and Evelyn, of course; and Carroll, too. We should invite Uncle Sime and Aunt Nellie, I guess. That's about six, plus you and Pa and me. Don't forget me, you can't have a wedding without me.

Maynard, how many in your family would you invite?"

For sometime Maynard had been pondering how he could suggest that the wedding be held at the Foreside house, and now he saw an opportunity. Even if he invited his three brothers and their wives, his mother, and Milton and Helen, that would make another nine people which would be too many to fit comfortably in the Tyler home.

"I had hoped to invite my son, Milton and his wife, and of course my mother, Annie Bird. However, if she comes, I would have to invite at least one brother to bring her, and that would cause problems. The other two brothers and their wives might feel offended if they weren't invited too."

He stopped and looked around at their faces. He could see that Jennie had already realized that her home would never accommodate so many people. It was a comfortable house, but she and Joe had never been ones for giving parties. The house just wasn't designed for it.

"I suppose we could have the wedding in a church and use the church hall for the reception," Jennie said rather tentatively.

Rose pitched in at this point, "Ma, you know it would have to be at the State Street Church. If I'm going to be married in a church, I couldn't be married anywhere else. And if we did that, then we're back where we started because we'd have to invite all those who associate us with that church, both my friends and Maynard's."

There was silence for a while. Maynard was about to suggest his house when much to his surprise, Rose addressed both her parents, "Maynard and I have discussed this to some extent." (They really hadn't, but it was an indication of how well Rose understood Maynard's thinking.) "What would you say to our having a small wedding at Maynard's home? There's enough room there for all the relatives we want to invite. We wouldn't be crowded and no one would be left out."

Maynard, who had already had visions of Rose dressed as a bride coming down the hall staircase, quickly followed up on her suggestion. "Would you mind terribly if we did that?" he said, addressing both Joe and Jennie. "It would solve all the problems of where to have the wedding and who we could invite. It would still be a small family affair."

Joe looked at Rose and smiled. "Rose, darling, is that alright with you?" Rose nodded. He then continued, "We appreciate your offer Maynard. It's very generous of you. I've got to admit it seems to be the only sensible thing to do." What Joe didn't say, but what Maynard understood perfectly, was that he and Jennie really weren't in a position to pay for a large wedding.

"Thank you Joe, and thank you Mrs. Tyler[94], for letting me do this. I only want, as you do, what's best for Rose."

So that's the way it was decided. The date was tentatively set for the first week in June, although the exact date, time and other arrangements were to wait until later.

◆   ◆   ◆

In March, shortly after they became engaged Maynard asked Rose to meet him in Boston to pick out an engagement ring. There he took her to Shreve, Crump & Lowe, Boston's most prestigious jeweler, where he had called in advance to make sure she would be shown rings in what he considered appropriate size and price range. Rose had protested that he should be the one to pick out the ring, but he felt that she would be happier with something she had chosen herself. The salesman, a dapper little man, with an air of smug superiority, escorted them into a private room where he made a big show of bringing out several trays of beautiful rings for them to look at. The rings had diamonds ranging between two and four carats many of them set with additional precious gems. Rose was a little overwhelmed at the size of the stones and their pretentiousness. Initially she picked out what appeared to be the smallest in the tray—a ring with twin rose-cut diamonds of one carat each surrounded by a wreath of smaller stones. It was obvious to Maynard that she wasn't pleased with that one so he kept urging her to pick out the one she truly liked. She tried on several more rings from the selection: an emerald-cut framed with smaller sapphires; a marquise-cut four carat stone surrounded with smaller quarter carat diamonds, which, when she put it on her finger, came almost down to her knuckle. "With this ring," she laughed, "you couldn't marry me. There wouldn't be room for a wedding ring on my finger." She sighed, "there are so many to choose from!"

Eventually she noticed a ring in another tray that had been pushed to one side. The stone of about three and a half carats appeared to Rose just like an opened flower—maybe a rose—with leaves in the form of small chip diamonds on either side of the bloom. The simpler platinum setting only enhanced the beauty of the stone. "May I see that one," she said to the salesman.

"Of course, Madam," and the tray was duly placed in front of her.

She put the ring on her finger and extended her arm so that she could see how it looked at different angles. Its simplicity appealed to her.

Maynard watching said, "Is that the one you like best, Rose?" He was a little surprised that she had not picked one of the larger, more elaborate stones. He remembered how Mary had always gone for the biggest and flashiest jewelry, but he was beginning to realize that for Rose, understatement led to elegance. He looked at the salesman about to tell him this would be their purchase when he noticed a frown on the man's face. "Is there something wrong with the ring?" Maynard asked.

All-in-One Tree of Rose M. Tyler

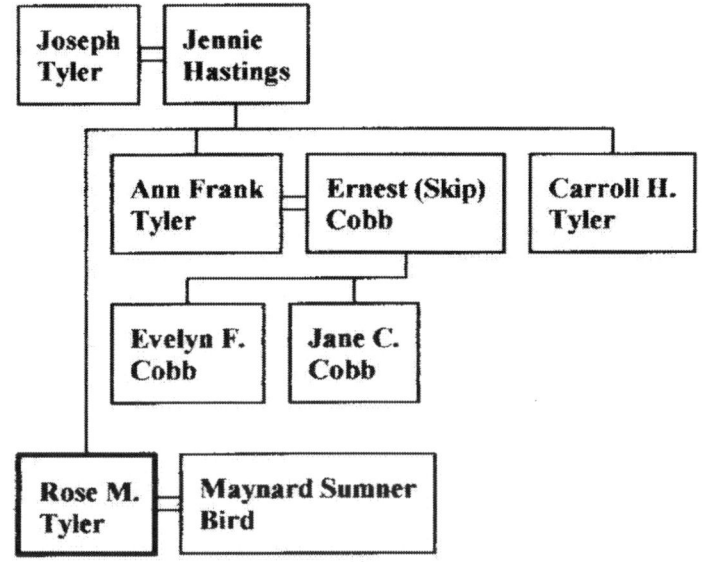

Tyler Family Tree

Rose M. Tyler

Rose M. Tyler Bird

Cumberland Foreside House

Jennie Tyler and Baby Rose

The salesman, who had either been too polite, or too eager to make a sale of a more expensive ring, answered in an embarrassed manner.

"Well, sir," the salesman stammered, "The diamond Madam has selected has a slight flaw in it, and is not the same quality in color as the others Madam looked at."

"What do you mean by a flaw?" Maynard inquired rather gruffly.

Taking the ring from Rose, the salesman proceeded to show Maynard with a jeweler's glass, that the ring had a tiny speck in it that reduced its value. He also mentioned that, although the number of facets in its cut gave it a marvelous sparkle, it was classified as a 'yellow' diamond rather than a 'blue' that was considered more desirable.

Rose had said nothing up to this point while the salesman and Maynard looked over the ring, but now she spoke up.

"I really like this ring the best even if it does have a speck in it. If it takes a magnifying glass to see it, no one will know about it if I don't tell them."

"And," she went on, "you told me, Maynard, to pick the one I wanted and this is the one I want." All this was said in a pleasant but firm tone, as she smiled alternately at both Maynard and the salesman. And that put an end to the matter!

◆　　　◆　　　◆

So far, the only acknowledgement of their engagement from members of the Bird family was the letter from her future mother-in-law and some congratulatory cards from Maynard's Rockland sisters-in-law. The winter weather had ruled out a trip to Rockland before she returned to New London. Although Rose had met Milton and his fiancée, Helen Cushing, briefly in Boston just before the couple's wedding, it had been a casual encounter without any hint of a future relationship. In early April when both Maynard and Rose were in Boston, Maynard took the first step of introducing Rose to his side of the family by arranging a luncheon for her to meet his son and daughter-in-law. Maynard had already talked to Milton about his forthcoming marriage, and had satisfied himself that his son had no objection. Milton had long since accepted the fact that affection between his mother and father had dwindled to the point, where, at her death, their relationship was one of habit and convenience. He also recognized that Mary's love for him had been a predominating influence in his life, and that it was his father's opinion that she had turned him into a 'mama's boy'. After his mother's death, he had been released from his father's domination by his marriage. Now, he was actually relieved that his father was remarrying since it lessened his feeling of obligation to continue at Bond and Goodwin. In fact, he and Helen had already been making arrangements to buy land in North Carolina, where they planned to move and raise peaches.[95]

Rose, on the other hand, was uneasy about how Milton would feel about her marriage to his father. She was now the one who saw the disparity in their ages as a hurdle that might not be so easily cleared. After all, Milton was only five years her junior. Some might say she was marrying the wrong man. She also wondered if the matter of Maynard's money would inject itself into the father's relationship with his son. The fact that Milton's wife's family was wealthy made Rose fear that they might see Maynard's money as her pretext for the marriage. The Cushing family, Rose knew, were part of the Boston social elite. Would they look down on her background and her profession as not worthy of their son-in-law's family? All these thoughts went through her mind as she accompanied Maynard into the Parker House dining room.

They need not have worried—the luncheon went off without a hitch, in part due to Milton's friendliness and charm. Helen was more reserved, and although not unfriendly, she was cold and lacked the outgoing personality so obvious in her husband. Rose found it a little difficult to keep up her end of the conversation with Helen while Maynard talked business matters with his son. Sticking to a safe subject, Rose explained that they were planning a small family wedding at the Foreside house.

"Yes," Maynard interjected overhearing Rose's remark. Then he looked at Milton in a rather self-conscious manner and without any preamble said "I'd like you to be my best man, Milton."

"Of course, Father, I would be proud to stand up with you."

Maynard smiled and there was a look of relief in his eyes. It was a rare moment—there had not been many—when he felt really close to his son. "Good, well that's settled," he said.

After lunch, the weather being quite spring like for April, Rose and Maynard strolled down Commonwealth Avenue toward the park. Maynard remarked, "I thought that went off very well, didn't you, Rose?"

Rose nodded. "Were you concerned that it wouldn't, Maynard?"

"Sometimes I never know how Milton will react. He was close to his mother, but doesn't seem to have any reservations about our marriage. In fact in some ways, he and I are closer now than when his mother was alive."

Rose smiled, and said rather apologetically, "I thought I was the one who was worried about being accepted, and here you were just as worried as I was. Milton is a lot like you, Maynard. Did you know that?"

Maynard shook his head. "No I don't see it, but you see him from a different point of view." Changing the subject, he continued, "How did you like Helen?"

Rose tried to couch her remarks tactfully. "She's very reserved and I'm afraid we don't have a lot in common. But if she's Milton's wife then I will make a point of liking her. Milton makes up in charm and conviviality what she lacks in sociability, but maybe she has other qualities that we don't immediately recognize and that appeal to him."

Maynard nodded his head, but said nothing.

Rose enlarged her comments by saying, "Milton certainly is an attractive man—very charming. That's what I meant when I said he is a lot like you. But because he has so much charm, I think Helen is worried that he may be attracted to another woman, and she would be intensely jealous if he were. By the way, how do you feel about her?"

In a tone so lacking in warmth and a manner so blunt that it shocked Rose, Maynard said, "I think she's a cold fish! Don't know what he saw in her—money I guess. He'll never earn much on his own, so he may need hers. Well, it could have been worse. He could have married someone without money and then he'd would have had to work for a living."

This was a side of Maynard that Rose had not seen before. She thought it best to drop the subject and not get involved in a father-son standoff if that was what it was going to be. Just the same, she made up her mind to be as nice to Helen as she could be and to encourage Milton's good relations with his father; she was sure there was affection there that needed nurturing.

For the rest of their walk their conversation was devoted to plans for their wedding and no more was said about their luncheon companions.

◆   ◆   ◆

Maynard had not yet met the Cobb family until Rose invited him to come to New London after one of his Boston business trips. He found the little family warm and welcoming. It was obvious that anyone Rose loved (and who loved her) would get a cordial reception in their home. Ann was like her mother both in appearance and disposition—rather quiet, but positive in her opinions. She was like her father in that she doted on Rose, but Maynard was beginning to realize that the whole family seemed to see Rose as someone special.

Skip was a perfect match for his wife—relaxed and affable; inclined to tease her a bit over some of her minor foibles. He had a salesman's disposition—gregarious and talkative. It was not long before he was regaling Maynard with stories of his experiences in the automobile business. He seemed to have made many friends in New London during the twelve years they had lived there. Also, Maynard could see why Rose was so fond of the Cobb's daughter, Evelyn. A smaller version of her father, she was alert, interested in everything and devoted to her 'Auntie Rose'. This was not surprising since whenever Rose came to stay, she brought Evelyn some little gift. The child loved the presents but seemed not to have been spoiled by the attention.

Rose was delighted to see how well Maynard got along with Ann and Skip—not that she had doubted it—but she wanted the approval of her choice of a husband. If she had been somewhat apprehensive that the Cobb's simpler life style would, in Maynard's view, reflect badly on them, she had still a lot to learn about her fiancé. It was part of Maynard's make-up that he hadn't forgotten his roots in Rockland, and his memories of country folk, some of them his own relatives, stayed with him all his life. He was never patronizing and, although he would later adopt some of the social habits of the circles in which he moved, he retained a certain down-to-earth manner that attracted people from all walks of life to him.

Of course they told Ann and Skip all about their wedding plans: they explained about the intimacy of the wedding. "We are not quite sure whether we'll have attendants or not," Rose said. "But if we do, you'll be my matron of honor, won't you Ann?"

"I'll be there whether or not I'm in it," was Ann's response. Secretly she hoped she could be Rose's attendant, but she wasn't going to let that diminish her excitement and anticipation of the event.

Nothing marred Maynard's visit. Saturday evening he took the whole family out to dinner at the best New London restaurant he could find. It had been a jolly evening with Maynard and Skip trying to outdo each other with tall stories about their 'downeast' experiences.

. Later that evening when they were alone together, Ann said to her husband, "I'm so happy for Rose, Skip. I think she's found a wonderful man—at last."

Skip nodded, "I agree, she should be as happy as we are, and we don't have the kind of money that Maynard does."

Ann looked up sharply. "I don't care how much money he has as long as he loves her and is good to her. And as for us, we have everything we need and love besides. Are you jealous, Skip?"

Skip laughed, and reached over and tickled Ann.

She squealed and slapped his hand playfully. "Now you just stop that, Skip Cobb!"

But he didn't, and their playfulness ended up with a kiss instead of a tickle.

When Maynard left on Sunday for Boston and Portland he felt that the visit had solidified his relations with the Tyler family to a greater extent than he had anticipated.

◆   ◆   ◆

In April, Maynard moved back to the Foreside house where by this time all renovations had been completed. It was only then when Rose returned to Portland that he had taken her to see his country home. The size and the extent of the property had astonished her. She had spent most of her life within city confines where large houses were placed on property limited by the restrictions of city living. Never having traveled abroad she was unprepared for Maynard's version of a small English country estate. As she looked at the house standing amid a grove of pine trees, she said, "Why Maynard," it's just like living in a 'pine bower'. And that was what the name—Pine Bower—they decided to call it.[96]

They first walked around the grounds so that Maynard could call attention to the beautiful view and point out where the flower garden was going to be. Then he escorted her through the main floor—even the kitchen and pantries much to Whiteway's disapproval but not to Ruth's. Their tour took them upstairs where Maynard showed her the master suite with its large bathroom connecting to what he called his dressing room.

"I thought you should have the larger room with the fireplace for your things, and there is a separate closet for your clothes beside the fireplace."

"Oh Maynard," Rose said rather breathlessly, "what a beautiful home you have! You have thought of everything."

"Dearest one, it will be your home, too. Everything must suit you." He already had a vision of Rose as mistress of his estate. "Now, I've brought a lot of the furnishings from Rockland, but those twin mahogany four-poster beds are new. I thought they were just the thing for our bedroom."

"They are really handsome, Maynard. I want Pa to see them. You know how he is about furniture."

"The decorator I hired from Boston," Maynard continued as they walked along the hall to the other bedrooms, "has just about finished her work here, but if you want anything else, or you're not satisfied with anything, I can get her back easily enough. You may want some of your own things—your piano, of course."

Rose had a small spinet in the Portland house, and a larger upright at Ann's. "The piano must go in the living room, Maynard. Perhaps over at the end opposite the sun porch. There will be good light between those two windows. I will want a cabinet for my music, too." She thought for a minute, then said, "otherwise, I have no particular choice in furnishings. Oh, of course I'll bring things like pictures and some of the little things I've collected over the years."

Rose had never been the kind of person who was interested in household furnishings, although she loved the furniture her father had made for their home. Understandably she was much more absorbed in her music, her voice training and protection, and how she presented herself. She had developed a stylish appearance by selecting clothes designed to enhance her height and figure; and she tried to pick bright colors that would highlight her eyes—so dark that they looked almost black. All of which relegated her taste in interior design to a rather low priority.

As they once again arrived on the ground floor, Rose put her hand on Maynard's arm and said in a voice filled with emotion: "The important thing is that <u>our</u> home should be a welcoming place. I hope, and I know you do too, that we will have children to occupy the bedrooms and to fill the house with joy."

Maynard smiled. There was nothing he wanted more.

Finally, they were seated in the living room where Whiteway served them tea.

After the butler left, Rose turned to Maynard and with a twinkle in her eye, said, "When I first met you, you impressed me with a chauffeur driven car. Now I find you have a butler as well. What other surprises are you going to spring on me, Maynard?"

"I just thought a place like this deserved a butler and maid," he said in an almost apologetic tone. He wondered if Rose thought him too pretentious. "Does having a butler bother you?"

"I don't think it will, although I wonder if I may bother him. After all, I'm used to my mother doing the cooking and letting me help with the dishes and cleanup after a meal. What would Whiteway think if I were to take this teacup into the kitchen, let alone wash it?"

"Don't worry about that, my dear. Just be yourself. But you should try to observe his traditions. You must remember, he and Nancy are new to America, and are adjusting too."

The staff of 'Pine Bower', as it was now called, had already adjusted to the move from Bowdoin Street to the Foreside. It generally suited both Whiteway and Nancy who found the country place represented a style of living that they had known in England. Mike had no objection to living in the country as long as he could get to the nearest Portland Catholic Church on Sundays. Maynard, who placed a high value on Mike's services, was happy to oblige by letting him take a car for transportation. (Maynard now owned two cars.)

As for Ruth, she was that much closer to her roots in Freeport and consequently felt more at home in the country than she had in the city. Maynard and Ruth subscribed to the same 'downeast' culinary menu. She could be relied on to serve the standard Maine fare of baked beans on Saturday night and creamed finnan haddie for Sunday morning breakfast. She wouldn't mind if after their marriage, Rose wanted to upgrade the menus a bit to include a greater variety of green vegetables and fresh produce from the vegetable garden that Ruth with Maynard's approval planned to plant. No one, however, dared interfere with her desserts for she was a superb pastry cook. She had a reputation among some of Portland's prominent dowagers for her confections and Maynard had already countered offers of higher pay to lure her away.

All in all, from Maynard's point of view, things seem to be working out well, and he felt sure that both servants and mistress would readily adjust to each other.

In Boston, Maynard made one purchase that did not involve the decorator: a Concert Grand Steinway piano that was to be his wedding gift to Rose. When it had been shipped and assembled in the living room of the Foreside house, a piano tuner was engaged to make sure that it was perfectly tuned. One day in May, when Rose had finally returned to Portland for good, Maynard took her out to 'Pine Bower' ostensibly to show her the progress made in planting gardens and shrubbery. But the point of the visit as far as he was concerned was to surprise her with the piano. He planned it so they first walked around outdoors, inspected the second floor, then the kitchen, the butler's pantry, the dining room and finally the living room.

As they came to the doorway, Maynard said, "Close your eyes, Rose. I have a surprise for you. Don't open them until I tell you to."

With that he took her hand and carefully steered her so that she was directly in front of the piano. "Now you can open them,"

When Rose saw the piano, she let out a gasp. "Oh, Maynard, Maynard," was all she could say. She turned and threw her arms around him and there were tears in her eyes. "You're too good to me! I've only dreamt that I might someday have a Steinway. How can I ever thank you."

For Maynard, just seeing her pleasure was thanks enough. "Your love is so precious to me, Rose," he murmured as he held her in his arms. "I want you to have everything your heart desires."

She immediately sat down at the piano giving Maynard a private concert of some of her—and his—favorite pieces. As she sang the high notes of *From the Land of the Sky Blue Water,* her voice could be heard throughout the house so that each servant stopped what he or she was doing to listen.

Whiteway and Nancy were in the butler's pantry polishing silver. As they heard the singing, Nancy smiled and remarked to her husband, "This is surely going to be a happy home with all the music and that beautiful voice."

17

Portland, Maine—Wednesday, June 2, 1920

PORTLAND BANKER AND SINGER MARRY
Miss Rose Tyler Bride of Maynard S. Bird

A very quiet wedding took place this morning when Maynard S. Bird and Miss Rose Tyler, both of this city were united in marriage, the Rev. Birney S. Hudson officiating. The wedding took place at Mr. Bird's beautiful home at Cumberland Foreside and the ceremony was followed by a wedding breakfast to which only a few very close friends were bidden. Mr. Bird and his bride left immediately after the breakfast for a motor trip to Quebec and other points of interest in that locality. The wedding is an important one as both the bride and the bridegroom are well known throughout the State. Mr. Bird through his business interests and the bride through her musical ability as she is perhaps one of the finest soprano soloists Portland has ever produced, and both are receiving the best wishes of a large circle of friends.[97]

The decision to have a small, quiet wedding came as a surprise to the numerous friends of the couple. Most surprised were Jennie and Joe Tyler when Rose told them in late May that she and Maynard had decided on June 2nd for a date. They had been expecting that the couple would be married the latter part of June, and had wondered why the date had not already been set.

Jennie was the first to ask the obvious question. "Isn't this rather a sudden decision? What's the rush?"

"It isn't a rush, really, Ma. We've been talking about it for a long time now, and it just seemed that the sooner we did it the better it would be," was Rose's rather defensive answer. "Besides, it fitted in better with Maynard's schedule. You wouldn't believe how busy he's been."

They were in the kitchen where Joe was repairing a table leg that had come out of its socket. He got up from the floor where he had been kneeling, dusted off his knees and straightened up. As he did so he looked directly at Rose. "Are you being up-front with us, Rose?" he asked.

Rose flushed at the implied meaning of his question. "Have I ever hidden anything from you?" she said defiantly. "You know me better than that, Pa."

Joe said nothing more and sat down heavily in one of the kitchen chairs. He would never quite understand this daughter of his. She had been independent all her life, made her own living, and had so much talent that he hated to see her give up her career. With a sigh he acknowledged that he no longer had any 'say-so' in the matter. He just hoped that Maynard knew that his wife would be a woman who, despite her sometimes submissive appearance, was one who would make her own decisions.

Jennie tried to smooth things over. "If that's what you and Maynard have decided—well, it's your wedding, after all. But what about Ann and Skip? I know Ann wanted to be in your wedding."

"I know, Ma, and I'm going to write to her and try to explain it. We want to invite them—all three of them—to visit us this summer. Also, we're going to have a reception for all our friends in July and we hope Ann and Skip will be here for that. I think they'll understand that it is more important to me to adjust to Maynard's schedule than to have a wedding that all our relatives can attend."

Rose went on to explain that they would combine their honeymoon with a motor trip to Canada where Maynard had some business matters to attend to. They planned to go to Rockland when they got back where she would be introduced to all his relatives—especially his mother whom she was anxious to meet.

◆   ◆   ◆

Dawn comes early in Maine as the days lengthen with the approach of Midsummer's Day. By five in the morning the pre-dawn grayness dissipates and the first rays of the eastern sun rising above the islands of Casco Bay touched the windows of Pine Bower that faced the bay. There was still a mist on the water that extended to cover the hillside in front of the house. The sky, as yet cloudless, held its watery blue color waiting for the sun with its warmth to deepen it to a darker shade. The weather had turned milder after several stormy days earlier in the week as if to announce its approval of the approaching nuptial event. The air was fresh with the mixed scents of new grass, pine needles, a few remaining lilacs and the ever-present sea smells. The maples still dressed in their light spring green rustled gently in a southwest wind dropping the last few seedpods from their branches. The joyous chirping of robins, finches and blue birds, mixed with the softer notes of mourning doves and the shrill cries of gulls, welcomed the beginning of a new day.

Ruth Brewster, whose farm youth had taught her the virtues of early rising, was already in the spacious kitchen. Following her customary practice, a pot of coffee was already on the stove, while a teakettle was close to boiling. "Those English people aren't any good until they get their morning tea," she remarked to herself, "Too bad they couldn't drink coffee like everyone else. At least, Nancy makes it for Whiteway saving me the trouble."

As she looked over the menu that she had proposed and Mr. Bird had approved, she was proud of her part in making it special. Methodically she checked off each item commenting where she felt comments were due.

Compote of fresh strawberries and cream—"Sent special from Pennsylvania, Mr. Bird said. Too bad it's too early for them lovely, sweet ones from round here. At least the cream came from Porter's farm in Freeport."

Individual omelets with hot creamed mushroom sauce—"put them mushrooms up myself last fall."

Blueberry muffins—"Picked those blueberries last summer, and put them up too."

Wedding cake—"One of my best if I do say so myself!"

Coffee and tea—No comment here.

"Mr Bird said he would take care of the beverage for the toast, and I'm pretty sure it will be champagne." Even with prohibition there were always ways of getting liquor, and Ruth was sure that the bottles placed in the Frigidaire the night before were not devoid of alcoholic content[98]. Anyway, that was Whiteway's job.

Whiteway and Nancy were already hard at work getting ready for the big event. Nancy was busy arranging flowers—a few cut from their own garden, some kept in the 'flower room' that adjoined the sun porch across the back of the house, and others delivered by a Portland florist the previous day. Arrangements were placed on either side of the fireplace and one on the mantelpiece in the living room where the ceremony would take place. A low centerpiece of white and pink roses, white stock and ferns adorned the dining room table, and additional smaller arrangements were placed in nearly every room. When she finished with the downstairs flowers, she took a bouquet of white violets up to the guestroom reserved for the bride. Here she checked the bathroom to make sure there were plenty of towels and anything else the bride would need.

In the meantime, Whiteway was putting the finishing touches on the table setting including a champagne glass next to the water goblet at each place. He had set the table the night before, so now it was only a matter of checking to see that no speck of dust had soiled the crystal or an inadvertent bump of the table had disturbed the precise positions of the silverware. Despite the early hour, he had placed two single candles in their silver candlesticks at either end of the floral centerpiece. He had not decided whether they should be lit or just be there to provide a fitting touch to the decor. As he consulted the seating chart to make sure the place cards were properly placed, he thought of the country house in England where he had been trained. There, before the war, he had worked his way up to a position as assistant to the head butler. But the war had come and an end to the kind of service he had been taught. Things were surely different in America. Never would he, Nancy and Cook have been invited to attend an affair like this wedding, as Mr. Bird had done yesterday. Whiteway was shocked by the invitation and turned it down for both he and his wife. But when Mrs. Brewster (he couldn't get used to calling her Ruth as she had suggested) said she wouldn't think of missing the event, he relented and told Nancy they could stand at the back of the room and watch.

He finished taking the serving dishes into the kitchen. There he changed from his striped working vest and butler's apron to his morning coat and accepted the cup of tea Nancy had made for him. He was now ready for the day that started with the sound of the doorbell shortly before seven-thirty.

◆   ◆   ◆

Maynard, too, was up early. He had slept restlessly his mind jumping about like a nervous horse.

He had reviewed the reservation he had made for the bridal suite at the Copley Plaza in Boston where they would spend the first night of their married life. Although he had previously stayed at the Palmer House, the Copley had more style and elegance and was better suited to the occasion. He had also decided to have Mike drive them, at least as far as Montreal or Quebec. This way, he and Rose would both be able to enjoy the trip along the Mohawk Trail and past Lake George and Lake Champlain.

He was still grateful that Rose had accepted his suggestion that they have the wedding quietly and that they arrange their wedding trip to Montreal in time to coincide with a conference of senior utility financiers that he had personally arranged. "I won't leave you alone long, dear," he had said to Rose. And then added, "afterwards we'll go on to Quebec City. I'm told that is like a city in France."

"Don't worry, Maynard," Rose had replied, "I'm sure I can find plenty to keep me busy in Montreal while you're having your conference."

Maynard's night thoughts included a lot of 'supposes': suppose Rose had changed her mind and didn't show up; suppose there was an accident and she was injured and couldn't get here. Every possible thing that could go wrong hopped through his mind like a grasshopper; he seemed unable to keep one idea in his mind long enough to work out an answer to each problem. Finally, at five o'clock he abandoned any further effort to sleep and got out of bed. This was to be a special day and the sooner it started the better!

He showered, shaved and dressed carefully in an oxford gray wool gabardine suit, a white shirt and blue, white and maroon striped tie. (This was not the day for a bow tie.) He packed his shaving kit and made sure that the rest of his luggage, packed the night before, was ready for Mike to pick up. Finally, he went downstairs, only to wander back and forth through the rooms getting in everyone's way.

He stopped in the dining room and spoke to Whiteway, noting that a champagne glass was at each place. He took little stock in this newest government interference with a man's right to have a drink. Maine had had a 'dry' law since just after the Civil War, but it didn't seem to have done much good (from Maynard's point of view) to cut down drinking. Now the politicians in Washington were going to try it on the whole country and he doubted that it would be any more effective than the state law. No liquor had been served at Milton's wedding and he and another guest had to go outside to get a sip from a flask of something stronger than fruit punch. He saw this as very demeaning; so he was going to have champagne to toast *his* bride at the wedding, by golly, and let the chips fall where they may.

Milton and Helen, who had come up from Boston the day before, came downstairs about seven and joined Maynard in the sunroom where Whiteway provided them with a 'pick-me-up' cup of coffee.

The Tylers—Jennie, Joe and Carroll—were the first to arrive bringing with them Mildred Ficket, an old and cherished friend of the family. Jennie went upstairs with Rose to help her change into her wedding dress. Joe, Carroll and Mildred were introduced to Milton and Helen in the sunroom where they were joined shortly by Rev. Hudson. The McDougalls were next to arrive followed by the Whitneys. Both Maynard and Rose had agreed that they wanted Helen and Edmund Whitney at their wedding since Helen had been the key to bringing them together.

As the grandfather clock in the hall struck eight thirty, Jennie came downstairs. The rest of the party moved to the hallway waiting for the bride's appearance. There was a hush as Rose's steps could be heard at the top of the stairs, gradually coming into view at the second landing. She was dressed in a cream-colored faille and crepe gown. Vertical bands of pale pink satin decorated the long sleeved bodice and the skirt that fell nearly to her ankles. Ruches of the same pink in tulle had been inserted in the square, low-cut neckline to give it a more modest appearance. A pink satin sash and a sleeveless tunic beaded with small artificial pearls completed her wedding gown.[99] She wore her hair as usual, parted in the middle, framing her face, waved along the sides and gently pulled back into a bun. Her face was devoid of makeup except for a faint coloring of her lips, but makeup was not necessary for her skin seemed to glow from within. Although her eyes had their usual sparkle, there was also an air of serenity in her manner as she gracefully descended the stairs. In her right hand she held the stair rail and in her left the bouquet of white violets.

Joe Tyler stepped forward when Rose reached the foot of the stairs. Offering his arm, with great dignity he escorted her into the living room where Maynard, Milton and the Rev. Hudson were waiting. The rest of the group followed seating themselves in chairs set in a semi-circle behind the bride and groom. The servants stood unobtrusively in a line inside the doorway with Whiteway at one end of the line and Mike Hanratty at the other—as distant as possible the English from the Irish.

The service was short and simple. There was no music, and the quiet in the room only magnified the responses of both bride and groom. What thoughts went through their minds are hardly describable. Chances are that both Maynard and Rose were too absorbed in the liturgy: so often repeated but seldom with as much meaning as when the words were spoken to them alone. As Maynard placed a circlet of diamonds on Rose's finger, he repeated the words, "With this ring I thee wed, and with all my worldly goods I do thee endow." He meant every word of that pledge.

As Rev. Hudson intoned, "I now pronounce you man and wife," Maynard kissed Rose gently, but with all the love and longing stored up in his heart. Then they turned and greeted their audience with smiles of joy and happiness.

The wedding breakfast came off without a hitch. Milton toasted the bride and groom with all the graciousness that came to him so easily. He mentioned the loneliness his father had suffered after his mother's death, and how happy he was to see that his father had found and married such a lovely and caring woman as Rose. Maynard appropriately toasted his bride and her parents, while Nelson McDougall endorsed the general sentiment that both Maynard and Rose were well suited to each other, and wished them long life and happiness. No mention was made of the alcoholic beverage, although Maynard was aware that neither

Rev. Hudson nor Joe Tyler, a longtime teetotaler, drank the champagne. Both raised their water goblets instead when responding to the toasts; Jennie, on the other hand, drank champagne with the others.

The arrival of the wedding cake brought oohs and aahs from the group, for Ruth had truly outdone herself in the decorating. She had made a three layer white cake with raspberry filling. The butter cream frosting was decorated in the center with a rose bush with one large pink bloom; a blue bird entwined in its branches had its head nestled in the petals of the rose. The cake was edged in a green and pink garland of rosebuds.

As the cake was placed in front of Rose and Maynard, Rose looked at Maynard and said, "It's just too beautiful to cut. We must thank Ruth, can she come in?"

"Of course she can," he responded and he signaled to Whiteway to ask Ruth to join them.

When Ruth arrived, Rose got up and put her arms around her. "How can I ever thank you, Ruth, for the wonderful gift of the cake."

It was too much for Ruth, who turned scarlet and mumbled something in reply. Then taking a deep breath in order to compose herself, she said, as if memorized for the occasion, "Congratulations, Rose, er...I mean, Mrs. Bird. We all hope you both will be very happy." With that she turned and fled back to the kitchen.

Shortly thereafter the breakfast broke up. Rose changed her clothes for travel, while the others chatted with Maynard waiting for their departure. When Rose reappeared she had changed into a gray two piece suit with touches of blue in a muted plaid under which she wore a light blue blouse with a ruffled jabot. A broad brimmed gray straw hat accented by a blue band to go with the suit completed her going away outfit.

As they got ready to leave, Rose kissed her mother and father, while Maynard shook hands with everyone and thanked them for coming. Then, at the last minute, Rose turned to Mildred Ficket, hugged her and said, "I want you to have these, Mildred," handing her the bouquet of white violets. "You've been a wonderful friend to me and all the Tylers. Keep these as a reminder of a happy day for all of us."

As they drove away, the sun beamed down, the trees nodded their approval as a slight breeze rustled their limbs and leaves, and the birds sang a hymn of joy to the newlyweds on their departure.

18

Postcard dated Williamstown, Mass. June 6 (?) 1–30P 1920
Addressed to: Mrs. E. M. Cobb, 34 School St., New London, Conn.

"Having a wonderful trip. Came through the trail [Mohawk] yester-day—here in Williamstown, Mass. today & on to Montreal tomorrow if pleasant, everything went of [sic] finely Thursday but (?) _____(illegible) you all might learn very soon. Love, Rose."

After spending their wedding night in Boston, Rose and Maynard set out on their motor trip the following day. Crossing northern Massachusetts, they entered the Mohawk Trail at Miller's Falls. They followed it to western Massachusetts; from there, as the postcard indicated, they went north to Montreal where Maynard planned to spend a day attending a public utility conference. He had felt rather guilty about taking time out of their wedding trip for business and had apologized profusely to Rose.

"We'll still have time to go on to Quebec City where we'll stay at the Chateau Frontenac overlooking the old city and the St. Lawrence River," he explained.

"Maynard, dear," she replied, "I can find something to do in Montreal. Don't you remember, I bought a guidebook in Boston that covers both Quebec City and Montreal. So I can go sightseeing while you're at your conference. As for Quebec City, the guidebook says it's just like France."

Neither of them had been to France, so they were both looking forward to the foreign ambience of French Canada. "One day doesn't mean that much to me," she added. "Besides, we have the rest of our lives to spend together. I don't begrudge you one day."

Maynard patted her hand. "You're a good sport, Rose. I won't leave you alone for long, I promise." He remembered how he had allowed his business to consume all his waking hours when he was married to Mary and Milton was little. He wasn't going to do that with Rose.

Rose was a great one for guidebooks; she had also found one about the Mohawk Trail which was one of the highlights of their trip. As they drove through Massachusetts on their way to the Trail's start at Miller's Falls, she entertained Maynard by reading excerpts from the book

"'The Trail stretches from Miller's Falls on the upper Connecticut River to the New York Line ending in the northwest corner of Massachusetts at North Adams near the college town of Williamstown,'" she read. "'The Indians of Mohawk tribe, one of the five tribes of the Iroquois Nation, and Pocumtuck tribe shared salmon fishing rights on the Connecticut and Deerfield Rivers,'" she paused and then in puzzled tone said, "Maynard, who or what are the other tribes of the Iroquois Nation?"

"I don't know," he answered, "but maybe the book tells you farther on." (They later found that the other tribes were the Senecas, the Onondagas, the Oneidas and the Cayugas, and felt very pleased with their newly acquired knowledge.)

Rose continued reading about the early settlers who found the Trail a convenient route between Boston and the English settlement of Deerfield. In order to make the trail accessible to horses and wagons, and to prevent ambush by the Indians, the settlers widened the trail by felling trees and cutting back the undergrowth of the dense forest. In the 18th century, the English and the Dutch (in New York) fomented a rivalry between the Mohawks and the Pocumtucks. Rose read on about how the Mohawks annihilated the Pocumtuck settlements and how they paid dearly for their victory because, while their attention was diverted, the Dutch seized Mohawk lands further up the Hudson.

Rose read on: 'In the 19th century the trail became a highway of commerce between eastern centers and the industrial city of North Adams in Western Massachusetts. The trail lost its usefulness, however, when railroads usurped its role in commercial transportation; and its loveliness forgotten, the forest resumed its predominance; but its scenic beauty was such that in 1914 it was designated as a scenic tourist route by the Massachusetts legislature. With the advent of the automobile in the 20th century, the trail once again flourished.'[100]

By the time they reached Miller's Falls, Rose and Maynard had covered the whole history of the region. Now they found the Trail roadway was dirt, but had been widened and graded, and guard rails had been built at some of the more acute and precipitous curves. Second growth deciduous trees, whose spring-soft greenery only waited for the hotter, dustier days of summer to assume a darker hue, had replaced much of the original lush evergreen forest. From the forest's depths they could hear the rustle of animals and the calls of larger birds.

◆   ◆   ◆

A honeymoon is a time for two people to learn more about each other. Maynard was finding that Rose, in addition to her musical talent, took particular pleasure in the natural beauty of her surroundings. Nature's gifts elicited moments of enthusiastic delight from her as when on seeing the gorge at Shelburne Falls or the distant peak of Hawks Mountain, she said excitedly, "Oh, Maynard, isn't it beautiful; it's just breathtaking. How did you know I'd enjoy it so much?"

Maynard enjoyed seeing new places, but he had never given much thought to the natural beauty of his surroundings; except perhaps the sea that was so much a part of him that he always wanted to be near it. Not just lakes and rivers, but real honest-to-goodness ocean water. The sea was part of his life from the time when he had sailed on the John Bird ships up and down the Maine coast; even to the part it played in his telephone adventure. The insurance and securities businesses were somehow related to the existence of deepwater voyages. He had crossed the Atlantic once and perhaps he and Rose would have an opportunity to do so again. Then there was the Pacific; wouldn't that be a trip to remember! Now, however, he was beginning to see his surroundings from Rose's eyes, and at the same time to appreciate this new and unexpected facet of her nature.

He was also discovering that Rose had a well-developed sense of intellectual curiosity as displayed by her interest in what the guidebooks told about the places she was seeing. Additionally, she was curious, perhaps interested is a better word, in Maynard's business affairs; asking repeated questions about the difference between notes, bonds and stocks. Whether she understood the answers she got didn't matter to him. It was her interest in what he did that pleased him. After so many years of Mary's indifference to his business life, he now had a wife who showed an awareness and concern in things that were important to him. She also evidenced a vein of practicality, which was not surprising considering that she had lived independently and managed her own affairs for ten years. She still could not get used to the luxury she now enjoyed. Even though she knew Maynard was wealthy, she insisted on knowing how much things cost. In selecting a gift to take back to a friend or relative, she debated with herself the relative value of the expensive versus the more moderately priced item. Sometimes she took so long to make up her mind that Maynard got a little impatient with her.

"Come on, Rose, take this one," he would say, pointing to the more expensive item. "It's a lot better than the other one or it wouldn't be priced higher."

"That's not so, Maynard," Rose would respond. "Sometimes there's very little difference in the quality, but a big difference in price. It doesn't seem right to spend the extra money for such a small difference. I find it hard not to place a value on things even though I know we have the money to spend." She paused and added thoughtfully, "Maybe being rich takes a little bit of the excitement out of buying things, especially gifts?"

Weren't things worth more if you had to save to get them, she wondered? Perhaps, if they had so much money some of it should go to people who needed it more instead of just being spent for their own pleasure. This was something she would have to talk over with her husband. But for the time being, she guessed she would just enjoy the opportunities to buy what she wished.

Rose, too, was learning about Maynard. She recognized that he had a deep sense of pride in his family, especially his late father and grandfather, the first John Bird. However, once he had formed an opinion about a person's shortcomings, whether a relative or friend, he was unlikely to change his mind. She had been surprised when in Boston he had so bluntly labeled his daughter-in-law a "cold fish". There had been other instances, too, when he had spoken disparagingly of family members, who had not quite measured up to the yardstick he held up to them. On the other hand, she knew that he had supported some of his less affluent relatives; and, because he appreciated the value of a good education, had assisted at least one cousin through college.[101] She was anxious to visit Rockland and meet his brothers, their wives and other family for she felt her exposure to them would lead to a better understanding of her husband. Most of all she wanted to meet her new mother-in—law, whose gracious note welcoming her as Maynard's bride she treasured.

On their trip they discussed going to Rockland when they got home. They also talked about having a large reception at the Foreside house where they could invite all their friends and acquaintances—whether business or social—who would otherwise have been invited to a large wedding. Rose was very anxious to have Skip, Ann and Evelyn come to visit—perhaps at the same time as the party. They had given some thought to combining the Rockland relatives with the Portland crowd, but that was quickly discarded. Maynard wanted Rose to see his hometown; so both agreed that the Rockland trip should come first.

◆   ◆   ◆

Rockland welcomed Maynard's new bride with open arms—or at least it seemed that way to Rose. They stayed at the Samoset and had arranged with the management in advance to give a large party for Maynard's many friends and relatives. The three brothers got together to host a family lobster boil on the Owl's Head side of the harbor where Henry had a cottage. Here Rose was initiated into the 1920s version of a cookout. She found the carefree, informal atmosphere of the party delightful and although she had been brought up in Maine, she was still a novice at handling a lobster—especially a live one. She also saw Maynard really let down his hair. He had found a pair of old trousers and a collarless shirt that his mother had evidently saved, and garbed in those, dove right into the business of picking the lobsters, putting them into the boiling sea water laced with sea weed, and serving them when they were done. As the afternoon progressed, the Bird men regaled the company with one story after another. Rose heard from Alan how he and Henry and some of their friends had started a business taking the bones of dead horses left by the lime-hauling teamsters to the rendering plant in Rockland.[102] Maynard told about how Henry killed the rooster next door, and Henry followed up with how his mother had entered him in a baby beauty contest.[103] Only Elmer seemed to have little to say.

There was no feeling of constraint when Rose met her new mother-in-law. She immediately told Annie, who she called Mother Bird, how much she appreciated the letter; and after that they got along as if they had known each other all their lives. As she got to know Annie better, she discovered some of Maynard's endearing qualities in his mother. There was a sense of practicality and down-to-earthiness about Annie that Rose recognized in Maynard. Also, he seemed to have inherited her thoughtfulness and concern for others. She wished she had known his father for she was sure that the qualities of ambition, wit and persuasion were ones he had inherited from Sidney. (At this point in her marriage her husband had no bad qualities as far as Rose was concerned.) Rose liked to think that Maynard was Annie's favorite son. There seemed to be an unusually close bond between them.

Although Alan seemed a little standoffish at first, Rose noticed that in the company of his close friends and relatives he was more convivial. She thought Henry was wonderful—so warm and friendly, but between the wives of the two brothers she was not sure which she liked best. She recognized in Adelaide an acute intellect—she was brighter and far more interesting than any other woman there, and she certainly differed from Henry's wife Edith, who was sweet and charming, but perhaps a little prudish. As for Elmer and his wife, Emma, she could not make up her mind. Elmer seemed a much rougher, unpolished version of Maynard, even though as the eldest he was head of the family business; there was none of the sophistication or drive that she found in her own husband. As for

Emma—well, she seemed to dissolve into the background; unassertive and quiet. Rose realized that it would take more time than just their brief visit for her to get to know all these people. For the time being it was enough to have been introduced to some of them and to get a feel for the environment her husband came from.

If it was enough for Rose to identify her husband's brothers and their wives, when it came to their children, she was swamped. She was not quite sure who belonged to whom. Alan and Adelaide had no children, so the two young boys and little girl[104] must belong to Henry. She was also able to identify Sidney, Elmer's oldest son, but she was not sure about Sid's wife and who were his children. It was all very confusing and it would take time to sort everyone out.

◆   ◆   ◆

In early July, Maynard and Rose entertained several hundred of their friends at Pine Bower; there were those connected with Maynard's business and Rose's many contacts in the artistic world. Although a tent had been erected to serve as shelter, the weather cooperated perhaps due, in part, to prayers sent upwards by every member of the Bird household. The day of their party turned out to be one of those sparkling Maine summer days with the temperature in the low 80s, the sky clear and cloudless, and the air fresh with the smell of salt water mingled with the scents of flowers, pine needles and new cut hay. The guests were able to stroll on the lawn where they had a splendid view of Casco Bay, and enjoy a delicious supper served under the tent at little tables placed around a movable dance floor. A small orchestra that had been engaged to play fashionable dance music also accompanied Rose, when by popular request, she sang several selections from her repertoire.

Originally, Rose had intended to have Ann, Skip and little Evelyn come in time for the reception, but their visit was postponed so that they would have more time for a happy family reunion. One day during their visit, when Maynard was tied up with business, Skip drove them down to Old Orchard Beach in his Studebaker touring car for an afternoon of sunning, swimming and entertainment. The adults, more timid about going in the water, splashed around on the edges of the beach as the tide came in. Evelyn felt no such hesitation and ran gleefully into the water up to her waist.

"It's so-o-o cold," she squealed as she came out gasping.

"She's used to the warmer water in the Sound (Long Island) near us," remarked Ann.

But the cold water didn't seem to deter the child, who promptly went back in and stayed until her lips turned blue and her teeth were chattering. The day ended with Evelyn getting a ride on the Merry-go-Round where she tried in vain to catch the brass ring and then they all went up on the big Ferris wheel.

While she was visiting, Ann confided to Rose that she thought she might be pregnant again. Rose was delighted. "Oh Ann," she exclaimed, "how wonderful! You are so lucky. I hope Maynard and I can have children some time soon. Right now Maynard wants to wait, but I want so badly to have a baby."

◆　　　◆　　　◆

The rest of the summer and into the fall was a whirl of parties—teas, luncheons, dinners and receptions—many of them to honor the newlyweds. Rose was a bit surprised by all the invitations they received from people and organizations throughout the state that wanted to honor Maynard and his new bride. Perhaps she had forgotten that he had served two terms in the state legislature and in twenty-five years had developed a network of contacts through his political and business associations. In Boston, Bond and Goodwin feted them on one of their visits to that city.

Reciprocity was in order, and Rose, a very social creature at heart, delighted in entertaining. She renewed her association with the Rossini Club, and invited her bridge group for a lunch and bridge with cards taking a backseat to the chatter and gossip of the day. It was good to be back in Portland and enjoy her friends. There were so many of them she thought she'd never run out of people to invite. She and Maynard hosted the occasional small dinner party, and were often mentioned in the social columns as attending this or that affair. One unanticipated consequence of their social prominence was a burglary that resulted in the theft of a diamond pin Maynard had given Rose. It also scared her pretty badly for she was the one who awoke and, seeing a strange man in their bedroom, screamed at the top of her lungs. The thief fled with only the pin and a pair of inexpensive earrings. But after that, Maynard hired a private security firm to patrol the property when they were in residence.[105]

That Fall Milton and Helen moved from Boston to North Carolina where, as previously anticipated, they planned to raise peaches. Maynard viewed his son's undertaking with some skepticism; he had never gotten over Milton's failure to show any interest in the security business. When Milton had worked for Maynard, which hadn't been often, he had functioned mechanically and it was obvious to his father, as well as to others, that selling securities was the last thing that interested him.

As Maynard put it to Rose, "I don't know why I spent so much money on his education if all he wanted was to be a peach farmer. Can you believe it—four years at Exeter and a Harvard degree—all for this."

"Well, dear," Rose demurred, "he does have his own money now," (Rose was aware that Mary had left Milton an inheritance) "and maybe he's happy. You can't really rule what your children want to do, you know."

Still Maynard was not mollified. "Mary didn't leave him that much. He's living on Helen's money, and probably always will," he said disgustedly.

Rose saw no point in pursuing the argument, but she noted her husband's respect for those who used their abilities constructively. Evidently in his lexicon constructive use was synonymous with business.

◆   ◆   ◆

For Maynard, the months since their marriage were the happiest he could remember. He delighted in Rose's presence, often teasing her about some of her foibles. When she had her friends over for bridge, Maynard christened the gathering "The Girls & Gossip Club", even though she insisted they really did play cards. He was proud of her graciousness when entertaining, whether their guests were social, business or political acquaintances. He remembered how Mary had turned up her nose at some of the small town political hacks she was forced to entertain. Rose on the other hand treated all their guests with the utmost courtesy no matter what their origins or interests. He watched her one evening listen to a local up-state politician expound on the price of potatoes in Aroostook County, knowing all the while that she had no idea what the man was talking about and couldn't have cared less; but her attention never faltered. The speaker was delighted to find that Mrs. Bird had such a depth of understanding in the potato agriculture of Aroostook County.

Later, when Rose asked, "Maynard, what did that man mean by futures?" he laughed so hard that it took him a few minutes to wipe the tears off his cheeks and regain his composure. The answer when it came elicited a shrug of the shoulders and "Oh, is that all!"

He delighted in buying her gifts, bringing her pieces of jewelry, monogrammed linen handkerchiefs or knick-knacks to display around the house. When she accompanied him to Boston, he suggested she shop for clothes; Rose needed no encouragement in this activity. Consequently, her wardrobe grew considerably to her own satisfaction and Maynard's pleasure. Occasionally, Maynard would buy her something she considered utterly useless and even ridiculous, as when he brought home a lady's hunting outfit complete with jacket, britches, boots, flat—top silk hat, and a side saddle skirt.

She looked at the collection in both amusement and amazement. "What in the world am I going to do with all this, Maynard? I don't ride horseback, there is no hunting to my knowledge around Portland, and besides, we don't have a horse that I could ride." [106]

She started to laugh, but stopped when she saw the expression of disappointment on his face. "Oh, I'm sorry Maynard, but really, I don't want to even learn to ride at this point."

Maynard looked rather sheepishly at the outfit, realizing that he had bought it with a picture in his mind's eye of Rose riding to the hounds, as he had seen women in England do.

"Well, I guess I could take it back if you're sure you don't want it," he said, hoping that perhaps she would change her mind. "You would look great in it," he said rather wistfully.

Rose came over and kissed him and whispered in his ear, "Take it back, dearest. We have other things we can spend our money on that would make me happier."

For the time being that was the end of the riding outfit. Maynard didn't take it back, but kept it with the forlorn hope that perhaps someday he would see Rose wearing the black riding clothes mounted on a chestnut hunter riding to the hounds.

◆　　　◆　　　◆

Rose, too, was enjoying married life. Even though Maynard's business took him frequently to Boston, he seldom stayed away more than one night. Her days were full starting with breakfast that she always shared with him when he was home. She made a point of practicing her music for at least an hour each morning. She was determined not to let her vocal skills get rusty, and she still had hopes of giving charity recitals or taking part in amateur performances. At present though, her schedule was too full to contemplate any such commitments. A car, with Mike to drive it, was available if she wanted to go into Portland. She often visited with her mother and father if no other engagement interfered.

In spite of her earlier reservations, Rose was adjusting easily to a household with servants. She thought Whiteway was a little overbearing and patronizing, but made up her mind not to let it bother her. Nancy was a 'peach', and of course Ruth, in the kitchen meant that she never had to worry about cooking herself. (Rose was not a cook and never presumed to be.) Whenever they entertained, an additional maid was hired to assist Whiteway, although Nancy was available for family meals.

Sunday dinners were still shared with her parents, but Jennie and Joe now came to Pine Bower. Both Rose and Maynard had been putting on weight, what with all the parties they were going to, so she tried to make the Sunday menus a little lighter with more green vegetables and fruit for desert. It was really impossible, however, to wean her father away from mashed potatoes and apple pie with a slice of good cheddar cheese on the side. She found she could succeed to some extent with Maynard when they ate at home, (which was rarely), but Joe Tyler was not about to change the habits of a lifetime. "You can't teach an old dog new tricks," he would remark as he heaped mashed potatoes on his plate or spread butter on the dinner rolls. Rose soon gave up on her father and anyway, he remained the same lean man he had always been.

As fall turned into winter, Maynard suggested that they move back to Portland to the house on Bowdoin Street. "We don't want to get snowed in here, Rose."

"Why not, dear," Rose replied with a girlish twinkle in her eye. "I think it would be fun to be out here with snow all around us. Think how beautiful it would be."

"Rose, be reasonable. You'd get tired of the snow in twenty-four hours."

She gave in to Maynard's common sense, but delayed their move to the city until after Thanksgiving. Fortunately, the weather cooperated and no snow fell until later in December.

For the first Christmas since their marriage, both Maynard and Rose were determined to make it a memorable one. The house in Portland was decorated with wreaths and garlands of pine and spruce boughs. A seven foot tree stood in front of the fireplace, loaded with decorations, strings of popcorn and cranberries and pomander oranges whose scent of cloves mingled with that of the evergreens and permeated the house. Small, colored, electric lights were strung all over the tree—an idea quite new to Rose, but Maynard said he'd seen this done in Boston and New York. He had dozens of pots of red poinsettias delivered to the house where they found their way into every room. Even the front door had wreaths both inside and out, and smaller wreaths were placed in windows facing the street.

It was a memorable Christmas for both of them. Gifts there were aplenty for all the family members. Gifts were sent to the New London family and to some of the Rockland relatives, although Maynard warned Rose not to try to remember all the Birds or she would wind up sending presents to all of Knox County. They hosted a gala Christmas dinner with Joe, Jennie and Carroll Tyler, and also Jennie's older brother Simon Hastings, known as 'Sime', and his wife, Nellie. Like Joe, Sime was a veteran of the Civil War, so these two old vets regaled their audience with tall tales of their war adventures. If their listeners had already heard the stories, they greeted them with enthusiasm and laughter as if hearing them for the first time.

The day ended with guests going home and host and hostess retiring.

Stomachs full, spirits happy and thankfulness in their hearts for a never-to-be-forgotten holiday.

As Maynard looked back on past Christmases, he felt lucky to have a wife he adored, and one who loved him in the same way. He was already thinking ahead about a New Year that would be full of excitement and most of all adventure. For he had a surprise for Rose that he was saving for New Year's Eve. Nineteen twenty had been a wonderful year. He was sure nineteen twenty-one would be even better!

19

Social Note from a Portland, Maine paper
Dated February 3, 1921

Mr. and Mrs. Maynard Bird left yesterday for an extended trip to the Far East. Mr. Bird is well known in Maine banking and investment circles. Before her marriage Mrs. Bird was the popular concert singer, Rose Tyler. They will visit Japan and China and make a stop in Hawaii where Mrs. Bird has relatives.[107]

Among friends and relatives, their journey was always known as THE TRIP. Although Maynard and Rose moved in cosmopolitan circles where lengthy journeys were not unusual, no one in their immediate family nor in their social group had ever ventured as far afield as the Orient. Needless to say there was considerable discussion on what had motivated the two of them to pick such remote destinations.

One acquaintance was heard to say, "I could understand it if they had gone to Europe and stayed there for a while. Rose would have enjoyed the music, especially in Italy, and Maynard would certainly have picked up enough business to make the trip worth while. But to go to Japan—or even China—where practically no one speaks English! What can he possibly expect to gain from that?"

A young and newly admitted member of the Rossini Club, who had heard others speak of Rose in glowing terms, timidly ventured a comment. "It sounds like a wonderful adventure to me," she said. I'd go in a minute if someone would ask me."

If there were patronizing smiles at the naivete of this opinion, is it possible that behind the smiles were unvoiced feelings of envy? One matron expressed the general feeling when she said, "I can't imagine my husband ever thinking of taking a trip like that. Why, if I even suggested it, he'd think I'd gone out of my mind."

The extended trip to the Orient was Maynard's New Year's surprise to Rose.

Although he may have casually mentioned business matters as the reason for the trip, it was certainly not the only reason, and, probably not the major reason.

He came from a family with the sea in their blood—almost like an infection that the Bird offspring caught from their Gregory grandmother, Clarissa. All his life he collected books about ships. There was one on sailing ships on Penobscot Bay; another called *The Down Easters,* and another on the clipper ship era. He treasured a print made from the original Currier & Ives lithograph of the *Red Jacket* that had been built in Rockland and hung in his study. He also had prints of a number of the Bird vessels, including one, the *S.M.Bird,* named after his father. Nor had he forgotten his Aunt Lorinda whose daughter, Clara Borstel, was born aboard a ship while it was at anchor in Calcutta harbor. And Clara was still going strong, or at least she was the last time he had heard.[108] For Maynard all life was, more than anything else, an adventure; and what was more logical than to take his new and beloved bride on the adventure of their lifetime. She might not have thought of the idea herself, but his sense of adventure was infectious so she welcomed the idea with enthusiasm.

As the time drew near for their departure, Rose's mind was buzzing with ideas and anticipation of their great journey. She went to the Portland Public Library for books about Hawaii, Japan and China so that she would know something about the history of the places they would visit. Her days were filled with making lists, sorting out the wardrobe she would take, and if necessary shopping—in both Portland and Boston—to make sure that both she and Maynard had all the appropriate apparel wherever they might happen to land. Luggage was bought or brought down from the attic; and Rose's room and Maynard's dressing room were periodically awash with tissue paper, open steamer and wardrobe trunks, hat boxes and other travel paraphernalia. Pictures and passports were duly obtained as were the appropriate visas. (It was Maynard's job to take care of the tickets for trains, ships and hotels.) Arrangements had to be made for the care of the town house as well as *Pine Bower.* Whiteway and Nancy were given a three-month vacation during which they planned a trip to England; it was expected that they would return in time to get the Foreside house open and ready for its owners' return. Mike and Ruth were given part pay and assigned care of the Bowdoin Street house and to check periodically on the estate.

The day of their departure finally arrived. Their first stop was New York City where they stayed at the Waldorf Astoria Hotel. The next day was spent in last minute shopping for Rose and business matters with the New York office of Bond & Goodwin for Maynard. He had been to the New York office a number of times and was beginning to be known to the various partners there. His best contact was James Auchincloss who currently held the Stock Exchange seat for the firm. His son, Hugh, was also a member of the firm but had not as yet achieved the standing accorded to his father. Maynard found Hugh, who was close to him in age, a congenial associate and made a mental note to promote their friendship whenever possible.[109] While in New York, Maynard was anxious to finalize some pending underwriting issues that he had been instrumental in initiating. Also, he was counting on the New York office to provide him with letters of introduction to the financial centers of China and Japan. In addition, he wanted to expand his contacts in Honolulu without relying solely on Rose's relatives for entrée into the upper echelons of Hawaiian business and society.[110]

That evening there were orchestra tickets to the Metropolitan Opera's performance of *Rigoletto*. Although Rose had hoped to hear the great Italian tenor, Enrico Caruso,[111] she had to be satisfied with Giuseppe DeLuca in the title role. She could not help but think, however, that she could have sung the role of Gilda just as well as Cora Chase. Despite knowing that that part of her life was over, there would always be the might-have-been of singing in the Gilda role at the Met. She looked a little guiltily at Maynard sitting beside her, and mentally scolded herself for having such thoughts. She had found a wonderful husband whose love and care for her was giving her life new meaning and whom she loved more every day. Enough of wishful thinking; she could still sing, but there was more to life now than concerts and opera. She was sure of that. In a gesture of affection as if to make up for her guilty thoughts, she reached over and gently squeezed his hand.

During the intermission, Rose noted that the following day there was to be a matinee of *L'Oracolo* with the incomparable Antonio Scotti playing his signature role of Chim-Fen. "Oh, Maynard, I've got to hear this one," she exclaimed as she showed him the program announcement. "Do you suppose I could still get a ticket?"

On checking the box office, Maynard was able to get not one, but two tickets. "Perhaps you could invite Mrs. Auchincloss to go with you—the younger one, I mean," he said as he presented Rose with the tickets.

It was not that he was unwilling for her to go to the Met alone, but from his point of view two birds could be killed with one stone; it would be a good opportunity to further their association with the Auchincloss family. "You might find her interesting, and it's someone with whom we should maintain a good friendship," he added.

Rose took Maynard's advice and invited Irene Auchincloss to join her and after lunching together, the two ladies were treated to the one-act opera that had become a favorite of New York audiences. In it Scotti had made the role of the villainous Chinaman his own, but "one most distant from his own natural elegance."[112] Rose would always remember every detail of Scotti's acting. "Not only in make—up and costume, but in pace, gesture and movement, the great Italian baritone gave a gruesomely realistic characterization" to the part. "Every detail of the portrayal, even to the forward inclination of his head, the indrawing of his shoulders and elbows, and the ghastly limpness of his pendulous fingers, show[ed] careful study and elaboration."[113] At one point, Scotti rolled three oranges across the stage, a bit of stagecraft that only he could do. "Few persons are likely to forget the uncanny sight Scotti presented as he sank, loose and spineless under the onslaught of his murderer, and later as he flopped forward in a heap and rolled over on the stage."[114] Rose was mesmerized and could hardly wait to get back to the hotel to tell Maynard all about it. For her it was the highlight of their stay in New York.

The next day they took the train for Washington. There they stayed one night at the Willard Hotel; the Portland congressman and his wife joined them there for dinner. Rose knew them both since they had attended the party at *Pine Bower* the previous summer. They also lunched in the Senatorial Dining Room on the second day with one of the Maine senators.

Rose had never been to Washington before and was impressed with the buildings, the malls and open spaces, and the air of power and influence that seemed to pervaded every corner of the Capital building itself. There were senators and congressmen who could be seen rushing about undoubtedly on business of national importance or so Rose supposed. In fact everyone seemed to be in a hurry, although she couldn't quite understand why. She and Maynard sat in the Visitor's Gallery and watched while the Senate was in session, but she was disappointed because she expected that more would be going on. In fact there were very few senators at their desks until a loud bell rang. This she was told was a bell to call for a quorum so that the Senate could vote on something. Then a lot of senators rushed back into the room, and the roll was called. Except that the senators answered with an "Aye" or a "Nay", it sounded to Rose like a teacher calling the role on the first day of school

That evening they said goodbye to the Nation's Capital and boarded their train for the West Coast.

◆   ◆   ◆

**Postcard dated: Los Angeles, Calif. Feb. 14, 1:30pm 1922
Addressed to: Mrs. E. M. Cobb, 34 School St., New London, Conn.
The picture on the front is of the Ambassador Hotel in Los Angeles, California.**

Had a fine trip so far. Motored from Pasadena this PM. & have dinner here before leaving for San F. Hope you are alright. Much love to you and a kiss from Auntie for her sweetheart. Rose and Maynard. It's very cold here.

Rose and Maynard traveled to the West Coast on the Twentieth Century Limited, later frequently used by movie stars. (This was the route celebrated in the song *The Acheson, Topeka and Santa Fe.*) They occupied a Pullman stateroom consisting of two lower beds that were transformed during the day into comfortable divans beside a large window the better to view the passing scenery. Unfortunately, there was little out of the ordinary to see until they reached the eastern part of New Mexico, but from then on they were treated to white-capped mountains, followed by miles of dry desert interspersed with buttes. The train continued its climb to the heights of Northern Arizona where the triple crowns of San Francisco Peaks greeted them. When they got off the train in Flagstaff Rose looked up transfixed by Mt. Humphrey in all its 12,000 foot snow covered glory.

"Little higher than Mt. Katahdin isn't it?" Maynard remarked.

Rose only nodded as she stared, awestruck, at the grandeur of the mountain and the scenery in its winter starkness and beauty.

There followed only one more night on the train before arrival in Los Angeles and then a short motor trip up the coast to Pasadena where they spent several days.

◆   ◆   ◆

**Postcard dated Yokahama, Japan, 01 Mar. 1921.
Addressed to: Mrs. E. M. Cobb, 34 School St., New London, Connecticut, U.S.A.
Picture on the reverse side is of the S.S. Nanking.**

Dearest Ann: Have been thinking about you & hoping you will be all right.[115] This is the ship we are spending twenty days on. Not as large as some, but comfortable—fine service. Much love from both [of] us to you and the two babies. Affect'y Rose.

The *S. S. Nanking* was a combination passenger and cargo liner; a two-stacker that burned coal. It put into port at Honolulu for refueling, but there was only time for a brief visit with Rose's Hawaiian relatives. A longer visit was promised on their return voyage.

During the three-week voyage they amused themselves by reading, playing games and, of course, getting to know their fellow passengers. In their cabin luggage were the books on their anticipated destinations and they occupied some of their time in reading and discussing their planned itinerary. Each morning Maynard, and sometimes Rose, would walk energetically around the promenade deck until the laps added up to a mile. If the sea was rough, Rose's stomach was often queasy and she would stay in the cabin, but Maynard, on the other hand, had long since tested his sea legs aboard ships of all sizes and makes, and found them reliable under the roughest conditions.

In addition there were the deck games of shuffleboard and badminton to play in good weather; cards and other games were saved for days when it rained or the sea was too rough to be outdoors. Maynard's favorite game was cribbage which he tried to teach Rose; but she found her self confused by her husband's quickness in adding up their scores. It seemed that she always came out on the short end of the stick and decided to stick to bridge. Bridge—the Auction kind—that had achieved great popularity first in England and later in the United States—appealed to her more.

They were a gregarious couple and made friends easily; so if there were contacts to be made—no matter what nationality—they took advantage of such opportunities. Some of their fellow passengers were Americans on their way to assume diplomatic or commercial posts in the Orient and welcomed the presence of other fellow countrymen no matter what their purpose or destination.

Thus the sea trip was enlivened not only by other passengers, but also by their own resources for self-entertainment.

◆   ◆   ◆

Postcard dated 01 Mar 1921, Yokahama, Japan.
Addressed to Mrs. E. M. Cobb, 34 School St., New London, Connecticut, U.S.A.
Picture on reverse side is of Yokohama Pier. It shows a large ship tied up with many cars and carriages waiting to receive some of the people debarking.

"This is just where we have landed. Have decided to go on to China—Shanghai & Peking & come back through Japan. Leave tonight at five. Hope you & our new baby are well. Maynard joins me in best love to all. Aff'y Rose."

The decision to go on to China was somewhat spur-of-the-moment. They found it would be easier to continue on the same ship rather than have to book passage on another one, and they were encouraged by several of their shipboard friends to join them for a few days (or weeks) in touring China.

"We are going to come back to Japan, anyway," Maynard said when discussing the change of plans with Rose. "This way we can keep our cabin and not have to move twice."

Rose was more practical. "I hope they haven't taken our hold luggage off, dear. That would really complicate things.:

Maynard assured her that he had already talked to the purser about the matter and had been assured that their luggage would continue with them.

◆   ◆   ◆

In the early 20's China was undergoing a nationalist movement led by Dr. Sun Yatsen. In order to consolidate the power of the Kuomintang (KMT), the Nationalist party, Dr. Sun had forged an alliance with Russia and the Communist party. After his death when Chaing Kaishek assumed the reins of the party, the Communists were forced north (The Long March) under the leadership of Mao Tse Tsung and the KMT became the ruling party until after World War II. Unfortunately, Chaing was never able to completely pacify the country, and it continued to suffer the depredations of warlords and Communist supporters until the resurgence of the Communists in the late 1940's. But when Rose and Maynard visited China, the country—at least the westernized coastal area—was quiet and at peace.

In Shanghai they found a cosmopolitan city divided by the British, French, German, and Russians into separate concessions each reflecting the culture and environment of its sponsor. In the British sector they found an excellent deluxe hotel where there was no language barrier to contend with. Shanghai was also a thriving commercial center, so hoping to find some business opportunities, Maynard made several calls on bank executives whose names had been given him in New York. Nothing particular emerged from these contacts, so he contented himself with his role as tourist and shared all the exotic sights with Rose. With

English speaking guides to show them the 'sights' they traveled around Shanghai and then took the train to Peking. There they stayed several days visiting the Forbidden City; they climbed the stairs to the Great Wall—a <u>must</u> on any tourist's itinerary—and were impressed by its length.

Before the end of March they were back in Japan.

◆   ◆   ◆

Postcard from Tokyo dated 29 March (?)
Addressed to: Mrs. E. M. Cobb, 34 School St., New London, Conecticut, U.S.A.
Picture on reverse side shows Japanese garden with bridge over water and several red maples in the background. Numerous female figures in traditional Japanese garb are shown. They wrote:

This is such a lovely public garden—the maples look just like this. How's the new offspring? We are hoping for news very soon but may not get any until Honolulu. Much love—Rose & Maynard.

◆   ◆   ◆

Postcard from Tokyo dated 29 March (?)
Addressed to: Miss Evelyn F. Cobb, 34 School Street, New London, Connecticut, U.S.A.
Picture is entitled "Hoodo of Byodoin, Uji. Four female figures in kimonos stand in front of a lagoon with a large Japanese temple on the further side. Rose wrote:

Auntie's Sweetheart
Wish you could see the little boys & girls here. They all wear very bright colored kimonos & no hats. The babies are all carried on their mother's back. Auntie bought a dollie for you, which has five different wigs. Love to Mother and Daddy & most for you. Aff'y Auntie.

◆   ◆   ◆

Postcard from Tokyo dated 29 March (?)
Addressed to: Miss Evelyn Cobb, 34 School St., New London, Conn. U.S.A
Picture is of a country scene. A Japanese woman peasant leads an ox with a
child and household goods on its back. Maynard wrote:

Mch 28/21, Dear Evelyn: It is considered quite a treat to ride this way.
How would you like it? There are more shops selling toys than of any other
one thing. That's because of so many children. Aunt Rose joins me in love to
you all. Uncle Maynard.

At the time Rose and Maynard visited Japan, the country was on its way to becoming a fully modern country even though to western eyes it still seemed very traditional in style and culture. In the postcard pictures, the kimono is still shown as the traditional woman's dress. On the other hand, Tokyo already had a working street railway and there were trains that ran between Tokyo and other major cities. When the Japanese defeated the Russians in the early part of the century (1904–1905), the world became aware that Japan possessed a modern and highly trained military establishment. The devastating earthquake that hit the Tokyo region in 1923, two years after their visit, left the city in ruins; but it served as a symbol for renewal. The Tokyo that emerged from the rubble was a far more cosmopolitan and modern city than the one Rose and Maynard saw.

In 1921, however, the two travelers found Japan more to their liking than China. Besides Tokyo, they visited Kyoto, the city of temples and shrines and in particular the Byodoin Temple, the 12th century structure that is the oldest in Kyoto. They also saw parts of the countryside and were awed by the majesty of Mt. Fuji. Maynard mentions the number of toyshops where Rose was busy buying toys for Evelyn and for Ann's new baby.[116] Rose bought, with Maynard's urging, a beautiful kimono that had floral embroidery in graduated shades of browns, tans, buff and ivory on a pale golden background.

As she caressed the kimono, she said rather wistfully, "I wonder if I'll ever have a chance to wear this as Yum Yum in *The Mikado* or maybe as Cho Cho San in *Madama Butterfly.*"

"I'm sure you'll have a chance to wear it when we get home," he responded, and noticing the sadness in her face he put his arm around her. "You're not sorry you married me, are you Rose?"

"Of course not," she laughed and shook her head. "What a silly thing to say. I'll find an occasion to wear the robe—at a concert or presentation—who knows. It's just so beautiful."

They stayed long enough in Japan to see the famous Japanese Cherry trees in bloom, and left around the second week April. Rose was not feeling well the last days in Japan and during the voyage to Hawaii she felt even worse. When they got settled at the Cooke's palatial estate, Rose took Alice Cooke aside and confided in her that she thought she might be pregnant. Alice recommended an obstetrician who confirmed Rose's suspicion, and told her that the baby would probably be born around mid-December. This was cause for great rejoicing for there was nothing that Rose wanted more than to have a child. Maynard, too, was overjoyed—perhaps this time it would be a girl—a girl just like her mother. With this news to impart to the family, they did not linger long in Hawaii.

◆   ◆   ◆

Postcard dated May 16, 1921 PM, Blue Canyon, Cal
Addressed to Miss Evelyn F. Cobb, 34 School St., New London, Conn.
Picture shows a train passing though Palisade Canyon, Nevada

Dearest Sweetheart—Aunty was so pleased with your two sweet letters & it won't be long before she will see you and your baby sister. We are on the train now and will soon be at the top of the world in the Sierra Mts. Love to all from Auntie & Uncle M.

They were anxious to get home. Like many women in their first pregnancy, Rose was coping with morning sickness. They both felt they had been away long enough and looked forward to being home with family and friends.

Rose wanted to have children. Maynard, for his part, wanted what Rose wanted, but he remembered Milton's childhood, and perhaps his own failings as a father. He had given Milton every material thing a boy could want including a first class education. If his son had turned out to be less than he had hoped for, part of the blame was Mary's. He knew that Milton had always been what the Rockland boys called a 'sissy', but wasn't that Mary's fault—she had overly mothered their son. Did he think of the times spent away from home—times when he was not there to counteract Mary's influence? If he did, did he rationalize his absences by the need, more often than not, to put his business first? If Mary complained his answer was always, "I work so that you and Milton can have the best of everything."

Now, he had a second chance with a wife so much different than Mary. Business was no longer a concern; he was wealthy enough to provide a family with all their needs as well as their desires. He told himself that it would be their baby and they would share in bringing up the child together. No, there were no clouds on his emotional horizon at the thought of once again becoming a father.

Maynard, had never taken a vacation as distant from the financial centers of the Western World as this one. Getting home meant getting back in the world of finance and investment; a world that he now realized he sorely missed. Although his career had been founded on investment banking and the underwriting of new issues, especially utility securities, he was now making some personal investments in the stock market. The decade of the 20's was a period of great, and some would say 'unbridled'—expansion in 'the market'. Maynard, however, considered himself an investor rather than a speculator: that is he considered judiciously trading stocks a means of adding to his personal wealth. Generally he made his investment decisions on the basis of thorough study and careful analysis looking for value and a satisfactory return on the amount invested; and as with his commercial affairs, he invested in stocks that posed a minimal risk of massive loss. This pattern of investment discipline served him in good stead later in his life when the stock market became wildly unstable and eventually crashed. Thus by the end of May 1921, he was looking forward to their return home with great eagerness.

After the transcontinental rail trip, their first stop was in New London so that Rose could see her new niece, Jane, named after the baby's grandmother, Jennie; and, of course, compare notes with Ann about her sister's pregnancy and her own. The Cobb family was excited by the gifts and enthralled as they listened to the tales of adventure from the two travelers. Then on to Portland where Joe and Jennie, grateful to see their daughter and her husband back home safe and sound, met them at the station with hugs, kisses and for the expectant mother, a huge bouquet of roses.

Once settled at *Pine Bower*, the couple resumed their former routine, albeit with some changes in expectation of their new arrival. The first order of business was to find a doctor for Rose. Maynard only wanted the best care available for his wife which lead him to Dr. Richard D. Small,[117] at that time Portland's leading obstetrician and highly recommended in the medical community. Small was an attending surgeon at Maine General Hospital, but more important as far as Maynard was concerned, he was on the staff of Lying Inn Pavilion[118] on Brighton Avenue, a division of St. Barnabas Hospital.[119] Lying Inn Hospital was considered the best obstetrical hospital in Portland.

Dr. Small examined Rose and confirmed the date (December 23rd) that the doctor in Honolulu had given her. Whether he also counseled her on diet, weight gain and exercise, as was the case in later years, as a singer, Rose was used to keeping herself in good physical condition. She had had a bout of typhoid when she was 16 and her family felt that, thereafter, she was never robust.[120] Rose herself pooh-poohed the idea that her earlier illness constituted a problem with having a baby. All in all both prospective parents felt there was nothing abnormal about her pregnancy.

◆   ◆   ◆

Shortly after their return, the couple made a trip to Rockland where Maynard conferred with Walter Ladd, who had handled affairs in the Rockland office during Maynard's absence. All things seem to be running smoothly; Ladd boasted of a number of new insurance accounts. Maynard's baby, The Security Trust Company, was showing increased deposits and growing assets. If there were any problems with his own affairs they were ones Maynard felt he could easily handle. While there, he attended a Board of Directors meeting of the John M. Bird Company where the principal business was to elect Sidney Bird, II, Elmer's oldest son, to the presidency of the company. This came as no surprise to Maynard—he had always known that Elmer would see to it that his boys got first crack at the family business. If anyone had asked him how he felt about Elmer's family dominating the family business, Maynard would shrug and remarked, "I knew this would happen. That's why I got out nearly thirty years ago."

Despite his family pride, Maynard wasn't sure that young Sidney was the best choice as president. He would rather have seen William (Case) Bird, now known as Bill and married[121] to a Rockland girl, as head of the company. William was smart and evidenced more leadership qualities than Sidney. If it had to be someone in Elmer's family, Maynard thought Adriel, the youngest of his brother's brood, showed more drive and salesmanship than his older brother.

Rose could hardly wait to tell Annie of the impending arrival of another grandchild. Annie was overjoyed at the news, since she realized how much a child must mean to both parents.

Of her four sons, only Alan remained childless. She knew that there was another side of this stern, remote, rather dour man: one that was obvious when surrounded by children he would play games with them or tell them stories. Although with his intimate friends he was known as a great storyteller, a characteristic inherited perhaps from his great-great-grandfather, William Gregory. 'Old man Gregory', as his descendants called him, lived to be 101 and was known to be a genial host and a great teller of 'downeast yarns'. But children would flock to Alan sensing perhaps the hidden child waiting to come out. Their favorite was the 'what's my name game'. Alan would start the ball rolling by saying "What's my name?"

And the children would shout, "Pudd'ntane".

"Where do I live?" would be his response.

"Down the lane," or sometimes it would be "Down the drain!" the children would cry.

Finally, "What's my number?"

Then there would be a chorus of, "CUCUMBER", winding up with laughter and shouts of glee as the word cucumber was repeated over and over again.

Annie watched with sorrow as the years went by and no offspring was forthcoming from the union between Alan and Adelaide. She could only assume that Adelaide had some physical failing that precluded having children. But now it seemed as if this new addition to Maynard's family could in some way make up for the gap she saw in Alan's family. She had known of Maynard's disappointment in Milton, and was hopeful that a second child would bring more happiness and satisfaction to him.

When Maynard and Rose returned to Portland, their lives settled down into a calm, anticipatory state that must befall all expectant parents. One night after dinner on a perfect Maine summer evening, as they were sitting on the terrace enjoying the view of Casco Bay, Rose broached a subject that had been on her mind for quite a while. Not being one to beat about the bush, she got straight to the point.

"You know Maynard, there is a lot of space on the third floor that has never been finished. The servants don't use it because they have their own quarters above the kitchen." She paused, took a deep breath as if to subdue some misgivings, and continued. "What do you say we fix up that third floor as a little suite for the baby? We could put a nurse's room up there and a playroom for when the baby got bigger. What do you think?"

Maynard smiled as he looked affectionately at Rose's earnest expression. "I bet you've even figured out how it's going to look and what furniture you're going to put in it, haven't you?"

It was Rose's turn to laugh. She knew he was teasing her, and she loved it. "Well not quite, but I did have some ideas about how it should look."

"Well, go ahead, spill the beans!"

"To start with," Rose continued, "we could make two rooms, one for the nurse and one for the baby. We would have to put a bathroom up there too. Would that be difficult? As the baby got older, we might need another room just for her, but for the time being we would need only two rooms and the bathroom."

"Hold on a minute!" Maynard interrupted. "You said *her*. How do you know it's going to be a *her*? What if it's a boy?"

"Well, little boy babies like to live in pretty places. I don't see that that makes much difference," she said rather defensively. Then she laughed, again. "You're just teasing me again. I just hope it's a girl because I think I would know how to handle a girl better. Would you be disappointed if it wasn't a boy?"

"Of course not, dearest," he replied. "You know I want what you want and if you want a girl, then a girl it's got to be! By the way, what have you decided on for a name for this little girl? We haven't talked about that yet."

Rose cast a rather sharp glance at her husband—wondering if he was still teasing her. Then, rather hesitantly, she said, "I had thought perhaps we could name her after Pa—Josephine."

Maynard turned this over in his mind. He was not sure that he wanted to saddle a child with a name like that. She would always be called Jo or Josie. It had sort of tomboyish sound to it and he wanted a girl child to be just like her mother—beautiful, feminine, intelligent and artistic—pretty much in that order. He had considered the possibility that they might name a girl after his mother—Ann or Annie—and that would kill two birds with one stone since they would also be naming the child after Rose's sister.

Before he could say anything, Rose continued, "But if it's a boy, he's going to be named after you, dear—Maynard S. Bird, Jr."

Maynard knew how much Rose cared about her father and decided not to press the point. If this was what she wanted, then she should have it. They would have other children with more opportunities to pick names. He hoped this was only the beginning.

As for the third floor redecoration—there was no argument about that. It was a good idea and Maynard had come to respect Rose's ideas. He would contact Seth Kimball, who was a master handyman, if there was such a thing, tomorrow and get the project underway. However, they reduced the plan to a single large playroom for the time being. On second thought, Rose decided that the baby, and the nurse they would hire, would do better closer to them on the second floor.

In the meantime, Rose went to an artist friend to explain her ideas for decorating what became known as "the baby's room". As the work progressed, Maynard became curious and pestered Rose to find out what was going on.

"I want the finished product to be a surprise for you, dear," she said firmly.

"I hope you're going to let me in on the secret before the baby comes," Maynard responded.

"Oh, you'll see it long before that," she said rather smugly.

The baby's room was finished to Rose's satisfaction around the end of October. One evening after dinner, Rose escorted Maynard up to the third floor and threw open the door of the room. What he saw was a playroom whose walls were decorated with paintings from children's stories. There were characters from Beatrix Potter's stories: here was Jemima Puddleduck wearing a shawl and poke bonnet with a legend underneath that read "she flew beautifully when she had a good start". Peter Rabbit was there, too, as well as Flopsy, Mopsy, and Cotton Tail. *Alice in Wonderland* was represented by the Mad Hatter's tea party that showed him with Alice, the door mouse and the grinning Cheshire cat looking down from a nearby tree.

Maynard was speechless. He kept going from one painting to another and when he didn't know a character, Rose would explain.

"Do you like it?" she finally asked.

"Like it! It's marvelous! What a wonderful world our child is going to live in, and what a wonderful mother she—or he (Maynard was beginning to think in terms of a girl now) will have. It's just great, Rose". He turned to her and put his arms around her. She was so precious to him that all he could say was: "I love you Rose. Don't ever leave me."

As if to underline his devotion, Maynard arranged during that fall for the well-known portrait photographer, Bachrach, to do a series of photographs of Rose. She was shown standing at the foot of the staircase; there was one of her at her piano; and several shots—both full face and profile. There was a picture of her in the flower garden; and the last one obviously taken outdoors, showed only her head and shoulders in a hat and fur coat. When Maynard looked at these pictures some months after they were taken, Rose's serenity and beauty struck him. In the last one, the photographer had captured the essence of her personality in a beaming smile. When the pictures were finished, he had them mounted in a large, blue, leather-bound gold embossed album. At the top of the cover was the single word *Mother* and at the bottom *1921*.

As fall came and the weather became brisk, Maynard was grateful that they had the house on Bowdoin Street to move to. It was closer to the hospital and resolved any problems that winter weather might present in getting Rose there when the baby came. Both of them enjoyed spending the winter in town since it meant they were closer to their friends and to Maynard's office on Exchnage Street. The staff had mixed feelings about the move. As always, Ruth preferred the country environment, while Whiteway and Nancy seemed to like the city better because they were closer to Portland's movies and nightlife. Mike came too, but was expected to do double duty checking on the Foreside house at frequent intervals.

As it turned out the winter of 1921 was a fairly mild winter without much snow by Christmas. Just the same, it was pleasant to be in the city and Rose took advantage of this by seeing more of her mother and giving small parties for her friends. In a letter dated December 19th to Ann Cobb, Rose wrote of having gone shopping with Jennie for andirons for the Cobb Christmas present. She also mentions that she hasn't been able to get around as much this year for presents. "I have thought of many little things I would like to send Evelyn but you tell her next year Santa will do better with play things."

Her letter also shows her impatience with waiting for the baby. "The doctor in Honolulu said Dec. 23rd. It doesn't make much difference to me except I am getting a bit tired of waiting and am so clumsy and heavy it is hard to get around."

In a more cheerful vein, she says, "Maynard is quite amused at me this year as I have all my cards addressed & gifts done up & ready to go for a week."

She closes this letter to her sister by saying, "Much love to you all & a Very Merry Christmas & Happy New Year from us both, Affectionately, Rose."

Their Christmas this year was quieter than the year before. Rose did not feel up to doing much decorating, but there was a Christmas tree with presents under it—many for the baby. Jennie, Joe and Carroll joined them as usual for Christmas dinner, and they called long distance to Ann and Skip. Evelyn, who believed whole heartedly in Santa Claus, broke into the conversation with "Auntie, Auntie, Santa brought me a doll with real hair and eyes that close when she goes to sleep." She was so excited that she hardly stopped chattering and Ann had to take the telephone away from her so the rest of them could talk.

For all of them it was a happy day. As they went to bed that night, Rose said to Maynard, "Just think, dear, next year there'll be three of us."

Maynard smiled and smoothed her hair on the pillow under her head. "This year has been pretty good with just the two of us, but I guess the baby will make our life together different." He had been about to say "more complicated" but changed his mind and added "more complete" instead. He looked down at her, seeing only her lovely face and eyes and then his eyes traveled down to the big mound under the covers that was their child.

"Sleep well, my dearest," he said, "maybe tomorrow will be the day."

20

Inez Turner opened her copy of the Portland Press Herald at the breakfast table on Tuesday, January 3rd and settled down to read the article on the front page about the New Year's Day reception given by President and Mrs. Harding at the White House. As she turned to the continuation on an inner page, her eye caught a familiar name below. Although in the same column as the news article, it was headed by DEATHS. What she saw brought her up short with a gasp. Hardly believing her eyes she read: BIRD—In this city, Jan. 2, Rose Tyler, wife of Maynard S. Bird. She read the article over a second time to make sure she hadn't made a mistake. No, there it was in black and white. After a moment, she looked across the table at her husband and said, very quietly, but in a voice choked with tears, "John, dear, Rose is dead", and with that she burst out crying.

The news got around quickly particularly to those in musical groups. As soon as she recovered her composure, Inez was on the phone to the members of the Rossini Club and her bridge club. Helen Whitney, when she recovered from the shock of the news, lost no time in calling other friends of Rose and Maynard. There was a slightly longer notice in Wednesday's morning paper giving the time and place of the funeral service.

Portland Press Herald
January 4, 1922—DIED

BIRD—In Portland, Jan. 2nd, Rose Tyler, wife of Maynard S. Bird. Funeral services Wednesday afternoon at 2 o'clock at her late residence, 72 Bowdoin street.

As soon as they heard the news, The Portland office of the Maynard S. Bird Company closed on Monday. It was left up to Nelson McDougall to break the news to the Rockland office, which also closed abruptly; and to notify Bond & Goodwin in the Boston office of the loss that had struck one of their principal business associates. But the hardest part for McDougall was to tell the Bird family in Rockland of the tragedy. Thinking that perhaps Henry would be the likeliest brother to break the news to Maynard's mother, he was called first. Henry

190

enlisted Alan's help so that they arrived together at their mother's apartment on School Street late Monday afternoon. Annie's distress on hearing the news of the death of her daughter-in-law was overwhelming.

"She was so lovely", she kept repeating. "And she was looking forward to this baby so eagerly. Ah my poor, poor boy. They were so much in love." She stopped abruptly and looked at both men. "What happened to the child?" With a touch of desperation in her voice as if the worst was still to come, she continued, "Did they lose the baby too?"

Henry reached out and held his mother's hand. "No, Mother, the baby is alive and well as far as I know. It's a girl and she will be named after her mother—Rose Tyler. So there will be another Rose to take the mother's place.

Annie put her handkerchief up to her eyes to wipe away the tears. Trying to smile and only half succeeding she murmured, "Poor little thing—to be without a mother. Poor little thing!"

In a later edition on Tuesday, the Portland Press Herald carried a long obituary in which Rose was praised as "one of Portland's most talented women......She possessed a voice of remarkable quality and was a leader of marked personaltiy."[122]

On Friday, the Rockland paper printed the final tribute to Rose in its account of the Wednesday service.

ROCKLAND, MAINE—COURRIER-GAZETTE FRIDAY, JANUARY 6TH

Funeral services of the late Mrs. Maynard S. Bird, whose sudden death was such a great shock to family and friends were held at her late residence 72 Bowdoin St., Portland, Wednesday afternoon. The beautiful home over which she had presided so graciously was the scene of a remarkable gathering of friends whose sympathy was outpoured in the form of condolences and a display of floral offerings in great number and of rare beauty. The service was brief and simple, the sermon being preached by Rev. Dr. Bradley. The interment was in Evergreen cemetery, the bearers being Henry B. Bird, Alan L. Bird, Milton Bird of Samarcand, N.C., Carroll Tyler, (a brother of the deceased), and H. N. McDougall. Mrs. Bird had been a frequent visitor to Rockland where her rare accomplishments and sweet and beautiful nature won her a place deep in all hearts. Nowhere is there felt a keener sense of sorrow at her untimely taking off than is felt here or a deeper sense of sympathy for the surviving husband and infant daughter, Rose.

◆   ◆   ◆

It was a sorrowful group on a cold bleak January day that crowded around the hillside lot in Evergreen Cemetery. Up to that time it had been a mild winter, but the day had been damp and as someone remarked, 'it smelled of snow'. As if to prove the truth of this prediction a few snowflakes began to fall as members of the group gathered to paylast tribute to one they had known and loved.

A tent had been erected on the grave site—about fifty feet back from the road and on the slight incline. Chairs for the mourners were arranged in several rows so that the immediate family would be under cover. Maynard, still in a state of shock, sat silently with head bowed staring at the coffin as it was placed above the grave. He had been crushed by Rose's death, hardly able to speak; as if some unseen hand had reached out to choke off his ability to communicate. At intervals, he would mumble "Rose, Rose".

Annie Bird sat next to Maynard, holding his hand just as he had held hers when Sidney died fifteen years ago. Did she think of the little boy, now a man, who stood beside her so long ago when they lowered her first born into the earth? Now it was her turn to offer consolation to her grieving son.

Beside them in the front row sat Jennie and Joe Tyler. It had been left up to them to handle the funeral arrangements as best they could, although Rose's brother, Carroll, had helped his father by taking care of most of the details.[123] Joe sat woodenly staring out across the hillside, teeth clenched and jaw jutting out—his face a mask of misery. Jennie's eyes were red with crying and as Reverend Dr. Bradley intoned the final words "Ashes to ashes; dust to dust", sobs wracked her body. Joe, put his arm around her and gently rocked her back and forth as she cried. Ann Cobb sat on the other side of Joe, her tears no less plentiful than her mother's.

Henry, Alan, Milton, Carroll Tyler and Nelson McDougall, all pallbearers, stood behind their wives, who sat in the second row .

Most of those who had attended the service at the house followed the hearse to the cemetery so that a crowd of mourners filled all the space from the gravesite down the hill to the street. Many of the women to whom Rose had been a cherished friend stood in tears as the final words were spoken. All of Maynard's office staff, saddened at the thought of what had befallen their employer, clustered together a little to one side. Ruth Brewster, her eyes red from crying and her work worn hands twisting her handkerchief stood beside Mike Hanratty on the edge of the crowd. Mike's arm was around Ruth's shoulders in an effort to give her warmth and comfort. Nancy and Whiteway, saddened by the loss of their mistress, did not go to the cemetery with the others; Perhaps they wondered what the future now held for them.

Other friends of the couple, both business and social, who had known Rose as a charming hostess and gifted artist, stood with bowed heads, each perhaps thinking of a moment that would crystallized their memory of her. For Mildred Fickett that moment would always be the wedding bouquet of white violets that Rose had given her as the newlyweds started out on their honeymoon.

At the end of the committal service as the crowd drifted back to their cars, the family members stayed unable to tear themselves away from the scene. Finally, as the Tylers descended the hill, Milton took his father's arm and said softly, "It's time to go, Father."

Maynard moved slowly down the slight incline, a bent and broken man. 'Rose is gone,' he thought. 'My beautiful, lovely, Rose. How could this have happened?'

◆　　　◆　　　◆

How could this have happened! These words were not only in Maynard's mind, but repeated over and over by friends and family alike.

Maternal death was becoming less frequent, and a death such as Rose's brought up questions that begged for answers. Unfortunately, few answers were forthcoming, either then or in the future. At the time, those closest to Rose were too overwhelmed by the loss, and too preoccupied with the baby to ask for details on her care while in the hospital, or to question the doctor on whether the death might have been avoided. Time passes and memories fade. Questions that might have been asked at the time later on no longer seemed pertinent.

It was a time when doctors were immune to criticism. Rose had had the best obstetrician in Portland, if not in Maine; Dr. Richard Small's record was impeccable and his reputation faultless. He died in 1934, an honored member of numerous professional societies and service clubs. Thus the answer to the question of what happened must depend on deduction from the few facts available.

Rose was apparently in good health, and had had a relatively normal pregnancy. The Bachrach pictures Maynard had taken of her in the fall show a healthy (and happy) woman. She may have gained a little too much weight, since she mentioned in her Christmas letter to Ann that she felt heavy and ungainly. She was having her first child at age 33—somewhat old to start having children. As a competent obstetrician, Dr. Small would have done a complete history on his patient, and he also would have been aware of earlier childhood diseases and any health problems that might cause complications during delivery. If her earlier bout of typhoid had left her less robust—as her family believed—he would have known about it.

According to oral accounts, Rose's labor began on Friday, December 30th and lasted for three days. Since it was a holiday weekend it was possible that the hospital was not fully staffed and therefore not prepared for a difficult delivery. Both Lying Inn (also known as Dr. Cousin's) Hospital and St. Barnabas, its parent institution have been demolished; therefore no written records remain.

Over a holiday weekend, Dr. Small may not have been immediately available. However, knowing that his patient was already late in delivering, it is difficult to believe he was not in attendance soon after her arrival at Lying Inn. Weather was not a factor in getting to the hospital for either doctor or patient, since newspapers of that date comment on the mildness of the winter.

The baby was in a breach position; breach deliveries are more difficult than when the baby is delivered headfirst. Any obstetrician, or even an obstetrical nurse, can determine this through a simple examination early in the labor process. To allow any woman to labor to the point of exhaustion before resorting to a surgical delivery is, of itself, asking for trouble.

The only official record of Rose's death is a "Certified Abstract of a Certificate of Death". This abstract is so full of errors that it is hard to believe that Dr. Small was even party to its certification. Nowhere does the husband's name appear, although 'Father's Name' was originally shown as 'Joseph Bird'. (This error was corrected on request to read Joseph Tyler). Dr. Small evidently did not sign the certificate, and the date of filing, by a clerk, Frank B. W. Welch, was a week after the death. Burial was shown to be in Calvary Cemetery (Catholic) in South Portland rather than Evergreen Cemetery in Portland. Even the cause of Death—Acute Myocardial Insufficiency Pregnancy—is suspicious since it wasn't Rose's pregnancy that caused her death. It was three days of labor that extended past the point where proper medical steps could have saved her.

Dr. Small was quoted as saying 'he was devastated' by the death.^{124} If the death certificate is any indication, he certainly seems to have divorced himself from the whole proceeding as quickly as possible.

There is, therefore, no satisfying answer to the question of "How did this happen?" The family wanted to believe that there was a completely unexpected situation and Dr. Small used his best medical skills to save his patient, to no avail. However, if Dr. Small waited too long to deliver the baby by caesarian section, as seems probable, he must be judged to have been negligent and irresponsible.

Whatever the answer, nothing could compensate for the tragedy of Rose's death.

21

The months following Rose's death were the lowest point in Maynard's life. Up to that time his career had been one of outstanding achievement and success.

He had found in his marriage to Rose the kind of love he had come to attribute only to younger couples. The difference in their ages only seemed to enhance the bond between them. It was a union of passion and contentment; a natural dependency of physical attraction bound up with emotional compatibility.

When he compared his two marriages, he realized that there had been an element of sincere affection in the first. He had been entranced by Mary's girlish prettiness and the aura of 'big citiness' that was part of her charm. They had been happy (at least he thought they were) during the first years of their marriage. Milton's birth had bound them more closely together until Mary's sexual interest gradually faded to non-existent, and her mother's persistent interference disrupted their home; then he found other outlets for his energy in business and the social contacts it produced. Although he continued to treat her with unfailing courtesy and kindness, Milton was the glue that held them together.

Mary's illness and death had been a difficult time for both husband and son. Maynard felt he had done everything expected of a devoted husband, but it was with a sense of sadness tinged with relief that he saw her buried in the plot in Rockland.

But nothing could compare with the desolation he now felt in losing Rose.

Rose's death—so unexpected, so inexplicable—had left Maynard in a state of physical shock. For days he was unable to speak even to his mother who had stayed in Portland to care for him. It seemed that his mind could not absorb the fact that Rose was gone. A curtain had been drawn across his memory enclosing it in a dark space where only periodic visions of Rose could intrude. He would remember her laugh, her sparkling eyes, how her voice sounded when she sang, how she moved through a room, and all the little idiosyncrasies of her personality. He constantly expected to see her seated at the piano, or perhaps arranging flowers. If he came into a room his eyes would search every corner expecting to find her. Sometimes he was sure he'd seen her. Then the curtain would open slightly and once again he would realize the enormity of his loss. Nighttime was

195

the worst. In their bedroom the scent of her perfume still lingered as a constant reminder. He could not sleep. His mind was too full of Rose so that when he dozed off his dreams were always of her. Often in the dead of night Annie would hear him up, pacing, always pacing. Occasionally she would hear moans, or worse yet, his voice talking to his lost love.

As the days passed, Annie became more and more concerned for her son's well being. She had thought that her presence would help him through the first shock of bereavement. But she found there was little she could do. The servants saw to the running of the house, answered the phone and took messages that went mostly unanswered. If visitors called, Whiteway would take their cards and tell them that Mr. Bird would acknowledge their visit later on. Nelson McDougall came dutifully each day bringing with him papers from the office for Maynard's review. But Maynard wasn't interested and barely spoke to him, his closest friend and business confidant. Nelson would leave downcast and disturbed. When he consulted Annie, it was more for the reassurance that she could give him that her son would recover, she hoped, soon.

Annie went each day to the hospital to see the baby. The nurses allowed her to hold the infant and even feed her at the regular times. Often whether by pre-arrangement or coincidence, Jennie Tyler would join her and the two grand-mothers would take turns fondling the child. But there was a limit as to how long the hospital would care for the baby. Jennie offered to take the baby to her home, but Annie felt that this was Maynard's responsibility and he must accept his role as father.

Something had to be done to shake him out of his emotional isolation. There were practical matters to be resolved; she wanted to go home to Rockland, but couldn't do so until the care of the baby was resolved. After a week during which Maynard had hardly acknowledged her presence, she decided to take the reins in her own hands. Fortunately, Rose had engaged a nurse, Mrs. Snow, to care for the baby. This very caring woman had been in touch with Annie ever since Rose's death; asking would they still need her and when should she come, indicating her availability at a moment's notice. The nursery was ready for the baby, and accom-modations for Mrs. Snow had been made in an adjoining bedroom.

So it was a very determined Annie Bird who confronted her son with her own decision: there was nothing for it but that the baby and nurse must come to the Bowdoin Street house where they belonged—and the sooner the better.

Cornering Maynard more than a week after Rose's death as he was seated one morning in the music room staring at Rose's piano, Annie placed herself on the piano stool so that she obstructed her son's view.

"Maynard", she said in a firm, almost stentorian voice, "there's something we must discuss."

Maynard appeared to look at her, but Annie felt as if he was staring past her at someone or something he saw in the distance.

"Maynard, Maynard, listen to me!" She was almost shouting now. "We have to bring the baby home. Do you hear me? Answer me, Maynard!"

Finally, Maynard shook his head and focused his eyes on his mother's face. "What is it you want of me, Mother?"

"I want you to wake up and act like a father! We must bring Rose's—and your—baby home from the hospital. It's all been arranged; Mrs. Snow is ready to come and her room and the baby's nursery have been ready for quite some time. I want Mike to take us to the hospital to get the baby this afternoon."

"Fine, you go and get the child." It was said as though it was something routine that didn't concern him.

Annie was shocked at his response, "You're coming with me," She persisted. "It's your child—yours and Rose's. It's named after Rose; you can't ignore your own daughter. What would Rose think of you as a father, not willing to bring her baby to the home she had made for her?" Her words held the maternal authority that her son could not ignore.

As she looked at Maynard, so despondent and so sad, there was one more thing to be said and she didn't hesitate to say it. "Maynard", she said, her voice trembling, "This child is Rose's gift to you. For the sake of her memory, you must love the child—Baby Rose—and devote your whole being to seeing that she grows up as Rose would have wanted her to; cared for by a loving father in memory of her beautiful mother. It is your obligation and you must accept it."

With that she stood up and marched out of the room in a manner that allowed for no dispute over her decision.

◆   ◆   ◆

Whether it was his mother's words, or perhaps having the baby in the house where he could see her and hold her, Maynard's depression over Rose's death gradually abated. The wound was deep, and would take some time to heal. Like all wounds, healing started from the surface and worked it's way down to the core where an internal scar would remain, forever a reminder of his loss. Work at the office and a child to come home to acted like bandages, covering the wound while it healed. Little by little as the days went by he put aside his grieving until moments when he was alone.

The baby was healthy and didn't cry excessively or at least didn't seem to. Mrs. Snow turned out to be an ideal nursemaid—gentle and loving yet efficient in her care of the child. The staff, too, lavished their attentions on the baby. Each evening when he returned from the Exchange Street office, Maynard would climb the stairs to the second floor nursery and ask if he could hold the baby.

"Perhaps you would like to have dinner with the staff tonight, Mrs. Snow, instead of eating alone up here," he would say on occasion.

Mrs. Snow would smile and acknowledge the not so subtle hint that Mr. Bird wanted some time alone with the baby. She felt so sorry for him, and wished that she could do more to ease him through this troubled period.

Alone, he would hold the baby, thinking of Rose and how she would have delighted in this small bundle of waving arms and legs. Nothing marred the baby's person. He would look at the little fingers and marvel at their perfection. When the child cried, he would rock her until she quieted down. These were precious moments; they were the closest he could get to his beloved wife.

When Maynard had to go to Boston on business, he tried not to be gone more than a day, returning by late afternoon train so as to be home by dinner time. If business necessitated spending a night in Boston, he would invite Joe and Jennie Tyler to come stay, so that the baby would not be alone with only the servants. Jennie, and sometimes Joe, would visit frequently just to see Baby Rose, or to spell Mrs. Snow so that she could have some time off. Saturdays and Sundays were days when Maynard was most lonely; so he resumed the habit of having the Tylers come to Sunday dinner and stay as long as they wanted to.

Rose's death had been almost as much of a shock to Joe and Jennie as it had been to Maynard. Joe, especially, felt the loss acutely. Rose had been his favorite and to live without hearing her voice and to enjoy their shared love of music was almost more than he could bear. For days he sat lonely and sad, gazing out the window as if expecting to see his daughter come up the walk at any moment. Jennie tried to compensate for her husband's sorrow by taking him at every opportunity to visit the baby. They were both grateful to Maynard for the opportunities of being with him and the child.

One Sunday as they sat in the living room after Sunday dinner, Maynard got out the folder that held the pictures of Rose taken by Bachrach the previous fall. As he leafed through the dozen or so prints, he realized that he had never had any of them framed. This was something he had intended to do before the baby came. Picking out the one of Rose bundled up in her fur coat and broad brimmed hat with the happy smile on her face, he turned to Jennie and said, "I think I'll have this one framed for my office or maybe on my bedroom dresser."

Jennie looked through the pile and pulled out a three-quarter length pose of Rose in her blue chiffon dress with her hand at her bosom, seated in a corner chair. "I like this one better, Maynard. It has a serenity about it that was so characteristic of Rose."

As they discussed the various merits of the two pictures and compared them with the others, Maynard turned and offered an idea that had been in his mind for some time.

"How would you two feel about having Rose's portrait painted from this picture—the one in the blue dress, I mean?"

Jennie looked questioningly at Joe, but Maynard mistook their response.

"You don't like the idea do you?" he said.

"No, no, that's not it. It's just that Joe and I had been thinking the same thing for some time but didn't know how to suggest it to you. We were wondering if you would mind if we took one of the pictures for a portrait. But you got to it first."

At this, Joe smiled—something he had rarely done since Rose's death—and nodded his head. "Go ahead! You have my blessing, and you two will probably do it, blessing or not." Then he added when he saw the look of dismay on their faces, "but it's a good idea."

At this point, Jennie took over. "We were thinking about Grace Burnham. She was a good friend of Rose's and I'm sure she would love to do it in memory of Rose."

"Well, is she good enough?" was Maynard's response. "Perhaps, I should check with the Portland Art Museum and see what they say. And I'd rather she didn't do it for nothing. If it's going to be done, I want it done well and professionally.

"You can go ahead and check all you want," Jennie said rather tartly, "but there isn't any better artist in Portland than Grace. Everyone will tell you so, including those people at the Museum. And I don't think she will take any money for the work. It will be a labor of love."

As it turned out, Grace Burnham was happy and honored to do the portrait. She, like so many others, had been saddened by Rose's death. Later, when the portrait was finished, Maynard had it framed in a gilded frame and hung over the mantle in the living room of the Foreside House where it stayed as long as Maynard had the house. It was a sad but cherished reminder to Maynard of his wife.[125] He later had Bachrach make a blue leather bound album to hold the rest of the pictures. The album had the word *Mother* in gold letters on the cover, and the date *1922*. This was for Baby Rose so that she would have a reminder of the mother she had never known.

◆   ◆   ◆

The winter in Maine, that had been mild at the time of Rose's death, turned cold and snowy during the rest of January and into February. March lived up to its reputation by coming 'in like a lion' and showed signs of spring by 'going out like a lamb'. In Rockland, where Annie Bird had been too long confined indoors since her return from Portland, the arrival of spring—mud and all—inspired her to once again be seen on Main street, shopping, chatting with friends and showing every sign of recovery from the winter's self imposed hibernation. So when she was asked to chaperone an April Fool's party for young people at the Masonic Hall, she accepted enthusiastically. Just getting out lifted her spirits and the idea of music and watching young people dance added to the anticipated pleasure of the occasion. Unfortunately, the evening turned out to be a stormy one with sheets of rain pelting any traveler from head to foot no matter how short the distance from one place to another. She managed to get to the hall without trouble, but by the time she returned home around midnight, she was soaked to the bone and shivering uncontrollably. She took to her bed, dosing herself with every remedy she could think of. Alan, whose office was nearby, stopped in to see her as usual the next day. When he found her sick in bed with a fever, he immediately called the family doctor. At first she seemed to be recovering nicely, but took a turn for the worse on Thursday, and despite the best medical attention Rockland had to offer, she developed pneumonia and died a few days later.[126]

His mother's death dealt Maynard another blow before he had even recovered from the shock of the first. To be faced with a his mother's death so soon after Rose's seemed to pile one misfortune on top of another. Her presence when Rose died gave him the strength and love he needed to get through those first terrible days. It was unbearable to him that now she was gone.

As he stood once again by an open grave in Achorn Cemetery, he remembered that beautiful summer day in 1875 when the casket containing Newbury's body was lowered into the warm waiting earth. He had stood by his mother then, confused and wondering at this first intimation of mortality. But his mother was there then to support and comfort him. He wondered if he had he comforted her by just being there. Once again when Sidney died, mother and son stood together, this time on a crisp autumn day, staring at the yawning hole that would receive his father's body. Who was the comforter and who the comforted that time? He suspected that there had been a mutuality of understanding, of the sharing of events, but most of all, a distinctive and unique relationship with his mother—one that transcended that of his brothers. This was the fourth time he had buried a family member at Achorn Cemetery, and as he looked at the group of mourners that included his brothers and the numerous offspring of his grandfather, 'Old John', he vowed it would be the last.

Standing beside the grave he realized that Rockland no longer offered him any new opportunities. His company was an established leader in both insurance and investment banking. He had founded the Security Trust Company that enhanced both the stature and the returns of his other undertakings, all the while producing a good return to its stockholders. Although he still owned stock in the Bell Company which paid him generous dividends and capital gains, he had not been active in the local operations for many years. There were no further business challenges in his hometown.

As he looked at Elmer standing beside him, he noted that, in his ill-fitting clothes, his brother appeared older than his 61 years and always would be just a small town New England businessman. Maynard was still a stockholder and sat on the board of The John Bird Company, but it was now almost entirely in the hands of Elmer and his family. From Maynard's point of view, Elmer had no 'git up and go'. He lacked the vision, the energy and just ordinary good business sense that had made his father and grandfather such dynamic individuals. Even though his son, Sidney, was assuming more of the burden of running the company, Elmer, during his tenure had not managed to expand the company as Maynard felt he could have. In fact, it seemed to be shrinking and would soon be back to what it had been nearly a hundred years ago—a simple wholesale grocery store. Young Sidney seemed to be doing reasonably well, but Maynard thought Adriel probably had more ambition and business sense than either his father or his older brother. Raymond, Elmer's middle son, had shown few signs of leadership, but would always have the support of his family and a sinecure in the company. There were rumors around town that he drank too much.

Maynard speculated that perhaps Alan had felt the loss of his mother more than either Elmer or Henry. Alan had developed into a competent small town lawyer. With the Bird name and the family backing he had established a busy and profitable practice in the Knox County area. He was also beginning to dabble in local Republican politics, and in this sense was following in the footsteps of his father. Maynard, who knew that Alan could be stubborn and hold a grudge, sensed a feeling of tension between Alan and Elmer, although as long as their mother was alive, there was no estrangements between the brothers.

Of all four of Annie Bird's surviving offspring, Henry had a gentleness and affability to a greater degree than his brothers. Maynard recalled that his mother had referred to Henry as her "Heaven Born Child". He smiled to himself when he remembered his mother and the annual Rockland Baby Beauty Contest in which she had entered Henry. Unfortunately there were no ribbons or prizes for his brother causing his mother to be "quite decided in her opinion that the judges did not know beauty when they saw it!"[127] Now Henry had a fine family, a handsome house on Broadway, and his business, The Medomak Canning Company, was thriving. This seemed to be the limit of Henry's ambition and horizons. He would remain a Rockland boy for the rest of his life. For this he could not be faulted, but it was not what Maynard wanted.

As the service concluded, he turned away and stared up at Dodge's Mountain. Through his mind ran the first line of the psalm read by the Reverend Browne, 'I will lift up mine eyes unto the mountain',[128] but it was not the mountain so much as the further horizon that Maynard sought. No, Rockland had nothing more to offer him. It was time to pull up stakes and move on.

22

In the spring of 1922 Portland was only slightly more welcoming than Rockland for Maynard Bird. The two deaths within the space of three months were barely offset by the birth of his baby daughter. He was now pondering whether it might not be better to leave Maine altogether. He had treasured his relationship with his mother, but now that she was gone, Rockland would no longer play a significant role in his life. Portland was so full of memories of his beloved wife; and the friends they had made would always remind him of her. A move to the Foreside house would forestall some of the unwanted attention from friends and give him time to think about his future.

By the beginning of May the move had been made and Mrs. Snow and Baby Rose were now settled in the suite of rooms on the second floor that, before her death, Rose had designated as the nursery. Sadly, neither he nor Rose's child would ever set foot in "Ye Play Room" or be told the stories of Jemima Puddle-duck. Without consciously acknowledging it Maynard no longer wanted to live in or near Portland just as with his mother's death, Rockland was no longer important in his life.

During the following two months he turned his attention to an accumulation of business affairs. These had been piling up since Rose's death and could no longer be ignored. Under the able direction of Nelson McDougall, and with the assistance of young Walter Hammons, who had taken to investment banking like a duck to water, the Portland office had handled its share of new incoming business. However, there were still many situations that required Maynard's attention and that involved travel to Boston and sometimes New York These were the cities where he was eager to develop new business even if that meant placing the Portland office on a secondary level. Little by little the framework of a plan began to emerge in broad outlines in his mind, one that he would be put into operation over the next months and years. Before he could take any steps to change his business structure, other matters of a personal nature had to be settled.

Despite the more permanent atmosphere of the Foreside house, (Maynard could never bring himself to refer to it as Pine Bower, the name Rose had given it), he knew that sooner or later a decision had to be made regarding the baby's future. As a single man with business demands, he was in no position to create a

203

permanent home for the child, much as he might want to. Perhaps at a later date he would be settled enough to do so, but right now the question of who should be foster parents to the baby was uppermost in his mind. Ann and Skip Cobb had volunteered to take the baby, but, as Maynard explained to Jennie and Joe Tyler, Ann was already burdened with a year old infant and an older child besides. He told them that he felt an additional infant at this time would certainly put a strain on the Cobb household in too many ways. Although he never voiced it to the Tyler family, he felt Skip Cobb's future as an automobile salesman was limited, and did not reflect the kind of financial, cultural or social future that he wanted for his child. He may have realized that others might see this as being snobbish and surely there was an element of condescension in his thinking, but to him it was the natural reflection of his present wealth and his future prospects. He knew he could provide far more generously for Baby Rose without embarrassing the Cobb family by loading them with his generosity.

More important he wanted his child to be a BIRD, and she should grow up knowing her Bird heritage. At present, if he could not make a home for her, she would be best off in Rockland where the Bird family amounted to something. Hadn't his grandfather started a successful business and been an outstanding member of the community? Hadn't his father continued to maintain and even enhance that reputation in commerce, banking and politics? Hadn't Maynard, himself, followed in their footsteps carrying on the tradition of business excellence taking the Bird name to new heights? In Rockland and in Maine the Bird name stood for something. In New London Baby Rose would be closer to the Cobb family and might never know or appreciate her Bird heritage. Even if his son had denied his roots in spite of growing up in Maine, his daughter surely deserved the chance to know and appreciate what her family there stood for.

Maynard mulled over this matter in the weeks following the move to the Foreside house, and concluded that the logical foster arrangement should be with his brother, Alan, and his wife, Adelaide. He recalled how good Alan was with children; how they flocked to him when he told stories and played games with them—almost as if he were a child himself. After twelve years of marriage they still had no children and it didn't look like they would. 'Probably something the matter with Adelaide!' Maynard thought. (Female physiology was still a mystery to him as it was to most men and some women at that time.) Surely the Bird men had never lacked the ability to have children. He had always thought well of Adelaide; she was bright, articulate and Maynard found her—of all his sisters in law—a good listener and very perceptive in respect to business matters. He liked intelligent women, and Adelaide was, in some ways smarter than Alan, although she tactfully suppressed her opinions when it appeared she might be upstaging her husband. She had made him a good wife and there was no reason to think she wouldn't be a good mother. He would talk to Alan—no, to both of them—when he was next in Rockland. That would probably be pretty soon since he and Elmer had to get together, as executors, to work on their mother's estate and finally close their father's affairs. The implementation of this decision was made easier by a telephone call from Rockland.

It was early on the morning of July 11, 1922 that the call from Alan reached Maynard at home before he left for the Portland office.

"Thought I'd better get to you right away," were Alan's first words.

"Why, what's the matter", Maynard responded. He knew that Alan wouldn't be calling this early unless something serious had happened.

"Sidney died," was the laconic answer.

It took Maynard a few seconds to connect Alan's message with the Sidney who was Elmer's oldest son. "I didn't know he was sick", was Maynard's response.

"They're not quite sure what he died of but they think it was something connected with the influenza he had two years ago."[129] Alan continued, "He'd been sick for a couple of weeks with what they thought was an upset stomach. No telling just what it was. The funeral's on Friday."

"How's Elmer taking it?" Maynard didn't really want to go back to Rockland again for another funeral, but he thought Elmer might feel hurt if he didn't attend this one. Elmer was difficult to deal with under some circumstances; now he was probably pretty broken up over this misfortune and would have to be handled tactfully when it came to matters concerning The John Bird Company.

"About as you might expect," was Alan's non-committal answer.

'Alan could be annoyingly obtuse when he wanted to be', was Maynard's first thought. But then he had better not leave Alan in limbo.

"Alan, I was planning to go to Boston on business tomorrow and stay over the weekend. I'll have to see if I can cancel some appointments. You'll be at the office, I assume. I'll be in touch with you there in a couple of hours. I'd better call Elmer too." With that, the brothers said goodbye.

Maynard's decision to go to Sidney's funeral was due in part because with work still to be done on their parents' estates he didn't want to do anything to alienate Elmer. Also, as he had earlier decided, a trip to Rockland would give him the opportunity to talk to Alan and Adelaide about Baby Rose.

After the funeral service, Maynard returned to Alan's home at 246 Broadway. As they sat in the living room—on horsehair chairs and a sofa that Maynard considered among the most uncomfortable he'd ever sat in—he brought up the subject of Baby Rose.

Looking more at Adelaide than Alan, Maynard tried to explain his situation. "You know, I can't really bring up a little baby even though I have a good nursemaid to care for her." He paused and waited to see if there was any comment forthcoming. Neither wife nor husband said anything so Maynard continued.

"I would like to have her brought up in Maine so she gets to know both sides of her family." Pause! Obviously they were not going to make this any easier. "Rockland is the obvious place—at least for the time being.

Here Adelaide in her usual positive manner interrupted. "Maynard, what are you getting at? Do you want to send the child down here, and if so, who did you figure would take care of her?"

"I wondered if you and Alan would like to be her foster parents—at least for a while until I am in a situation where she can come and live with me." This was said in a rather diffident tone, trying to allow them to turn the offer down if they wanted to.

For a moment there was a stunned silence; then Adelaide rose from her chair and went to Maynard, where, in a completely uncharacteristic gesture, she threw her arms around him and said in a voice choked with emotion, "Of course we'll take her. Nothing would make us happier, and we promise we'll be good parents to her."

Alan, also overcome with emotion, only shook Maynard's hand vigorously. In a gruff voice, he managed to say, "We appreciate your confidence in us. Don't worry, we'll take good care of her and keep her safe."

And so the matter was settled.

◆　　　◆　　　◆

Business matters consumed the rest of the summer of 1922 so it was not until fall that the first steps were taken to send Baby Rose to Rockland. In the meantime, Maynard had rented a comfortable apartment in the Beacon Hill area of Boston so that travel between Portland and Boston did not consume as much of his time.

His first move was to dispense with the services of Whiteway and Nancy. While Rose was alive he had justified their employment because of the considerable entertaining they had done. (Besides, he wasn't above using an English butler as a status symbol.) With Rose's death, that need vanished. Neither husband nor wife had enough to do which only increased Whiteway's natural tendency to laziness. Though Nancy was energetic enough, she was, after all, his wife. They were given good references and would have no trouble in relocating.

Ruth Brewster would stay until the baby went to Rockland. In the meantime, she doubled as housekeeper with the assistance of an occasional cleaning lady. Mrs Snow had already indicated her willingness to continue to care for the baby; she had grown very fond of little Rose, who, under her care was developing into a healthy and inquisitive child. Mrs. Snow also enjoyed the country surroundings. "After all, she said, I'm a country girl at heart. Grew up in Topsham; married in Topsham; and buried my Albert there. Can't get much more country than that, can you?"

Mike Hanratty, reliable and nearly indispensable, occasionally turned up bleary-eyed after a Saturday night's Irish outing; but he was always available when needed. With Maynard traveling by train and staying in Boston so frequently, Mike's duties as chauffeur had diminished. Instead he had turned into an all round handyman and gardener, caring for the grounds and doing odd jobs around the place. His presence on the estate provided protection for the property and its occupants. When the baby was taken to Rockland and the house closed, Mike, now in the role of caretaker, lived on in a small cottage on the property.

On a cool, crisp November day, Maynard and Mrs. Snow carrying the baby, set off for Rockland by car with Mike driving. Their arrival had been anticipated and a room in Broadway house had been redecorated and rearranged as a nursery to greet the baby's arrival. Maynard stayed for a few days to see that his daughter had adjusted to the change, Mrs. Snow also stayed to give her advice and any assistance—whether needed or not—to the new foster mother. She could not help boasting a little when giving up her charge.

"You'll find she's just the best baby that ever was," she said to Adelaide. "She never cries—or at least not much and then only when she's wet. Now, I've written down all the things she can eat. She's a real good eater."

Adelaide didn't doubt that for a moment as she looked down at the little round face with the large brown eyes and the smile that showed several teeth poking through the gums. She could hardly believe that she now had a child of her own—even a foster one. It was the answer to her prayers.

◆　　　◆　　　◆

The unexpected death of Sidney Morse Bird, II at such a young age presented problems not only to Elmer and his family but also to the Bird family as a whole. For a number of years Elmer had been training Sidney as his successor to be head of The John Bird Company. In fact, Sidney was acting president when he died. Elmer, already past sixty—a ripe old age in those days to be active in business—had spent his entire life in the family wholesale grocery business. He had counted on Sidney as his successor with Adriel, eventually, as second in command. Raymond, his middle son, would always have a job with the JB Co. but at present did not seem to have either the interest or the capability to handle any executive position. With all this in mind, Elmer felt, not unreasonably, that if he were to continue to run the company he wanted to own the majority of the stock. There was nothing unfair about Elmer's behavior. Maynard, still a minority stockholder, did not protest Elmer's handling of the company or the accumulation of its stock.[130] He had long ago recognized the nepotistic nature of the company and wanted no part of it; but as long as his mother was alive he had retained his seat on its Board of Directors.

Sidney's death postponed the final settlement of both Annie Bird's estate and that of her husband, the first Sidney. Elmer was once more taking an active part in the Bird Company business, while Maynard, preoccupied with his own affairs, focused to a progressively greater degree on his Boston and Portland offices. Therefore the two brothers found it difficult to cooperate in their executors' duties. It was not until December, 1923, that a final accounting was filed with the Probate Court.[131].

The net result of the final settlement, after some discussion among the brothers, was that Elmer got both his and Alan's share of his father's stock in the company. Henry, had received his share earlier when he had started the Medomak Canning Company in 1917. Maynard accepted his share and continued to sit on the Board.[132]

Alan, who had been general counsel for the firm, but had recently resigned due to a falling out with Elmer, was persuaded to exchange his shares of. the family company stock for 379 shares of the Rockland Water Company also held in the trust account. Elmer felt that Alan's Bird Company stock was vital to his ability to run the company. Alan, for his part, was angry with his brother over an earlier argument and now felt he was being shut out of the family business. When he appealed to Maynard for help, the latter found himself caught in the middle.

"Alan," Maynard said, "you'll be better off with the Water Company stock. You can sit on the Board of the John Bird Company without the stock if you want to. Face it, Elmer's going to have to run the company because there's no one else to do it and I can understand why he wants to have as much stock as he can get."

"Elmer wants to shut me out." Alan was adamant.

Maynard was tempted to point out that if Alan hadn't gotten into a fight with Elmer, they wouldn't be having this conversation; but there was no sense in alienating Alan further, so Maynard changed the subject.

"Believe me, Alan, you'll be better off with the Water Company because utilities' earnings are up and going higher. I'm not impressed with the condition of The John Bird Company. Now that Sid is dead and Elmer has had to take it on again, I don't see the business growing. There's no spark there."

Alan took Maynard's advice and as things turned out it was good advice. The Water Company did well in the next few years and Alan prospered.

Eventually, all the heirs signed off on the will and it was filed for probate on December 4, 1923. The settlement of his father's estate contributed to the rift between Alan and Elmer and his family; there may have been other factors, but from that time on Alan never again spoke to Elmer, nor did he have anymore dealings with The John Bird Company.

Although he was aware of Alan's anger over his treatment by Elmer, Maynard, perhaps, did not appreciate the fact that Alan never forgot a real or perceived offense. It was a characteristic that Maynard should have taken more seriously for it would influence their dealings together at a later time. Trying not to get involved in family feuds, Maynard was probably glad his mother was not alive to see two of her sons fighting with each other.

After the final accounting of Sidney's will, a curious incident took place. Belle Cullen, a former employee of The John Bird Company, had been hired by Elmer and Maynard, as executors, to do some clerical work in connection with the will. She had already been paid an agreed upon sum, but in 1924 she presented Elmer with a bill for $350 for additional work dating from 1907. Elmer wanted to pay this out of the estate. Maynard objected, noting that the will had already been filed, and that he and Elmer should pay it out of their own pockets. Elmer refused and took the matter to Probate Judge Oscar H. Emery. The judge refused to allow Elmer's request, and advised Elmer to pay it himself. Maynard, on hearing of the judge's decision shook his head. 'What had Elmer expected, he wondered?' It was just one more evidence of Elmer's poor judgement.

◆   ◆   ◆

During the course of the next two years, the plan Maynard had conceived at the time of his mother's death, began to take shape. Basically, it involved divesting himself of the Rockland and Portland operations and establishing himself in either Boston or New York where he knew there were greater opportunities. He had not found the way to do this until one day in December (1923) he had lunch with his old friends, Ed Fenno and Charlie Meyer of Bond & Goodwin[133] at the Union League Club in Boston.

The Christmas holidays were not happy times for Maynard and he relished the chance to join these two old friends from the Rockland days when he was just starting out in the security business. He had felt for some time that B&G, as he called the company that had given him his start, had become stodgy, which both his luncheon companions verified at least by inference.

"You know, Maynard, the investment business is changing from what we used to know," Ed Fenno remarked over a delicious plate of baked scrod. "But, I guess you know that. You keep up on things more that we do."

Maynard nodded. He knew that he had brought in more clients to the Boston office of B&G than others—including the partners eating lunch with him. He was also aware that if he owned a business like B&G he would get a greater percentage of the net profit on all transactions. That was the reason he had never wanted to become a partner: for him there was no financial advantage in partnership. It didn't seem appropriate, however, to mention these thoughts to his old friends.

Charlie Meyer picked up the conversational ball. "You know, Ed and I are thinking of retiring. I wouldn't be surprised if others would take the opportunity of getting out too. 'Course if we do, there'll have to be an evaluation of the company's assets."

As Maynard looked down at his plate of scrod, the fish seemed to have dollar signs at the head and tail with the word "securities" engraved on its middle. He closed his eyes and shook his head to get rid of the apparition.

Then, looking up, he said in a completely casual voice, "Do you have any idea what kind of value the assets of B&G might bring?"

"Not really," Ed Fenno remarked. "I haven't really looked at our inventory for six months or more. I do know that there are quite a few holdings of utilities and other securities that the company has had in its portfolio for a number of years. No one seems to have paid much attention to them."

Charlie put in his two cents. "If we offer the portfolio to one of the big firms like Lehman Brothers, you know what we'll get—just skin and bones."

Ed Fenno, now came to the point of the conversation, "Maynard, we've worked with you for nearly twenty years. You've always been straight with us, and I think you feel the same way about us, don't you?"

Maynard nodded. He knew what they were getting at.

Ed continued, "How would you like to take this thing over?"

Maynard hesitated. He didn't want to seem too eager. "Let me look it over," he responded, "so I can get some idea of its value. Then I'll get back to you."

After lunch, as he walked across the Common toward his apartment on Beacon Hill, Maynard reflected on the afternoon's events. Here was his chance to cut his ties with Maine and get started in New York. He would not be satisfied with just the B&G portfolio; he wanted the company, especially the prestige associated with an existing name. It would take some doing, but he thought he knew how to manage it. If all went well, by next Christmas he would be well on his way to being the head and principal stockholder of Bond & Goodwin.

23

For Maynard the years that followed Rose's death and the birth of their child were years of both recovery and achievement. They were years in which his emotional balance was gradually restored after the almost concurrent losses of his wife and mother. They were also years of great business activity and the accumulation of wealth. It was the latter, perhaps more than anything else, that gave Maynard's life purpose and direction.

In the 1920s all businesses boomed. New technology and inventions demanded new investment. A growing population, long deprived during the war of consumer goods, now eagerly gobbled up each and every new product that came on the market. Railroads were the best investment one could make. They needed capital—provided by investment bankers like Maynard—to extend their tracks and rolling stock. (A strike in 1922 of workers on the Pennsylvania Railroad that lasted two months did little to dampen enthusiasm for railroad stocks.) Besides carrying passengers, railroads carried the produce of the Midwest and Far West to eastern and western markets. At ports all over the country ships were taking on cargoes of wheat and other staples to feed a hungry Europe, while returning with European goods to be sold in the United States; thus reducing to some extent the war debt of those countries. Skylines of big cities were changing with the construction of more and taller skyscrapers. In the late 20's the Chrysler Building in New York was the tallest building in the world; only to be exceeded five years later by the Empire State Building. Automobiles were more popular than ever with Chrysler, Studebaker and General Motors dominating the higher priced market. Ford, of course, was still turning out the ever-popular Model T always in black; but even that was being replaced by the Model A which now came in several muted colors. Telephones were ubiquitous in homes and all places of business. Household appliances such as refrigerators (called 'Fridgidaires' after their maker), washing machines and other household appliances were making their appearance. Radios had caught on and progressed from the crystal set to cabinet style. To fuel the manufacture of all this new technology public utilities were seeking investment capital. Power companies needed funds to produce electricity. Water companies had to raise capital to extend the public supply of water. A voracious economy clamored for more and more raw material to fuel all industry. In short, demand for investment funds was greater than ever, and Maynard Bird was not the kind of man to allow tragedy and grief to extinguish his appetite for the challenges of this dynamic business world.

◆ ◆ ◆

As a result of his post-Christmas lunch with Ed Fenno and Charlie Meyer, Maynard set about working out a plan to acquire Bond & Goodwin—not just its assets but its name as well. In reviewing the company's inventory, he found that, in addition to stocks and bonds of well-known, listed companies, there was a wide variety of securities and notes. There were partnerships, preferred stocks and joint ventures, many unheard of or forgotten, even deeds to couple of lots on West 68th Street in New York come by, no one knew how. Maynard could see that this portfolio was going to be tough to analyze and dispose of, and would require months of work ahead. He would also need a sizeable loan to buy out the Bond & Goodwin partners.

For the loan he contacted his old friend Charlie Higgins at American Trust. John Boone had long since retired and Charlie had replaced him as Vice-president and Senior Loan Officer. (Maynard liked to think that the utility deal he had brokered ten years ago had contributed to Charlie's success.) In spite of his promotion, Charlie still retained his youthful zest, and greeted Maynard with the enthusiasm of a longtime friend.

Maynard explained to Charlie his plan to take over the Bond & Goodwin firm: outlining the contents of the portfolio and emphasizing that the portfolio would be put up as collateral. In addition, he planned to personally guarantee the loan.

The response was immediate. "How much do you need, Maynard?" Charlie had no reservations about his client's reliability.

Maynard named a seven-figure amount that he felt would be sufficient.

Charlie hardly blinked at the figure. "You work it out with the fellows down the hall," he said. "Give them all the figures and a repayment schedule, and I'll present it to the Loan Committee at their next meeting." The deal was made.

During the next two years Maynard concentrated all his efforts on the takeover of Bond & Goodwin and divesting himself of his Maine commitments. Walter Hammons, whose rise in investment banking had been only slightly less spectacular than Maynard's, bought the Portland office and changed the name to Scott Corporation.[134] Concurrently, the Hammons family also purchased the Foreside house in April 1925.[135] In Rockland, the Maynard S. Bird Company became McDougall-Ladd Company[136] when Nelson McDougall and Walter Ladd bought out Maynard's interests. Finally, he resigned from the board of the Security Trust Company and in due course sold his stock He continued to hold a large block of stock in the Bell system and it's successor A.T.&T. From all these transactions Maynard realized sizable gains.

Though he had previously dealt principally in the Boston securities' market, Maynard planned to make New York his headquarters once the loan with American Trust was paid off. When Jim Auchincloss, the managing partner, resigned his seat on the New York Stock Exchange in October of 1922[137] the rest of the sales force, who were principally commission salesmen, either found employment elsewhere or remained with the company under Maynard's direction. During the course of the changeover, the major Boston partners retired after they received their share of the Company's assets. This left Maynard the sole owner of Bond & Goodwin and, as it turned out, a very wealthy man.

◆   ◆   ◆

Although Maynard had some regrets about leaving Portland, where success and happiness during so many years of his life had been followed by loss and grief, there was no question in his mind that his future lay elsewhere, probably New York. He had made many fine friends in the city and state of his birth and these he would still cherish. Wherever he finally wound up, Maine would always be the essence of his character and personality. He never lost his 'downeast' accent, and in later years he cultivated some of it's more colorful phrases and unique inflections, finding that they gave him a distinction in both business and social circles. For now, however, he felt constricted by what he saw as the State's provincialism and lack of opportunity.

Leaving Jennie and Joe Tyler was the most difficult of all the breaks that Maynard had to make. At 77, Joe had aged considerably; the loss of his favorite daughter was surely a contributing factor. Maynard did his best to reassure the couple of his continued concern for them and their granddaughter, and especially of his commitment to the child: that she would be brought up knowing her mother's heritage as well as that of the Birds. In the following years they were the recipients of various gifts that contributed to their comfort and wellbeing.[138] Also, Maynard set up a trust fund for Baby Rose with he and Alan as co-trustees so that in the event of his death, the child would be well cared for.[139]

◆　　　◆　　　◆

In the meantime, while still separating himself from his Maine commitments and engaged in the details of the Bond & Goodwin reorganization, Maynard made Boston his home base. The apartment he had rented on Beacon Hill needed redecorating in a style more suitable to his advancing position. On one of his increasingly frequent business trips to New York in late 1923 he made the acquaintance of a fellow financier, William Watson, (always known as Billy), and was entertained at the Watson's New York apartment. Admiring the décor, Maynard inquired about the decorator the Watson's had used and was referred to a New York firm run by a pair of dynamic women. This led to one of them, Addah LaHines, being engaged to decorate and furnish the Beacon Hill apartment.

Addah LaHines was a businesswoman at a time when women were seldom found in executive positions in the business world. Women were pretty much confined to career opportunities in the nursing, teaching, and social work professions; and they were almost universally single, as was Addah. Descended from French Huguenot stock, with a generous helping of Scottish thrift in her make up, she had grown up in Kansas City. After her mother died and her father remarried she lived with her oldest sister, Minnie Potvin. From her father's second marriage she had a half-brother, Paul LaHines. Another sister, Elizabeth, always called Lize, was married to a man of Italian descent, Joseph Onorato, and lived in New Orleans. These three siblings completed Addah's immediate family. Somehow there was enough money to send her after high school to a finishing school where her artistic talent and taste made her stand out among the other young ladies and gave her opportunities for employment when she graduated. It is not clear how she got to New York, but by 1923, at thirty-five, when she met Maynard, she and her partner had become well known as talented interior decorators to the moderately wealthy. They catered to a clientele, whose business addresses on Wall Street and summer homes on Long Island and nearby Fairfield County, Connecticut, bespoke their rise in New York society.

Addah was not a pretty woman and certainly by comparison to Mary or Rose she might have been called plain. About five foot five, she had black hair with some natural wave so that when she wore it parted in the middle and loosely drawn back into a bun, as was fashionable at the time, it had a softening effect on her broad forehead and determined chin. Her eyes, deep brown almost black, radiated intelligence and were her best feature tending to draw attention away from her too long, fleshy nose, and thin lips. Despite these physical drawbacks, she was an attractive woman who made the best of her natural endowments; she dressed well and fashionably, and by using her innate sense of style selected clothes—well made and expensive—that enhanced her figure—one of her best features. She had developed over the years a charming social presence—people liked, trusted and respected her. All of this allowed her to cut a fine figure in the social circles she frequented or aspired to.

In their contacts, both in Boston and New York, over the furnishings of the apartment, Maynard found her a bright, perceptive person. It was his first serious exposure to a woman who had made a life for herself in the business world. He appreciated the fact that she was interested in many of the intricacies of finance that had bored Mary and eluded Rose. Her quickness with figures rivaled his. She was competent and organized the redecorating assignment with skill and efficiency.

As long as Addah was involved with the Beacon Hill apartment, Maynard would find opportunities to invite her to dinner, concerts and plays. When the redecorating was completed and she returned to New York, he missed her company and took every opportunity of seeing her on his trips there. Absorbed as he had tried to make himself with his affairs, to the exclusion of any social life, he was beginning to realize that work would never erase the loneliness and need for female companionship that had always been an essential part of his nature. Feeling that he was—or soon would be—at the peak of his career, he was unconsciously considering how he might enhance his living style and social contacts.

Addah welcomed Maynard's attentions enthusiastically. At first her assignment provided common ground for conversation. Little by little she found herself looking forward to their meetings until the time spent with him consumed all her attention outside of her business affairs. She had never met a man with whom she could share her thoughts, and who showed her the respect as an equal she felt she deserved. In some ways she realized that they were alike for they were both ambitious. But they differed in their views of themselves. Maynard's self confidence came from the security of his Maine heritage, where family and community contacts had paved the way for his achievements. Addah lacked this kind of inherent security. She knew that her success was built on her own efforts, for there had been little if any family support. Her mother's death when she was ten meant that she had to rely first on the goodwill of a stepmother, and when that didn't work out, being taken in by sister Minnie, whose drunken and abusive husband made both women's lives miserable. Subsequently she lived periodically in New Orleans with her sister Lize, and it may have been there that she developed her taste for all things French—clothes, food and of course, décor. That she had established herself in New York, able to earn a living and live at a level far above that of her youth was a tribute to her intelligence, determination and ambition. Her position in the business world gave her opportunities to travel abroad as a buyer for her firm—mostly to France where she became fluent in French and knowledgeable in period French furniture. Thus, as Addah saw it, family heritage was a mixed blessing. If she had learned one thing it was that one's social contacts and material goods were important contributing factors to success in the world she wanted to live in.

Maynard, whose only European travel had been to England and whose Maine education and accent defied any effort to learn a foreign language, was impressed with the breadth of Addah's travel, her sophistication and her assured cosmopolitan manner. As time passed and the circumstances of his life changed, he saw her more and more as a suitable wife. He truly cared for her—not with the youthful infatuation of his marriage to Mary, nor with the unquenchable love and romance that Rose had brought him—but with a deep feeling of fondness and companionship that somehow made up for the lack of his former emotions. Furthermore, he had never given up the idea of being a real father to Little Rose. The child was fine staying with Alan and Adelaide for the time being. (In spite of his business obligations, Maynard visited Rockland frequently to see his daughter.) However, he owed it to his beloved Rose—or so he convinced himself—to make a home for the child and give her all the material benefits that his wealth would make possible. In this he believed that Addah would make a good stepmother for his daughter.

Addah's perception of Maynard was one mixed with practicality and genuine emotion. He would make her an ideal husband, and when he asked her to marry him, she happily accepted. Besides sincerely caring for him, she also saw in him the fulfillment of all her dreams. A home, social position and wealth—all the things she had longed for since childhood. She would accept being a stepmother, despite her own unhappy experience with one of that breed, and as she always did, made up her mind to be a good one.

If there was any impediment to their union it was her religion, for Addah was a Christian Scientist, and a devoted one at that. Religion to Maynard was something you were born with—just as he'd been born with brown eyes and straight hair. It is difficult to attribute to him any deep religious faith. He was a Christian; his parents had been Baptists and he had stuck with that denomination until he joined the Congregational Church in Portland where he had found Rose. (If he had withdrawn somewhat from active churchgoing, he excused it on the basis the church's failure to reach out to him on Rose's death. Perhaps he should have asked himself if his own attitude wasn't a contributing factor to this rift.) As for other religions, he knew a few Catholics and some Jews with whom he had done business. Although he admired, perhaps envied, the latter's business acumen, they did not figure in any part of his personal life; they had their own people and their own way of living that certainly would never touch his. Christian Scientists, on the other hand fell somewhere in between. As Maynard understood them, they were Christians who didn't believe in modern medicine or using doctors. That was all well and good for some people, but he had had too much experience with sickness and death to deny the need for medical care under any and all circumstances. So if Addah wanted to impose her religious beliefs on him or his daughter there would be no marriage. On this he was firm.

In spite of her faith, Addah was not a proselytizer and her marriage to Maynard meant more to her than any attempt to convert him. She readily agreed that her religion should play no part in their relationship. Because she was truly committed to Christian Science, she told him that she would continue to practice her beliefs for her own peace of mind, making sure, though, that they didn't interfere with Maynard's well-being or that of his daughter.

◆　　◆　　◆

On January 1, 1926 it was official: Maynard Bird had purchased the assets of Bond & Goodwin with headquarters at 65 Broadway, New York City. The reorganization had gone well, and with a rising stock market, Maynard had become a very wealthy man.

On March 16, 1926, at the age of 57, Maynard Sumner Bird married Addah Louise LaHines in a small, quiet ceremony at the New Orleans home of the bride's sister, Elizabeth Onorato. Milton Bird, as best man for his father, was the only member of the Bird family to attend the wedding. It was Maynard's third marriage and his last.

24

'The Roaring Twenties were at their peak when Maynard married Addah LaHines. In many ways these were the most dynamic, exciting years that anyone could remember. They were times when the industrial and commercial wealth of the United States was engulfing a segment of society whose affluent life style knew few limits. True, there was still a large portion of the population that only benefited, if at all, at a much lower level.

After the war, immigrants, principally from eastern Europe, provided cheap labor for the steel mills, the coal mines and industry and commerce in general. An equally large number of these new immigrants settled in the cities where the women worked in the sweatshops of the garment district's needle trade. Scandinavian and other northern European arrivals were available, especially in the north, as household help, and in so doing commanded relatively higher wages and consequently a higher standing in the labor pecking order. The labor movement was growing, but not to the extent that union demands affected the corporate bottom lines. In the South's more rural environment, the black population was severely restricted by the white ruling class through Jim Crow laws and poll taxes, and by the Ku Klux Klan who took the law into their own hands. Workers in the states below the Mason Dixon line were predominantly black and their wages accordingly lower. The Midwest was still the breadbasket of the country. Cities like Chicago, Detroit and St. Louis, had been affected less by immigration than by the influx of southern Negroes looking for better paying jobs and better living conditions during and after World War I. The Far West was still emerging. New Mexico and Arizona, the last territories to become states were only beginning to grapple with immigration; labor, when it was needed, was drawn from the Hispanic community and occasionally from the numerous Indian tribes. California had long since utilized Chinese and Japanese workers despite the uproar over the 'Yellow Peril' so abhorred in the early part of the century. These immigrants formed their own communities in cities like San Francisco where they worked hard and in a relatively short time founded prosperous ethnic communities.

In New York—the largest and most important city in America—the dividing line between the 'haves and the have nots' was easily visible should one care to

219

take notice. Below 34th Street, to the east and west, there were pockets of gentrification. Gramercy Park maintained its air of refined if somewhat dated living, while the area around Washington Square, known as 'The Village', attracted a more bohemian crowd of writers and artists. But there were also blocks and blocks of tenements populated by newcomers who crowded into cold water flats, and whose lives were devoted to unrelenting work and the dream of a better future. At the tip of the island of Manhattan was Wall Street, the financial heart of America, with its stock exchanges, brokerage houses and international banking establishments. The prosperous, well-to-do section of the city lay to the east of Fifth Avenue, between 34th Street and Harlem, with the unmatched beauty of Central Park as its western boundary. Here there were numerous fine hotels, elegant shops, and up-scale restaurants, which, had they been in Paris, would have merited stars from the Michelin Guide. All the cultural and entertainment attractions were to be found in this part of Manhattan—theaters, opera, museums, art galleries, and that newest diversion, 'the movies'—all the things that make a metropolis such as New York, for those who can afford it, a wonderful place to live. Here too were the "speakeasies" whose existence lent an aura of illegal liquor, crime and prostitution. East of Fifth Avenue there were the grand townhouses of the fabulously rich, and the handsome apartments and apartment hotels catering to the not quite so wealthy.

◆   ◆   ◆

After a month long honeymoon in France, where Addah introduced her husband to the historic elegance and artistic beauty of Paris and its surroundings, the couple returned to New York. Here they settled down in a luxurious apartment at the Drake Hotel on Park Avenue, whose prestigious address came close to fulfilling many of Maynard's dreams of status. He had finally arrived! No longer the small town boy from Maine, he now associated with many of the leaders of business and finance. Each day he went to his office down town on Broadway in the Wall Street area in his Studebaker town car driven by a liveried chauffeur. He dressed for dinner every night in a tuxedo or tails depending on the destination of the evening. Addah had a closet full of evening gowns, some of which she had acquired in Paris. Their social life included the opera, the latest plays and musicals, and of course entertaining and being entertained by their growing circle of friends.

Since Maynard's business didn't run by itself, there were still details and decisions to be made that could not be left to junior associates or staff. While he was abroad, he had been able to communicate by cable and if necessary by transatlantic telephone with Jim Auchincloss' son, Hugh, who had been temporarily put in charge. (How times had changed since his first adventure in getting the telephone cable laid between Rockland and Vinalhaven. In Paris he had actually telephoned New York via the transatlantic cable.) Once back in New York, there were many business affairs—and some new opportunities—that required his attention. The summer of 1926 was spent mostly in New York, although both he and Addah recognized that year-around living in the city was out of the question. Their friends, the Watsons and the Auchinclosses, had both built homes along the shore of Long Island Sound in the Fairfield County (Connecticut) town of Southport. This area was on the verge of becoming almost as exclusive as the Greenwich-Darien enclaves. Next to Southport the town of Fairfield included an area called Greenfield Hill. These exurbs were beginning to attract summer residents whose elaborate homes and estates gave meaning to the word 'exclusive' It was on Greenfield Hill that Maynard and Addah found an eleven acre parcel of land that met their aspirations.

The site they chose was superb. Located on the highest point of Greenfield Hill it presented a breathtaking vista of Long Island Sound. Maynard had always needed to be close to water; the Foreside house had allowed him to get an unimpeded view of Casco Bay. Here he was farther away, but still able to see water that led ultimately to the vast expanse of the Atlantic Ocean he had known in Maine. Already, Addah was thinking of the kind of house they would build: a French manor house of a style she had frequently seen in the French countryside. For her it would be a dream fulfilled.

Construction began in the spring of 1927. There were already several buildings on the property; here they stayed on weekends during construction in a small two-bedroom cottage that later became the caretaker's house. Another small building was temporarily converted into guestrooms where Lize and Joe Onorato stayed when they visited that summer. Milton and Helen also put in an appearance; for they were in the process of moving to the town of Norwell, south of Boston. (Helen had inherited part of an estate from her Aunt Florence. They had evidently found peach farming in North Carolina unprofitable.) In the fall of 1927, with construction well underway, Addah and Maynard made another trip to France to buy furnishings for their new home. With her business experience, sense of style and former connections in France, Addah took advantage of lower European prices to accumulate many valuable antique pieces—furniture, art works and other decorative items.

The house was ready for occupancy by June of 1928, although the landscaping was still a work in progress. An arriving visitor would drive through existing stone gates to a fork in the gravel drive. Bearing to his right, through a leafy archway of beeches and maples, he would see the house stretched along the eastside of a forecourt where the drive circled a rectangular grassy area. Later clipped privet hedges enclosed the drive, completing the framing effect of the house. The French manor house motif was unmistakable. The façade in the symmetrical style with its centered entryway was both elegant and simple and was dominated by a massive hipped roof out of which protruded two large chimneys. Balanced wings at either end of the central portion extended the structure to give the building additional size and distinction.

The interior of the house was as elegant as the exterior. Formal rooms were furnished with the antiques and period pieces brought back from France. The dining room was distinguished by panels, on three walls, of oil paintings of French pastoral scenes done in a Louis XV style. A circular staircase led to the second floor. Three bedroom suites offered luxurious privacy; one suite in the south wing was reserved for Little Rose for the day she would come to live with them. The north wing on the second floor over the kitchen and pantry areas housed the servants' quarters.

Maynard selected the landscape architect—a Maine woman, Louise Payson—he had known in Portland. The French style was reflected in the terraces, the parterre, and a reflecting pool reached by a pair of semi-circular steps from the upper terrace. There were numerous clipped hedges, a formal flower garden and two *allées* of linden trees clipped yearly to form an arbor.

Maynard's rose garden was the outstanding feature of the grounds—a reflection of his love for Rose, but on another level his need to return to the days of his youth when everyone lived so much closer to nature. Whatever the reason, it became Maynard's passion, and he made it into a showpiece of the area. There were more than two hundred hybrid teas, planted according to their type and color, in beds facing each other; the beds were separated by a grassy, slightly sloping walk that ended at a small pool and fountain. Trellised arbors held climbing roses of different varieties. Maynard could always find rest and relaxation in the tending of his roses. Up early as was his custom, he watered, sprayed and pruned the plants assiduously, furnishing his home—and the homes of many of his friends—with blooms from Memorial Day to Thanksgiving. He exhibited his roses at Garden Club shows and at the annual Grange Fair winning ribbons and prizes at both events. Some years after his retirement, he was invited to lecture at various garden clubs on the growth and cultivation of roses. His lectures were illustrated with drawings and samples of roses, and even a three-dimensional cut-away showing the way soil should be prepared for a rose bed.

In an area nearer the caretaker's cottage and extending eastward, he oversaw the planting of a kitchen garden. The vegetables harvested here provided fresh produce in summer and were available for canning in the fall. Additionally, peach, apple and pear trees provided fruit to be eaten fresh or canned. The only live stock Maynard wanted on his 'gentleman's farm' was the annual batch of 3-day old chicks that grew into broilers, egg layers and eventually roasters, providing another source of food. He remembered all too well having to milk cows and groom horses in his childhood. He would have none of that at his new home and left the care of the chickens—and an occasional duck or goose—up to the caretaker.

How did Maynard feel about this beautiful domain once it was finished? Certainly, he was proud of it, and never questioned, as others might have, the extravagance in its creation. If Addah's influence predominated in the style and design, Maynard, nevertheless saw the estate as the hallmark of his success. He had the money to spend and had decided there was no better way than this estate to express his social and financial achievement. He was proud of Addah's role in its creation and never missed an opportunity to praise her taste and ability to create—as he saw it—this masterpiece. She also gave the estate its name. It was called it *Mon Repos.*

◆   ◆   ◆

Shortly before his marriage, Maynard learned of Joe Tyler's death in Florida where he and Jennie were spending the winter. For Maynard it meant just one more link with Rose was broken. He still cherished the memories of Sunday dinners with Joe and Jennie and the afternoons spent with the old veteran, listening to the stories—probably exaggerated—of his wartime escapades. (In Joe's mind there had been only one war and that was the Civil War.) Unable to attend the funeral, Maynard made a point of going to Portland as soon as they returned to New York after their marriage; even leaving Addah for a few days to make the trip. On their return from Europe, business affairs in Boston gave him the opportunity to stop off in New London where Jennie was staying (temporarily) with the Cobbs. It was important to Maynard then, and for the rest of his life, to maintain close ties to Rose's family—both for himself and for the sake of their daughter.

During the first year and a half of their marriage, while Addah devoted most of her time and attention to the house in Connecticut, Maynard had business and other affairs that demanded attention. He still made business trips to Boston and Maine—Portland usually but occasionally to Rockland, where there were still a few loose ends, and where he would have an opportunity to visit his daughter. He had not divested himself of his interest in The John Bird Company where he was still a minority stockholder and a director.[140] The company was doing reasonably well, even though Elmer had resumed the presidency. The last time Maynard had seen Elmer in September of '26, he noticed evidences of illness in the pallor of his brother's skin, the hoarseness of his voice and a shrinking of Elmer's usually sizeable girth. Maynard remembered seeing the same symptoms in his father nearly twenty years earlier. It was not unexpected, therefore, when Henry called him one February (1927) morning to tell him of his brother's death.[141] Although they had not been close as children, Elmer's death seemed to Maynard just one more sign of the chipping away of family structure. Now he would be the only one who remembered the birth of Henry so shortly before Newbury's death; and how the loss of her first born had had such a devastating effect on their mother. In his mind's eye Maynard could see himself and Elmer standing on either side of their parents each clutching a parental hand as Newbury's coffin was lowered into the grave. Alan and Henry were left now, but they wouldn't have the same memories that he and Elmer had had. Although he was saddened by his brother's death, he would not go to the funeral; he had had enough of Achorn cemetery and the sad memories it evoked.

By the summer of 1927, with the start of construction of the house, Maynard decided it was time to introduce Addah to his family in Rockland, and at the same time see how things stood with The John Bird Company. Adriel had taken over the leadership after his father's death and as far as Maynard could tell was handling things well. Although Maynard thought the company really needed new blood and would benefit by outside leadership, he found that Adriel and the rest of Elmer's family, as majority stockholders, were not interested in non-family participation.

Maynard was anxious for Addah to get to know Rose and to meet his Maine relatives. (At this point, Maynard no longer referred to his daughter as "Little Rose", but only as "Rose". It was unfair, he felt, that Addah be constantly reminded of his earlier wife.) Shortly after they arrived and had settled at the Samoset, he brought the child to meet Addah. What she saw was a five-year-old with big brown eyes, straight hair cut in a Dutch bob topped with a big yellow taffeta bow. The child seemed tall for her age as far as Addah could tell, but she looked nothing like her father. Addah assumed Rose would eventually look like her mother and in that she was right.

"How-do-you—do", Addah said as she made an effort to shake hands with Rose.

Rose didn't respond, but merely stared at Addah.

"I'm going to be your stepmother. Do you know what a stepmother is?" she asked.

Rose nodded her head, and said in a small voice, "Cinderella had a stepmother."

This was not what Addah had expected and it left her a little non-plussed. Maynard came to the rescue.

"But Cinderella's stepmother was wicked. This lady is a good stepmother. You know that I'm your father and since she's my wife that makes her your stepmother. And I would <u>never</u> marry someone who wouldn't be a <u>good stepmother.</u>"

They planned to have tea in the Samoset salon so Addah resumed getting ready. The child stood shyly beside her without saying a word watching while she brushed and arranged her hair powdered her face and put on some lipstick. Only the rapt attention reflected in those big brown eyes as she stared at her new stepmother; indicated how fascinated the little girl was by these actions.

Later, they would decide that Rose should call her new stepmother, Aunt Addah in order to minimize any confusion in the child's mind; she was already in the habit of calling Adelaide, "Mother". If Addah was a little disappointed that she couldn't be called mother, she was sure that in time, Rose would understand and give her the title she deserved. In the meantime, Rose was Maynard's daughter. Addah loved the father; she would love the daughter too.

During their visit, Henry and Edith gave a party for Maynard and Addah at their cottage on the shore at Owl's Head. In retrospect, the party was one of the last gatherings of the Bird family for many years. It included mostly those members descended from the first Sidney's branch: Elmer's widow, Emma, and her sons, Raymond, with his wife Katherine, and Adriel. So were two of the three children of Sidney, their dead older brother. Alan and Adelaide came despite their estrangement in recent years from Elmer's family; and William (Case) Bird, the descendant of the first Adoniram, and his sister Madeline were also invited. This William was a particular favorite of Maynard's, who had earlier recognized William's ability and intelligence. At this time, William's marriage to Ruth Gurdy had ended in divorce and it may have been during this summer's visit that

Maynard offered to help him obtain a position in New York at the brokerage firm of Goldman Sachs.[142]

A long table, set on saw horses and covered with oilcloth, was set up outside the kitchen door of the cottage. The table was set with the usual cutlery: shell crackers and picks; dishes for drawn butter and plates of lemon sections. All were placed on the table where they could be shared. Each place had a coarse quality cotton napkin large enough to be tied around the neck as a bib. Several large buckets were strategically placed on the ground—at either end of the table and on each side in the middle. Edith and Adelaide with aprons covering their summer dresses oversaw the kitchen cooking which included fish chowder, native beans and salad of local greens. The men cooked the clams and lobsters over an open fire on the beach. Homemade pies—apple and blueberry—made up the dessert: all in all the standard Maine Shore Dinner.

Maynard had warned Addah that the party would be a quite informal, but Addah with her Midwest background, her French and Southern affectations, and her New York sophistication, was quite unprepared for the casualness of the event. She had dressed in the simplest dress she had, but she still felt overdressed compared to the other women present. She was seated at one end of the table between Henry and his oldest son, Fred, all went well at first. She declined the steamed clams because she may have misunderstood what was meant by 'steamahs'. She enjoyed the fish chowder, which was delicious, and made a mental note to ask Edith how it was made. It was with the arrival of the lobsters—hot and steaming, encased in their bright red shells—that she began to question her ability to cope with this so-called delicacy. Of course she had had lobster before—Thermidor, Newberg, Mousse, and Homard a la Francaise—but nothing quite like this. Since she had never seen cooked lobsters in their shells before, she had no idea how to eat them. Certainly you didn't eat the shell, but how did you get the meat out?

It was young Fred Bird, sitting next to Addah, who, having seen the expression of dismay on her face, came to the rescue. "Here, let me show you how to handle this thing." With that he picked up her lobster with both hands and broke it in two—the tail in one hand, the body with the claws in the other. As the 'juice' squirted out on to the plate, Fred plucked Addah's napkin from her lap and tied it around her neck.

"There", he said, "that will keep your dress from getting splashed and all smelly."

"Thank you," Addah said in a weak voice. "What do I do with it now?" She felt embarrassed to ask this young man, who seemed to be the only one paying any attention to her, to help her with her food; when he tied the bib around her neck she felt like a small child.

"I usually take the meat out of the tail first and leave the claws to the last." As he said this, Fred picked up the tail portion of her lobster and, tearing off the tail fins, deftly pushed the meat out with his forefinger.

"You crack the claws with the crackers and pick out the meat with a pick or a fork. You can also eat the green stuff under the body shell; it's called tommale, although you may not like it. Not everyone does."

Addah tried to follow Fred's directions, and although she found the lobster meat sweet and tasty, her enjoyment of the meal was marred by the table manners of the other guests. Most of them, including her husband, saw nothing wrong in using their fingers to dip pieces of lobster in butter or to drink the 'juice' directly out of the shell. But the most disgusting thing, from her point of view, was pitching the shells in to buckets. She watched as a shell would go sailing behind someone's back landing in a bucket with a clang. Occasionally, when a particularly good throw hit the bucket, the pitcher would be applauded with a chorus of, "That were a good 'un".

◆   ◆   ◆

If, on her first trip to Maine, Addah had hoped to impress her new relatives with her sophistication and *savoir faire* and they her with their 'downeast' life style, the visit had proved a disappointment to both.

25

Nineteen twenty-eight and nineteen twenty-nine—these two years—represented the apogee of his career to Maynard. He had achieved success in business beyond anything he had imagined when, in 1898 he had financed a telephone cable between Rockland and Vinalhaven. This had proved to him that you could raise untold sums for all manner of businesses if you just knew how to go about it; and <u>you could make money doing it!</u> Now, established in New York, he was affiliated with some of the most prestigious members of the banking community, and his wealth was opening doors of acceptance in social circles as well.

He and Addah spent their winters in the New York apartment at the Drake; they visited New Orleans for Mardi Gras where they received invitations to several of the balls; and they made occasional trips elsewhere when Maynard's business permitted his absence. They had their wonderful estate in Connecticut for a summer residence—at least for the present. 1928 was their first summer there and Addah had hired a house staff through a New York agency that consisted of a cook, a downstairs maid and an upstairs maid; in addition, the chauffeur and caretaker were full time employees. (The staff would be increased the following year with the addition of a kitchen maid and a second downstairs maid.) This was also the first summer that Rose came to stay with them in Fairfield, so an *au pair* was engaged to take care of her. (Maynard and Addah made a chauffeur driven trip to Rockland to get Rose and bring her to Fairfield. It was nearly the last visit to Maine that Addah would make.)

In Fairfield their circle of friends grew as a result of joining several clubs. Maynard was not particularly athletic, but he saw the advantages in business and social contacts that club membership could provide. They joined the Sasco Hill Country Club in Southport and the Black Rock Yacht Club in an area between Fairfield and Bridgeport. It didn't matter that Maynard was a real duffer and had no yacht, although it is possible, given his nautical heritage, that he had contemplated such an acquisition. He and Addah used their memberships to attend the frequent dinner dances at both clubs, and Rose took swimming lessons at the Black Rock club pool. (Later he and Addah would find membership in the Fairfield Beach Club more congenial.) They also joined the Fairfield Hunt Club;

bought a horse for Rose—an overage, retired polo pony named Major—and enrolled Rose in riding lessons.

Weekdays, Maynard commuted to New York by train from the Southport station at 8:00AM and returned around 6:00PM. In both directions the train carried a 'Club Car'; the privilege of riding in it was available to him and other businessmen by invitation only. Weekends were spent socializing with their new friends, and, of course, overseeing the progress made on landscaping of the estate—in particular the creation of the rose garden.

Addah's time was taken up with the house and shopping in downtown Fairfield. The town was now beginning to take on the distinction of an up-scale exurbian community. The Post Road—the main thoroughfare between New York and points further east—ran through the middle of town with shops on either side of the road. It still had some of the characteristics of a country town of bygone days with a blacksmith on one corner and hitching posts at intervals along some of the curbs. Since Addah didn't drive, she relied on the chauffeur to take her everywhere; she would dress appropriately, including a hat and white gloves, for her sally into town to shop for weekly provisions. The specialty grocery run by the Mercurio family got most of her trade although she would occasionally stop at the A & P for the more every day necessities.

During their first summer in Connecticut, Addah joined the local garden club where she made a number of friends and gained a reputation as an expert in the art of flower arranging. Later, as the gardens at *Mon Repos* matured, she invited some of her club members to lunch and an after lunch tour of the gardens enlivened by discussions of horticultural subjects. She also found other friends who shared her interest in mah jong, Bridge was another game in which she and Maynard shared a mutual interest; when they entertained at dinner parties for eight, two tables of bridge in the living room followed dessert and coffee.

New York was still the focus of shopping for clothes and other items unlikely to be found in the 'country'. Addah still bought most of her clothes in "the city", and with Rose now a part of the family—at least for the summer months—she felt it necessary to take her to New York to be outfitted. Local stores in Fairfield and Bridgeport did not carry clothing that suited their Fairfield life style. Of special importance, from Addah's point of view, was the condition of Rose's hair. (In Rockland, Morris Derry, Adelaide's brother-in-law, was a barber. He was considered skilled enough to cut the hair of most of the children in town; little boys got clipped up the sides leaving a tuft on top of their heads, while little girls sported Dutch bobs.) Nothing would do but to have Rose's hair styled at Best's, (an upscale New York department store), children's hair salon. Addah found a great deal of satisfaction in shopping for her stepdaughter and she spared no expense in procuring the best and most fashionable childrem's clothes available. She was undoubtedly trying to copy the styles she had seen on children in France, never thinking that such clothes would be out of place in a small Maine town where Rose would spend most of the year.

◆   ◆   ◆

On July 16, 1928, Maynard celebrated his 59th birthday. If he looked in his dressing room mirror that morning, he saw a man whose hair had thinned somewhat and was now sprinkled with gray as if a silvered comb had left evenly distributed streaks. His face was full—perhaps a little fuller than it should be—as was his waist. Although he disliked the term, he was looking rather portly—a concession to good living. His eyes under heavy brows were still expressive of intelligence and humor, and could assume a look of cold, hard bleakness when angered. He didn't anger easily, but when he did he could demolish his adversary with words that left his opponent without an effective response. His neatly trimmed, graying mustache still covered the rather sensual mouth; the chin below was firm with little evidence of the flabbiness that comes with age. The lines from his nose to the corners of his mouth were the sole features of a man past fifty. He had never liked the shape of his nose, which might be referred to as 'Roman' with a high bridge and a downward pointing tip. Nevertheless, three generations were sufficient to wipe out any self-consciousness and he no longer gave this genetic characteristic any thought.(Maynard always attributed his nose to his grandfather, John Bird, but it is more likely that the shape came from Clarissa rather than her husband.)

He dressed, as always, meticulously; a practice he had followed since childhood. The same London tailor, who made semi annual visits to New York, had served him for many years. Maynard's wardrobe consisted of clothes appropriate to every occasion, perfectly fitted and made from the best materials available. He knew he presented a tasteful, dignified, but unpretentious appearance that proclaimed his level of success.

He was not thinking as much of his appearance that morning in July as he was taking stock of his personal and financial situation in relation to his age. In another year he would turn sixty; his father had pretty much retired in 1900 at 60 and Elmer would have retired at that age or slightly older if his son, Sidney, hadn't died so unexpectedly. Both father and brother had been dead in less than ten years after retirement and Maynard didn't want that to happen to him. He was healthy, albeit a little overweight, and there was still a lot he wanted to do. He looked forward to more travel, especially in the Far West. Except for the train trip to the West Coast with Rose, he had seen nothing of the great national parks that had become renowned throughout the country. There was a lot more of Europe to see as well; only Germany would be omitted, since he made no secret of his dislike for Germans—a hangover from the war.

In business, Maynard was concerned with the Wall Street environment of recent years. The bull market had attracted hordes of young speculators, traders and investors seeking a share of the wealth flooding into the market place. Many had amassed substantial fortunes before they turned thirty, and they viewed the possibility of a market collapse as a thing of the past—inapplicable to their situation. Maynard, however, with the wisdom and experience of more than thirty years in the ups and downs of the securities' market, could see storm clouds on the horizon and did not intend to be around when the lightening struck. He had recently declined several offers for underwriting new issues. Some of these were attempts to refinance old debt. In addition, the stock and bond issues appearing on the market were not soundly supported; and their value would inevitably fall with very, very substantial losses to investors. Securities were being bought on margin with as little as 10% down; the balance came from loans arranged by brokers or underwriters, who thus earned substantial profits. From Maynard's point of view, all of this contributed to his reservations about the soundness of a market that seemed, more and more, to be functioning 'on margin', and trading as if it were a gambling casino.

During the course of his career, Maynard had always taken advantage of the leverage inherent in the handling of loans and borrowings. In the coming months, he made sure that he, personally, stayed only with those stocks and bonds he knew enough about to feel secure—taking profits wherever possible. He worked on getting himself and his company out of contingent liabilities by demanding more margin payments from his investors or, if necessary, selling stock on accounts unable to raise their margins. He also counseled some of his clients whose investments showed gains—and there were plenty of gains to be had in a market where stock prices were doubling and sometimes tripling in a year[143]—to sell and take their profits. By the following July (1929), he had been able through such transactions and others to considerably reduce Bond & Goodwin's debt to banks from whom he had borrowed money to lend to other investors. Additionally, he had managed to sell his underwriting interest in a number of issues to other brokers, further reducing his and his company's exposure to a market reverse which he now felt sure was coming. His own personal portfolio showed numerous sales and transfers of funds to government bonds and holdings of secure stocks, like "Ma Bell", insurance companies and, of course, utility companies—those areas of business that had been the foundation of his success. Altogether, he was satisfied with his personal financial position when, after their second summer at *Mon Repos,* he and Addah moved back to New York in the fall of 1929.

When the stock market crashed on Wednesday, October 23rd, continued down the next day, always known thereafter as 'Black Thursday, and then went down, down and down in the week that followed, Maynard was personally in relatively good shape. Only the severity of the crash surprised him. Bond & Goodwin had been hurt by the crash, but the steps he had taken in the past year to reduce risks and shore up what remained, had left it solvent if much diminished in value. From past experience, he expected that after a few months the market would rebound, and that he could perhaps continue with the investment banking business in a more limited way. He was finding that he just didn't want to go out of business on a negative note. He knew that, whether from good judgement and experience or just plain luck, he had weathered the worst financial storm the country had ever seen. Others had not been as fortunate. There were a number of his acquaintances in the banking community, who resorted to suicide rather than face a life of indebted impoverishment. There were many others including, as he later found out, some of his Fairfield neighbors, who had been left practically penniless.

And the market did rebound slightly; but by the spring of 1930 with four million unemployed, breadlines appearing in New York and thousands now on relief, it became obvious to everyone, including Maynard, that this was no run-of-the-mill financial panic. There was a "contagion of fear"[144] which, by the fall of 1930, had turned into terror. All over the country unemployment was rising, soup kitchens and bread lines were commonplace in all cities, and relief, or the dole as it was also called, had become a way of life for countless destitute families. Unemployment had risen to eight million by March of 1931 and was still rising and eventually reached at least 20% of the work force. Mortgage foreclosures reached unheard of levels and homeless families found shelter wherever they could—in railroad box cars, in flophouses, in parks and even by building tarpaper shacks in communities that became known as "Hoovervilles".

What was the federal government doing? Practically nothing! Hoover, in a statement in February 1931, allowed that federal aid would destroy the principles of self-government—of individual and local responsibility and mutual self help—on which the nation was founded; and that he had faith that that day would never come.[145] So the Hoover administration expected states and communities to provide relief to the millions who needed help. Unfortunately, local credit and fiscal resources were drying up and local relief was overwhelmed.[146]

As a staunch Republican all his life, Maynard probably agreed with Hoover's distaste for government interference in the form of economic aid to the homeless and the hungry. His Maine heritage had always stressed individual responsibility and abhorred the idea of public assistance in any form. That was reserved for those who lacked the motivation or the intelligence to pull themselves up by their boot straps. Maynard was not an uncharitable man; he was generous in his contributions to private charities feeling that this was sufficient support for those who could not care for themselves. But that was the extent of his largesse. Government simply should not interfere in people's lives or their businesses.

By the summer of 1930, Maynard had concluded that the financial markets were not going to recover sufficiently to warrant continuing his involvement in the investment banking business. It was time to finally close Bond & Goodwin and get on with his retirement life. The times also dictated the economy of his personal assets. He and Addah discussed their financial situation and agreed that it would be prudent to cut their expenses wherever they could reasonably do so. Maynard had great respect for Addah's business judgement and had adopted the habit of including her in all major decisions. (This was something he had never done with Mary, and he had not been married to Rose long enough to know whether she would have wanted to be included.) They were solvent, debt free and far better off than many they knew, but there was no harm in taking precautions while they were available.

The first decision was to give up the apartment at The Drake and spend the winter in Fairfield. Maynard could still commute to New York a few days a week, which seemed to be all his business now demanded. The Club Car had been discontinued due to lack of subscribers of which he was one. Memberships at Sasco Hill Country Club and The Black Rock Yacht Club had been cancelled; the latter replaced by the Fairfield Beach Club at a lower fee. In the fall Addah discharged the kitchen girl and the second downstairs maid with good references, but without any thought as to their future employment. That was the concern of the agency from which they had been hired.

Mon Repos, Greenfield Hill, Fairfield, Connecticut

Addah LaHines Bird (1888–1952)

Maynard with Daughter, Rose (1943)

Second Greenfield Hill House

One major change in the pursuit of economy was to dispense with the services of a chauffeur. Ever since Mike Hanratty, Maynard had made a practice of hiring Irishmen to drive whenever possible on the theory that most police in Boston and New York were Irish and having an Irish driver was protection against unwanted tickets or interference from city police. However, the latest driver, Joe Ziminski, was of Polish origin and not particularly smart or a very good driver. Addah didn't like him and it was mostly for Addah's convenience that they had a chauffeur. In discussing areas of economy, Addah was the one who suggested they get rid of the current driver and she would learn to drive.

"If I can't drive better than Joe," she said in a manner that brooked no contradiction, "then it would serve me right if I couldn't go anywhere."

So Addah learned to drive. She turned out to be a good and careful driver albeit a rather unique one. Once she felt comfortable behind the wheel of a car, she became her own backseat driver, commenting on the proper way to drive and castigating other drivers for their failures. If she was alone in the car, other drivers might notice her lips moving and conclude that she might be singing; but this was not the case: she was talking to herself usually out loud. If she was not alone, she was perfectly comfortable sharing her automotive comments with her passengers unless there was something else to talk about.

They still needed a permanent, live in caretaker who could double as a gardener. Joe Link, a young man of Hungarian descent, who had heretofore been employed as a gardener on a part time basis, filled this position. In addition to a modest salary, he and his wife were offered the occupancy of the caretaker's cottage. This turned out to be a fortuitous decision for Joe and his wife, Martha, became a fixture on the Bird estate making it their home for many years.

The economy was still depressed and if anything getting worse in the spring of 1931. With economies of lifestyle in place and Bond & Goodwin all but liquidated, Maynard was now free to concentrate on his own personal investments. No one else could have done it better.

26

Maynard and Addah were at home in Fairfield in the summer of 1931 awaiting the arrival of Rose from Maine. The previous summer, when Rose had her tonsils out at Boston's Children's Hospital, they had gone there to bring her to Fairfield. This year, they had worked out an arrangement whereby Alan and Adelaide would take her to Portland for a visit with her grandmother. Then Carroll Tyler would put her on the train to Boston where Milton would meet her and transfer her to the New York train; she would then be met at the Bridgeport station. Maynard looked forward eagerly each summer to his daughter's arrival; he was considering having her live with them year around. Now that he and Addah had been married five years and had a stable marriage, there was no longer any reason for them not to provide Rose with a permanent home. Since business demands had lessened—due in equal parts to his retirement and the depressed state of the economy, he reasoned that living with him Rose would have greater opportunities than if she stayed in Rockland. He remembered, too, his mother's words to him after Rose's death: *"For the sake of her* [Rose's] *memory, you must love the child—Baby Rose—and devote your whole being to seeing that she grows up as Rose would have wanted her to."*

And Rose was growing up! When she arrived that summer Maynard noted that she resembled her mother more and more, and since her tonsillectomy, she was shooting up like the proverbial weed. All signs pointed to her becoming a tall young woman, and he had high hopes that she would have her mother's voice and her mother's attributes as well as her appearance. He had concluded that Rockland was not the place to achieve this. Hardly a day went by that he didn't think of his beloved dead wife who had been the romance his life had never known before or since. In his efforts to be the kind of a father she would have wanted, he convinced himself that training and educating his daughter for a future consistent with his wealth and social position was a worthy goal.

Maynard considered a good education to be the most valuable asset a person could have. He had always regretted his lack of advanced schooling; one year at Exeter had only whetted his appetite for more of the same. Despite his disappointment in Milton, he didn't begrudge the education he had given his son. In fact he was very proud of Milton's recently attained advanced degrees.[147] While he cared about his Rockland family, he was particularly proud of those who had made good elsewhere. William Bird, who he'd helped both at college and in the business world was, in Maynard's eyes, the shining example of this kind of achievement. So he intended to pay special attention to Rose's education which he hoped would infuse her with a pride of family and motivation to achieve.

Even before Rose arrived, he and Addah had been discussing plans for the coming fall and winter. They could not fail to see, although living in comparative affluence, that the economy was not only depressed, but also relief was nowhere in sight. Although they were well off by anyone's standards, it cost a great deal to keep up the large house. Several New York acquaintances had gone to live temporarily in Europe where they found costs considerably lower. It was probably Addah who suggested that they consider such a course, but when she mentioned that they too go abroad, Maynard, thinking about Rose's future, demurred.

"You know we talked about bringing Rose to live with us permanently, and going to Europe—I suppose you mean France—well, that would postpone having her here for another year at least."

Addah had not considered this eventuality, but but it took only a moment's thought before she said, "Why couldn't we take her with us? What better opportunity than for her to have a year in France or Switzerland! She could learn a foreign language that would certainly be good for her later on. And I don't mind seeing that she keeps up with her American school work."

"You mean you'd spend all your time teaching her?" Maynard seemed a little baffled by this.

"No, of course not. She could go to school wherever we decided to settle. There are plenty of private schools that cater to foreign students. All I meant was that I'd be willing to see that she didn't fall behind in whatever studies she would have had here."

"I'll think about it," he said, "but I want Rose to be with us. I don't want to see her shipped off to a school where she'll be away from us. That would be too hard on her."

"No, of course not," Addah responded. If Maynard wanted Rose to be with them, then that's the way it would be."

"Let's not rush into anything," He still seemed dubious. Then, as if to soften his objections, he said, "In the meantime go ahead and write to your friends and see what they can tell you about housing and schools."

As Maynard pondered Addah's suggestion, it occurred to him that to take Rose to Europe might make it easier for her to adjust. Especially, since the change in surroundings would be new to all of them. Spending a year in France would be a great experience; Rose would be one the few children living in either Rockland or Fairfield who could boast of being educated abroad. The idea appealed to him for other reasons. He remembered his seafaring forebears, some of whom took their families with them when they traveled to all parts of the globe. Perhaps that is where his love of adventures had come from. The more he thought about spending a year abroad, the more he saw it as one more adventure with the advantages that went with it. If he took into account how Alan and Adelaide would react to Rose's leaving them, essentially their child since birth, he did not give it particular weight in making his decision. He was grateful to them for helping him by taking the baby after Rose's death, but there had never been any question, at least in Maynard's mind, (and he assumed in theirs), that his child would eventually come to live with him. Nor did he consider how a move away from the people she always thought of as mother and father would affect her.

Once he had made up his mind, he wrote to Alan, trying tactfully to suggest that it was time for Rose to live with her father and stepmother. He outlined all the opportunities Rose would have in education and culture, and noted that since he was retired, he could now give his daughter the attention that had not been possible earlier. He did not mention the European trip for he was beginning to have concerns as to how his brother would accept the idea of losing Rose.

Maynard had not really expected Alan to acquiesce without an argument. By return mail Alan wrote that he and Adelaide had discussed the matter but felt that Rose was still too young to make a change. The tone of Alan's letter alerted Maynard to the fact that his brother was going to be stubborn about giving up Rose. But he could be stubborn too! If he still had any hopes of persuading Alan to accept his decision amicably, he would have to do it face to face. His next letter reiterated his decision that Rose should come to live with him, but included an invitation to come to Fairfield so they could discuss the matter directly with each other. Maynard still had not mentioned the trip abroad, sensing perhaps that it would further aggravate the problem.

Alan accepted the invitation and he and Adelaide arrived in Fairfield shortly thereafter.

◆　　　◆　　　◆

They met in Maynard's study. Alan and Adelaide both stiffly erect and apprehensive sat on the sofa; Maynard, seated in the leather chair behind the large mahogany desk, appeared relaxed but confident. Addah sat perched rather uncomfortably on the edge of a chair, across from her husband. She had made up her mind that she would try to stay out of the conversation that might become contentious. She had even suggested that she should not be present at all, but Maynard vetoed that idea.

"You're my wife and Rose's stepmother. You've been good to her and I know you think of her now as <u>our</u> daughter. There's no reason that you shouldn't have a say in all of this."

Despite his effort at inclusiveness, Addah felt uneasy about the situation that she feared would pit brother against brother; she didn't want to aggravate the issue by her presence. She knew her husband had made up his mind and was also sure that the streak of obstinacy he had identified in Alan, also ran, if not as strongly, in his own character.

To Maynard's surprise, Adelaide was the one who spoke first on the subject about which they were all concerned.

"I want to explain our thinking about Rose's future and why we feel that now is not the right time for her to be uprooted from the surroundings she has known all her life," she began.

Maynard felt a momentary wave of relief. Perhaps they would be reasonable after all.

"You may not realize, Maynard, but Rose thinks of us as her parents and we love her as though we were," she continued. "She understands you are her father, but that is not the same as 'feeling' you are her father. She has grown up in Rockland; that's where her friends are and where she feels secure. I know that Addah has been a good stepmother, but in Rose's mind I am her mother—the only one she has known. Whether you like it or not, there is a bond between us that will be difficult to break. If it is broken at her present age, it may do her untold damage. Perhaps in a few years as she grows older, she will have a better understanding of her family's relationships, but at present she is just too young and immature emotionally.

She paused to marshal her thoughts, and Maynard took the opportunity to interrupt. "Adelaide, you have been a good mother to Rose. I am eternally grateful to you and Alan for taking Rose at a time when my life had been almost destroyed by her mother's death. But…," and here he paused long enough for Adelaide to do her own interrupting.

"I haven't finished, Maynard," she said rather sharply, and continued with her proposal. "We recognize that you only want what is best for Rose—as we do. With that in mind, we suggest that she stay with us until she is ready for high school—that's only four more years. Then we can leave her further education up to you; you may want to send her away to school, and of course we would have no objection.

As she spoke she looked at Addah as if she were saying, 'I _am_ her mother, please don't take her away! Can't you understand that?' But Addah's kept her eyes on her clasped hands lying tensely in her lap and said nothing.

It was now Maynard's turn, and it was almost as if he hadn't heard his sister-in-law. Or perhaps her words had only touched the surface of his mind as he concentrated on how to say what he must say about their decision to go to Europe. From what Adelaide had already said, he was sure that there would be opposition. Nevertheless, he started out in a conciliatory if slightly patronizing tone of voice.

"Adelaide, I understand your feeling about the bond you have formed with Rose, but you and Alan must acknowledge that I am her father and that my decisions about her future take precedence."

He paused, momentarily, trying to frame what he wanted to say in a reasonable and placating manner. "Yes, I recognize that the break from Rockland may be traumatic, and for that reason, we have decided that the break will be easier if we take Rose with us to Europe this fall for an extended stay—maybe up to a year. There she can adjust more easily to a different way of life with us as her parents."

There was an appalled silence and, as Addah noted, a look of dismay appeared on both of her in-law's faces.

Alan, who had been silent up to this point, was on his feet and in a voice choked with rage he pointed a finger at Maynard. "Why didn't you tell us this before? Did you think you could hide this from us? What are you trying to put over on us? We did you a favor when you needed one. We took your child in when you didn't want her, and were too busy with your money grubbing to do what a father should have done—give her a home. Well, we gave her a home and we're the only family she has ever known, and now you say you want her back. You don't give a damn about Rose; you just want a child to satisfy your own ego. And to drag her to Europe to boot! You must be out of your mind!"

Adelaide tugged at his sleeve: "Alan, this isn't getting us anywhere. Perhaps we should ask Rose how she feels about going to Europe with them."

"Yes, that would be a good idea," said Addah, forgetting her vow not to get involved in the affair. "I'll go and get Rose; she should be part of this decision." With that she hastily left the room before either Maynard or Alan could stop her.

Maynard had been angered by Alan's accusations—justly so he thought, but he had managed to contain his anger. If Rose was going to be a party to this decision, and it looked like she was, it was important that she not witness a family fight. He didn't want to turn her against Adelaide who obviously loved the child. Maynard was almost positive that Rose would choose Europe—France—over Rockland if he put the question to her in a way she couldn't refuse. While Addah was gone to find Rose, he addressed both Alan and Adelaide: "When Rose comes in it is important in the interest of fairness that she not hear us arguing or get the feeling that it is anything but her decision."

They sat in silence until Addah returned with Rose. Addah resumed her seat leaving Rose standing alone in the middle of the room. The little girl looked around at the faces staring at her, but she was not aware of any element of tension. These were grown-ups after all, and sometimes they acted strangely.

"Rose, dear," Maynard spoke in a quiet, friendly voice that he hoped would gain his daughter's attention and interest. "How would you like to go with Aunt Addah and me to France this fall? We would stay there a while and you could go to school, learn to speak French and have lots of fun."

Rose looked around the room. Mother (Adelaide) wasn't smiling, and neither was Lannah (her pet name for Alan). She turned the question over in her mind; nobody else said anything. 'Surely someone would say something if they didn't want me to go', she thought. 'It would be an adventure, just like the story she had read about in the *French Twins*.¹⁴⁸ Maybe she'd better find out a little more about this trip. "How would we get there?" Even as she asked the question she knew the answer, but let them tell her anyway while she thought some more.

"We'd go on a great big ocean liner, just like the ones you've seen pictures of in that book you were reading last week," Maynard responded.

She couldn't think of anymore questions right now, but she stalled a little; she didn't want to appear too eager. "And I'll go to school there? Will I have any friends my age?"

"Of course you will, dear. Aunt Addah has already looked into schools that take American girls your age."

"Well, I guess it's ok. Now can I go back to my book?"

When her father nodded, she ran off with a skip and a jump. What an adventure it would be! She didn't know anyone who had ever been to France except her father and Aunt Addah and they didn't count; she'd be the first. How exciting!

"Maynard," it was Adelaide speaking again. "The child doesn't understand what she's agreed too. I'm asking you, pleading with you, don't take her away from us!"

But Maynard was adamant. "I'm her father. You surely didn't think I'd leave her with you for the rest of her life." He was looking directly at Alan as he said this. "And you know perfectly well, Alan, that when you agreed to take her, there was no question of my being able to make a home for her. Do you resent my doing well and being wealthy? I haven't noticed that you turned down the money I gave you to pay for things for Rose. I paid for her tonsillectomy; I've paid for the braces on her teeth that she has now so that she won't have buck teeth like Ted Bird[149]; and I've sent presents to both of you and Rose."

If Maynard had stopped at that point, he might have salvaged some modicum of amity. But he went on, ignoring the consequences. "And besides, I don't want her growing up in a small town like Rockland. Look around you and see what has happened to our family. Those who have made something of themselves have left Rockland. Isn't that so?"

This time Alan spoke in a controlled yet furious voice. "So that's the way you feel about us—about your family. We're not good enough for you or your daughter. Rockland isn't good enough for you anymore. You've changed Maynard! Look at you living in your fancy mansion, with a wife who doesn't like us—or Rockland. No wonder she wants to get Rose away from us. You've taken up with some high society friends, but I'll bet they don't know that your grandfather was illegitimate and that Mother was pregnant before she married Father. You've obviously forgotten where you came from."

It was Maynard's turn to explode. "How dare you insult my wife that way and in her presence too. I was right, you're not fit to take care of my daughter. I have nothing more to say to you on the subject. Rose stays with us."

"In that case, I never want to see you or speak to you again." Alan was still standing when he said this and turned to his wife. "Come on Adelaide, let's get out of here."

As they left, Adelaide, her face white and wet with tears, looked desperately at both Maynard and Addah hoping for some word of apology. Something—so they wouldn't leave on this angry note which seemed to doom any future relationship. But neither Maynard nor Addah said a word.

Within a half an hour their bags were packed and a car was made available to take them to wherever they wanted to go.

Subsequently, Maynard came to regret the harshness of his words. In time he made up with Adelaide so that Rose could and would renew her relationship with them in the years after she returned from France.

Alan kept his word. He never spoke to or saw Maynard again.

27

The Birds prepared to sail for Europe in mid-September, 1931. Maynard had booked first class passage on the Italian Line *M/S Augustus*. He had closed the office at 65 Broadway and referred pending matters to one of his former associates. Rose's horse had been shipped to Milton's place in Norwell. Joe Link was put in charge of the Fairfield house, and would continue to live in the cottage and care for the property.

Addah took Rose to New York to buy new clothes for the trip and at home attended to the packing. Servants were dismissed; silver was stored in a bank vault; and furniture covered with sheets. By the time they were ready to leave they had twenty-one pieces of baggage including a portable Victrola and a carefully packed box of records.

They spent their last night ashore at a New York hotel where they were met by Lize (Addah's sister) and her husband, Joe Onorato, who had come from New Orleans to see them off. Their stateroom aboard ship was full of flowers and telegrams sent by friends and relatives, and Maynard had ordered champagne and hors d'oeuvres to make the occasion a festive one. After a final call of "All ashore", the visitors left the ship to wave goodbye from the dock. As the ship pulled slowly out into the channel and headed down the Hudson River past the Statue of Liberty, the Birds' adventure had begun.

Their route took them directly to the Mediterranean, and because the weather was mild and the sea calm Addah avoided her usual seasickness. The leisurely voyage reminded Maynard of the trip he and Rose had made to the Far East. With no business matters on his mind, he had time to relax and enjoy shipboard life.

The crossing was uneventful and ten days later the Bird party disembarked at Villefranche-sur-Mer on the French Riviera, where a tender took passengers ashore. As Addah approached the top of the wooden boarding ladder, she could see the tender, far below, rolling in a slight swell. In fear and trembling she backed away; but after a few moments to calm her self, she began the perilous descent; and, with a seaman in front of her grasping each arm, she finally reached the tender. Maynard and Rose had already descended with agility while Maynard struggled to maintain an air of serious concern for his wife.

The taxi drive to Cannes, fifteen miles away, further stressed them all. The car, piled high with roof luggage, swayed dangerously as it rounded each curve on the Lower Corniche Drive. To calm both wife and daughter, Maynard put his arm around Rose and gently patted Addah's hand as they careened from one side of the road to the other. By evening, though, they were settled in a comfortable suite at the Hotel Victoria, and Addah's nerves were soothed by a shot of whisky from Maynard's flask. "Purely for medicinal purposes", he said, with a wink, when she looked with some surprise at the container.

After taking a few days to adjust to their new surroundings, Rose was enrolled at Cours Maintenon, a private school for girls, where she was placed in a special class with other English speaking girls her age under the tutelage of the headmistress' daughter, Dazah Palet. Rose progressed rapidly, learning the language quickly and adjusting to her new environment. Maynard felt relieved that the transition had gone so smoothly. Ever since his fight with Alan, he had kept Adelaide's predictions in the back of his mind hoping that her warnings of harm to his daughter's life would prove untrue.

Next, Maynard and Addah found the Hotel Bristol located a few blocks from Rose's school. It had been built in the late 19th century when wealthy and important visitors from all over Europe made the Riviera their winter playground. Having seen better days it now catered to a mixed clientele of middle class refugees from the cold damp of the English winters, and a few Americans, like themselves. Their suite on the first floor included a large bed-sitting room with an attached full bath and an adjoining single room for Rose. There was a toilet room across the hall from Rose's room that she could use when necessary. Breakfasts and dinners were included in the pension rate; lunches could be eaten wherever they pleased, while Rose had hers at school.

Their next requirement was a car. A Model A Ford sedan was duly purchased at a price Maynard thought was a bargain. It turned out, when the car was resold in Paris at the end of their trip, that the 'bargain' was not quite as good as he had thought. Just the same, the car was reliable and gave them good service throughout the stay. Addah's fluency in French never quite rubbed off on Maynard. No matter how hard he tried, he could not remember more than a few words of the language. When he had to get gas from the local filling station, it was all he could do to say, "Dix litres, s'il vous plâit", and when the tank was full, say "Combien?"

◆   ◆   ◆

This was a happy time for Maynard. He realized that his whole life, except for the brief time with Rose, had been devoted to the pursuit of business and the accumulation of wealth. Despite Alan's remarks that still rankled, he was proud of his affiliation with prestigious members of his community both in New York and Fairfield. He thought less and less of Maine and had no regrets about putting it behind him. He intended to make up for lost time by devoting himself to his daughter—something he had failed to do with Milton.

Addah was an interesting and enjoyable companion. Their stay in France gave them unlimited opportunity to be with each other. They poked around the shops in Cannes and nearby Nice; they visited museums; strolled on the Croisette, sampling different cafes and bistros; and made day trips to many of the picturesque towns and villages in the rugged mountains a few miles inland. On the winding roads of the Middle or High Corniche Drives[150] they had spectacular views of the coastline and the sparkling blue Mediterranean Sea. On weekends, when Rose was with them, they visited the perfume center of Grasse, and explored the winding, narrow streets of hill towns like Eze on the Middle Corniche. They visited Monte Carlo and the Oceanographic Museum there. They took Rose to the opera at the Cannes Casino; and on winter Saturday afternoons to showings of American movies; Laurel and Hardy and Charlie Chaplin were their favorites. This was a rare treat for Rose who had not been allowed to see movies in Rockland. Evenings were often spent playing records on their portable Victrola., ("You see, Addah," Maynard would say, "we are using it even though you didn't want to bring it!"). On one or two occasions, Maynard made tentative efforts, with mixed results, to teach Rose to dance. They had brought a number of songs by Frank Crumpet and Julia Sanderson. Rose's favorite was "Around the Corner and Under the Trees" which she memorized and sang at the top of her lungs. They made friends with a number of other residents at the Bristol; and found that bridge was just as popular with the English visitors as with the Americans. Maynard kept up with the news through the English language edition of the Herald Tribune.[151]

The most exciting event that winter was the wedding, over the Christmas holiday, of Rose's teacher, Mlle. Dazah, to which all Rose's class was invited. No one in the Bird family had ever been to a French wedding, and it is doubtful whether Maynard had ever been to a Catholic service. Not only was he delighted that the family had been invited, but he was impressed by the elaborate invitation in the form of a small booklet, detailing the genealogy of both families. Addah agreed that it must be an important affair since the religious service[152] would take place in the centuries old Cannes Cathedral and the reception afterwards at the Carlton Hotel—the most prestigious hotel on the Croisette. The event gave the whole family an opportunity to wear their best clothes: Maynard noted approvingly that Rose, who was "decked out" as he put it, in her best dress, patent leather shoes and white knee high stockings, resembled her mother. She had her mother's coloring, her nose and her mouth; only her eyes were different—they were more like the Bird family eyes.

On arrival at the cathedral, they were escorted to seats on the bride's side midway down the aisle. Rush-bottomed chairs with pullout kneeling stools replaced the familiar pews of American churches. Not even the chill of the cold damp December day in the unheated church could detract from the pageantry and beauty of the affair. Candles illuminated the interior; flowers banked the sides of the steps to the chancel; flowers were also on the altar and on either side of the central aisle. The bride, arrayed in a long-sleeved gown, covered with lace, and with a long train held up by two little girls, was preceded by a procession of ushers, bridesmaids, flower girls and a ring bearer. Compared to a Protestant wedding—the kind Maynard was used to in the United States—the service was long, lasting more than an hour. At one point the bridesmaids in their handsome cerise taffeta dresses, their shoulders covered with ermine stoles, passed their muffs, now transformed into furred baskets, for a collection. Maynard considered this custom to be not only unusual, but also not entirely appropriate since they had already contributed a costly gift. He gave a small amount, however, for he was getting used to the fact that the French seemed to do everything differently.

The reception at the Carlton Hotel was equally elaborate with plenty of champagne, wine and a sumptuous buffet. When they went through the receiving line, Rose, who had been practicing all week saying "Meilleurs felicitations" and, curtseying, uttered the congratulatory words without hesitation or error. Maynard, was proud of her poise and facility with the language, but for himself made do with the usual 'Congratulations' in English.

◆　　　◆　　　◆

That winter, during the months of January and February, the Riviera weather turned cold, damp and very often overcast. On Mardi Gras, the crowd that assembled along the Croisette to watch the annual Parade of Flowers was bundled up in coats and scarves as protection from the cold. The Queen and her attendants riding in horse drawn open barouches had coats or capes over their elaborate costumes that tended to interfere with their ability to toss flowers to the onlookers.

Maynard who had not anticipated the cold, found the gray days depressing. Other factors contributed to his mood especially the news from home through newspapers and letters. As he read about the bank failures, the closing of factories and the enormous number of unemployed that now amounted to nearly twelve million, he wondered what had happened to the rosy predictions of only a year ago. There had been a lot of talk then about how business would solve all the problems and there was no need to encourage the wild ideas of Labor and Liberals that a planned (government?) economy was what the country needed to get back on its feet. He read in letters from Rockland that The John Bird Company was having a hard time. Only the spice and coffee divisions were operating He worried about his baby, The Security Trust Company. Would it be strong enough to withstand the demands of depositors for their money? Perhaps the most worrisome of all the current news was that Samuel Insull's utility empire was thought to be crumbling.[153] Utilities had been Maynard's bread and butter business; they simply couldn't fail. It was probably those holding companies that were over extended.

It was these thoughts that went through his mind one evening when he and Addah were sitting by the fire in their room after Rose had gone to bed. He had been reading, but put his book down and said, almost as if he was thinking out loud, "Maybe we should go back to the States now before it gets any worse."

Addah had been occupied with knitting a sweater. She recognized the remark as neither a positive statement nor a casual comment. She had become accustomed to her husband's moods and often knew his ideas even before he expressed them. So after a brief pause, she said, "What would you do if you went back now?"

"Oh, I think I could help reorganize some of the companies. There's the Central Maine Power Company for one that seems to be in trouble."

"Perhaps," Addah replied. "But you wouldn't get involved unless you were asked, would you"?

Maynard stroked his chin with his thumb and forefinger—a habit he had developed when he was not sure of where he stood. "I suppose not, but I still feel so helpless over here with nothing to do."

"It isn't as though there was nothing to do. For a man 62 years old, you've kept pretty busy: I notice you go to the American Express office nearly every day so you can watch the ticker tapes, and we do have a lot of social obligations."

Here she paused, because she could see that she had not been able to change his conviction that he wasn't doing anything worthwhile.

She picked up her knitting again, but laid it down after a minute or so. "If we were to go back now, it would mean taking Rose out of school and finding another school for her in the middle of a school year. Really, Maynard, that wouldn't be fair to the child. She needs several months in the class she's in now or she won't have gotten anything out of her French education." (After Christmas, Rose had been placed in a class of French children more or less her age in which all instruction was in French.)

"I've been thinking," she continued, "that after Easter we could then take Rose out of school and make a motor trip through France to Paris. There is so much more to see, and I know that you, with your love of history, would find many places fascinating."

After some further discussion, Maynard agreed with Addah's suggestion. (In fact he was beginning to think the whole thing had been his idea.) A few days later they came home loaded down with travel books, maps and even a book for Rose on the history of France. Afternoons and occasional winter evenings were now devoted to planning their trip. Maynard became absorbed in selecting stops where they could see a variety of scenic and historical attractions, while Addah busied herself with picking out hotels and routes.

One afternoon, Maynard put down the travel book he had been reading and looked up at Addah, "Did you know there are cave paintings 30,000 years old along a river called the 'Dordogne'?" I've just read about them and we must see them!" Every time he found something of interest, he made a note to include it in their itinerary: the Palace of the French Popes at Avignon, the walled medieval town of Carcassonne, the Roman ruins around Nimes and Arles, and of course the caves.

They decided that they should make an extended stay in the Chateaux Country of the Loire Valley. (Addah had traveled this area previously on trips before her marriage, and was enthusiastic about the places they would see.) Their search for accommodations in the Chateaux Country ended fortuitously with an introduction to a charming lady, Madame, la Comtesse de Pierre, who's finances compelled her to take in paying guests at her villa on the Loire river in the town of Amboise

By the end of March their plans were in place and they only waited for Rose's Easter vacation before starting off. In the meantime, after at first having a difficult time in her new class, Rose had been doing exceptionally well. Maynard saw this as justification for staying in Cannes through the winter, and their decision to see more of France. In fact he was so enthusiastic about their coming trip that he had nearly forgotten his earlier desire to return home.

They said farewell to the Riviera on a glorious, bright, warm day—the air redolent with the smells of the sea mingling with the last, lingering fragrance of mimosa and the springtime scent of lavender. Maynard drove with Addah beside him so she could read the signs and give instructions—needed or otherwise—about driving. Rose, who had developed skill in map reading, sat in the back, maps on her lap, hemmed in by their overnight luggage. Some luggage was in the trunk; but, with the recollection of the taxi drive from Villefranche to Cannes, there was no baggage on the roof of the car this time.

Their route took them through the sun-dappled fields of Provence where farmers were busy planting spring crops. Fruit trees were in bloom and fields of flowers intermingled with the freshly tilled earth. As they approached Aix-en-Provence they could see Mt. Ste. Victoire on the northern horizon but were unaware of the painter, Cezanne, who had been a resident of Aix, and whose paintings of the mountain would make it famous. Their journey took them to the towns of Avignon and Nimes where they went to a bullfight in the Roman amphitheater. In Arles women could still be seen in their traditional costumes and here they took a picture of Rose dressed in one of them. They showed no interest in the art of VanGogh and his famous painting of L'Arlesienne.

On they went to Carcassonne and then north to the Dordogne Valley and the caves. The roads were not crowded and they might go for ten minutes or more without seeing another car. The Ford was reliable; it never had a break down, and seemed to demand only that it be fed on gas, water and an occasional dose of air in its tires. It was easy to stop along side of the road for lunchtime picnics or just to rest and relax. When they finally arrived at Amboise and the Villa Violetta, they had been on the road for nearly three weeks and were happy to unpack and settle in.

By the middle of June they had visited nearly every chateau in the region, and although Rose was always eager to see one more, both Maynard and Addah felt they had seen enough. Their stay with Madame la Comtesse had been delightful and had given them all a chance to enjoy the experience of living in a genuine French home. Once more they loaded up the Ford, and with fond—and in Rose's case tearful—farewells to Madame and the staff of the Villa Violetta, set off on the day's trip to Paris.

In Paris they took up residence at the Hotel Atala, a small hotel conveniently located a block off the Champs Elysees and two blocks down from the Arc de

Triomphe. From the balcony of their rooms on the top floor they had a panoramic view of Montmartre dominated by the immense Basilica of Sacre Coeur.

They had no sooner unpacked than Maynard, who had been looking forward eagerly to their arrival in Paris, started making calls on American banks and brokerage houses, or their representatives in Paris, whom he had met on earlier trips. At Goldman Sachs' Paris office he inquired about William Bird and brought himself up-to-date on the state of the financial world. There was also a Paris branch of the Guarantee Trust Company that he planned to visit. Although he was pretty much divorced from the securities business, he knew his reputation would open many doors, and, who knew, perhaps he would find something worthwhile to market in the States. Addah, too, wanted time on her own to revisit some of her contacts at the antique galleries with whom she had done business in the past. There were also the couturiers where, even if she didn't buy anything, she would have the opportunity to see the latest styles. For those times when they couldn't be with Rose, they hired a companion—a young French woman, Francoise, who was a student at the Sorbonne.

The time spent in Paris was rewarding for all. On his business visits, Maynard was greeted warmly—often with the words, whether in French or English of "welcome back, we are delighted to see you again". The financial news from the other side of the Atlantic was not good, and the political outlook, from Maynard's Republican point of view, was equally dismal. The Depression,—as it was now called—was as bad if not worse than ever, and the Hoover administration seemed to be incapable of doing anything to make things better. However, as a result of his contacts, he and Addah were invited to numerous dinner parties and events, including an afternoon at the races at Longchamps where even Rose was included in the party.

They took Rose to see all the sights of Paris: Notre Dame, Sainte Chapelle, Napoleon's Tomb and the Eifel Tower where, not surprisingly, Addah declined to go with them to the top. They picnicked in the Bois de Boulogne and visited Versailles; they bought Rose a toy sailboat so that when Francoise took her to the Luxembourg Gardens, she could sail her boat on the pond there with the other children.

There were renewed acquaintances with American expatriates whom they had met on earlier visits. This gave them a chance to learn more about the political situation in Europe. In May, while they were in Amboise, a shocking event, particularly disturbing to the Americans, had occurred. A Russian Communist had assassinated Doumer, President of France. There was also a good deal of talk about a man named Hitler in Germany, whose party, the National Socialist

Party—called the NAZIs—had gotten 37% of the popular vote for Adolf Hitler for president. Of course, according to their friends, von Hindenburg won, but this new party might be just the thing Germany needed to get rid of the Communists who were so dangerous. Did Maynard and Addah know that the new chancellor, Franz von Papen had refused to include Hitler in his cabinet?

"Well, those Germans will just have to sort it out," Maynard remarked when he was told this bit of news. "They've had enough problems since the war; it's time they settled down to a stable government and maybe this Hitler fellow can do it."

After six weeks in Paris, Maynard wanted to go home. They had been away long enough, and he wanted to be back home where people spoke a language he understood. The baggage that had traveled separately to Paris was repacked and forwarded to the Holland America Line. They hired a car and driver to take them to Amsterdam, stopping overnight at the shore resort of Ostend in Belgium. They visited the mediaeval town of Middelburg where they watched the clock figures on the town hall strike the hour; and there they bought Rose a Dutch costume and Maynard a pair of wooden shoes that he took home with him to wear for gardening. They stayed in Amsterdam several days before boarding the S/S Veendam in Rotterdam for the six-day voyage to the United States. The crossing was uneventful and they arrived back in New York by the middle of August—eleven months after their departure.

In the years to come, Maynard always thought of that year abroad as his last great adventure.

28

Maynard had not realized how glad he would be to return home. He couldn't wait to get back to doing something more useful than just being a visitor in a foreign land. With a store of energy, accumulated during the past months, he was anxious to get to New York; to renew acquaintances and contacts there; and to once more feel the pulse of the business world. However, he needed a week or two to catch up on the state of things at the Fairfield house and enroll Rose in her new school. (They had selected Unquowa School, a small private day school located in the eastern section of Fairfield, where she was placed in sixth grade.) In the meantime, Addah had hired a cook and a maid; arranged to resume mail delivery and telephone service; and supervised the unpacking. Finally, Maynard was free to go back to New York.

Things had changed more than he realized as he quickly discovered on his visit to the Guaranty Trust Company; the bank that had been the focus of much of his banking business in earlier years. Here he found that officers with whom he had formerly dealt were no longer there. They had either retired or simply left the bank and had been replaced by younger men who were either new to the bank—and to Maynard—or had advanced from lower levels of management to leadership positions once held by Maynard's friends. This same pattern of change repeated itself as he visited several other investment houses with which he had formerly done business.

Finding that William Bird was still at Goldman Sachs gave Maynard a lift. Here at last was a tie to the old days—not only of business but also of family. Over lunch in the executive dining room, William was able to bring him up-to-date on the state of the banking industry.

"You know, Maynard, the whole damn banking system is in jeopardy," William said in response to one of his cousin's questions.

"I had read about bank closings in the papers abroad, but I didn't know it was that serious," Maynard replied. "Do you have any information on the Security Trust in Rockland? I would hate to see that go under after all the effort I and my partners put into it."

"From what I hear, it's right on the edge. So far it hasn't had to close its doors, but a good run of withdrawals would probably put it under. Like most small

253

banks, foreclosures haven't helped because people have no money to pay their debts," was William's rather gloomy assessment.

Pulling at his chin with his thumb and forefinger, Maynard said, rather tentatively, "I wish I could do something to help."

"Don't waste your time or your money, Maynard," was William's response. "It would be like pouring money down the drain. Don't you see, the whole system needs repair; the RFC[154] has money to prop up some of the larger banks, but not nearly enough to take care of the smaller ones throughout the country."

"Sounds to me as though the government is meddling in business. Doesn't that sort of smack of socialism?"

"What else can we do, Maynard?" was William's answer. "The country is in such bad shape financially that the government had to do something. It's a question whether it will be enough to get us out of this depression. So far it doesn't seem to have helped."

Maynard decided to change the subject to something pleasanter. "I hear you're getting married again, William."

William's face shown with pleasure. "Yes, I'm marrying a charming, wonderful woman from Springfield, Massachusetts. Her name is Julia Fisher"[155]

Maynard congratulated William and their luncheon talk switched to family subjects and news of Maine. When he left New York that day He was pleased with William's obvious success at Goldman Sachs, and his coming marriage that boded well for his future happiness. On the other hand, as he told Addah that evening, the country was in even worse shape than he had realized. They were lucky to be reasonably well off financially. In fact, William had told him that he (Maynard) had retired at the right time. Maynard hoped he was right.

Politics was also a matter of concern to both of them. Their Fairfield crowd was overwhelmingly Republican; so, of course, all political conversation was directed against the Democrats who had nominated Franklin Delano Roosevelt as their presidential candidate. No Democrat would have been acceptable to Maynard and his friends; but the selection of Roosevelt, a man who had disgraced his heritage by lining up on the wrong side of the political fence, was like a slap in the face to their inherited self esteem. "He's a traitor to his class!" was the common epithet among the stalwart Republicans of Fairfield County.

A native of Maine, Maynard had never known anything but the Republican Party; it was just as much a matter of genetics as of ideology; not that he didn't believe in the latter. He had never really known a Democrat, although he had probably known some without realizing it. But he was too much of a realist not to be influenced by the state of the country as a whole. He wondered if the

Hoover administration had understood the political implications of the bonus marchers when federal troops had been sent in to break up the shantytowns, called 'Hoovervilles'[156], around Washington. The word had gone out that communists and criminal elements had infiltrated the protest movement; but that didn't make up for the 11,000 marchers who would go home to swell the ranks of unemployed—over 12 million at last count—and undoubtedly vote against Hoover. Just the same, from Maynard's point of view, the worst Republican was better than the best Democrat. He was disappointed, but not unduly surprised, when Roosevelt and the Democrats won by a landslide that November. He was stunned, however, to learn that Maine not only went to the Democrats, but elected a Democratic governor. When Roosevelt, in order to put new Treasury regulations into effect, declared a seven-day bank holiday, one of the first steps taken after his inauguration, Maynard grudgingly conceded that the move made sense. Although major banks were allowed to reopen, he was saddened to learn, later on, that the Security Trust Company, in order to survive, had merged with the Knox County Trust Company.[157]

In the months following the election, Maynard started to consider just what the future held for him. He wanted to get back into some kind of business activity, but the investment and banking businesses were out of the question. He still held directorships in several companies and their meetings allowed him to keep up with current business issues. While in France he had acquired authorization to market, in the United States, a cleaning fluid called La Zembine. His effort to promote this product to firms in New York and elsewhere were unproductive; none of his contacts were interested in dealing with a new product, no matter how good it was, in the depressed business climate of the time. By 1934, he had given up on La Zembine and for all intents and purposes he was out of business. Several years later, he once again undertook to market, independently, another product—a baby food called Cerevim—with little more success. Eventually, after insisting that Addah, Rose and even the cook and maid eat the cereal regularly for breakfast, he found a buyer for the manufacturing rights in a large corporation that had other lines of baby food.

Although he was discouraged by his inability to re-establish himself in business, Maynard's self-confidence was not diminished. With a generally optimistic outlook, he accepted the fact that, even though the country seemed to be pulling out of the worst of the Depression, (no thanks to Roosevelt, of course), there was little he could do at his age to start a new career. Never one to allow his energy and talents to be idle for long, he remembered how his father had contributed so much to Rockland and to Maine as a whole. Was it not possible for him to contribute similarly to the Fairfield community? He and Addah had a beautiful home to enjoy why shouldn't others enjoy it too? His rose garden continued to be an all-consuming passion; and with the help of Joe Link, he nurtured the grounds so that the estate became a showplace for the area. Frequently, *Mon Repos,* as Addah had named it, (Maynard disliked the name thinking it pretentious), was opened for charitable events. When the hurricane of 1938 demolished the steeple and damaged the sanctuary of the Greenfield Hill Congregational Church, of which Maynard was a member, he helped organize a committee to raise funds for its restoration. The following June the gardens were opened for a successful garden fair at which copies of an etching by a local artist of the church, as it would appear when restored, were sold.

They renewed their activities at the Fairfield Beach Club where Rose could take swimming and tennis lessons; some years later, Maynard became a board member and in due course was elected club president. Through some of his contacts he was appointed to the Fairfield Zoning Board of Appeals and to the board of the Visiting Nurse Association. Although he never aspired to run for political office, he became active in town affairs and was appointed to a commission set up to review the operation of the police department. This commission's recommendation, that the police department be removed from the Board of Selectmen, resulted in a department shake-up.[158] In all of these undertakings, he made friends who admired his personality, his tact and his intelligence. He gained a reputation as a man of great capacity and integrity, and was admired for his thoroughness in handling whatever job he undertook.

He became the consummate 'country gentleman'. In this new role, he decided it was time to change his style of dress. Suits were saved for trips to New York; otherwise he dressed casually in tweed or corduroy sports coats and gray flannel slacks in the winter. Linen, cotton and seersucker coats and trousers were worn in warmer weather. Both he and Addah had abandoned the habit of formally dressing for dinner, even though they frequently changed clothes at the end of the day or when company was expected. Although they still entertained a good deal, they and their friends had given up the ostentation of the 20's life style. Maynard also stopped wearing four-in-hand ties except with suits or on special occasions; he now wore bow ties made out of gingham or small patterned cotton with only slightly widened ends. For Addah or Rose these ties, hand made and lined with linen strips, became staples for Christmas and birthday gifts. As always, he presented a dapper appearance with a signature rosebud in the buttonhole of his jacket. On pleasant evenings in the summer, neighbors might see the couple, each with a walking stick, strolling along Hillside Road—the very image of landed gentry.

◆   ◆   ◆

In the years following their return from Europe, Maynard's thoughts and goals centered to a large degree on his daughter, Rose. He wanted to give her every social and educational advantage possible. He could see that she was already the 'spittin image' of her mother. Unfortunately, she did not share her mother's musical abilities. When Maynard realized this, he decided that the deficiency, (as he saw it), could be compensated for by training her in all the social graces that she might need to take a place in society. Addah, who was more attuned to the importance of social position, agreed with him wholeheartedly; she even visualized Rose as a debutante sometime in the future. Maynard, while not discouraging her, placed the idea on a low rung of his ladder of priorities. He fervently hoped, instead, that Rose would grow into a woman who would attract a husband of wealth and social standing, one with the intelligence and motivations to achieve success—as he had—in business.

This kind of training was frequently reflected when the family ate dinner together:

"Rose, dear, do sit up straight at the table." Addah would say, "Don't slouch and for goodness sake, keep your left hand in your lap when you're not using your knife." Or: "Don't chase your food around the plate, Rose. You have some bread on the butter plate; use it as a pusher."

"Rose, have you got a broken elbow?" Maynard, in an attempt at humor, would jokingly remark. "No! Then why is your elbow on the table? Maybe that's the way they ate in Rockland, but here we have better manners. A lady never eats with her elbow on the table." A second offense of this kind would bring the threat of a cast on the putative broken limb.

Eating in the kitchen was another custom Maynard deplored; he frequently warned Rose that to be a "kitchen eater" would consign her to a very low position on the social scale. Of course with a cook and a maid the opportunity for her to eat in the kitchen was minimal.

Deportment was also considered essential in the making of 'a lady'. This included the appropriate way to shake hands: never a limp, sweaty hand; a person of character always shakes hands firmly while looking the other person straight in the eye. The way one walked and carried theirself was also important. To achieve the proper, graceful walk—head held high, back straight, gait even—Rose, when she was eleven, was required to spend fifteen minutes a day in good weather walking up and down the terrace walk with books on her head and a cane through her elbows behind her back. This may or may not have had an effect on her dancing. At dancing class this young girl, who was tall for her age, stood head and shoulders over boys with whom she danced. As a result, she tended to lead her male partner because she, rather than he, could see where they were going.

Besides the swimming and tennis lessons at Fairfield Beach Club, Rose was introduced to the sport of sailing at the Pequot Yacht Club. Maynard had no intention of buying a boat, but he could not conceive of his daughter growing up without some experience with ships and sailing similar to that of his own youth. If he was disappointed that she showed no outstanding ability in any of these activities, he was satisfied that she was competent; and who knows, he thought, someday all these lessons might pay off.

All of this was meant to instill in Rose a sense of pride and a desire to achieve. Any lapse in behavior, any failure to meet pre-set standards was viewed as letting down the family. (In spite of putting his Maine connections behind him, Maynard still retained a strong attachment to the Bird family and its history.) So instead of praising Rose for what she had accomplished, more often than not she was left with a nagging feeling of guilt over not having lived up to her parents' expectations. She was a compliant child—whether by disposition or from fear of harsher restrictions, and since she had no siblings, there was no one with whom she could compare notes. Maynard, whose childhood memories were of another time and place, had no understanding of the needs of a child approaching puberty: the need for love, for acceptance and for a feeling of self-worth. Addah, who remembered her own youth as without family support except for her older sisters, understood even less than Maynard the dynamics of childhood. Both father and stepmother sincerely believed that they were doing well in raising Rose. If later events indicated a tendency on their daughter's part toward subterfuge and mendacity, they were unable to associate it with any failure on their part.

◆   ◆   ◆

Maynard also set great store in education since his own had been curtailed after a year at Exeter. He had little patience with stupidity or dullness of intellect. So far, Rose showed an alert and inquiring mind, and he hoped that she would turn out to be intellectually—if not brilliant, then at least brighter than average.

The selection of Unquowa School turned out to be an excellent choice. Rose seemed to handle the work there well in spite of having spent the year abroad. By the fall of 1934, when she was in eighth grade and doing well, Maynard and Addah decided to go south for the winter, seeking greater warmth than Connecticut could offer. They rented a house in the town of Pass Christian, Mississippi, just across Lake Pontchartrain from New Orleans. Rose would live with Lize and Joe Onorato in the city during the week while going to school at Metarie Park Country Day School; weekends would be spent with them at Pass Christian. The winter of 1934–35 turned out to be one of the coldest in memory all over the country. The cold dampness from the Gulf of Mexico and lack of heat in the house they had rented—essentially a summer place—reminded Maynard of the winter months on the Riviera—but worse. It was probably better than staying in Fairfield, but Maynard allowed as how he'd never go back there again. If he had to be cold, he'd take a decent, honest, New England cold any day.

When they left in the early spring their trip north included visits to boarding schools for Rose once she graduated from Unquowa in June. It is a tribute to Maynard's judgment that, after visiting a number of so-called society schools[159], they settled on Emma Willard School in Troy, New York. What he wanted for Rose, even if she was a girl, was a first class education comparable to the one he had given Milton. Although his decision was based on references from Fairfield friends, and parents of former or current students, the school's reputation for academic excellence was more important to him than a 'finishing school' environment. He recognized that Emma Willard was not only turning out young ladies, but young ladies with brains. In this perception, he was correct, and perhaps, in his ambitious goal for Rose's education, a little ahead of his time.

◆　　　◆　　　◆

During these years when Rose was growing up and her future was so much on his mind, Maynard had not forgotten that her roots—and his—were anchored in Maine. For Rose's benefit he had kept in touch with the Cobbs and Jennie Tyler. Jennie and her granddaughter, Evelyn Cobb, had both been occasional guests in Fairfield, and they had taken Rose for frequent visits to New London.

But it was Rockland that more than anything else that occupied Maynard's thoughts. He missed the town and the people he had known there; he missed the family roots and the feeling of belonging that came with them. He was proud of his Maine heritage and wanted Rose to feel the same as he did. Fairfield was fine, and it was his home now, but it could never take the place, mentally or emotionally, of Rockland. Even though he came to regret the breach with Alan, he also knew that his brother would never change his mind and that the break was irreparable. (It evidently didn't occur to Maynard that he had the same streak of stubbornness, if not to as great a degree, that he attributed to his brother.) He carried a vivid mental picture of Adelaide's face when he had last seen her—white and streaked with tears. For the present these and other memories made it impossible to go back.

Rose had corresponded regularly with Adelaide and her niece, Barbara Derry. (Barbara had been Rose's closest friend in Rockland.) If Adelaide would invite Rose for a visit, it would be almost like going back himself. So, in the spring of 1934, Maynard swallowed his pride and wrote to Adelaide, (he knew it was hopeless to write to Alan), suggesting that Rose would like to visit them in the summer when school was out. The response was immediate: they would love to have her. Rose's visit that summer was the beginning of regular visits in years to come. On these annual jaunts to Maine, Rose very often stopped to visit Milton and Helen. It was important, Maynard felt, for Rose to maintain contact with her brother. Besides, Rose seemed to enjoy the stops in Norwell where she could ride her horse Major.

Each time she set off for Rockland, Maynard would suggest someone in the family she should see. "Why don't you pay a visit to Harriet Bird," he would say. "I think she lives in a Home for the Aged on Rankin Street, but Adelaide can tell you if it's someplace else."

"Who's she?" Rose would ask, and her father would detail the genealogical connection for her.[160]

Then one year there was this directive: "Go see your Aunt Emma."

Again, Rose wanted to know who Aunt Emma was.

"You mean you don't know your own aunt!" Maynard was astounded. "She is my older brother's widow. I'm surprised you've never heard of her."

He had perhaps forgotten that Alan had also had a fight with Elmer and had never spoken to him afterwards. It was beginning to run in the family, and Maynard wondered what his mother would have said about her sons' fighting with each other? He knew the answer to that: his mother would have put a stop to it as only she could. It made him very sad to think of what had happened to his family. Only Henry seemed to stay on good terms with everyone, and for that, Maynard was grateful.

Rose now became one of her father's lines of communication to Rockland and Norwell. With her reports of the people she had seen, what she had done, and snatches of gossip she had overheard, Maynard felt more in touch with his family than he had for a number of years. He still subscribed to The Rockland newspaper, The Courier Gazette, and his spasmodic correspondence with Henry kept him further abreast of the town's goings-on. He still wanted to go back, but that would have to wait.

◆　　◆　　◆

About this time (1938), Milton notified Maynard that he and Helen had sold their place in Norwell and were moving, permanently to Mount Dora in central Florida.

Maynard was baffled. He had been encouraged when Milton had taken a teaching job at a junior college in Boston, but it appeared that he was just dabbling in a profession; after a two or three years, he gave it up altogether. He and Helen had spent the last two winters in Florida, as did many people who could afford it. There was nothing wrong with that from Maynard's point of view, but to sell the fine estate in Norwell, where the Cushing name stood for something did not make sense. Was there more to this abrupt departure than met the eye? Rose hadn't visited Norwell that summer so there was no report on how things were going there. "Why this sudden move?" he asked himself.

Maynard did not possess an introspective disposition. He had always been too busy with his own business and personal affairs. Now his thoughts went back to the many times that he had been disappointed in Milton: there were his many warnings to Mary that she was turning the boy into an effeminate sissy. His son had no boyhood pals and seemed alienated from the Bird the family; up to now he was more attached to Helen's family.

Maynard disliked the Cushing family. As he saw it, they exhibited all the pretentiousness of the Boston Brahmins, of which Helen was the perfect example and as 'homely as a mud fence' to boot. From her affected, nasal, Boston, upper-class twang to her appearance, she was a caricature of the Bostonian he found most distasteful. Her clothes were an affront to a man like Maynard, who prided himself on his personal appearance. They were always expensive, but looked as though the style had been selected in 1928, and the same one worn ever since. And it wasn't as though she couldn't afford attractive clothing: the Cushing family was extremely wealthy.

Was it the Cushing wealth that rankled Maynard or the fact that Milton lived on it parasitically? Maynard was proud that his wealth had been made through his own endeavors, and he admired others who had done the same. Conversely, he looked down on those who had lived off of other people's efforts; and who, like Milton, had married for money. That, as Maynard saw it, was a disgrace to him and his family.

Milton's character and the Cushing wealth and snobbery did not explain the reason for their sudden their move. Maynard knew that Helen dominated his son's life. In this respect she had replaced Mary as a mother figure. Their marriage had always seemed an odd one. Perhaps this was Helen's decision; but again, Maynard wanted to know "Why?"

He decided that if he was ever to get an answer to this mystery, it had to be through a face-to-face encounter. It had been many years since his son and his wife had visited Fairfield: their absence due, in part, because neither Helen nor Addah liked each other. In this situation, however, Maynard's curiosity got the better of him; and with Addah's concurrence, they were invited to visit Fairfield before leaving New England.

They arrived late one Friday afternoon in early November. After cocktails and dinner, where the conversation was limited to political matters and the worsening situation in Europe, they moved to the living room for coffee. Now, thought Maynard, was a good time to bring up the subject of their move.

Looking directly at Milton, Maynard said, "We were surprised to hear that you had sold the Norwell place. What brought that about?"

Milton answered. defensively, "Well, we've bought some property in Mt. Dora and we still have a place in Coral Gables if we find Mt. Dora too isolated. And then there's the tax matter. Also, Florida tax laws are better for us than Massachusetts." If he expected some objection from his father, he was not disappointed.

"I can't see moving to Florida permanently just for a tax break," Maynard said in a critical tone.[161] "That seems like a pretty poor excuse since your taxes probably don't amount to much anyway."

"We've put some money into buying land in Central Florida where we plan to raise cattle," Milton added.

"Cattle!" Maynard exploded. "You mean to tell me you're going down there to raise cows? What in Sam Hill is that going to get you?"

Addah had said nothing up to this point, but she recognized the signs of Maynard's rising anger. "Maynard, let Milton explain."

"They're beef cattle, Father. You may not know it, but beef commands a pretty good price. We think......"

Maynard interrupted. "Milton, in the last twenty years you have sold securities, raised peaches and taught school. Not one of these ventures was successful. Now you say you want to raise cattle. How long will it be before you decide that doesn't work out either? You're lucky your wife has money, because it's obvious you can't even support yourself let alone her."

Helen decided to enter the conversation. "Maynard, why don't you just mind your own business. We're tired of you trying to run our lives."

It was good advice, which, unfortunately, Maynard didn't heed. Again, his customary tact and control failed him in a family dispute. "Helen, I would think you'd want your husband to amount to something instead of living like a leach on your inheritance."

Helen now as angry as her father-in-law replied, "Maynard, you don't even know your son. You have tried to control his life ever since he was a child, and if he has become someone you don't like, then it's your fault."

"How dare you say that! I've given Milton everything—every advantage—and what has he done in return? Nothing!"

"Yes, you've given him everything, except the one thing he needed—love. You want to know why we're leaving Norwell? Why we left North Carolina, as well? It's because Milton got into a scrape with another man in both places."

Maynard was speechless, and Addah's mouth dropped open in surprise. Before either one could say anything, Helen continued.

"I know that neither of you like me, but I have given Milton the affection and security he needs. I care about him even with his faults, and I'll protect him to my dying day.

Maynard sputtered, "What do you mean he got into a scrape with another man?"

Helen was now in control. "You know what I mean, Maynard. You're a big boy. Or do you want me to spell it out for you?"

There was silence in the room. Milton, flushed and embarrassed, looked down at his shoes. Addah rose and left the room, unable to endure any further revelations. Helen stared stonily at her father-in-law.

It took Maynard what seemed an eternity before he could speak again. Finally he broke the silence and said in a choked voice, "Milton, you have disgraced our family. Not just me, but all of the Birds. As a result, I can no longer acknowledge you as my son."

Almost in unison, Helen and Milton stood up.

"I had hoped you might understand and show some compassion, Maynard," Helen said. "We will leave now as I'm sure you would rather we didn't spend the night."

◆   ◆   ◆

Once again, Maynard had allowed his temper to override his good judgement. The result was that this time he had lost his son—permanently. Only when faced with a similar situation with Rose some years later, did he finally learn his lesson!

29

The summer of 1939 saw two major changes in the lives of the Bird family. In mid-June, accompanied by Jennie Tyler, Maynard and Addah, traveled to Troy, New York to attend Rose's graduation from Emma Willard School.

The beauty and dignity of the school's campus always appealed to Maynard. The impressive Tudor-gothic buildings standing in a rough square around a grassy area, intersected by walks to form a triangle, gave the campus an air of tradition and permanence. The rough textured stone buildings with their crenellated rooflines, their grayness softened with the passage of time, and the occasional tower and mullioned windows, reminded him of places he had seen and been impressed with in England. He hoped that Jennie would be as moved as he was with the surroundings he had been able to give her granddaughter during the past four years.

As Jennie listened to Maynard extolling the educational and social advantages of Emma Willard, the phrase "all the things that money can buy" floated through her mind. She wondered what Rose would have thought of all this affluence, and she hoped that Maynard had not forgotten the gifts of love and caring that her granddaughter had missed with the loss of her mother.

In her four years at Emma Willard, Rose had done well. Although she didn't graduate with any particular honors, she stood in the upper quarter of her class, and had been active in a number of extracurricular activities. She had made friends at the school, and, as Maynard noted, her friends were girls from the 'right kind' of families. Just to see his daughter graduating from this fine school, and with the expectation of further college education, filled him with pride. Rose had applied to Smith College and Connecticut College for Women in New London, and expected to hear from both later in the summer. As it turned out, she was accepted at both and decided on Smith. She would be the first woman in the Bird family to graduate from a four year college.

Commencement started with a procession, to the strains of Elgar's *Pomp and Circumstance,* of the seniors from the gymnasium to the Slocum Hall auditorium. Each girl was dressed in white, the dresses similar but not identical, and each girl carried a large bunch of red roses. When Maynard saw Rose in the line, it was as if he was once again seeing his beloved wife: she was the image of her mother. He looked at Jennie Tyler to see if she had the same impression, and as their eyes met, they exchanged looks of sadness that the mother of this lovely girl could not be there to share in the joy of the occasion.

Before their trip, however, Addah had come home one day from a Garden Club meeting overflowing with excitement. She found Maynard in his study and could hardly wait to tell him her news.

"What's on your mind, Addah? Has the Queen of England invited you to tea?" Maynard joked. He knew her well enough to know when she had some bit of gossip or news that couldn't wait.

"Better than that, Maynard," she replied, "I ran into Margaret Field today."

It took Maynard several seconds to place Margaret Field in the landscape of his memory. He finally remembered that the Fields were related to the Warner clan, who were major stockholders in the Warner company that made ladies' underwear—brassieres and corsets and such. 'Now, there was a business that would always have a market', he thought.

"So! I didn't know she had replaced the Queen of England in the pecking order." He loved to tease his wife because 'she would always bite'

"Oh, Maynard, be serious," she said in a tone of exasperation. "You know who I mean: John Field's wife. She asked me if we might be interested in selling this place." The words came tumbling out not allowing any interruption. "Of course, I told her we had never even thought about selling, but she insisted that we consider the idea."

Maynard's expression was one of surprise. "That is interesting," he remarked, now serious. "Why, do you suppose they want to move up here? I thought they lived in a perfectly good house in Brooklawn Park near the Country Club."[162]

Addah explained what little she had gleaned from her conversation. Evidently Mrs Field's family—the Warner branch or some other distant relative in the family—had, at one time, owned all the property on top of the Hill. They would like to buy some of it back.

Although the Depression had eased somewhat by 1939; eight million men were still unemployed and hard times were far from over. Maynard realized that it was highly unusual to have an offer—any kind of an offer—on property as valuable as theirs. In fact, he questioned whether this was really a bona fide offer. But Addah was positive that it was genuine, and with her usual good business sense, Maynard had no reason to doubt her.

"So, how did you leave it?" he asked.

"I told her that we were going away and couldn't talk about it until we got back."

Maynard could think of several reasons to sell the house. It was really too big and too hard to keep up with just the two servants and a gardener. Their entertaining was not, nor could it be, on the scale they had originally expected. Then there was the anticipated expense of putting Rose through college, and their income, while still ample, was being eroded due inflation. It was an expensive place and he was not sure that anyone would pay the amount he thought it was worth. Another consideration was that all his houses—whether built or bought—reflected his opinion of himself and the way he wanted others to see him. Would moving to a less pretentious home diminish his standing among his Fairfield friends? Probably not. He still derived great pleasure and pride from just living on the estate he and Addah had so lovingly created. It was truly the epitome of all the homes he had owned.

These and other conflicting thoughts occupied his mind while they were in Troy. If the offer was serious, and if it could be arranged to their financial advantage, they would be foolish to turn it down. He and Addah would decide jointly, for it was she who had had the time, knowledge and skill to make their home the show place that it was.

After their return, Rose left for a houseparty in Savannah given by one of her school friends. It was then that they got in touch with the Fields to see if their offer to buy the place was serious. Maynard was still skeptical about it. They might have changed their minds, or it might have been just something that came up in casual 'women's type' conversation. As it turned out, the offer was valid and they started meeting with John and Margaret Field.

Addah's willingness to be flexible and her skill in bargaining, more than anything else, produced an agreement satisfactory to all the parties. Maynard and Addah would get the Field's present house in Brooklawn Park and a substantial cash payment for only ten acres of the Greenfield Hill property. Since neither of them wanted to give up living on Greenfield Hill, the eleventh acre would be retained on which they would build another house. In the meantime, they would live in the Field's Brooklawn Park house while their new one, designed by the noted local architect, Cameron Clark, was being built.

The day that they signed the final agreement with the Fields, Maynard said to Addah in a tone of satisfaction mixed with a bit of awe, "I think we'll come out of this on the plus side, all things considered. If it hadn't been for your agreeing to take their barn of a house in trade, dear, we could never have arrived at a settlement with them. What did you see in it?"

Addah smiled rather smugly at this comment. "That house is worth far more than you or they realize, Maynard. It is a great family house, and most people with a large family couldn't care less that it is ugly outside."

(Maynard had not thought of the house as ugly. Only that it was too big and reminded him, unpleasantly, of the house he and Mary had owned in Rockland. 'Was it the brown shingled exterior?' he wondered. Well, it would only be a temporary address after all.)

"It's also in a fine neighborhood that will appeal to people who want to move up," Addah continued. "When I finish with it inside, a prospective buyer will think he's bought a palace."

When they moved into the Brooklawn Park house that fall, Addah had transformed it with paint both inside and out, and a few inexpensive changes here and there to prove her point. As she had predicted, when they sold it a year and a half later after the new house on Greenfield Hill was completed, they profited many times over from the face lift she had given it. It was her first venture in real estate, and it wouldn't be her last.

◆   ◆   ◆

When Maynard turned seventy on July 16, 1939 he knew that, although he still could get around as nimbly as ever, seventy was an age that was considered advanced by the standards of the day. He tried, with Addah's help, to eat moderately, cut down on smoking and get a good bit of exercise by working outdoors whenever possible. Even so, he had put on weight that required some tailoring adjustments around what had once been his waist. He didn't feel all that old, but the lines on his face—on either side of his nose down the sides of his mouth—and on his forehead, plus the thinning hair and the loosening jowls, said otherwise. His eyes showed the alertness of a younger man; and his wit and humor were still intact. The doctor had advised a morning dose of Metamucil to cure him of occasional abdominal pains, and a restricted diet that eliminated corn on the cob and lobster. He took the Metamucil religiously along with his morning bowl of Cerevim, but no one could possibly expect a son of Maine to give up eating lobsters-occasionally. With the repeal of Prohibition in 1933, he could enjoy his bourbon old-fashioned before dinner with a dividend straight from the bottle, without feeling that he was breaking the law. (Not that he had ever seen himself as a law-breaker, anyway.)

He decided to give himself a birthday trip to Maine in the interval before moving to the Brooklawn Park house, and planning for the new home on Greenfield Hill. He had not been to Maine for nearly a dozen years, partly because of Addah's aversion, expressed in no uncertain terms, after their visit there in 1927. But things had changed; he wanted to see the places he had known as a boy, as a youth and as an up and coming young man. An added inducement to go was an invitation from his old friend, Billy White and his wife, Dot. They had retired from the hustle and bustle of New York to Rockland, where they had built a house overlooking Chickawauka Pond. Addah agreed to go because they could stay with the Whites who were also her friends. Rose had already left for her usual visit with Alan and Adelaide, so the trip became a leisurely one with a visit to the Cobb's in New London and stops to see friends in Massachusetts and Portland. Here they stayed at Maynard's old haunt, The Lafayette Hotel, now much seedier than he remembered.

He spent a solitary fifteen minutes at Rose's grave in Evergreen Cemetery remembering their brief life together. The marker that had been erected, after he had recovered from the shock of her passing, paid tribute to her voice. It read: *"I know that only as a singer* [can] *I come into Thy Presence"*. He wondered if something should have been added that mentioned her as a wife and a mother. No, this was the way she would have wanted it. Besides, he would be buried here next to his beloved so that they would once again be together.

In Rockland they told Rose of the house sale and trade, but she seemed much more interested in her new beau, Ted Richardson, than in a move to a new home. He took note of Rose's interest in the Richardson boy whose family had originated in Rockland. He knew Ted's father, Arthur Richardson, who, from Maynard's point of view, was another example of a Rockland boy who had succeeded elsewhere. Arthur was an executive at Standard Oil of New Jersey and had had a number of foreign assignments. In the following two years during in which Rose dated Ted, Maynard envisioned a match that would be the culmination of all his hopes and expectations for his daughter's future. Here was a boy (he could not yet call him a man), of Maine heritage, educated in England and now a senior at Princeton with a bright future through his father's connections. What more could a father ask for his daughter? Unfortunately, for reasons Maynard never understood, the romance cooled a year or so later when Ted, upon graduating from Princeton, went to work for his father's company, and was shipped off to India where he stayed until the war, which was so imminent in the summer of 1939, was over.

As he had expected, Maynard found that Rockland had changed during the Depression years. But what place had not? The lime business no longer supported the town and lime was now quarried exclusively for the use of the concrete plant in Thomaston. No one seemed to miss the lime kilns along the harbor front and the air was certainly cleaner. McDougall Ladd Insurance (Maynard's original firm) was now W.C. Ladd & Sons[163], Nelson McDougall having moved to Portland where he became a banker.[164] Of course Maynard had enjoyed a visit with Nelson when he was in Portland and basked in the aura of his protege's success. As Maynard was fond of saying then and in later years, "All his boys were doing well".

The same could not be said of The John Bird Company. Under Adriel's management the company now dealt almost exclusively in spices and coffee. Three Crow brands were still produced in Rockland, but coffee was now sold under the brand name of La Touraine with headquarters in Boston. In fact, Adriel seemed to spend most of his time in Boston, and Maynard wondered if he had the best interests of the company at heart. It was also obvious that his grandfather's and his father's company no longer held a significant place in the Rockland business community.

Henry still operated the Medomak Canning Company, headquartered near Waldoboro, and Maynard was pleased to find that it was doing well. Theodore, Henry's youngest, was now active in the business, and his brother, Fred would soon join him. He did not see Alan, nor did he expect to. Perhaps he could have called on him, but the scars left by their fight had not healed to the extent that he wanted to reopen the wounds again—which was sure to happen if he saw his brother.

When he left Maine, perhaps for the last time, Maynard was satisfied that he had broken the ties with his family when he did. No point now in looking back.

◆   ◆   ◆

September 1, 1939. German Troops Storm Poland.

Every newspaper in the country carried this headline. Americans kept their ears glued to the radio stations anxious to hear the latest bulletins. On September 3rd Britain and France declared war on Germany, too late to save Poland. Russia by secret agreement with Germany stayed out of the conflict. By Tuesday, the 5th, stocks on the New York Stock Exchange soared as investors saw war profits looming.

For Maynard it was like a repeat of 1914 only this time he had been on the sidelines for so long that the best he could do was to invest in stocks he judged would produce war profits. It was better than nothing, but a far cry from his activity in the early days of WWI. In the years since their return from Europe, both he and Addah had been very much aware of the inexorable take over of Germany by the Nazis: the absorption, first of the Rhineland, then Austria and finally Czechoslovakia. The invasion of Poland came as no surprise although hopes had been high that Chamberlain's[165] Munich meeting with Hitler would put an end to the German's land grab. There was still the feeling among Maynard's friends, however, that a war in Europe was none of America's business. Maynard was not so sure; he remembered all too well how our country was dragged into the first war; and he was fearful that some incident or other would propel the United States, once again, into foreign entanglements. Although, he was appalled by the attacks on Russians and then on Jews by the Catholic priest, Father Coughlin, he paid scant attention in general to the Nazi's treatment of the Jews. Like many others, he felt it was a problem in many countries and maybe this was just a little more extreme. What did concern him was Lindbergh's support of Hitler. Here was a national hero who was supporting German aggression. This was anathema to Maynard who had vivid recollections of German barbarity and cruelty in WWI.

In the fall of 1939, he and Addah were heavily involved in moving and the design for the new house. By November, when Rose came home from college for Thanksgiving, they were comfortably installed in the house in Brooklawn Park. They would live there for nearly two years while a smaller, but elegant version of a French style manor house was built. Landscaping was less elaborate than formerly, but a semicircular drive leading up to the balanced façade with its centered entryway, and two large chimneys at either end of a hipped roof, gave the impression of a structure larger than it actually was.

When they moved back to Greenfield Hill in the fall of 1941, the war showed no sign of lessening. The Germans had overrun most of Europe; Italy had entered the war on the side of the Germans as had Japan. Paris had fallen in June 1940 and France was divided with the Germans occupying the northern portion, and the southern half a supposedly independent France. Winston Churchill, whose oratory had aroused the English and spurred evacuation of 340,000 troops of the British Expeditionary Force from beaches of Dunkirk before the Germans could annihilate them, was now Britain's Prime Minister. In the fall of that year, German planes bombed British cities and the Battle for Britain was underway. In the U.S. Franklin Roosevelt had been re-elected, handily defeating Wendell Willkie for a third term—the first time ever in the history of the country that a president had served more than two terms. A peacetime military draft—also a first—had been instituted in November 1940 and men were being called up for a year's service in the Army. All signs pointed to America's eventual involvement in a Second World War, especially when Germany invaded Russia in the summer of 1941, severing the non-aggression pact between the two countries.

Considering his political background, one might have expected Maynard to be an isolationist. However, unlike some of his friends and associates, a background of foreign travel and the experience of living abroad had given him a broader, more internationalist point of view. He had not adopted the attitude of many, who had served in World War One, of boasting that the United States had saved Europe in that war and then turned their backs on further European involvement.

He and Addah were both concerned with the fate of their friends abroad—principally those in France. She would often remark, "I wonder what has happened to Madame la Contesse? Villa Violetta is on the German side of the Loire. Poor Madame!" Maynard too wondered about their expatriate friends in the north. Had they managed to escape through Portugal as so many others were doing? Although Maynard and Addah no longer had strong connections in England, they joined their friends and neighbors in deploring the plight of the English. "Bundles for Britain" engaged the women in knitting, sewing and contributing clothing to those in Britain who had been bombed out of their homes. Knitting and sewing get-togethers were held at many homes where scarves, mittens, sweaters, and the ubiquitous balaclava helmet, a hangover from WWI, were turned out in great quantities. Parties were also given to collect funds for the needy in Great Britain.

However, the war did not prevent Maynard and Addah from setting out in late November to drive to Florida, where they were renting the home of their friends, the Scudders, in Delray Beach. They were there when the Japanese bombed Pearl Harbor on December 7th. Rose joined them for Christmas vacation arriving in West Palm Beach on one of the last commercial flights before civilian air travel was discontinued. They would leave their car in Florida when they returned by train to Fairfield in the spring. Since they could only get gas rations for one car at a time, it was more sensible to keep one in each place.

There seemed to be no way that Maynard could contribute to the war at his age: draft boards, air raid security, ration boards and other quasi government boards were not seeking men in their 70s even on a volunteer basis. At least not unless things got a lot worse. Outwardly, their lives went on undisturbed except for contributions to worthy causes in support of the war. Since they held no positions that warranted increased rations, they made do with the minimum allotments of ration books: A-book for gas, and A books for nearly everything else including food and clothing. Gas rationing did mean, however, that they, and their neighbors, were limited in their contact with the town, its stores and community activities. To lessen this isolation, Maynard and other Greenfield Hill residents chartered a small school bus, paid a driver (a woman), and with a gas allotment for public transportation, established a bus route between Fairfield center and the Hill. Twice a day the little bus would make the three-mile trip carrying mail, groceries, and even domestic help to the Hill residents; return trips often carried passengers and made deliveries at intermediate stops. The bus and Addah's knack for economy enabled them to use their limited resources to great advantage. Mary, the maid and Trudy, the cook, left to take war jobs for reasons of patriotism and remuneration. Addah made do with daily help when she could get it. She had never learned to cook, but with her usual determination, mastered the culinary arts with success that bordered on excellence.

For Maynard, as for many of his friends, the war was putting a strain on their financial resources. It was now that Addah's business acumen again came into play. During the second winter (1942–43) that they spent in Florida, they rented a small house on the west side of town. This house was a far cry from the comfort and luxury they had enjoyed at the Scudder's place the previous winter, and it was quickly obvious to both of them that if they intended to continue to winter in Florida, a more suitable place must be found. Addah started looking for a better home almost as soon as they arrived in Delray that October; as a result, she located a two-story house on the east side, within walking distance of the center of town (with gas so scarce that was an important factor). The house was in good condition; perhaps a little larger than they needed, but that wasn't a deterrent; the lot was large stretching down to N.E. 7th Street, and behind the house was a row of several run down apartments.

"What in the world do you want that place for?" Maynard had asked when she took him to see her 'find'.

"Don't you see, Maynard, the house itself is in good shape, and we can get those apartments fixed up and rent them. There's a tremendous demand for housing for the families of the men at the Boca Raton Air Base."

When Maynard thought about it, he realized that here was an unexpected and welcome source of additional income. He remembered what Addah had done with the Brooklawn Park house and how it had sold for far more than he had expected. They could use the money, but he wondered what they would do with the apartments after the war.

"Don't worry about that, Maynard", Addah said confidently. "We can convert them into something else if they're not rentable. In the meantime, let's make the best of the housing market while we can."

The following year, after some renovations that included painting and collecting basic furnishings, the apartments were fully rented for the duration of the war, and they found the main house a vast improvement over their previous lodging.

Addah's second venture into real estate, turned out to be as profitable as she had predicted

The war would continue for two more years. Maynard and Addah split their time between Florida and Connecticut. Except for the restrictions imposed by the war their pattern of life was little changed.

30

In June 1943, Maynard and Addah traveled by train to Northampton (Mass.) to attend Rose's graduation from Smith College. Attendance at the event by parents was limited due to wartime travel restrictions and the lack of public accommodations in the town.[166] They were fortunately able to stay with William Bird who now lived in a lovely home adjacent to many of the college facilities. (William had left Goldman Sachs in the mid-thirties to become the head of the Prophylactic Brush Company, a division of Warner Lambert.) Despite the wartime limitations, the ceremony was impressive. A number of juniors, dressed in white, had been selected to escort the commencement procession to the college auditorium. The faculty in their multicolored hoods designating their college or university of origin led the procession; then came the graduating class with hoods in the Smith colors of yellow and white over their black gowns. Although somewhat diminished by wartime dropouts, the class still numbered nearly four hundred. At the conclusion of the graduation program, each girl received her diploma, and as an indication of having achieved a bachelor's degree, switched the tassel on her mortarboard cap from left to right. Maynard reflected that this was the first time he had seen a child of his achieve this distinction. (Milton had joined the navy without finishing his last year at Harvard—the diploma had been awarded *in absentia*.) It was with a sense of pride and satisfaction that he saw Rose, perhaps for the first time, as a mature young woman who would reflect well on her parents.

Maynard expected that Rose, on graduation, would join the WAVES, (the title given to the women's branch of the active naval reserve). Although she had majored in Zoology, in her senior year, she had also completed a course in cryptoanalysis that would qualify her for officer's training and service as a naval officer for the duration of the war. Much to his disappointment, however, Rose failed the physical examination. He was always concerned when she showed any indication of poor health, (her mother's untimely death continued to haunt him); so on their return to Fairfield, he insisted that she see the family doctor. The result of further tests was the same as had been noted by the naval doctors. Maynard was somewhat reassured by the doctor's conclusion that there was basically nothing wrong with her that wouldn't clear up in due course.

It was time, he realized, for Rose to be on her own. He had fulfilled the goal he had set for himself of giving his daughter the best education possible; now he was relieved of the financial burden of college, even though he still chose to give her a modest allowance. He did not object to her plan of finding a job in New York City, where she proposed to live with her old school friend, Helena Plumb, if they could find an apartment. He suggested—it was more of an order than a suggestion—that the girls look for an apartment in a suitable location, preferably to the east of Fifth Avenue. As he recalled from his days of living in the city, any housing west of Central Park tended to be inhabited by people, especially women, of poor reputation who were suspected of loose living. Furthermore, he cautioned that any apartment the girls found should be one with an elevator and doorman; this he felt would be a further precaution against incursions by unwelcome males. Rose found a job at New York University's medical school in the Department of Physiology as a research technician; later she transferred to the Chemistry department. After a couple of weeks of hunting, she and Helena were lucky enough, and perhaps to Maynard's surprise, to find a one-bedroom furnished apartment on East 52nd Street between Lexington and Third Avenue—with an elevator and a doorman!

Despite the fact that Rose was 21 and now living independently, Maynard still had concerns about her. He knew that wartime was a time of great social upheaval; it had been so with WWI and this war gave indications of being much longer than the earlier one. Ordinarily, he would have expected her to be engaged or married by this time. Since wartime marriages didn't usually turn out well he was not anxious to see her commit herself just yet. He did worry, however, about the associations she would have in New York, and how she would handle them. He told himself that if Rose used her good sense and kept her feet on the ground, everything would be all right.

Addah was not as sanguine. Having lived as a single woman in the city for many years, she was more acutely aware of the pitfalls to which a young woman could be exposed. (She may have exaggerated them somewhat to make an impression on Maynard.) After Rose was settled in New York and talked about going to dances at the Officers' Clubs, Addah visualized all kinds of men Rose might meet: Catholics, Jews, even colored—God forbid. They came from all over the world. Who knew what they might be? Just because they were officers, didn't make them acceptable

Maynard tried to allay his wife's worries. "That girl she brought home one weekend—what was her name? Martha someone?[167] She was alright, wasn't she?"

Addah couldn't dispute this. She had found the girl quite acceptable and was further relieved to find that Martha was also a Smith graduate.

However, during the fall of 1943, when Rose invited a young naval officer named O'Gara, whom she had met on a visit to Maine the previous spring, to Fairfield for a weekend, Addah voiced her concerns to Maynard about the young man being an Irish Catholic.

Maynard started to pooh pooh her worries. "Just because she wants to have him spend a weekend here doesn't mean there's anything serious," he said.

When Addah persisted, he finally gave in. "I'll speak to her about it, he responded rather irritably. "But I really think you're making a mountain out of a mole hill, Addah. Rose says he's going overseas shortly, and that will probably be the end of it."

"It's just that she never sees any of the young men she knows from around here." Addah was still worried. She felt that Rose was living a different life from the one she and Maynard had tried to make for her, and she didn't like it.

After the young man left, Maynard brought the matter up with Rose in what he hoped was a bantering tone. "I hope there's nothing serious going on between you two. You certainly wouldn't want to be known as Rosie O'Gara for the rest of your life, would you?"

"Oh, Daddy," Rose replied in an obviously annoyed tone, "why do you always think that anybody I go out with I want to marry. Or for that matter, wants to marry me. The way you give any man I date the third degree, makes it impossible for me to bring anyone home."

Maynard resorted to his usual excuse—one that seemed less and less relevant these days. "I'm just thinking of your welfare, my dear. You have been brought up to have the best and to want the best; I don't want to see you accepting anything less than the best."

Rose turned and left the room leaving her father to wish that he could talk to her without always feeling he had made her angry. He was sure that if he tried to tell her how it was in his youth, she would look at him blankly; and if she said anything, it would probably be, "Oh, Daddy, things have changed. You're so old fashioned."

Was he old fashioned? Was it wrong for him to question her dates about their background? He knew, from his own experience, that boys still could get away with as much—more in wartime—as they had in his youth. He also remembered some of the tales told by men who had been in France during WWI, and he didn't want to have his daughter get 'in trouble'. Rose didn't seem to understand that when he said, "Boys will be boys!" and "It's the woman who pays!" he was coming as close as he dared to speaking explicitly about sex.

◆   ◆   ◆

During the last two years of the war, things seemed to go along without incident. Maynard and Addah, and others like them lived quietly within the constraints the war imposed on them. They spent their winters in Florida where they volunteered occasionally at the Red Cross; they were unable to do much volunteering in Fairfield because of the limitations on gasoline. They heard occasionally of the death or wounding in battle of someone's son or grandson, but their friends and their friends' children were all too old to be in service. Thus they were spared the distress of the war's impact that so many younger parents endured.

On May 7, 1945 Germany surrendered unconditionally. Although the war was over in Europe it was still raging in the Pacific. Rationing was still in force and things had not changed significantly in their lives. In June, Rose spent a few weekends in Faifield because she was having trouble breathing. The asthma-like symptoms would disappear when she returned to the city on Sunday; the source seemed to be something she was working with in the laboratory. Maynard, as usual, was concerned about his daughter's health. When he realized that the problem was work related, he recommended that she quit her job. This she did at the end of July and spent the remaining weeks of August visiting Alan and Adelaide in Maine.

The headline read: Japan surrenders; war is ended all over the world. After the United States had destroyed the cities of Hiroshima and Nagasaki with atomic bombs, the Japanese sued for peace. Maynard and Addah, like most of the American people, could not comprehend how a single bomb could destroy a city. Neither they, nor others, disputed the right or wrong of the atom bomb at that point. It was enough for everyone that lives had been saved by not invading Japan, and the war was over. Parties were held everywhere celebrating the surrender and victory; later on, as the troops came home, there were parades in every large city in the nation. The feeling of relief was palpable. People hoped, Maynard included, that now they could go back to ordinary life without the ration books and shortages of everything; and to some extent they were right when gas and fuel oil rationing ended on August 15th.

Maynard and Addah greeted the Allied victory with relief and celebration. Using some of their precious food ration coupons, they entertained a number of their close friends at a dinner featuring a whole ham; they would have had lobsters had they been available. Maynard made applejack cocktails from a gallon jug recently discovered in a forgotten hatbox in the attic. Spirits were high both from the celebration as well as the bottle. Maynard laughed when he recalled how some of the ladies wove their way into dinner. "That applejack sure made everyone pretty loose," he remarked to Addah the next day. "Did you see Bess Klotz? She hasn't had such a good time in ages."

When Rose returned from Maine, she applied for a job with the American Red Cross as a Field Assistant, and was assigned to Fort Dix, New Jersey. Maynard wasn't quite sure what she was doing—mainly office work she said—but at least it wasn't work that exposed her to health hazards; and she was making more money than before; allowing him to discontinue her allowance. (Although he never admitted it, his income was suffering from higher taxes and an increase in expenses.) He and Addah had hoped that, with the war over, Rose would stay home and resume her place in Fairfield society; join the Junior League or something like that. He didn't see a career for Rose in the Red Cross, but for the time being, she seemed happy with what she was doing. She continued to work at Fort Dix until the following July when she abruptly quit her job at the end of the month and returned to Fairfield.

That summer (1946), Maynard was puzzled by Rose's behavior. She made a trip to Chicago, shortly after leaving the Red Cross, to visit a family whose son she had met at Ft. Dix. On her return, after stopping to visit her college roommate in Buffalo, she showed no further interest in the people she had visited. Maynard had promised Rose a car when new ones became available. In August, on her return, he made a $400 down payment on a small Ford business coupe with the understanding that she would pay the balance on a monthly basis. This enabled her to get around without using the one car they now had in Fairfield.

Unlike other summers, Rose did not go to Maine, but stayed close to Fairfield. She was to be in the wedding of her former New York roommate, Helena, in September; bridal showers and pre-nuptial parties took up some of her time. With her new car she visited the Cobbs in New London for several days. While she was there, Addah took a call from a man who identified himself as Rose's friend and asked where he could get in touch with her. Addah gave him the Cobb's phone number without thinking much about it, but when Rose returned, all she would say was that this was someone she had met in Maine a year ago.

"Why don't you want to talk about him?" Maynard inquired. "We are interested in what you are doing. It's not just out of curiosity, Rose." He truly wanted know what she was doing, so he tried to make his tone as pleasant and non-confrontational as possible. He remembered her outburst over the O'Gara incident.

"I don't <u>not</u> want to talk about him, Daddy. It's just that I don't like him any more. Maybe I did once, but he's just not a very interesting person. He bores me!"

After that, Maynard kept his questions to himself. He was still concerned about his daughter. She was often away from home during the day without telling them where she was going. He assumed that she was either at the Beach Club or visiting friends. He knew that she had made several trips to New York and he inferred they were for job hunting, although there didn't seem to be anything in particular that she was looking for. When he asked her what she planned to do in the fall, she put him off by saying she was going to get serious about getting a job after Helena's wedding. He asked Addah several times if Rose had confided in her, but Addah was just as much in the dark. He wanted to trust his daughter, but the feeling was growing that she was evading him, or even, possibly, lying to him.

The Tuesday after Helena's wedding, Maynard ran into his good friend, Sid Talbot at the Beach Club. Sid mentioned, during the course of conversation that he'd seen Rose getting mail out of a post-office box the day before. "What's the matter, Maynard?" Sid said. "Post Office not delivering mail to the Hill anymore?"

Maynard was puzzled but decided to pass it off as a joke. "We get so much mail, Sid, we have to have two places—one for bills and one for real letters."

He wondered what in the world Rose was doing with a post office box. A feeling of unease followed him the rest of the day. He decided that before he asked Rose about it, he should talk with Addah. Their discussion that evening did nothing to ease his concerns. They agreed this was a problem that demanded clarification.

At breakfast the next morning Maynard took the bull by the horns.

"Rose", he said bluntly, "I want to know what is going on? You have been getting mail at a post office box. Are you hiding something from us?"

There was silence. Rose looked down at the bowl of cereal—'Cerevim of course, would they ever stop eating the stuff'. When she looked up, both Addah and Maynard were staring at her waiting for an answer. Maynard sensed her distress and decided a little patience might elicit a more forthright response; he wasn't sure now whether it was one he wanted to hear.

Her voice came out strained and apologetic. "I know I should have told you sooner, but I just couldn't." Then in a rush of words: "I'm going to get married."

Dead silence followed for what seemed like an eternity. A strangled sound of disbelief came from Maynard. Addah gave a gasp, but kept quiet.

Finally in a controlled, emotionless voice he said, "Who do you plan to marry? Where did you meet him? And for heaven's sake, tell us the truth."

Rose was engulfed by a feeling of relief. 'There', she thought, 'I have said it'. It had gone much better than she had expected. A burden of fear had been lifted from her shoulders. Maybe they <u>would</u> understand. She started by saying, "Daddy, I'm marrying a wonderful man. His name is Ed Waterman and I met him last spring at Fort Dix."

"Why didn't you tell us about him?" Maynard interrupted. "Why, if he is so wonderful, didn't you bring him home so that we could meet him?"

Rose's answer was simple and to the point. "Because he's Jewish and I knew you would object."

Addah's face mirrored her distress. "Oh, Rose," she gasped, "how could you do this to your father?"

Maynard looked at his wife and held up his hand to quiet her, saying, "Addah, let me handle this."

He was upset enough without having Addah interfere. That the man was Jewish was a problem and he suddenly understood why she had been so secretive. However, no matter what happened, he didn't want his anger to cost him his daughter as it had his brother and his son. It took a lot of self-control but his next question was not derisive. "And when did you plan on getting married?" he asked.

"Tomorrow!" Rose, whose nervousness had abated somewhat, responded firmly.

This was a further blow. "And how do you figure to do that?" He could not control the sarcastic tone in his voice.

There was no going back now. "Ed arrives tonight," she said in a now positive voice. "He's flying in from Chicago, and I will meet him at LaGuardia Airport. We have all the papers ready to get the license in Stamford. All we have to do is find a judge or justice of the peace there to marry us." She knew that this was the last thing her father wanted to hear.

And on this she was right. Maynard's expression changed from one of anger to one of apprehension. There was still one answer he needed—one that would determine how he would handle the situation.

"Rose, are you pregnant?" This was said in a manner that brooked no evasion.

Rose's response was immediate, as if she had been anticipating the question and was relieved that it had finally come.

"No, "I am not," she said, almost defiantly. "You should know that if such a thing happened, you are the first one I would come to for help."

For a moment, Maynard sat in silence, his eyes closed. It was as if the voice of his beloved dead wife was speaking to him. *"Please, Maynard, don't drive her away. She's our daughter and she love's you. Don't destroy her opportunity for happiness."*

Maynard relaxed. Now he knew what he wanted to do; and was confident that Addah would back him up with all the good grace she could muster.

Decisively, but in a saddened tone, Maynard said, "Rose, you may not realize it, but we have always put your happiness and well being first. I won't have you running off to get married like some poor girl whose parents don't care about her. You will bring Edward here, and we will see that you are married in your own home in a respectful and dignified manner."

Rose looked up at her father with a broad smile, and in a voice trembling with emotion said, "Thank you Daddy. I love you!"

31

Maynard awoke at 5:30 in the morning the day after Rose had dropped her bombshell. He had slept little and restlessly: his mind whirling ceaselessly through the events of the past twenty-four hours. Once Rose had left around noon for New York to pick up Edward—he couldn't call him 'Ed' as Rose did, and didn't want to call him 'that man' as Addah did—he had spent the rest of the day and evening discussing with her how best to proceed. Around 11:30 that night they heard Rose return and, from the occasional sound of voices and movements, knew that their prospective son-in-law had arrived and was staying in the guestroom.

Addah had some misgivings about Maynard's resolve that Rose should be married at home, but, because she had no other reasonable suggestion, deferred to her husband. She agreed that a quiet wedding would be the best and promised to fulfill her part in the arrangements. Rose was, after all, his daughter; in this instance she felt separated from her husband and his decision; but she understood his need to keep Rose as part of the family. The burden of being a stepmother had never weighed more heavily on her shoulders.

They decided that he would get a minister to perform a Protestant service, but that depended on whether the groom agreed, as they assumed he would, to a Protestant wedding. Maynard would also talk to Sam Glover, the Fairfield Town Clerk, about having the marriage license transferred from Stamford to Fairfield. Addah suggested that since they must have witnesses, they should invite Sam and his wife Helen to the ceremony.[168]

Beyond this nothing could be done until they met the groom. What would this man be like that Rose had chosen in such a secretive manner? It was his being Jewish that disturbed them. Addah, with her more critical sense of social status, was concerned about what people would think. She thought about her sister Lize's Jewish friends in New Orleans and how they were accepted at everything except the Mardi Gras Balls. Although the Jews she knew in New Orleans were 'fine people', Addah knew that her friends in Fairfield did not share the same outlook. Here even a marriage between a Catholic and a Protestant was a source of gossip; she could only imagine what talk would ensue about the Birds who had a Jewish son-in-law.

283

Maynard, during the course of his career had known a number of Jews in the financial world. He respected their intelligence and their business acumen, but could not envisage his daughter married to one. Rose had said Edward came from Maine. From Maynard's point of view, this was a plus even though most Jews whom he had encountered there were merchants or shopkeepers. (Was there a certain irony in that his grandfather, John Bird, had started as a shopkeeper?) Rose said Edward had also worked in a government job in Washington to put himself through college. Always valuing industry and hard work in a man, Maynard thought, "Good for him!" And, as Addah pointed out, he had been an <u>officer</u> in the army; that counted for something. She had forgotten her recent reservations about officers when Rose had gone to Officers' Club dances in New York.

"At least his name isn't obviously Jewish", Addah said, implying that if it were it would present problems in their social relationships. "I just hope that he's presentable."

"I can't imagine Rose marrying a man who wasn't", Maynard responded. He was earnestly trying to see the positive side of the situation. "It doesn't matter anyway, I'm not going to lose another child just because her husband doesn't look right." By this time Maynard had long since come to regret his anger and stubbornness in severing his relations with both Alan and Milton, and wished he could undo the damage.

In a more hopeful vein, he said, "She must see something in him or she wouldn't have wanted to marry him," I just wish she had told us about him sooner."

Both of them knew that if that had happened, they would have done everything possible to discourage the match. Maynard, remembered how his brother, Henry's, daughter, Eleanor's marriage to a man her parents thought unsuitable had been obstructed. That was an instance of no one being good enough for their child. Henry and Edith had quashed the engagement leaving Eleanor, maybe the smartest of their three children, to live the life of a spinster schoolteacher. "No", thought Maynard, "I'm not going to have Rose end up that way."

Just the same, he wished he could think of some way to breakup the match. Perhaps Rose would come to her senses and see that a Jewish husband would never fit in with her friends in Fairfield; the Maine relatives might even ostracize the couple. Maynard wondered what Alan would say. Probably, that this would never have happened had Rose stayed in Maine as he and Adelaide had wanted. He must find out more about Edward, and although he had no intention of being outwardly rude to him, he hoped he might find a way—if there was one—to put a stop to the whole affair.

These and other thoughts plagued him throughout the night. Around 6:30 he got out of bed and started dressing. Addah, who had slept no less fitfully, awoke and dressed, and they went downstairs to breakfast.

◆   ◆   ◆

Maynard and Addah had finished their breakfast but were still sitting at the table when Rose entered with Ed behind her.

"Good morning, Daddy", Rose greeted her father.

Ed echoed her greeting with an all inclusive, "Good morning."

"Sit over there, Ed," Rose said, motioning him to a seat between Addah and Maynard on the far side of the table, while she sat down opposite him. "I'll get you some breakfast. "Are eggs and toast alright?" She didn't wait for an answer, but got up and went to the kitchen.

With Rose out of the room, there was silence as if each person was waiting for the other to speak first. For Maynard, it was a chance to take the measure of the man who wanted to marry his daughter. What he saw was a man of about medium height, well built and well dressed, although casually, in an open-neck sport shirt and navy blue slacks. Black curly hair framed an oval face with a broad forehead, dark eyes and high cheekbones. He had a well-shaped nose over a generous somewhat sensual mouth; the firm chin was marked by a centered cleft. Reluctantly, Maynard admitted to himself that the man was handsome, and he also recognized a maturity and air of self-confidence that he had not anticipated.

Still, no one spoke. Both men seemed to be challenging the other to speak first.

Rose finally returned with two plates of scrambled eggs and toast. She poured coffee for each of them, and helped herself to some jelly that was on the lazy susan in the middle of the table. Neither of them seemed particularly hungry but went through the motions of eating.

The silence was finally broken when Maynard said, "Rose tells me you come from Maine, Edward." Even though he already knew the answer, he continued by asking, "Where in Maine did you originate?"

"I was born in Portland and lived there until my family moved to Bangor when I was twelve," was the polite answer.

The ball was now back in Maynard's court. The conversation continued with Maynard asking the questions, and Ed giving answers, but volunteering no additional information. Meanwhile, Rose seemed to relax as if she knew that Ed was now in control and there was no cause for further worry. She realized that her parents were more uncomfortable than either she or Ed.

Maynard finally brought Addah into the conversation, saying, "Mrs Bird and I have discussed plans for you to get married tomorrow here at our home."

"That is very kind of you," Ed responded, "and I'm sure Rose appreciates it as much as I do."

"Rose tells me that a marriage license has already been issued at Stamford," Maynard continued. "If you are to be married here, the license should be transferred to the Fairfield Town Clerk, Sam Glover, who is a friend of ours."

"We can go get it this morning and take it to Sam, Daddy," Rose volunteered. She had been silent up to this point but now seemed to welcome a chance to become part of the conversation.

Not to be left out, Addah said, "Have you any objection to having a Protestant minister perform the ceremony, Edward?"

"Not at all, Mrs. Bird," Ed remarked agreeably. "I am sure whatever arrangements you and Mr. Bird wish to make will be just fine with both of us. But, if you have no objection, I would like to ask my brother, Bernard, who is presently stationed in Washington, to come if he is available."

"Of course, by all means," Maynard agreed. "It's only right that you should have a member of your family present."

With that, the extended breakfast hour finally came to an end. Rose and Ed had errands to do including the license transfer, while Maynard and Addah prepared for the events of the next day.

As they were parting, Maynard said to Ed, "I hope you and Rose will be back here in time so that we can have a talk before dinner."

◆   ◆   ◆

It was Maynard's habit to have a cocktail—usually an 'old fashioned' before dinner each evening. (The doctor had told him that there was no harm in an ounce or two of whiskey each day for a man his age—not that he ever thought there was. He liked to tell the story of old Alvin Heard, his mother's rather disreputable cousin, who lived in a shack on the road to South Thomaston in Maine. Alvin lived to be almost a hundred and attributed his longevity to the fact that he drank a pint of whiskey every day.)

While Rose and Addah were getting dinner, Maynard ushered Ed into his 'study'. He brought in several old fashioned glasses already made up with ice, a generous amount of bourbon, a half slice of lemon and orange in each glass topped by a maraschino cherry.

"You're not a teetotaler are you Edward?" Maynard asked in a jocular manner that obviously assumed the contrary.

"Certainly not, Mr. Bird. And why don't you call me Ed? Most people do." Ed could understand that this was a difficult time for Maynard, and it didn't cost anything to make his future father-in-law feel more at ease.

As they sipped their drinks, Maynard sought to find out a little more about the man who would, by tomorrow, be Rose's husband. "Tell me a little more about your family, Ed? Your brother in Washington—is he still in the Army?" (By this time most of the men who had been drafted had been released from active duty.)

"Yes, he's a career officer—a graduate of West Point—and a colonel in the regular army. He's two years older than I am, which makes him quite young to be a full colonel." Ed continued to give Maynard details about his family including the fact that he had two uncles, both lawyers, one of them a patent attorney in Washington. He also mentioned that his brother's wife was a Smith College girl knowing that Maynard would be impressed.

The conversation continued to lead up to the question Maynard most wanted to ask: "Why do you want to marry my daughter?"

In a thoughtful way, Ed said, "Mr. Bird, up to now, I have been too young, too busy with work and school to think about marriage. Even before the beginning of the war, I knew I'd be in the army, and I didn't want to leave a wife, or even a sweetheart, to worry or be worried about. It wasn't difficult because most places I was sent, there were no attractive women anyway. Rose is the first girl I've met that I care enough about to really want to marry."

It was not quite the answer Maynard expected, but it was a good answer. This was a man who thought things through; was mature enough to wait until an appropriate time to make a life-changing move. Maynard was reassured, even though he still had some questions about how they would live and what were their financial resources.

At that moment, Rose entered the room. "Have you got a drink for me, Daddy?" she said.

"The glass is right there, help yourself, dear.

Rose fixed herself an old fashioned, and as she did so said to Ed, "Old fashioneds are my father's favorite drink." Then, noticing that their glasses were almost empty, she said, "Aren't you going to offer Ed a dividend, Daddy?" She then seated herself next to Ed on the love seat and reached over to hold his hand.

Once additional bourbon was poured, the conversation continued but now Rose was included. They planned to live in Chicago where Ed had a job. It didn't seem to be much of a job, but Ed was optimistic that there were more and better opportunities available to returning service men—especially in a city as large as Chicago. Ed had been able to find an apartment in a hotel on the prestigious Lake Shore Drive. He spoke of his grandmother and his family in general, and how he knew that Rose would receive a warm welcome.

After that there didn't seem to be much more to say. Except that Maynard had a few words of caution. Perhaps thinking of his marriage to Mary, Maynard said, "I'd like to ask you not to have any children until you've been married for two years. Every couple needs time to adjust to each other before they take on the responsibility of a family."

This was not an unreasonable request and both Rose and Ed nodded in agreement.

As Maynard looked at them sitting close together, holding each other's hand, he saw in their faces the love and affection that united them. There was a closeness, an air of commitment, that reminded him of how he had felt about Rose's mother. He longed for her to be here; to see her daughter as he now saw her. Had he been the kind of father she would have wanted him to be? Would she have been pleased with how her child had turned out? Would he ever know for sure? He hoped so.

Then, because he couldn't think of anything else to say, Maynard spoke directly to Rose. He wanted her to know that he had accepted her decision, albeit with reservations. "I hope your marriage will work out; your mother and I want you to be happy." (Did he mean her real mother or Addah? He was not sure. Maybe both.) Then, so as not to be seen as giving in too readily, "There's never been a divorce in the Bird family and I would hate to see yours be the first."

At this point, Addah called them for dinner.

◆   ◆   ◆

The events of the wedding day went smoothly due in large part to Addah's efforts. Ed's brother, Bernie, arrived around one o'clock. He was dressed in full uniform, with eagles on his shoulder tabs and several rows of war ribbons on his chest. His handsome appearance did much to dispel Addah's concerns over the social status of Ed's family. Maynard, too, was reassured by Bernie's appearance, and quickly engaged him in conversation that no doubt reduced the awkwardness of the occasion.

The minister who would perform the ceremony, Mr. Esquirol, pastor of the Southport Episcopal Church, arrived. Maynard had hoped to get the services of the Rev. Houston, pastor of the Greenfield Hill Congregational Church where Maynard was a member, but found him to be absent at a church conference. When on the previous day he had become somewhat distracted at having to approach a clergyman of another denomination, and one with whom he was not particularly familiar, he carelessly ran his car into a bridge abutment on his way to meet Mr. Esquirol. Although no serious damage was done to either car or driver, Maynard was shaken up and Addah was inclined to blame the incident on what she felt was the needlessly rushed plans for the wedding.

While Ed and Rose joined the clergyman in a brief prenuptial conference in the study, the Glovers arrived and were introduced to Colonel Waterman. Shortly thereafter Rose, Ed and Mr. Esquirol emerged from the study. Addah pinned a large white orchid on Rose's suit and Maynard presented Ed with a small white rose boutonniere. It was time for the service.

The short ceremony was conducted in front of the living room fireplace. At either end of the mantle piece Addah had made two beautiful matching arrangements of white flowers and green ivy. As Maynard watched the couple take their vows, he could not help but think of another small wedding, also performed in front of a fireplace adorned with white flowers, some twenty-five years earlier when he and this bride's mother had been married. The memory of that day was as vivid as if it had been yesterday; the sensation of loss almost overwhelming. Now this Rose was leaving him, and he realized, not for the first time but more acutely than ever before, how much the daughter had been a substitute for the mother.

At the conclusion of the service, Rose and Ed turned to greet the family and friends. Then Addah led the way into the dining room where the table was set with lighted candles in silver candlesticks, a centerpiece of white flowers and a decorated cake that she called a "bride's cake". Rose and Ed cut the cake; Maynard poured champagne and toasts were offered. After a few minutes of general conversation, it was time to leave. (The plan was for Rose and Ed to take Bernie with them to New York where he could catch a train back to Washington and where they would spend the night.) At the front door, Maynard speechlessly embraced Rose while she murmured her thanks to him, and then to Addah. Maynard, again overcome with emotion, shook Ed's hand.

As the wedding party got in the car and prepared to leave, Maynard suddenly realized that he had meant to give Rose a going away present. In the rush of the last two days he had forgotten this. As the car started, he rushed out to shove a twenty-dollar bill through the window into Rose's hand. It was all he had in his pocket.

32

With Rose's marriage and departure, Maynard's life entered a new phase. Not obvious at first, were the gradual slowing of pace and the easing of responsibility. It was as if he had fulfilled the final obligation to his dead wife: to see that their child was given all the love and care that they together would have lavished on her. For all that the burden had been lifted, Rose's departure left an emptiness he had not anticipated. He continued to write to her regularly—not every week as when she was away at school, nor even every month as when she had sent him an accounting of her expenditures in anticipation of the next month's allowance, but still regularly enough so that they didn't lose touch. He wanted to be reassured that she was happy and he wanted her to know that she still had a father who cared. He was pleased when her letters recounted the warm response from Adelaide (and presumably Alan). It would be some time, Maynard knew, before she would come east and visit the Maine relatives. By that time, he was sure, the element of surprise would have faded and acceptance by the Bird clan would be easier.

Physically, Maynard was showing his age. Although his health remained reasonably good for the late seventies, the normal changes were taking place, muscles were beginning to sag, and the more wrinkled skin had assumed the mottled appearance characteristic of advancing years. The jowls had softened the firm, sharp line of his jaw, while the sunken cheeks accentuated his high-bridged nose with its downward curve. The hair, once black, then gray, now totally white was now only a thin covering of his scalp above the broad forehead. His eyes, however, under the hereditary hooded lids were keen and intelligent and still exhibited delight over a good joke or a humorous incident.

Mentally, he was as sharp as ever. He kept up with current events and in particular Republican politics. It was, therefore, a shock when, in the 1948 election, Truman defeated Dewey. Both he and Addah had been so sure that they would finally see a Republican in the White House. Although his activity in community affairs had diminished, as president of the Beach Club in 1947, he inaugurated a number of new activities, designed to appeal to all segments of the membership—in particular the younger members and their families. (He had been heard to remark, with no sense of irony, that the club was too full of old fogies.) He

291

introduced the Fourth of July Lobster Dinner, which became the high point of the club season. He would personally order the lobsters from Maine, and when they arrived, would oversee their preparation. This event soon became a Beach Club tradition.

There were other high points in Maynard's life now. In 1947, Rose and Ed made the first of many visits to Fairfield. Rose seemed to be happy in her marriage, and their visit gave Maynard an opportunity to get to know his son-in-law. The trauma brought on by their marriage had subsided, (not that Maynard would ever like the idea of a Jewish son-in-law), and the visit inaugurated an amicable relationship between the two. Maynard found Rose's choice an interesting and intelligent man, and he also found that Ed was someone he could talk to about stocks, investments and financial matters that had been his life-blood. They would drive around Fairfield and neighboring communities with Maynard pointing out houses and estates of people he knew. And it was no doubt, with considerable satisfaction that, on occasion, there was a home where his comment about its occupants was the disparaging, "Those people are living on their capital."

◆   ◆   ◆

Addah and Maynard were in Florida when they got the news that Rose was pregnant. Maynard's elation over the prospect of finally becoming a grandfather was tempered by the recollection of the tragedy associated with Rose's birth. However, the baby was born in June without difficulty: a little girl named Elizabeth Bird Waterman, who would always be called Buffy by her family. When Rose, Ed and the baby arrived for a visit in September, this lovely three-month old baby was held, coddled and cherished as the entranced grandparents were sure no other child had ever been before. At Addah's suggestion and with no objection from either parent, the baby was christened one Sunday in the Greenfield Hill Congregational Church. Grace Paulding, a close friend of Maynard and Addah, contributed, for the occasion, a beautifully embroidered white, lawn, christening gown that she had treasured because of its use for herself and her daughter in years past. As Maynard watched the brief ceremony in which the infant, swallowed up in yards of white fluffy material, was anointed, he tried to remember Rose's christening but couldn't. Once again, waves of sadness engulfed him with the memory of those agonizing days of birth and loss.

These summer visits continued for another two years as Maynard watched his granddaughter develop into a curly-haired toddler and then a cute, inquisitive two-year old. In 1951 a second granddaughter, Clarissa Gregory Waterman, named after her great-great-grandmother, was born. This time there was no need for Maynard to worry over pregnancy or delivery; Rose seemed to handle having children as a normal occurrence. This, he reflected, was the way it should have been when she was born. For her part, Addah, now twice a grandmother took advantage of the occasions at which she could exercise her new bragging rights against other grandmothers.

There was no visit the summer of 1951 after the second grandchild was born. "Too difficult to drive five hundred miles with an infant and a three-year old," Rose said. Besides, she and Ed wanted to take a vacation by themselves to celebrate their fifth anniversary. Maynard understood. He would miss them, but looked forward to the next year.

◆　　　◆　　　◆

At fifty-eight in 1946, Addah's health was good, although, as a Christian Scientist, she never saw a doctor. She never hesitated to call the family physician if she thought Maynard needed care, but she depended on daily readings of the Bible and its companion volume, *Science and Health* by Mary Baker Eddy, for her own physical as well as spiritual well-being. Should she become ill, she could always call for a Christian Science Reader[169] who would presumably impart the wisdom of Mrs. Eddy's understanding of biblical healing power. Addah also had an old and dear friend, Ida Lockwood, from her Kansas City days, who was a certified Science Reader, and it was through correspondence and her occasional visits that Addah received periodic doses of spiritual guidance. She knew that Maynard didn't like Ida, although he had never objected to her visits; he merely treated her with a polite coolness. Nevertheless, in the years following Rose's marriage, the correspondence between the two women grew as the visits diminished.

In appearance, Addah showed the usual signs of matronliness common to her age and her life style. She no longer wore her iron gray hair in a bun at the nape of her neck, but had had it cut short allowing the natural curl and wave to take over. Her skin had coarsened, as was to be expected, and her complexion had assumed a more florid look. She had gained weight, but she encased her figure in reinforced undergarments that did double duty of smoothing out the natural bulges and holding up her stockings. Depression and war had altered some of her earlier practices: she no longer bothered with a hat and gloves when going to Fairfield to market, although she still retained the hat for New York shopping trips.

Her style of dress had kept up with the current trends toward the casual, but she observed certain limits in keeping with her age. All in all, she represented the woman she was—a middle aged matron of an affluent, educated society.

Once the turmoil over Rose's marriage had died down, (it had been impossible to keep the news out of the Bridgeport Sunday Telegram which featured headlines about the wedding), Addah was surprised to find that there was very little comment about it. She had been prepared for, and apprehensive about, snide remarks on the hasty wedding, but so far there were none. Her friends were, she thought, either extremely tactful or simply didn't care. She assumed it was the former. Of course she, herself, never mentioned Ed's religious origin. If it was common knowledge it was uncommon enough not to get back to her. She continued to occupy herself with Garden Club and Beach Club by exhibiting beautiful arrangements in flower shows and presiding at social events at the Beach Club.

Shortly after Rose's wedding, Addah's sister, Lize, arrived for a short visit. Lize's husband, the congenial, charming Joe Onorato, had died in the early 1940's leaving his widow almost destitute. Never having had to work in her life, (unlike her younger sister), Lize was reduced to taking a clerk's job during the war at the New Orleans Naval Base Post Exchange (PX). Her visit to Fairfield, (probably paid for by Addah), was a welcome relief and a demonstration on the part of Addah and Maynard of their affection for her. On Lize's return trip she changed trains in Chicago where she had lunch with Rose and her husband. Reporting to her sister, she was enthusiastic about the newly married couple and in particular her opinion of what a fine man Rose had married. For Addah, this sign of approval relieved her concerns about the marriage to some degree. Unfortunately, it was the last time Addah was to see her sister who died the following year.

There was no doubt that Addah's life revolved around her husband. As a couple they had always exhibited a strong attachment to each other—one that was marked by elements of deep affection, companionship and a mutuality of interests that set them apart from many other couples of their acquaintance. They had always shared thoughts and ideas, particularly those dealing with their financial affairs. As time went on Addah played an ever-increasing role in how they invested and spent their money. It was a common joke between them that while Maynard poured over the financial news in the Wall Street Journal to select his investments, she selected hers for more esoteric reasons. Her purchase of stock in Coca-Cola in the 1930's was made because Joe Onorato drank a lot of it and so did his friends in the south. Her selection proved to be a winner, while Maynard's simultaneous investment in a roofing company never managed to show a profit. In Florida after the war, she converted the apartments that had served for military dependents' housing during the war into garages that were easier to rent and required less of a landlord's time and maintenance.

When once again in 1948, they were approached by the oldest son of the family who had bought the big house nine years earlier. This time, the offer was for the second one, and it was Addah who brought the news to Maynard and pushed for the sale. As she and Maynard discussed the offer, Addah was certain that they could get a top price for the property. Theirs was one of the last houses built before the war halted all home building and real estate development. Designed by an outstanding architect, constructed with care and with a wealth of fine detail, it was a quality home; and it sat on the choicest piece of land on the Hill.

"We would be foolish not to sell," she told Maynard. "Besides, with the war over, the cost of everything including gas has gone up and it is getting difficult to get into town to shop, and still go to the Club." As a clincher she added, "Did you know that Mercurio's is charging an outrageous amount for delivery these days."

Maynard looked at his wife and shook his head. He had long ago learned that when Addah made up her mind about something, she had usually thought it through to its logical conclusion, and there wasn't much point in arguing with her unless he had a very, very valid objection. But he decided to make a show of throwing in roadblocks

"And where, pray tell, do you plan to move us?" Not another Brooklawn Park house, I trust." This was said with a touch of derision.

"You know me better than that, Maynard," she responded with an air of injured pride. "There's a house off of the Old Post Road on Beach Road downtown that just came on the market. It's the one next door to Helen and Sam Glover's. I just heard about it from Marion Cornwall,"[170] she ended up rather triumphantly.

"My God, Addah," Maynard said in complete surprise, "that's a pre-Revolutionary house. Have you even been inside it? It would probably cost a fortune to heat. And how do you think all your French furnishings are going to look in a house of that type?"

"Well, we haven't bought it yet. I'm just telling you it's available, and you know I won't do anything without your complete agreement. Don't worry about the French furnishings," she continued, "it might look colonial from the outside, but it will be French inside."

They wound up buying the house on Beach Road at what both considered a very good price. The house on the Hill was sold to young John Field at considerably more than it had cost to build. By the time Addah had "smartened up" (a term she thought appropriate) the house downtown it was as she had predicted French inside, but retaining its handsome colonial exterior. Once again, her ability to create a lot out of little through decorating was the envy of her friends. In the spring of 1949 they returned early from Florida and by mid-May had moved into the house on Beach Road. She hoped, however, that this would be their last move. As she admitted to herself and hinted to Maynard, it had taken more out of her than she had expected.

◆   ◆   ◆

Addah's ventures in real estate were not limited to Fairfield. In Delray Beach in 1949, a smaller, one-story house on the lot adjacent to their two-story home had come on the market. With the war over and life returning to normal, winter visitors were once again flooding into the Florida East Coast. It seemed to Addah that carefully chosen property in Delray could produce a new source of income. Goodness knows, she thought, we could use it. Dividends from stocks and interest on bonds and other securities had not kept up with rising prices. Already, she had economized without jeopardizing their life style for she knew it meant a lot to Maynard to maintain certain standards. Furthermore, she had noted that her husband now found the stairs in the Fairfield house left him short of breath; he tired more easily, too. Although she didn't mention the latter consideration, she discussed with Maynard the economic benefits of buying the smaller house and having it available for rental. With his agreement they purchased the smaller house, and once again, their investment in real estate proved fortuitous. By the winter season of 1950–51, Addah was able to rent the smaller house at a reasonable rent for the whole winter.

However, on returning to Fairfield in April of '51, Maynard suffered what the doctor termed a mild heart attack. They were told that there was no reason to be alarmed by the diagnosis, but he would have to take it easy. No rushing around and it would be better if he didn't go upstairs more than once a day. Under these circumstances, Addah decided to try to rent the two-story Delray house, and occupy the smaller one themselves. The tenant she found was, by coincidence, an old acquaintance of Maynard's from his Portland days—Dr. Herbert Drummond and his wife, Margaret. Maynard was delighted with the arrangement and Addah relieved that the burden of renting had gone so easily. They returned to

Florida as usual in October and took up residence in the small house with the Drummonds in the larger one. Addah found them both companionable, especially when of a morning, Herb Drummond would stroll over and chew the fat with Maynard while Addah went shopping with Margaret.

Maynard's health did not improve noticeably that fall. In fact he was having low-grade chest pain as a result of any exertion. This was diagnosed as "angina", and Dr. King, their Delray doctor, gave him medication to minimize the pain. All this limited his activity. He slept later in the morning, and because the house had two bedrooms separated from each other by the living-dining room, Addah often slept separately in the front bedroom so that she wouldn't disturb him when she got up earlier in morning. They had a good, reliable, colored woman, Cora, who came in regularly to do the cleaning and make lunches for Maynard if Addah was out.

This didn't mean that Maynard gave up all activity. He and Addah maintained their social contacts, going out occasionally for dinner and enjoying a customary bridge game. They had made many friends in Delray who frequently came to visit. Then there was always Doc Drummond with whom Maynard could reminisce about the 'old days' in Maine. If Addah went marketing she would frequently leave Maynard, who seldom drove anymore, at the beach where he would sit on a beachfront bench gazing out to sea. How different the Atlantic looked here compared to the same ocean in Maine. Here it was so much calmer; never much surf to speak of, and only when it stormed in the hurricane season did the sea reveal its hidden power to destroy. There were not many ships to be seen, although Maynard's eyes were still good enough to spot the occasional tanker or freighter far out to sea. Often as he sat there, his thoughts would drift back to his boyhood days: the Rockland harbor so full of sail—everything from Friendship sloops to three and four masters. The lime burners were long gone, of course, as were the Bird Company's fleet of smaller ships that had delivered groceries to all the towns up and down the jagged Maine coast. If Maynard missed his Maine roots, he still had memories of an exciting life—a life of adventure. Although his life was now restricted, after eighty-two years it was still a pleasant, interesting one.

In January Addah was not feeling well. She couldn't understand why she should so often feel light-headed or why her heart seemed to be beating faster than usual. The Christmas holidays had not been as hectic as usual. They had had Christmas dinner at the Drummonds so that she did not have the burden of cooking a big dinner. They had attended fewer holiday parties and those mostly in the afternoon or early evening. (Maynard went to bed much earlier these days, so they frequently avoided going out at night.) Henry and Edith had bought a small place in Coral Gables and drove up occasionally to see Maynard. Of all his relatives, Addah found them the most congenial, and she realized that the shared family memories meant a lot to both brothers.

Everything now seemed to be on an even keel, so why didn't she feel better? She was not sleeping well and had moved more or less permanently into the front bedroom so she wouldn't disturb Maynard. (She had given him a bell so he could call her if he needed her.) Most upsetting of all was that she found it difficult to read; the words would often blur or she would see them doubled. Initially, she had consulted Ida Lockwood, who had written her many long, long letters offering all the spiritual support she felt her friend needed. Things didn't get any better, so after two weeks of being unable to read either her Bible or *Science and Health,* Addah called in a local Science Reader.

One morning in late January, Maynard awoke as usual around eight-thirty. He could hear Cora in the kitchen rattling some dishes, and called to her for some breakfast. Addah did not come in to see him, but he assumed that she had gotten up early and had already left the house. By lunchtime, when Cora brought him a sandwich, Addah still hadn't appeared. Finally, he put on some clothes and went to see what was the matter. As he made his way across the living room, he could hear the sound of a voice—but it was not Addah's. Entering the bedroom he found, to his complete amazement and consternation, Addah, stretched out on her bed, eyes open but unseeing, and barely breathing. In a chair at the foot of the bed was a woman he had never seen, holding a book from which she was reading aloud.

"Who are you, and what are you doing here?" were the first words Maynard could summon.

"I'm a Christian Science Reader and your wife called me to help her through her illness," was the reply.

"Help her! Help her! Good God woman, can't you see she's unconscious." Maynard was so angry he could barely contain himself. "Get out of here. She doesn't need you, she needs a doctor!"

Without a word, the woman got up and left, brushing by Cora who had appeared to find out what the commotion was all about.

Maynard's next words were to Cora. "Call Dr. Drummond and tell him I need him. It's an emergency." Then he pulled up a chair to Addah's bed and took her hand, talking to her, trying to arouse her. There was no response, however. When Drummond arrived Maynard was still seated by the bed, head bowed with in an attitude of utter desolation.

A quick look at Addah told Herb Drummond that there was little hope. The family physician, Dr. King was called, but there was nothing he could do except to tell Maynard what he already suspected. Addah was near death.

Addah Bird died that January night. She was sixty-four years old; she had been married to Maynard for twenty-five years. She had been a good and loving wife, stepmother and companion. But by failing to take care of her own health, she committed an uncharacteristic act of selfishness. She left her husband alone, without her support and care at a time when he was completely dependent on her for his wellbeing.

33

For Maynard, the immediate result of Addah's death—so sudden, so unexpected—was physical collapse. Temporarily bed-ridden, he was unable to attend the funeral service arranged by the Drummonds. Dr. King treated him with sedatives and painkillers to minimize the effects on his heart, and arranged for a practical nurse to stay with him. Rose arrived from her home in Illinois and did what she could for the few days she was with him. But he was an old man, once more alone, facing the grim prospect of a life without the support of a wife or family

In the days following Addah's death, many of their friends came to offer condolences. Dressed and seated in a chair, Maynard appeared outwardly calm and composed as he accepted their expressions of sympathy. But inwardly he struggled as he tried to come to grips with what her loss meant to him. She had been a wonderful companion. She no doubt loved him and had devoted herself to him. She had made him happier than he otherwise would have been. Had he loved her? He supposed so, but in a different way. No one could dim or replace his enduring devotion to his beloved Rose. Unlike Rose's tragic death that had devastated him emotionally, this loss affected him in a more practical way. He began to recognize his total dependence on Addah, and the extent to which she had become the decision-maker and the planner who had implemented nearly everything that they did. What would he do now?

The problem was solved in part by the devotion of his friends. Over the years, he had always made friends, but it was now, when the need for help was so acute, that his warmth and friendship for others was requited. The Drummonds, of course, played a major role in straightening out his domestic affairs. Within a month they had obtained a full time caregiver, Frances Lafferty, a divorcee in her fifties, a woman of good reputation, and most important, from Maynard's point of view, a 'lady'. (Maynard treated her as one of the family, but always referred to her as Mrs. Lafferty, perhaps out of concern that if he used her first name, it would imply a more familiar relationship.) She was a woman who was healthy and capable of handling the multiple chores of housekeeper, nurse and companion. There was only one drawback: she was extremely deaf. This was no problem in the daytime for she had a high-resolution hearing aid that she wore around her neck. At night she placed a small box-like contraption under her pillow that was

300

connected to Maynard's bell and would vibrate instead of ringing when he needed her.

After a month during which he slowly recovered from his latest loss, Maynard once again took over the handling of his finances. It soon became obvious that with the added expense of Mrs. Lafferty's salary, a change in his investments was needed to enhance his resourses. He decided not to return to Fairfield; he would stay in Florida the year around where the weather was better. In Connecticut, his lawyer, Bradford Boardman, handled the sale of the Beach Road house and the disposition of its contents. Rose got most of the furnishings and items she wanted. (She had already been given Addah's jewelry in order to prevent it from being included in the estate.) The remainder of its contents was shipped to a New York auction firm for sale. Whether or not Addah had overestimated the value of their belongings or perhaps the market in French antiques was at a low point, the sale did not net Maynard as much as he had anticipated. Sale of the house, however, yielded a gratifying return and the proceeds were invested in high-grade securities. In ridding himself of his Fairfield possessions, Maynard also instructed Boardman to personally oversee the destruction of his personal papers, dating back to the early years of the century, that were stored in the attic. (This was mainly an act of vanity that went beyond reason; it was prompted by a wish to be remembered for his wealth and prestige. It is hard to understand how the retention of these records could have sullied his reputation.)

It was also necessary to dispose of the house the Drummonds were renting. Once again Herb and Margaret Drummond came to his rescue by purchasing the property. Although Boardman remained Maynard's principal lawyer and adviser, a Florida lawyer was retained to take care of his Florida affairs. Thus by the end of 1953, Maynard had divested himself of all real estate except for his current home, and had become a permanent Florida resident. To his surprise and pleasure he found that there were tax advantages to this arrangement

◆   ◆   ◆

For the next five years under the competent and watchful eye of Frances Lafferty, Maynard lived comfortably. He was past the eighties mid-point, and there seemed to be only a slight diminishing of his faculties. He had been getting deafer for many years, but would not admit it and wear a hearing aid. His eyesight was dimming, although not to the extent that it limited his love of reading; he expressed himself lucidly; and from his letters, his elegant handwriting was still firm. His gait had slackened but he could still walk outdoors and about the yard, as well as the short distance to the car. Mrs. Lafferty occasionally took him for rides up and down the coast to see the changes taking place as a result of the post-war building boom. They would often stop for lunch at some little restaurant he knew from reviews in the newspapers or referrals from friends. If the restaurant was one where he was still remembered, he would be greeted with a genial "Welcome back, Mr. Bird". It might be noted that his appetite was still good.

Friends and acquaintances kept Maynard in touch with the rest of the world and kept him going. There were frequent callers, many of them women whose husbands had passed away. This did not phase him for he had always enjoyed female company. In the winter, friends from Fairfield, some of whom owned property in or near Delray, came to call. From them he would catch up on all the Connecticut news and gossip. He was always interested in what was going on at the Beach Club. One winter, Mrs. Pennell, who had been the club's manager when Maynard was president, came to see him. She was now retired and had bought a home down the coast in Deerfield.

"Are they still having the Lobster Party at the Club on the Fourth of July," he asked her?

When told it was one of the most popular events of the season, Maynard smiled at the memory of the first party in 1946 that had started the tradition.

He learned of family news and the goings-on in Maine from Henry and Edith, who now regularly spent their winters in Florida and came to visit once or twice a season. While Edith talked to Mrs. Lafferty, Henry and Maynard, sitting in their rockers on the patio, discussed business affairs in Rockland. According to Henry, the Medomak Canning Company under the aegis of "his boys", Fred and Ted, was doing well. Blueberries and beans were the backbone of the company. There had been talk about getting into the frozen food business, but "the boys" didn't think that was the way to go. "Can't preserve the flavor of the fruit in freezing and besides, people are used to getting food out of cans," Henry said.

Maynard was not so sure. Always the entrepreneur, he thought maybe Henry's boys were missing the boat. Mrs. Lafferty had told him that more and more food was frozen. It was a bit more expensive, but faster to cook and as far as she could tell, there was no difference in the taste. But he decided not to dispute Henry's statement. Changing the subject, he said, "I guess you never hear anything about the Bird Company, do you?"

"No," Henry replied. "Adriel sold it for what he could get for it and that was only the Three Crow Brand name, and whatever good will he could persuade the outfit in Bangor to give him." Henry's answer displayed his obvious unhappiness with whole affair. "I guess Adriel pretty much milked the company for what he could get for himself and his family before he died."

Maynard sighed. When he thought about the auspicious beginning of his grandfather's company, it hurt to see it disposed of in such an ignominious way. In 1949, before Addah's death, Adriel had paid them a visit. Maynard had been anxious to meet Adriel's new wife, Marion, and had looked forward to the visit. But when Adriel arrived he was drunk and the meeting was a fiasco. Maynard was angry that Adriel had the effrontery to show his face in such a condition. He had hoped Adriel would carry the Bird name (and the Company) to new heights. The fact that Adriel died within a year[171] did not lessen Maynard's opinion that his nephew had wasted his abilities and cast a blot on the Bird name.

Occasionally, he would ask Henry about Alan. But it was obvious from the little he said, that Henry wanted to stay out of the quarrel between his brothers. "You know, Maynard," Henry said, "Alan will never change. He's as stubborn as Old Man Perry's mule. You remember that one, don't you?"

Yes, Maynard remembered that mule all right—the one that had to be beaten over the head to get his attention—and they would both laugh at the shared recollection and talk about something else.

In the winter of 1955–56, Rose, Ed and their two oldest children, Buffy and Clarissa, came to visit. Rose now had three children, all girls, but they had left the baby, Terry, behind since she was too young to make the trip. This was Maynard's first opportunity to see little Clarissa—now and forevermore called Rissa. He thought he saw some resemblance to Rose in Buffy, but Rissa, he was sure, would look more like Ed when she grew up. Her dark coloring and almost black hair worn in pigtails, her big dark eyes in a face that was shaped more like her father's, all spoke more of Ed than Rose. He had three grandchildren now—more than he had ever expected. He wondered if somewhere his lovely lost Rose was looking down at them sharing his joy in their presence.

◆　　　◆　　　◆

By springtime, 1956, Frances Lafferty was tired. She had been taking care of Maynard for more than four years, and although she had taken a couple of short vacations, at which time she would engage a practical nurse to take her place, the twenty-four hour job was becoming a burden and her own health was suffering. Her patient now needed more nursing than she felt capable of giving and a nursing home was the obvious solution.

Maynard didn't like the idea of giving up his comfortable home, although he recognized that his health had deteriorated to a point where it was not sufficient to have only the Visiting Nurse come in three or four times a week to bathe him and check his medications. There was another circumstance that called for change. His lawyer had told him that the expenses incurred in living at home including the salary he paid Mrs. Lafferty, was draining his resources at an unacceptable rate. He would be better off financially to move to an institution where he could get good nursing care at less than he was currently paying.

This news was a bitter pill. He was a man who had always prided himself on his independence; and who had known great wealth and presented an affluent front, even now, to those who knew him. To acknowledge the necessity of living in a nursing home, dependent on strangers, was disturbing. But he had no choice. Mrs. Lafferty wanted to go and he could not keep her; she would not leave, however, until she got him settled in a new place.

When told of Maynard's decision, Dr. King suggested that The Cuyler Pavilion Nursing Home in Lake Worth would be a suitable place for him. It was close enough to Delray so that he could visit Maynard from time to time, although it would probably be necessary to use another doctor in Lake Worth for regular calls. With this advice and reassurance, a comfortable patio suite was reserved for him and he prepared to move in June.

He had written Rose of his impending move. Much to his surprise, she and Ed offered to have him come live with them in Park Forest. He gave this offer some consideration and he appreciated their thoughtfulness, but he was not yet at a point where his pride would allow him to appear to be dependent on his daughter as others might assume him to be if he moved north. Besides, he had lived too long in Florida to be transplanted at eighty-seven to the cold winter climate of Illinois. 'How strange,' he mused, 'that the husband I thought so inappropriate for Rose has turned out to be so kind and understanding. Never mind the pedigree and money of the Cushings, if only Milton had found a wife as good as Ed is a husband.'

So the move was made. With the help of Maynard's longtime friend, Jeff Davis[172] and Mrs. Lafferty, he was comfortably settled in a bright, sunny bed-sitting room with access to a pleasant patio at the Lake Worth home. Rose came for a few days to see that he was well settled and cared for, and Mrs. Lafferty stayed at the house for a while to dispose of any personal belongings that he had not taken with him. When the house was sold later in the year, it was the first time in his lifetime that he had not lived in a house he owned, (except for those first years with Mary and the Bowdoin Street rental), or in one owned by his family.

Life at the nursing home proved to be better than Maynard had expected. As long as he paid the weekly fee,[173] his telephone bill and the bills for his medications, he had no other recurrent expenses. The home provided routine nursing care, the food was good and the place was clean. Furthermore, he was not always alone as he had been at times in Delray; there were other residents whom he usually joined in the dining room. He regaled his table companions with stories of his life on Wall Street; and if he exaggerated a bit and dropped a few names of important people, whether he knew them or not, who was to know the difference? His next door neighbor, Elbert Marsh, was companionable and the two old men found much in common. About this time Maynard discovered television and bought himself a set so that he could watch the news and weather programs. At least those were the only programs he admitted to at first. Later on he found some of the evening sit-coms funny and interesting. He frequently invited Elbert to join him so that they could share the humor of the "I Love Lucy Show" and other sit-coms. His winter friends had not forgotten him either, and he entertained some of the ladies with tea or a little whiskey and crackers when they called.

Another visitor in October was Henry's son, Fred, and his wife, Dot, who had been visiting Henry and Edith. During the course of conversation, Maynard reminisced about his younger days in Maine, especially how he got into the telephone business.

Fred was fascinated with the story. "I never heard about that, Uncle Maynard, and I'll bet my brother and sister haven't heard it either. I wish you'd write some of this down so it can be passed down in the family."

Maynard readily agreed and spent many hours composing a history of his early activities in the insurance, telephone and banking businesses. He called these episodes "Adventures". He sent them off to Fred, who later transcribed them for his children. As Maynard looked back on his life, he realized that he'd had a lot of "adventures" and contemplated writing more, thinking Rose might be interested. Unfortunately, he never got around to it.

Although time seemed to pass more quickly than it had when he had lived at home, Maynard was aware that friends from Delray and other East Coast towns, who had occasionally visited him, were becoming fewer and fewer. Some had died while others aged and were unable to get transportation to the nursing home. Only Jeff Davis came regularly.

Each Christmas Maynard would receive a reel of homemade movies from Rose showing the entire Waterman family, but most especially, the three girls. Rose and Ed lived in house they had built in 1953 from a sketch by Cameron

Clark, the architect, who had designed Maynard and Addah's second house on the Hill. The movies gave Maynard a glimpse into the daily life of his daughter and her family and the house where they lived. He thought Addah would have enjoyed looking at the films that often showed rooms with some of her furnishings. He would rent a projector; the Cuyler staff would set up a screen; and other residents were invited for an evening's viewing. Later when Jeff Davis or others came to visit, Maynard would show the movies over and over again.

In the winter of 1958 Rose and her family, vacationing at Fort Meyers Beach, drove over to visit him at the nursing home. It was his first opportunity to see all three of his grandchildren, and was a rare treat for the old man. The visit also provided him with many hours of conversation with other residents, who would listen more or less politely but interrupted with stories of their own grandchildren and even great grandchildren.

Rose's visit included a surprise visit from Milton. Maynard knew that Helen had died the previous fall, and he had sent Milton a condolence card, but there had been no reply. So he was dumbstruck when his son entered the room—it was as if a stranger had come to call. After twenty years, it was an awkward scene; neither father nor son knew what to say and both sat mute most of the time, while Rose and Ed did their best to carry on a conversation. Maynard wanted desperately to reestablish a bond with his son but seemed unable to find the way to do it. Milton showed no such interest and appeared to be merely paying a duty call. He stayed only as long as courtesy required—a half-hour at the most. They said goodbye cordially enough, but there was no warmth to their parting and they never saw each other again. (Afterwards, Rose admitted to having persuaded Milton to come, hoping that the visit would repair the break in their long estrangement.)

Maynard celebrated his 90th birthday on July 16th 1959. There was a party, a cake and the local newspaper took his picture with his friend, Elbert Marsh, who earlier had celebrated his 96th birthday. The picture shows Maynard, sitting in a chair, looking frail and wan. But his head is still held high and there is an alert look on his face.

◆   ◆   ◆

In the spring of 1960, Maynard was worried. The cost of living at the Cuyler Pavilion had nearly doubled since he had moved in four years ago. A look at his checkbook told him that he was fast using up his resources. He didn't know what to do. He knew Milton had inherited the Cushing money when Helen died, but asking for his son's help never entered his mind. His pride would not allow it; nor could he ask Rose and Ed for help; not after once having turned down their generosity. Anyway, he didn't think she and her husband were that well off. He was becoming increasingly obsessed with maintaining the respect and high regard of those people most important to him in earlier times. He failed to realize that their number was diminishing and their memories also failing. He would do as he had always done: handle the problem himself. In so doing he did not take into account that he was also concealing his anxieties from those who cared most for his welfare. They would have routinely concerned themselves with the need to ensure his comfort and peace of mind—providing for him as discreetly as he might have wished.

With the help of Jeff Davis, his ever-loyal friend, he was able to find another nursing home in Lake Worth. This one was not as nice as Cuyler's, but, if he were willing to share a room with another man, the cost would be considerably less. Sometime after his 91st birthday party, with Jeff's help, Maynard packed up and moved to the new place. He only told the Cuyler management of his intentions at the last moment so that he would not be subjected to any long drawn out controversy. Without telling Rose or anyone else, by the middle of August he was situated in the new nursing home.

The move took a lot out of Maynard. He stayed in bed most of the time now, although the nurses and aides would get him up to sit in a chair each morning. Getting dressed was difficult and he couldn't always get an aide to help him; so it was easier to have his meals brought in on a tray. His roommate's mind was disturbed, so there was little opportunity for conversation. Maynard's mind, however, was still lucid, but he had no energy to do anything. His eyes were troubling him and he had difficulty reading. He still watched television—more to pass the time than from any real interest in the subject matter—but even the television images were fuzzy. The evening news that had always been his favorite no longer evoked much interest. He could not even get excited about the coming presidential election.

In September, when he had been at his new home about a month, his old friend, the manager of the Beach Club, Mrs. Pennell, came to call. She was the first (other than Jeff Davis) to see him in his new surroundings. Maynard was surprised to see her and wondered how she knew where he was. (He had forgotten that he'd had to leave a forwarding address with the Cuyler people.) Mrs. Pennell was appalled that this man, for whom she had the highest regard and always thought of as a well-to-do member of the club, was sharing a two-bedded room in what she considered a third rate nursing home. Without realizing what effect her words might have, she thoughtlessly blurted out, "Why Mr. Bird, you don't belong in this place!"

From someone whom he'd always thought of as somewhat in the servant category, this observation completely destroyed the barrier of self-esteem he'd built up around himself. Had he made a terrible mistake by moving? What was he going to do? He had practically no money left and no friends to whom he could turn. He had a son who didn't care what happened to him and a daughter, dear as she was, who was too far away. (He had evidently forgotten that he hadn't even told Rose about his move and she didn't know where he was.) Emotionally he was devastated, and, as so often happens, his physical health collapsed as a result.

That night and the following days, Maynard started down the slippery path to the end. His mind kept saying, *What will I do? What will I do?* And there was no answer. *I must get hold of Rose.* And the answer was: *which Rose? They aren't here anymore they've gone!* He would have intervals of lucidity; he took the pills and medications he was fed; his pulse and blood pressure were taken several times a day. He was aware of all the movement and the voices around him, and he would respond to any questions.

Gradually the fear left him and his mind seemed to float backwards in time. He was home again in the big house at the Highlands. He could smell the new-cut hay that mixed with the scent of piney woods. The winds off the ocean carried with them the shrieking calls of seagulls. There was the sound of the foghorn when the fog rolled in and the gauzy feeling of not being able to see your hand in front of your face. He heard the clank of the bellbuoy off of Owl's Head and the pounding of the waves as they broke against the rocky barrier of the Rockland breakwater. These sounds were music to his soul. Were these daydreams or had he dreamt them as he slept? In his more lucid moments he understood that these were fantasies, but he didn't really care anymore.

He heard a voice saying, "Mr. Bird, can you hear me? Your daughter called and is coming to see you."

He tried to say, "Yes I hear you," but the words wouldn't come out as he expected them to. Then, before drifting off again, he said, quite distinctly, "Rose is coming," and smiled.

Yes, Rose was coming. That was what he had been waiting for. His beloved Rose was coming. They would be together again and this time nothing would keep them apart.

He felt a hand on his forehead, and a voice that said, "Daddy, it's me, Rose. Daddy, can you hear me?" Then he was aware that someone was sitting by him, holding his hand. He tried to turn his head, but it was difficult to move it, so he just stared up into the void.

Again, the voice said, "Daddy, it's me, Rose. I've come to be with you."

No, it's the wrong Rose. That's not her voice. She had a beautiful voice; everyone said so. There was no one who could sing like my beautiful Rose. Sing to me again, Rose, let me hear your voice once more.

The voice that wasn't his Rose went away, and he was left alone. But he wasn't as alone as he had been. Rose was out there somewhere, he was sure of that and he knew she would come to him when it was time.

There was no time anymore only the fog rolling in from the sea. *How strange,* he thought, *I don't hear the foghorns. Should hear the foghorns!* He didn't know when it happened but gradually he could see through the fog. And joy of joys, there was Rose. His Rose dressed in the blue dress he loved so much. She was reaching out to him urging him to join her. His heart was so full of love as he moved toward her that it was almost unbearable. *At last,* he said, *I'm coming, wait for me.* She waited until he had reached her and took his hand as they moved silently together into the enfolding arms of the fog.

EPILOGUE

Portland Press Herald, October 2, 1960
MAYNARD S. BIRD

ROCKLAND—Committal services for Maynard S. Bird, 91, founder of Rockland telephone services and investment house operator, who died in Florida Monday, will be held at Evergreen Cemetery in Portland, Oct. 3.

Bird was born in Rockland, July 16, 1869, son of Sidney and Annie Heard Bird. He is also survived by a son, Milton of Lake Worth [sic], Fla., and a daughter, Mrs. Rose Waterman of Chicago. He was the brother of attorney, Alan B. Bird and Medomak Canning Co. head, Henry B. Bird of Rockland.

The day was clear and bright and surprisingly warm for early October. The air was fresh with only a hint of the colder weather still to come. Fall colors of the few deciduous trees among the evergreens of the cemetery lightened the somber burial of Maynard's ashes next to the grave of his long dead wife.

When Rose arrived at the cemetery she was surprised at the number of people who were there. Her father had left Portland more than thirty-five years ago, so she wondered how many of these people had really known him. Henry and Edith had driven up from Rockland, but, as expected, Alan and Adelaide had not come. The Drummonds, who still lived in Cape Elizabeth, were there; but Rose did not know most of the others. After the brief committal service, Henry introduced Rose to many of those present. Among them was E. Clifford (Cliff) Ladd, the son of Walter Ladd who had succeeded to the head of the insurance company Maynard had founded. There were a number of others whose names meant nothing to her.

As people began to disperse, a stocky man in his sixties approached Rose. He carried his cap in his hand and was dressed in an inexpensive, but neat dark suit. He wore a white collar and a dark patterned tie suitable for the occasion. His hands, hardened by years of manual work, projected a little further from his coat sleeves than was necessary. His white hair, that framed a round face, still showed hints of its original auburn color. His blue eyes were accented by little smile wrinkles; a ruddy face and a pug nose, across which could be seen the remnants of

311

youthful freckles, suggested his Irish origin. He introduced himself rather diffidently to Rose who forgot his name almost instantly. But she would not forget what he said:

"Mrs. Waterman, I worked for your father for many years when he lived in Portland. I was his chauffeur. I knew your mother, too. She was a beautiful lady, and how she could sing." He paused as if searching for the right words. "Your father was very good to me; he treated me well. He was a fine man."

Once again he stopped; his brow furrowed as he searched for the words that would convey the depth of his feelings. At last, haltingly, but with deep emotion, he said, "He was a real gentleman."

Endnotes

1. Robinson, Ruel, *History of Camden and Rockport,* p. 251

2. There is some question as to when the store was opened. Robinson states that John Bird moved to Rockland in 1832 but that the store had been started in 1825.

3. Hanson P. Gregory has been credited with inventing the hole in the doughnut. For many years Camden held a "Doughnut Day" festival.

4. Information on the family of Ann Eliza (Heard) Bird's family is from *Descendants of William Heard and Abigail Crockett of Ash Point, Maine,* by Charles S. Candage, 1987.

5. A clipping of the obituary, discolored with time and barely legible, was discovered recently among the leaves of an old Bible in the attic of a Rockland house once belonging to the Keene family.

6. Information on the Bird family's ships was provided by Willis Snow to Henry B. Bird and printed in the *Bird Genealogy.* This genealogy was compiled by Henry B. Bird with the help of his grandson, John Bird.

7. Portland Sunday Telegram, *The Bird House,* Sept. 17, 1961.

8. *Rockland Courier Gazette,* Obituary for Sidney Morse Bird, Sept. 21, 1907.

9. *A Goodly Heritage*, Mary Ellen Chase; Henry Holt and Company, Inc. c 1932; p. 248.

10. *Shore Village Story,* pp. 275–283,

11. Ibid p.283

12. *MSB Papers.* The Exeter education is from an autobiographical paper written by Maynard S. Bird to his nephew, Frederic H. Bird in 1956.

13. *Bird Genealogy*, p. 9 The John Bird Company

14. *Shore Village Story*, p. 116. The Limerock Railroad

15. *Shore Village Story,* p128. The clipper ship *Red Jacket* was launched on November 2, 1853. She subsequently set a record in January 1854 for the fastest crossing under sail from New York and Liverpool of 13 days 1 hour and 25 minutes, which was unmatched until the time of modern steamships.

16. Ibid, p. 133

17. *Bird Genealogy,* p. 10, <u>The John Bird Company</u>

18. General Journal for years 1889–1899 of The John Bird Company–owned by Robert Bird of Thomaston, Maine.

19. *Shore Village Story,* p. 160. The hotel was later renamed "The Samoset"

20. *The Vineland Press,* September 9 & 10, 1891.

21. *Rockland Courier-Gazette,* September 10, 1891.

22. *Bird Genealogy,* p.9 for the complete statement.

23. Belle Cullen was a long-time secretary to Sidney Bird.

24. This example of "Venture Capitalism" was the first time Maynard indulged in this means of financing his undertakings.

25. Little is known about Mr. Rice. By 1897 the name of Rice had been dropped from the firm's masthead.

26. <u>*Night Train at Wiscasset Station,*</u> Text by Lew Dietz, Photographs by Kosti Ruohomaa, p. 30.

27. Now the True Value Hardware, 1998.

28. *MSB Papers.* Transcript edited by Frederic Bird, July 1, 1968. "First Adventure" page 1.

29. Courier Gazette, February 1904.

30. Op. Cit. *MSB Papers.*

31. Ibid, page 3

32. E. Clifford Ladd, *How W. C. Ladd & Sons Came To Be.*

33. *Courier-Gszette* September 1906.

34. *Shore Village Story* p. 193. The Security Trust Company became The Knox County Trust Company in the 1930's. In 1958 it merged with Depositors Trust Company of Augusta.

35. The building now houses "The Harbor Square Gallery".

36. Courier Gazette, May 19, 1900.

37. Ibid, October 1905

38. Ibid.

39. *Courier Gazette*, November 1907. Advertising article entitled To Investors.

40. *Shore Village Story;* Chronology.

41. Morris, Edmund; *Theodore Rex*; p. 365.

42. *Night Train at Wiscasset Station;* Text by Lew Dietz; Photographs by Kosti Ruohomaa; pp. 98–103.

43. Later renamed Tillson Avnue

44. *Shore Village Story*, p.160–161. In 1940, the Samoset was sold to Adriel Bird, Elmer Bird's youngest son, who with a partner from Boston, ran it until it was conveyed in 1945 to the Hotel Corporation of America.

45. The Bird Homestead was torn down in the late 1960s and replaced by an unimpressive 2-story colonial.

46. *Shore Village Story*, p.34.

47. Courier-Gazette, April 20,1917. Obituary for Mrs. Maynard S. Bird.

48. *Will of Sidney M. Bird;* Knox County Court House; Probate Section: Files #6107, 6142 & 6143. There is one curious bequest to Elizabeth B. Avery (formerly Hall) of Athol, Mass: $500 for the education of her children. No one seems to know who this person was or how she related to the deceased.

49. Ibid.

50. Personal letter from Edward G. Hellier, dated 8/15/1998.

51. *New York Stock Exchange Directory; Jan. 1908.* Thomas F. Baxter and Edward F. Fenno, Jr. were both partners in the firm of Bond & Goodwin in 1907. Baxter held the firm's membership on the Exchange.

52. The *S.S. Mauretania,* a Cunard Line ship, made her maiden voyage in 1907 capturing the speed record between England and New York with an average speed of 26.06 knots. Until *The Titanic, The Mauretania* was the largest ship in the world.

53. The Harjula family was, and still is, a prominent Finnish family living in St. George, Maine.

54. *Portland City Directories*, vols. 1911–1925.

55. Personal communication from Lawrence A. Bird, August, 2002.

56. Phillips Exeter Academy transcript in letter dated 8/12/2002 to the author.

57. The only Rockland contact that Milton Bird maintained in later years was a friendship with Kitty Spear Sharpe Lowe.

58. Harvard transcript of undergraduate grades from years 1913–1917.

59. Ibid

60. *Portland City Directory, 1915.* He was listed as student in later issues.

61. *The Luisitania* sank with a tremendous loss of life.

62. Mary's death certificate shows cause of death as "general carcinomatosis" without designating a specific locus. It must be assumed to have been either ovarian or uterine cancer.

63. Cumberland County Registry of Deeds. File B980/78 and 980/87. Closing on the property took place on October 16, 1916.

64. *The Zimmerman Telegram,* by Barbara Tuchman, p. 175

65. Ibid, p. 184.

66. Rockland Courier-Gazette. Obituary

67. Boston Technology is now M.I.T. (Massachusetts Institute of Technology).

68. Personal communication from William's daughter, Mrs. Jane Bird Stearns.

69. Maynard Bird to Walter Ladd postmarked May 30, 1952.

70. See Cumberland County, Registry of Deeds; File B:980/78 and 980/87.

71. *Portland Monthly Magazine,* Summerguide, 2002.p. 148–149. .

72. *A Field Guide to American Houses,* by Virginia & Lee McAlester, c1984; p387.

73. *FLU: The Story of the Great Influenza Pandemic and the Search for the Virus that Caused It.* By Gina Kolata; Farrar, Straus and Giroux, c1999. Page 20.

74. Ibid p. 5

75. Milton Hawkins Bird married Helen Cushing in Boston, Nov. 29, 1919. Helen was the daughter of Dr. Harvey Cushing, a general practitioner, and not to be confused with the famous brain surgeon Dr. Harvey Williams Cushing (1869–1939), a distant cousin.

76. *The Portland Maine Sunday Telegram,* May 17, 1961. An article featured the house and its history.

77. The church is now known as *State Street United Church of Christ (Congregational).*

78. The Cross is made out of peach or apple wood. It reads "Lee Surrenders to Grant" on one side and "April 9,1865, J. Tyler, 20th Me Rgt" on the other.

79. *The Passing of the Armies* by Joshua Lawrence Chamberlain; Morningside Bookshop, Dayton, Ohio, 1982. Pages 260–264.

80. Little is known about Joseph Tyler's first marriage. Jennie Tyler never mentioned it to the author, although others in the family were aware of it.

81. Joseph Tyler was a skilled cabinetmaker and had earned his living working in firms that made carriages and sleighs. He made much of the furniture in the house at 169 Longfellow Street.

82. Gioacchino Rossini, 1792–1868. Composer of operas the most famous of which is *"The Barber of Seville".*

83. The Damrosch School referred to here was operated by Frank Damrosch, Walter's father, and was known as the Institute of Musical Art. It was founded in 1905 and later became by merger, the Juilliard School.

84. Portland Press Herald, Jan. 3, 1922, p13.

85. Mrs. John Hupper Turner was a soprano who Rose had replaced at the State Street Church, and a member of The Rossini Club. There is a newspaper record of a Bridge Party she gave for Rose in 1916 on one of Rose's visits to Portland.

86. Rose Tyler was born on October 14, 1888. Maynard could not have known at the time he met her that she had just celebrated her 31st birthday.

87. James O'Neill, the father of Eugene O'Neill, made a career of playing *The Count of Monte Cristo* in touring companies throughout the United States.

88. Evelyn Frances Cobb (MacDougall), born May 20, 1915.

89. *The Damrosch Dynasty*, by George Martin, p. 255. This was the last year in which the Musical Art Society performed having suffered from a change in taste as a result of the war.

90. The history of the Hammons family herein is fictional, although the family was not.

91. Unknown to his family, Adriel may already have been married. He married Esther Brock just after his WWI military service.

92. By 1900 the phonograph, invented by Thomas Edison in 1877, was the most popular home entertainment device in the U.S. The Victrola, new in 1906, was the trade name for the phonograph made by the Victor Recording Company.

93. The best account of the role of the 20th Maine can be found in *The Twentieth Maine: A Volunteer Regiment in the Civil War*, by John J. Pullen, c1957.

94. Maynard called Jennie Tyler, "Mother Tyler" after the marriage, but continued to call his father-in-law by his first name.

95. *Harvard Class of 1917, Twenty-fifth Anniversary Report.* .

96. This was before properties were numbered. The address was: Pine Bower, Cumberland Foreside, R.F.D. Portland, Maine. It is currently identified as 57 Foreside Road, Cumberland, Maine.

97. *Portland Press Herald (?).* Copy as shown above

98. The 19th amendment to the Constitution went into effect on January 16, 1920. However, many people with money and connections were able to obtain, with little trouble, good liquor and wines from Canada or elsewhere.

99. The description of the gown is taken from one Rose wore for a concert in 1916.

100. Information on the Mohawk Trail is from Massachusetts Tourist Board Internet publicaton.

101. This was William Case Bird.

102. *Henry B. Bird Papers.* Letter from Alan to Henry on his 80th birthday, 1955.

103. Ibid.

104. Henry and Edith's children were Frederick, Eleanor and Theodore. Their ages at that time were 13, 11, and 10 respectively.

105. *Portland Press Herald* "Burglar Gets Valuable Pin".

106. A horse and some sort of carriage was kept at the Foreside house, where a barn served the dual purpose of garage and stable. The horse if it was a saddle horse was not a hunter.

107. Fictitious quotation.

108. *Bird Genealogy.* Clara Borstel was born in 1867 and died in 1953

109. Letter dated 12/3/1999 from Steven Wheeler, Archivist, New York Stock Exchange. It mentions only the senior Auchincloss, but events some years later make it evident that there was a son involved in the Bond & Goodwin firm.

110. Jennie Tyler's brother, Frank Hastings, served as the last U. S. Consul General to the Kingdom of Hawaii in the early 1890s. His daughter, Alice, married J. Platt Cooke, a descendant of the Cooke family that was one of the original Congregational missionary families. The Cookes made a fortune in general Hawaiian commerce.

111. Caruso performed at the Metropolitan twice in the fall of 1920, but there is no further mention of him in the rest of the 1921 schedule. He died in April, 1921.

112. *The Golden Age of Opera* by Robert Tuttle; p. 102–103. Scotti retired in 1933 to his native Italy. There he died in 1936. *L'Oracolo* was never again produced.

113. Ibid

114. Ibid

115. Rose's sister, Ann Cobb was due to have her second child in March.

116. Jane Carroll Cobb was born on March 23(?) 1921

117. *Portland Press Herald,* Sept. 12, 1934. Obituary of Dr. Richard D. Small.

118. *Portland Press Herald,* Jan. 3, 1922 Also known as Dr. Cousins' Hospital.

119. Information on the hospital was obtained from Sister Therese Pelletier, Archivist for the Catholic Diocese of Portland. The hospital was torn down many years ago to make way for an apartment building.

120. Personal communication from Jennie Tyler to the author.

121. William Bird married Ruth Gurdy. They were divorced sometime in the 1920's.

122. *Portland Press Herald,* Tuesday, January 3, 1922, p.13

123. Because Maynard was not a resident of Portland, and therefore was not entitled to buy a lot in the city-owned Evergreen Cemetery, the lot-actually four lots-had been acquired in Joe Tyler's name.

124. Personal communication from Evelyn Cobb MacDougall

125. The portrait was later given to Rose's daughter, Rose, and stayed with her until the end of her life. *Grace Burnham* is a fictitious name, since the artist's name has long been forgotten.

126. Rockland *Courier-Gazette,* Tuesday, April 11, 1922. The obituary states that she died of pleuro-pneumonia.

127. From a letter written by Maynard Bird to Henry Bird on the occasion of the latter's 80th birthday.

128. Psalm 121

129. *Rockland City Hall, Death Certificates.* The certificate says "Intestinal tuberculosis following influenza two years ago. Age 38, 11 mos. 2 days".

130. Elmer may have picked up small amounts of stock from John Bird, Jr.'s heirs, William Bird and Addie Bird MacIntyre.

131. See probate record of the will of Sidney Morse Bird, Knox County Court House, Rockland Maine. Files #s 6107, 6142, and 6143.

132. It is not known when or how Maynard divested himself of his stock.

133. *NYSE(New York Stock Exchange)* letter dated 12/3/99 gives the names of the partners of *Bond & Goodwin* dating from 1907 to 1922 when the firm relinquished their seat on the Exchange.

134. *Portland Monthly Magazine,* Summerguide 2002. "To The Manor Born". Dorothy Whitney, a former employee of Walter Hammons, is the source of information on the firm's name.

135. See Chain of title for 57 Foreside Road, Cumberland Foreside, Maine in the records at the Cumberland Co. Court House, Portland, ME.

136. E.C.Ladd paper dated 1–27–88 on the history of the W. C. Ladd & Sons Company.

137. Letter from Steven Wheeler, Archivist, *New York Stock Exchange,* dated Dec. 3, 1999

138. The author has been told that Maynard provided money for a winter vacation in Florida for the Tylers. He may also have contributed to paying off the mortgage debt on the Longfellow Street house.

139. The trust agreement contained a clause that stated that if one trustee left the State of Maine, the remaining trustee would have exclusive authority to manage the fund. Maynard was to regret this clause in later years.

140. It is unclear when, and to whom, Maynard gave or sold his Bird Company stock.

141. Elmer died, while on a business trip to Dover-Foxcroft, Maine, of cancer of the throat.

142. Personal communication from Jane Bird Stearns, William Bird's daughter.

143. *The Crisis of the Old Order,* Arthur M. Schlesinger Jr., The Riverside Press, 3rd ed. 1959, p. 157. By September 1929, A.T.& T. was up to 304 and General El.ectric at 396 had tripled in eighteen months.

144. Ibid, p.168

145. Ibid, p.170

146. Ibid, p.172

147. When Milton and Helen moved north in 1927, Milton returned to Harvard where he got his Masters degree in education, and a Ph.D., also in education, in 1930.

148. Rose had a series of books about twins who lived in countries all over the world.

149. Theodore Bird, also known as Ted, was Henry Bird's youngest son.

150. The Corniche Drives are scenic drives at three levels that skirt the mountains between Nice and Monte Carlo.

151. Now known as The International Tribune

152. In France, as in many other Latin countries, there is a civil service that precedes the religious service.

153. Schlesinger, Arthur M, Jr., *The Crisis of the Old Order*, c1957, The Riverside Press, pp. 254–255.

154. The Reconstruction Finance Corporation, created in January 1932, established a $2 billion line of credit to help prop up industry and create jobs. In July of that year a $49 million line of credit was authorized of which nearly $33 million went to banks.

155. William's first marriage to Ruth Gurdy, ended in divorce during the '20s.

156. General Douglas MacArthur commanded the troops. He had as his aide the future general and president, Dwight D. Eisenhower.

157. *Shore Village Story*, 1976, p193.

158. *The Bridgeport Telegram*, October 4, 1960 "Services Tomorrow for Maynard S. Bird".

159. Among those visited were Foxcroft in the hunt country of Virginia, and Madeira, a school catering to daughters of diplomats and Washington society.

160. Harriet Bird, Maynard's first cousin once removed, was the daughter of A.J. Bird, and the great granddaughter of the first John Bird.

161. In 1938 income tax was not a significant factor, even to the very wealthy.

162. Brooklawn Park is an area of Fairfield immediately adjacent to Bridgeport.

163. Communication from E. C. Ladd, 1998: The "Sons" were E. R. Ladd and E. C.(Clifford) Ladd.

164. Ibid. McDougall became president of the National Bank of Commerce and later Chairman of the Board of the Maine National Bank.

165. Neville Chamberlain, Prime Minister of Britain.

166. Smith College and the town of Northampton, Mass., had become the headquarters for a Women's Naval Officers' Training Center. Naval personnel were using most public accommodations.

167. The person's name was Martha Barrett who was a co-worker with Rose in the lab at NYU.

168. Sam Glover was married to the former Helen Plumb and was stepfather to Rose's friend, Helena.

169. A Christian Science Reader is a person who has reached a level of understanding and expertise in the practice of that religion that enables him/her to teach and counsel Scientists. They function as both pastor and religious healer, and they are paid professionals.

170. Marian Cornwall, a real estate agent, was Addah's friend.

171. Adriel U. Bird died of cancer April 14, 1950.

172. Jeff Davis had worked as handyman for Maynard for a number of years, and had become a reliable friend.

173. In 1956 the fee at the Cuyler Pavilion Nursing Home for Maynard's accommodation was $100 per week.

0-595-34572-7

36477653R00201

Made in the USA
Middletown, DE
14 February 2019